Siren Land
AND
Fountains
in the Sand

Siren Land

AND

Fountains
in the Sand

By

NORMAN DOUGLAS

London : SECKER & WARBURG : *1957*

Martin Secker & Warburg Limited
7 John Street, London, W.C.1

Made and printed in Great Britain by
William Clowes and Sons, Limited
London and Beccles

SIREN LAND
First published (J. M. Dent) 1911
Second edition 1923
Third edition (New Adelphi Library) 1927
Reprinted 1929
Fourth edition (Penguin Books) 1948

FOUNTAINS IN THE SAND
First published 1912
Second edition 1921
Third edition (New Adelphi Library) 1925
Reprinted 1928
Reprinted 1936

COMBINED EDITION
First published 1957

CONTENTS

Siren Land

Fountains in the Sand

v

CONTENTS

SIREN LAND

I

SIRENS AND THEIR ANCESTRY

IT was the Emperor Tiberius who startled his grammarians with the question, what songs the Sirens sang? I suspect he knew more about the matter than they did, for he was a Siren-worshipper all his life, though fate did not allow him to indulge his genius till those last few years which he spent among them on the rock-islet of Capri. The grammarians, if they were prudent, doubtless referred him to Homer, who has preserved a portion of their lay.

Whether Sirens of this true kind are in existence at the present day is rather questionable, for the waste places of earth have been reclaimed, and the sea's untrampled floor is examined and officially reported upon. Not so long ago some such creatures were still found. Jacobus Noierus relates that in 1403 a Siren was captured in the Zuider Zee. She was brought to Haarlem and, being naked, allowed herself to be clothed; she learned to eat like a Dutchman; she could spin thread and take pleasure in other maidenly occupations; she was gentle and lived to a great age. But she never spoke. The honest burghers had no knowledge of the language of the sea-folk to enable them to teach her their own tongue, so she remained mute to the end of her days—a circumstance to be regretted, since, excepting in the Arab tale of "Julnar the Sea-born", little information has been handed down to us regarding the conversational and domestic habits of mediæval Sirens.

In the royal archives of Portugal are preserved the records of a costly litigation between the Crown and the Grand Master of the Order of Saint James, as to who should possess the Sirens cast up by the sea on the Grand Master's shores. The suit ended in the King's favour: BE IT ENACTED—THAT SIRENS AND OTHER MARINE MONSTERS EJECTED BY THE WAVES UPON LAND OWNED BY THE GRAND MASTER SHALL PASS INTO THE POSSESSION OF THE KING. This would show that Sirens were then fairly plentiful. And one of the best authenticated cases is that recorded by the veracious

1*

Captain John Smith—he of Pocahontas fame. "I cannot here omit to mention", says he, "the admirable creature of God which in the year 1610 I saw with these my own eyes. I happened to be standing, at daybreak, on the shore not far from the harbour of St. John, when I observed a marine monster swiftly swimming towards me. Lovely was her shape; eyes, nose, ears, cheeks, mouth, neck, forehead, and the whole face was as that of the fairest maiden; her hair, of azure hue, fell over her shoulders. . . ." Altogether, a strange fish. The rest of the quotation will be found in Gottfried's *Historia Antipodum*.

Consult also Gessner, Rondeletius, Scaliger, and other good folks, from whose relations it appears evident that Sirens were common enough in their days and, doubtless for that reason, of little repute; for whatever is common becomes debased, as the very word "vulgar" proves. This perhaps helps to explain their fishy termination, for the oldest Sirens were of a bird kind. The change took place, I imagine, about the time of Saint Augustine, when so many pagan shapes began to affect new vestments and characters, not always to their advantage. It influenced even those born in Hellenic waters, whom we might have supposed to have remained more respectable and conservative than the others.

Thus Theodorus Gaza, whose name is a guarantee of good faith and intelligence—did he not write the first Greek grammar?—once related in a large and distinguished company (Pontanus was also present) how that, after a great storm in the Peloponnesus, a sea-lady was cast up with other jetsam on the beach. She was still alive and breathing hard; her face and body were "absolutely human" and not uncomely. Immediately a large concourse of people gathered round, but her sighs and heaving breast plainly showed how embarrassed she was by their vulgar curiosity. Presently she began to cry outright. The compassionate scholar ordered the crowd to move away and escorted her, as best he could, to the water's edge. There, throwing herself into the waves with a mighty splash, she vanished from sight. This one, again, partook rather of the nature of a fish than of a bird.

In Greece, too, Sirens of every kind have ceased to sing.

I remember a long-drawn, golden evening among the Cyclades. A spell had fallen over all things; the movement of Nature seemed to be momentarily arrested; there was not a sound below, but, overhead, the sunbeams vibrated with tuneful melodies. Janko, the fisherman, had dropped his oars, and our boat, the only moving

object in that preternatural stillness, was drawn by an invisible
hand towards the ruddy pool in the west. But athwart our path lay
a craggy islet, black and menacing against the background of
crimson conflagration. Soon it came in upon us in swarthy confusion of rock and cloven ravine, a few gleams of emerald in its
sheltered recesses. Here if anywhere, methought, Sirens might still
dwell unmolested. The curly-pated rascal steered with cunning
hand towards a Lilliputian inlet; like a true Greek, he appreciated
curiosity in every form. But he resolutely refused to set foot on shore.
I began my explorations alone, concluding that he had visited the
place before.

It was no Siren islet. It was an islet of fleas. I picked them off my
clothes in tens, in hundreds, in handfuls. Never was mortal nearer
jumping out of his skin. Janko was surprised and shocked.

Now, whether these fleas had inhabited the island from time
immemorial, being degenerate descendants of certain heroic creatures that sailed thither in company of Jason and his Argonauts, or
had been left there by shipwrecked mariners of modern days; how
it came about that they multiplied to the exclusion of every other
living thing; what manner of food was theirs—whether, anthro-
pophagous-wise, they preyed upon one another or had learned to
content themselves with the silvery dews of morning, like Anacreon's
cicada, or else had acquired the faculty of long fasting between
rare orgies such as they enjoyed on that afternoon: these and other
questions have since occurred to me as not unworthy of consideration. Mr. Hudson, in his *La Plata*, has vexed himself with similar
problems. But at that moment I was far too busy to give any thought
to such matters.

Ay, they have deserted Greece, the Sirens. It was never more than
a half-way house to them. But they stayed there long enough to
don new clothes and habits. Nothing indeed ever entered that little
country but came out rejuvenated and clarified. A thousand turbid
streams, pouring into Hellas from every side, issued thence grandly,
in a calm and transparent river, to fertilize the world. So it was
with the Sirens. Like many things, they were only an importation,
one of the new ideas that, following the trade routes, crept in to
feed the artistic imagination of the Greeks. Now that we know a
little something of the ancient civilizations of countries like Egypt
and Phœnicia that traded with Greece, we can appreciate the
wonderful Hellenic genius for borrowing and adapting. Hermes,

the intelligent thief, is a typical Greek. For whatever they stole or appropriated—religions, metals, comforts of life, architecture, engineering—they stole with exquisite taste; they discarded the dross and took only what was of value. All traces of the theft quickly vanished; it looked absurd, as Monsieur du Presle has pointed out, to acknowledge indebtedness to others for things which they might as well have invented themselves. For the rest, the stolen material was re-modelled till its original creator could hardly have recognized it. The grotesque, the cruel, became humane. Borrowed gods of frantic aspect put on fair and benignant faces. And every item was forthwith stamped with the hall-mark of Hellas: temperance. All these *objets de vertu* have been handled a good deal since those days; they were sadly knocked about in the uproarious Middle Ages; but this hall-mark is not thumbed away: connoisseurs know it.

I question whether Phorcus himself, the father of the Sirens— or was it Achelous? these old family histories are delicate ground— would have recognized his girls again. How did they look on entering Greece? Ask Messieurs Weicker, Schrader, De Petra, Corcia, Klausen, and their colleagues. They will tell you everything, for they have performed the unknightly task, suggested by Anaxilas, of "plucking the Sirens". In the interests of anatomy it was no doubt desirable, since it enabled them to count the vertebræ and teeth, and perhaps to decide whether the Sirens were really cannibals or not; artists and poets complain of unnecessary mutilation. Dreamers are always complaining. How they looked? They were the personification of sultry dog-days when Sirius (whence their name) burns fiercely in the parching firmament; they were vampires, demons of heat, of putrefaction, of voluptuousness, of lust. But Hellas clothed them anew in virginal hearts and garments and sent them westward—in bad company to be sure, for it seems they travelled with the Telebœans or Taphians, incorrigible cut-throats and cattle-stealers. It must have been something like "the Baby and the Burglar".

Yes; from the minute specialized researches of scholars it is quite clear that the Sirens were nowise indigenous to Greece; they belonged to wilder, non-Hellenic cycles, "remaining", says Butcher, "as foreign words borrowed into a language, but never wholly nationalized". Like other animistic conceptions common to many seas and lands, they drifted into Hellas and were *deodorized*. Our familiar Sirens are not demons of putrefaction; they are creatures full of charm and go to prove the humanizing influence of the Greeks; not of the Greek crowd, as is sometimes inferred (for a more intemperate set of bigots and ruffians never breathed), but only of its teachers, who resented ugliness as a sin and ever held up to them the ideal of nemesis—measure.

Homer began the work, and nothing is more true than that saying of Herodotus, that "Homer arranged the generations of the gods". The *Odyssey*, which sweeps along its current the legend-wrecks of multitudinous extra-Hellenic races, has wafted down to us a fragment of the foreign and cannibalistic old Siren-lore—

> In verdant meads they sport, and wide around
> Lie human bones, that whiten all the ground;
> The ground polluted floats with human gore,
> And human carnage taints the dreadful shore. . . .

but there is no further elaboration of this ungracious aspect; on the contrary, their song, which follows, is conceived in the true spirit of beauty and quite at variance with this primeval picture of crude bloodthirstiness. A characteristic hellenization, caught in the act. This first step towards purification accomplished, later poets and philosophers dwelt ever more on the human attributes of the Sirens, on their charms of voice and feature, till finally the "whitening bones" and other harsh traits faded from sight.

After Hellas came the Alexandrian period with its philological and historical vagaries, and the prodigious syncretism of gods in the second and third centuries; then mediævalism, which dwarfed Hellenic shapes into caco-demons and with their glories crowned its saints.

The Siren Parthenope escaped by taking refuge during mediæval storms in the narrow confines of an amulet, such Siren-charms as are still seen in the streets of Naples and credited with peculiar efficacy against the evil eye. In this, I seem to see the homœopathic principle at work, for the Sirens themselves were witches at the time—sea-witches, and to this day the bathing population may be observed to cross themselves devoutly before plunging into the water, in order to paralyse these malevolent genii of the deep. Others, such as Venus, sheltered themselves behind musty saints; Santa Venere is in high repute as Healer of certain diseases.

And another point of general interest becomes clear from these

scientific disquisitions: that the Sirens of Homer must be sought in
the West rather than where Gladstone and others have located
them. A variety of speculations are now converging to show that
the Odyssean fable is the record of one of many westward processions
of gods and men and is, indeed, only another example of that
suggestive "westing" law first propounded, I believe, by the
Russian naturalist, Von Baer. Curiously enough, Baer himself
asserted that the adventures of Odysseus, including the Siren episode, took place in the Black Sea; but this may have been due to a
kind of patriotism on his part—if we always knew from what
motives our profoundest convictions have sprung! An interesting
phenomenon, by the way, this of exact thinkers relapsing, in old
age, into hazardous theorizings. So Baer, the physiologist, discourses about the legendary Phæacians; Virchow, the pathologist,
about prehistoric man; Wallace, the biologist, about the world of
spirits. And sometimes the weariness, the acquiescent mood is
premature: Lodge, the mathematician, has already begun to preach
the æons and ethics. It is the way of individual man and the way
of nations; none exemplifies it better than Hellas: from "pillars
of unwrought stone" to Aristotle and back again, via Plato, to the
logos, which is obscurity once more. But not all of us follow this
natural curve; some are born old and others never attain maturity,
the discords being adjusted in some posthumous or antenatal
existence.

The Greek Sirens, at least, are stamped with features of eternal
youth. They linger on sea-girt rocks, lyre in hand, or rise from the
gleaming water, clash their cymbals, and again vanish. So you may
see them pictured on Greek vases. There is a vagueness, remoteness,
and restraint about them which permits of multifarious interpretations and constitutes the charm of so many of these Hellenic
conceptions. They are not the product of one mind, but a complex,
many-faceted growth which reflects the touches of various layers of
culture superimposed upon one another—fair but elusive shapes.
Here is one aspect. Long ago, the Sirens engaged the Muses in a
singing-contest. They were worsted, and the Muses decked themselves with their enemies' feather-plumes. Who is not tempted to
detect in this legend the victory of disciplined music over the wild
improvisations of natural song? And another: the three sister-Sirens
drowned themselves out of love for Odysseus. This is the impress of
strong human feelings—a hopeless passion, you perceive: no school-

girl sentimentality. Picture a "demon of putrefaction" casting itself into the sea for a mortal! Oh, they had changed considerably in the air of Hellas. The purification—the hallmark. The "*chaste Parthenope*" found a resting-place and an honoured tomb on the spot where now stands Naples. For a thousand years she dominated its social and religious institutions. She dominates them still. Is Parthenope dead? Who, then, is Santa Lucia? The madonnas of Naples are all sea-queens whose crowns shine with a borrowed lustre; the Madonna della Libera, the Stella di Mare—they are all reincarnations of antique shapes, of the Sirens, of Leucothea, Euploia, and the Nereids, and their cult to this day is pagan rather than Christian. You will not find such saints in Tuscany.

A large Siren literature has sprung up within recent times. But I would still like to see a book which should develop the idea as a whole, tracing their genealogy from birth through all the changes of character they have undergone since ancient days—a book which might be entitled *Les Sirènes à travers les siècles* (why does it sound better in French?), and which would afford an interesting measure of the corresponding state of the human intelligence. For we create our gods in our own likeness.

There is an imp of the imagination called the familiar spirit or guardian angel, who often runs parallel to these eerie water-ladies. Like the Sirens that occur everywhere—in Chinese and Saxon tradition, in Brazil and in the grey-green reaches of Polar seas,* the attendant demon is of animistic growth, springing up, independently, in Burma, among the old Irish, the Eskimos, the Chilians.

Our particular Sirens are probably of Phœnician origin, while our particular guardian angels come from the Chaldæans. The crystal spaces of their æther were alive with fluttering divas who grew in holiness as they receded from earth; Hellenic and Roman culture took them over from direct contact with the East, but Christian Europe received them indirectly as a legacy from the Jews who had imbibed this poetic demonology during their Babylonian sorrows and had enriched their sacred books with these terrible and lovely creatures of air, which the Gnostics and Sabæans

---

* Henry Hudson's crew saw one when seeking a passage to the North Pole near Nova Zemblya. She was like a woman above, "her skin very white and long hair hanging behind, of colour black". Her tail was speckled and shaped like that of a porpoise.

elaborated into a glittering hierarchy. So the seven planetary spirits of Persian mythology melted into the seven arch-angels of Cabbalistic dreamings; but our ideas of ordinary ones, of winged forms intermediate between God and man, are purely Chaldæan. Christians were actually forbidden by the Council of Laodicea to call upon the angels, and it was not till the second Council of Nicæa that this "idolatrous practice" was sanctioned; Byzance indeed, rather than Rome, is the mother of angel worship.

Even as the Sirens soon took on fixed æsthetic attributes, so the guardian angel was early installed in his moral functions. Every man had his own; angels and gods likewise; the graves of the dead likewise, and high divinities were sometimes pleased to play the part with deserving mortals like Tobias or Telemachus. Pythagoras, strongly tainted with Orientalism, made his *daimon* perceptible to the senses, whereas the familiar of Socrates was invisible, the "divine voice" of reason. This point of time is approximately the high-water mark of both conceptions—hence onward there is the exuberance of decline. And as in Homer we can designate the precise poetic touch which raised the Sirens from their lowly place, so in Plato we may note the very blunder whereby the familiar became gross once more. For the master can hardly have meant by "a divine something" that which his disciples thought—interpreting literally an allegorical remark of his, they built up that anthropomorphic theory which stultified Socrates and re-materialized the *demon.*

It is characteristic of mankind that only then did he, like the Sirens, become "popular". Xenophon, Menander, Apuleius, and the rest of them waxed eloquent in explanations; Diogenes and Apollonius also began to consult private devils, and of course Plotinus, the ape of Socrates, had one too. And soon the curious spirit of Alexandrian pedantry was at work upon them, dwelling, with erudite dilettantism, upon the origins and meanings of the Sirens, while Philo mixed his astounding *salade russe* of Greek and Jewish demons.

The Romans, busy and honest, had no use for things of beauty, save as plunder of war to decorate their temples and villas. They rejected the Sirens, but the stern Pelasgic cast of their religion led them to identify the *demon* with what philosophers called the idiosyncrasy, the genius. Enlarging upon this sober notion, they gave congenial spirits to corporate bodies and towns, the grandest being that of Rome itself; the patron saints of modern Italian cities and villages are so firmly rooted only because they represent the lineal descendants of these old tutelar deities. And sometimes a good and a bad genius lived conjointly in the body of one man, striving for the mastery: a problem which already confronted these Chaldæans whose religious cursing-tablets (models of what such literature ought to be) are largely taken up with conjurations for the expulsion of malefic demons in favour of beneficial ones. The dilemma was inevitable—one of the two antagonistic forces must preponderate— and so these imaginary introcorporeal mannikins are a microcosmic illustration of the pitfalls of dualistic creeds.

Mediævalism came, and the familiar or paredral spirits went through the same degrading metamorphosis as the Sirens. They grew common; philosophers like Simon Magus, saints like Teresa, poets like Tasso—everybody had one or more of them. That of Cornelius Agrippa lived in the shape of a black dog (Faust) : on his death-bed at Lyons the sage thus cursed it—*Hence, beast of damnation, that hast wholly damned me!* (whereupon it vanished), and his great disciple Wier, who also believed in them, is sharply reprimanded for doubting this particular tale. The idea commingled with a host of mandrake legends; idols, of which numbers were sold in England under Henry VIII, were carved out of this plant and gravely consulted.

I think the Crusades and the Western domination of the Arabs, in whose lore the attendant genius plays a conspicuous part, may have helped to spread the superstition throughout Europe, which was then in a fit condition to believe anything. The familiar lived no longer inside man, prompting him to moral actions; he was imprisoned in capsules or rings (Parthenope in her amulet) and could be constrained to appear or dismissed from service (Ariel). Up to this day, *homunculi* in glass phials are bought in German fairs and kept "for luck"—I have seen them hawked about the streets of London—and the following will show that this trade, like others, had its risks: "In the year 1650 a merchant of Augsburg kept some of these quaint spirits sealed up, like flies or ants, in bottles, intending to bring them to the fair of Leipzig; but when, by means of a letter, it was discovered that he was about to offer them for sale, he denied the whole matter—*perhaps they themselves had whispered to him* that he might have to answer awkward questions on their account." Awkward questions!

Despoiled of their pristine ennobling qualities, these beings were still sociable and not without hopes of heaven; the familiar had become realistic, swayed by passions like mankind, sometimes lovable and often tinged with a vein of sadness, while Sirens like Undine and Melusine were strangely human in tears and laughter. We were not yet wholly afraid of these our creatures. But soon enough, by that process of deterioration of which the word "demon" is itself an example, they were absorbed into the essence of the Evil One and became his slaves—past redemption. Witches only, and not philosophers, kept familiars in the shape of cats, and the belief was merged into that of incubi, Satanic Pact; the Church warning its adherents against them: *Ipse simulat se captum, ut te capiat; a te inclusum, ut contra te finaliter concludat.* Thus the rebellious angels confined in copper vessels by the great Lord Solomon have degenerated into a bottled imp, an infant's toy; and from the voice of reason of the Greek sage, from the guardian angel that watches over the slumbers of innocent childhood, from the genius of divine Augustus and eternal Rome, we descend to the "harmless, necessary cat".

I rather question whether the familiar spirit would have maintained its strong fascination if it had not lent itself to practical purposes, and one may speculate how much of the worldly prestige of men like Mahomet, Numa, or Carbajal was due to their fiction of a ghostly counsellor, which justified actions unintelligible to the vulgar. The familiar has lately appeared in a new guise: the control of the medium.

Will he quite die out? No more than the Sirens. The pious Silvio Pellico addressed a prayer to his spiritual custodian; the Catholic Church, however, has never favoured this individualistic tendency, convinced that the rôle of guardian angel is more properly performed by confessors or one of the thousand saints appointed for that purpose. Protestantism, meanwhile, has reverted to the "still, small voice", though in neurotic men, like George Fox, a vision is required to supplement the conscience. All those who fail to attribute their well-being to natural causes will crave for something of the guardian-angel type, even as simple mariners, in moments of danger, may wonder whether there is indeed no truth in those tales of spiteful she-devils lurking in the depths. And if this were a philosophical age, I would endeavour to show that the whole invisible-companion-idea is merely an exemplification of Lotze's views, as to that striving of the human personality to extend and consolidate its sphere of domination which has induced us to carry walking-sticks and to wear tall hats; while the Sirens are—well, no matter. Fortunately, metaphysics are out of fashion just now.

It seems to me that the Sirens, like other old Hellenic ideals, are coming to honour again.

During their westward progress they tarried long about the headland of Athenæum, which is the southern horn of the Bay of Naples now called Punta Campanella, and about its islands. A snowy temple, one of the wonders of the western world, rose in their honour near this wave-beaten promontory—for promontories were sacred in oldest days from their dangers to navigation; colonnades and statues are swept away, but its memory lies embedded in the name of the village of Massa Lubrense (*delubrum*). A wondrous mode of survival, when one comes to think of it: a temple enshrined in the letters of a word whose very meaning is forgotten, handed down from father to son through tumultuous ages of Romans and Goths and Saracens, Normans, French, and Spaniards, and persisting, ever cryptic to the vulgar, after the more perishable records of stone and marble are clean vanished from the earth.

A good idea of the country can be obtained from the well-known Deserto convent above Sorrento or, nearer the point of the promontory, from the summit of Mount San Costanzo which, if I mistake not, ought to be an island like Capri near at hand, but will probably cling to the mainland for another few thousand years. The eye looks down upon the two gulfs of Naples and Salerno, divided by a hilly ridge; the precipitous mass of Sant' Angelo, stretching right across the peninsula in an easterly direction, shuts off the view from the world beyond. This is Siren Land. To the south lie the islets of the Sirens, nowadays known as the Galli; westwards, Capri, appropriately associated with them from its craggy and yet alluring aspect; Sorrento, whose name has been derived from them—I wonder some adventurous scholar has not identified it with the Homeric *Surie*—lies on the northern slope. A favoured land, flowing with milk and honey; particularly the former: Saint-Non mentions as proof of its fertility the fact that you can engage wet-nurses there from the ages of fourteen to fifty-five.

I am not going to describe its natural features; the thing has been done by five hundred travellers already. Imagine to yourself a

tongue of limestone about three miles across and six long, jutting
into the sea; a few islands hanging upon its skirts; villages and
farms whose inhabitants reflect the various cultures that have been
imposed upon them during the last two thousand years of political
changes. A microscopic territory; but overgrown with hoary
traditions of which that of the sea-maidens is only one. We need
merely think of those quaintly carved vessels which in olden days
sailed in between Capri and Point Campanella, bearing westwards certain gods and letters and aspirations—much of what is
best, in fact, in our own modern civilization. And more recent
memories, grim and glorious, cluster thickly about its rocks and
inlets. . . .

It was no doubt during one of those spells of deathlike summer
stagnation, known hereabouts as *scirocco chiaro* or *tempo di bafogna*,
that Odysseus encountered the Sirens—

> While yet I speak the winged galley flies
> And lo! The Siren shores like mists arise.
> Sunk were at once the winds; the air above,
> And waves below, at once forgot to move.
> Some dæmon calmed the air, and smoothed the deep,
> Hushed the loud winds, and charmed the waves to sleep—

for scirocco is the withering blast whose hot and clammy touch
hastens death and putrefaction.

This passage may have suggested to Cerquand the idea that the
Sirens "*sont le calme sous le vent des hautes falaises et des îles*", an interpretation which he subsequently discarded. Loosely speaking, this
would imply that *some* thing had been created out of nothing; even
as, on the same principle, Pan has been called the personification
of the midday hush that can be felt. The Swiss painter Boecklin,
whose Gothic exuberance often ran on lines antithetical to what
we call Hellenic serenity, has yet divined the psychology of the
matter in *Das Schweigen im Walde*—the shudder that attunes the
mind to receive chimerical impressions, the silence that creates;
though I cannot but think that the effect of this particular picture
would have been improved by the omission of Madame Boecklin.
So may those pioneers of navigation have felt when, becalmed in
the noonday heat amid pale-shimmering cliffs, they grew conscious
of the unseen presence. Sirens dwell here! For the genii of earth and
air were ready enough to commune with untutored men of early
ages, to whom everything unknown was marvellous. Such fruitful

shadows cast by inanimate nature upon the human phantasy are not rare; the secondary stage is reached when the artist endeavours to fix in stone these wavering shapes, or the bard in verse; the third is that of the philosopher or grammarian who explains them as the splashing of waves and what not.

What not, indeed? The Sirens, says one, are the charms of the Gulf of Naples. No, says another; they were chaste priestesses. They were neither chaste nor priestesses, but exactly the reverse. They were sunbeams. They were perilous cliffs. They were a race of peaceful shepherds. They were symbols of persuasion. They were cannibals. They were planetary spirits. They were prophets. They were a species of Oriental owl. They were the harmonious faculties of the soul. They were penguins.

Penguins! That is the final pronouncement of commentatorial erudition.

Yet I must add my own mite of conjecture regarding the so-called "eyed Sirens". These, I hold, may well represent a pristine version of the Beasts in the Apocalypse. And Eustathius has already explained how they came by their feather-dresses. They used to be young girls like any other nymphs or naiads, but Venus was so annoyed at their persistent chastity that she changed them into birds. Just like Venus—the Venus of the grammarians.

So may they have felt, those ancient mariners, spell-bound in drowsy scirocco-chains; but I question whether this was the true genesis of the Sirens. The bird-termination. . . . It recurs in the harpies, of Egyptian origin. Those Egyptians, too, had that notable conceit of the dead body being visited by its soul in the shape of a human-headed hawk (*Die Seelenvögel*), and it was also—says Doughty—"an ancient opinion of the idolatrous Arabs, that the departing spirit flitted from man's brain-pan as a wandering fowl, complaining thenceforward in deadly thirst her unavenged wrong". Leucothea, a Phœnician goddess, could likewise assume the bird-form,* and—who knows?—some crazy enthusiast may yet succeed

---

* Professor Correra gives various reasons for supposing that the cult of Leucothea was more widely diffused in these regions than is generally believed. So, for example, he refers to this divinity the statue of a sea-lady seated upon a marine monster which was found in the ancient Villa Pausilipon and is now in the Naples Museum. I observe that in the Blacas collection there was a gem which exactly reproduces this statue—King has figured it under the title of *Venus Euploia* whose temple is supposed, though not by Beloch, to have stood near the site of this Villa at the western point of the Bay of Naples, facing the Athenæum promontory on

in establishing a cousinship between the Sirens and those enigmatical swan-maidens who winged their way from snowy Himalaya
to grace the bridal couch of northern hero-kings.

For the rest, such days of heavy-lidded atmospheric brooding
are rare in Siren land.

They are clear-eyed and caressing as a rule, these summer
breezes; caressing and cleansing; they set all the shining leaves
a-tremble and scatter town-memories and the fumes of musty
learning. How the bizarre throng of water-witches and familiars
grow uneasy in that brave light, and wan—how they fade away,
like the ghosts they are!

the east. This identical gem is also photographed as "Nereid or Thetis" in the
beautiful work of Furtwaengler, who thinks that the several gems depicting this
subject are antique copies of a stone dating about 400 B.C. Here are three different
versions of one figure: Leucothea, Venus, and Nereid; whence we may conclude
that the sages have not yet quite disentangled the genealogies of these wave-born
divinities. It used to be thought that some of them, like the Sirens, Leucothea and
Aphrodite, had come to these shores with their old Phœnician worshippers. These
traders have doubtless left their mark in certain South Italian local names, such
as Megaris (their depot at Naples), Marata, and Sama—Megaris, Marathon, and
Samos in Greece are also of Phœnician origin—but their gods, as we now know
them, only entered the country later on, under Hellenic auspices.

II

UPLANDS OF SORRENTO

WITH the exception of Capri, which is the only spot within a hundred miles of Naples where a foreigner is reasonably well treated, no accommodation in the septentrional sense of the word can be found in Siren land save at Sorrento and Sant' Agata, the idea being that "foreigners must first come" before anything can be done to welcome the few that flee into these solitudes from the din and confusion of that fair land whose frontier-station bears the ominous name of Chiasso (noise). Massa is rich and populous, but contains not a single hotel or even restaurant; it is a community of peasant-proprietors who live, some of them, in fine country houses built in pre-Bourbon days by Spanish and Neapolitan grandees—indeed, it is one of the surprising things in this district to see mouldering structures with ample courtyards, arched galleries, and noble escutcheons over their gates, now inhabited by mean-looking folk whose manners, at least, are still in harmony with their dwellings. Massa is full of them, but even the humblest village can boast of one or two. The terrors of a century of Bourbonism reduced this country to direst distress. Capri, after the discovery of the Blue Grotto, began to thrive in spite of its sovereigns, but the mainland portions are only just now recovering from the blight. Neapolitans have grown rich again and seek the fine air of the hills as of yore, while the inhabitants themselves bring much money from New York; and from Argentina, where a good half of them are periodically employed in selling potatoes to the Spaniards, who apparently eat nothing else. "Good people" they call them, because they are easily gulled in the matter of weights and measures.

One consequence of this revival is that the price of land is rising once more and new houses are being built. This would be satisfactory, were it not that the style of architecture has changed for the worse. That harmonious medley of small vaulted chambers with their vine-shaded loggia in front, so becoming to this climate and charming to look upon, has been displaced by hideous *palazzi* constructed with iron beams, asphalt, and roofing tiles—things formerly unheard of. No person with a sense of the fitness of things will ever fall in love with these new dwellings, although they are built, as the architects will tell you, according to the latest *regola d'arte*. When a Southerner discourses upon *regola d'arte*, he is generally up to some mischief.

Even the colossal hand-made house-keys of the olden days, now replaced by weedy cast-iron abominations, were not without a certain austere beauty: there was a smack of Saint Peter about them. And they had their uses, too. Three years ago a wealthy landowner, returning home at night, was attacked by two ruffians with knives. Having no ordinary weapon of defence, not even a walking-stick, he began to wield his house-key with such dexterity that one of his assailants was brained on the spot, while the other crawled into the fields, where he was found dead next morning— at least, he ought to have been.

The ridge of backbone which divides the gulfs of Salerno and Naples is called *Le Tore*—an obscure and venerable word which is common all over this region and takes us back to Mount Taurus in Cilicia and to the Celtic and Sinaitic Tor. Perhaps the poet Statius was referring to these Tore when he spoke of the "green Taurubulæ" of Sorrento or Capri, but unfortunately nobody can tell us exactly what he meant, as in the whole of ancient literature the word occurs only in this one passage. A modern scholar derives the *Tore* from the Greek τα ὄρη, the mountains; which, if not correct, is at least simple. There is a village called Torco on the southern slope of the ridge just below Sant' Agata, whose name has been drawn by some from the Latin *torqueo*, because the road "turns" there, and by others from the Greek *theorica* because, they say, a religious procession of youths and maidens used to wend thither in olden days. Though the church of Torco is one of the oldest in the district, there are no classic remains whatever in the neighbourhood, and I rather disbelieve this tempting theorica-derivation, although it is adopted in his *Magic and Astrology* by Maury who copied it, I suspect, from the old Sorrentine writer, Onofrio Gargiulli. It seems more natural to connect the word Torco with this backbone or Tor.

It is not a crest but a rounded plateau, and as the divide

approaches far nearer to the southern shore, the rocks on this incline needs must rush precipitously into the sea, with perilous paths into grottos, and thrifty olives on the middle heights grasping the limestone ledges or climbing warily down the gullies; the northern slope, on which Massa and Sorrento lie, is a gentle declivity planted with vines and oranges and walnuts, and refreshed by streams that run through the heat of the dog-days. The Tore reach their highest elevation immediately behind Sorrento. Here, in the early morning, when sea-mists on either side shroud the two gulfs from view, the wanderer has all the illusion of being on some lonely Alpine meadow—not a sign of human habitation or handiwork; a chill nip in the air; browsing cattle with deep-toned bells round their necks, and real, close-cropped turf under foot. This, I imagine, is the track which the wolves follow when they leave their fastnesses of the Sant' Angelo in winter to scour the richer country.

A path, the *via delle Tore*, runs along the whole summit, passing through Sant' Agata and ending at Termini, which is the last village on the peninsula. An ideal summer walk, for those who do not feel a little dry heat. But if you sit down, it is well to seek out the shadow of some wall or an umbrageous carob, for the reverberation of the light may induce a sun-stroke.

The olives make scanty shade: they are too ferociously pruned hereabouts. The whole of the southern incline is planted with them wherever a little soil can be scraped together, and their oil is excellent —better, says Pliny, than that of Venafrum—probably because the inhabitants know the secret of preparing it. As soon as it is plucked, the fruit must be pressed in those picturesque rustic mills where, by the dim light of a lantern—the work is nearly always done at night— half-naked, Praxitelean shapes of men and boys may be discerned turning the heavy stone wheel which crushes the berry to a clammy pulp. Alas, these trees are now remorselessly uprooted wherever the soil will feed the more profitable grape; Capri has lost half its olives, Ischia all: a consummation to be deplored since the vine, however gladsome in its summer greenery, is bare for six months in the year when its straggling limbs have a peculiarly unkempt and disreputable appearance. Were the landscape alone to be considered, I could wish that some new scourge like phylloxera might be introduced, for there is enough wine in the country already. At this moment it is being sold for three francs a barrel (forty-four litres) on Ischia, whereas the oil-crop has failed altogether; there has been

no rain, the grub has invaded the fruit, and the preceding winter
was too mild (the olive likes a good shiver once a year). These trees
are small in size, mere pigmies beside the writhing monsters of
Spain and Greece and Apulia; their upper limbs are stretched in
a nervous tension which is the despair of artists, but in those
tumid roots there sits—to all appearances—a deep repose. Yet
who can tell what passionate alchemy is astir in that subterranean
laboratory, sustaining life and fashioning fruit through those
scorching summer months, among stones that are often too hot to
handle?

At this season the olive's complexion wanes to a yellowish green;
with the autumn rains it becomes blue-grey; the plant also varies in
tint according to locality. This may help to explain the contradictory colour-epithets which the ancients bestowed upon it. Even
now it is still revered as emblem of peace and plenty, a sprig of olive
being attached to boats and houses after the Easter blessing. There
is this peculiarity in its leaves, that they can make no fluttering
movements like those of most plants; they are affixed to the stem
like metal plates, and if the wind blows it is the whole limb of the
tree which sways. And so a pretty effect may often be seen upon
these olive-coloured slopes: the branches bending with one accord
to the breeze expose the white under-surface of all the leaves, and
the hillside is clothed in silver.

Here, on these remote uplands, I prefer to turn my back on the
green undulations of Massa and Sorrento, on Vesuvius and Naples,
Ischia and the Phlegræan Fields; all these regions are trite and
familiar. I prefer to gaze towards the mysterious South, the mountains of Basilicata and the fabled headland Licosa, where Leucosia,
sister-Siren of Parthenope, lies buried. At this height the sea's
horizon soars into the firmament smooth as a sheet of sapphire, and
the eye never wearies of watching those pearly lines and spirals that
crawl upon its surface, the paths of silver-footed Thetis—a restful
prospect, with dim suggestions of love and affinity for this encircling
element that reach back, for aught we know, to primeval days of
Ascidian-life. There is a note of impotence in the sea's wintry
storms, for it can but rage against its prison bars or drown a few
sailormen, an ignoble business: true grandeur is only in its luminous
calm.

Licosa is the furthest point visible but, on rare occasions, other
lands with peaks and promontories unknown loom upon the sky-line,

and sometimes, by the same atmospheric witchcraft, the volcanic cone of Stromboli is projected out of the waves. Early mornings in spring and autumn are most propitious for these delicate trickeries. So Hehn saw the island of Ischia from Monte Cavo near Albano, though it must have been well below the horizon. Dream-pageants, swift-fading. . . .

This is essentially a land of line, of irreproachable contours, and your painter had best begin by throwing away his palette and striving to see it aright: a land of classical parsimony, limestone and blue sea, whose chastened beauty none save a really great craftsman, with disciplined hand and heart attuned to eternal melodies, can hope to disentangle from among the prejudices and traditions of his own mind. What caricatures are the works of even world-famous artists who have painted on these shores; what faulty draughtsmanship, meretricious effects, and lack of decent restraint! How they fail to see the simplicity underlying those complex natural formations! For the loveliness of this landscape is not that of Phryne, and the painter errs who thinks that his inmost thoughts are met half-way by a smile of encouragement. The smile is there, but not for him. It is for the constraining mortal who disregards it; who stands to his work in the relation of God to man.

A gradual change is taking place in the orographical modelling of the Bay of Naples. Capri and the other limestone portions must formerly have presented a smoother aspect to the eye, as they were covered with trees and soil which gave them a rounded look. The trees being felled, the earth slipped down, exposing the jagged asperities of the rock. With the volcanic districts it is generally the reverse, for these craters are of soft material, and the longer they are exposed, the smoother they become. The lower eminences of Baiæ and Ischia are now merely a jumble of curving lines, and a small crater near Fuorigrotta is in the last stage of liquescence; soon the rain and the plough will have merged it into the earth whence it arose—the limestone tracts, meanwhile, grow more peaked every day.

Capri is a microcosm whose perfection of *décor* and hieratic lineaments can only have been the inspiration of some divinely frenzied Prometheus. But its beauty, though vital and palpitating, is now cramped and impaired by the encroachments of humanity. Rocks are blasted away for driving roads; shrubs are cut down;

high walls and houses everywhere invade its primitive comeliness.
The place is too small to endure these affronts without prejudice.
It must have been different in the days when the Sirens were its only
inhabitants; if, indeed, it was really their island. For I cannot help
thinking that commentators of the Homeric cosmography take the
"islands" too seriously, and thereby involve themselves in needless
trouble. Ancient navigators were inordinately fond of islands, and
slow sailing without a compass may well turn an indented coastline
or promontory into a group of them. This is plain from *Sindbad the
Sailor*, and from Hanno's *Periplus*. People living on continents are
more likely to locate marvels in islands—India and America were
also "islands"; so was Paradise, according to Lambertus Floridus;
to say nothing of Atlantis—and the ingenious Pelliccia has written
a book to prove that the whole Sorrentine peninsula was likewise
an island in olden days. He argues thus: The Sirens dwelt at Capri;
Circe, the enchantress, lived on another island near at hand;
Sorrento is near at hand; therefore Sorrento must have been the
island of Circe—falsifying geography and geology in order to
vindicate a prehistoric sailor's yarn. What strange creatures we are,
placing more faith in deductions than in facts—why? God created
the facts and they may take care of themselves, but the deductions
are our own, to be clung to with parental attachment. Even so
Vargas, that monster of misapplied eruditions, insists that the Siren
Parthenope was not worshipped at Naples, because—well, it would
injure his pet theory about the Semitic races.

A wonderful discovery was made on Capri three years ago: the
bones of mammoth, hippopotami, and other improbable beasts
embedded together with human weapons of the earliest palæolithic
ages. Inasmuch as a pair of mammoths would soon nibble away the
last leaf on a rock of this size, we must presume it to have been
joined to the mainland in those days. These relics were found below
the ashes of the terrific Phlegræan convulsions which may have
done the work of detachment later on.

Capri is curious also for its Tyrrhenian fauna and flora; it is part
of the wreck of that submerged continent whose ruins still lift their
head above the water here and there, and whose configuration is
being patiently mapped out by the labours of men like Suess,
Blanchard, Parato, and Forsyth Major. The remains of the fallow-
deer, a Tyrrhenian creature, have been unearthed here; certain
snails and various Tyrrhenian plants still occur on the island, such

as the *convolvulus cneorum* with its creamy blossoms, and the wild palm, which used to hang in exquisite clusters, untouched from time immemorial, on the rocky ledges, but is now ruthlessly torn down to decorate gardens, in which ninety per cent of them perish.

How much of this drowned world still saw the light of sun and stars when the Sirens sang, I, for one, would be glad to know. For it can hardly have vanished with a *Hey, presto!* like Graham's Island; doubtless it sank slowly; Odysseus may yet have drawn up his ship on beaches that are now, for aught we can tell, slumbering beneath the waves. We have all heard that story of Plato's, and how the priest of Sais told Solon of the mighty island of Atlantis which lay beyond the Pillars of Hercules and was engulfed by the sea. An old Orphic tradition runs to the same effect. Of the former existence of this true Atlantic continent there are abundant grave indications —may not this legend have become amalgamated in the course of ages with that of the Tyrrhenian catastrophe? Humboldt seems to have thought so.

It is easy to see, from the summit of the Tore, that Capri is merely a prolongation, a dependency, of the mainland. And in point of shape, too, it is almost a repetition—on an enlarged scale, of course —of the mountain of San Costanzo, which terminates the peninsula and is itself something of an island. That the chief beauty of Capri, its insular position and the noble line of cliffs fronting the town on the west, should be due to what they call a "fault", proves that scientific nomenclature is not always appropriate for ordinary purposes.

I often gaze down upon Siren land from those inspiring heights of Faito on Sant' Angelo which afford, from splendour and associations, one of the finest prospects in the world. It is cool up here among the mountain pastures, and there are still ancient beech trees and firs that look strangely out of place—relics of the autochthonous woodlands that have now been stripped of their timber like that once famous Sila forest, which is being eradicated so conscientiously that its chief town already lies in a desert of glaring rocks and to gather a handful of firewood there entails a scramble of half a day. Conceive what this means in a winter of Northern severity, how it makes for misery and depopulation, and how easily it could have been avoided!

It is a relief to think that the wooded tracts above Siren land have fallen into the hands of a man like their present owner. For they are an historical monument worth preserving: they display the flora of the Italian continent as it was in the days when the pious Æneas sailed hitherwards. We are apt to forget that the whole appearance of Italian scenery has been changed owing to imported plants—the very cypress, the orange and maize and a hundred others great and small, which we regard as so characteristic, are aliens to the soil.* And the idea of preserving such tracts, absurd as it may seem to modern Italians, is really not inherently preposterous: certain civilized nations, such as the French, Americans, and English, have already by private gift or public subscription enclosed delectable woodlands to be an eternal delight and precept to their children; and only the other day the German Emperor rescued, in the very heart of Italy, the hoary oaks of Olevano from their impending fate. These, unless I am much mistaken, will be monuments more acceptable and more intelligible to posterity than the forests now growing up in Italy: forests of trousered political nonentities in bronze and marble, whose doctrines, often enough, became a derision before their protagonists were yet fairly in their graves.

The stealthy teachings of the sea, the Sirens' abode, still lie open to all, but those of earth-nature have been sadly misread of late and thwarted; and although we have heard much concerning the hygienic and economic advantages of properly controlled woodlands, there is room for another benefactor to mankind—for him, namely, who would proclaim their ethical significance, their influence as a refining and civilizing agency in the education of the human race. Who will deny that forests, once they have abandoned their hostile attitude to man's progress upon earth, exercise a benignant power, subtle and profound, upon the mind of a people; that music, architecture, and other generous arts have in forests sought, and found, high inspiration; that some of the sublimest efforts of literary genius could not have been conceived in regions as denuded of timber as Italy, Greece, and Spain now are? Rentzsch ascribes the political decadence of Spain almost wholly to the destruction of forest. Even if this be going too far, I cannot but think

* So, for instance, the spiky agave which they call *mal' occhio* because its point is a defence against the evil eye; the mesembryanthemum, known as *unghia di iannara* (witches' claws) from the shape of its leaves; or the grotesque Indian fig— one of God's earliest attempts at tree-making—which Preller, by mistake, depicted in his "Homeric Landscape". The *kaktos* of the Greeks seems to have been a kind of artichoke.

that in sweeping away woodlands many deeply rooted humane aspirations, interwoven in their leafy solitudes, are likewise swept away, and a legion of gracious phantoms, who wandered freely among those solemn aisles ready to converse with all, banished for evermore. Shakespeare's England can still be found by those who look for it, but they who would discover the Italy of her poets must go far afield. Communion with nature, which exalts and purifies the mind, has ceased and in its place has arisen that pest of the South: futile inquisitiveness concerning man in his meanest manifestations.

It was not without an intuition of this truth that the ancients contrived their exquisite fable of Eresichthon, and whoever yet remembers the elves and fairies of his childhood may be envied of a talisman indeed. It would hardly profit us, I think, to withhold from our children the contemplation of woodland marvels, with their tender symbolism of leaf and flower, birth and decay; the wonder-period of our remote ancestors, through which we must all pass in youth, that fleeting hour of nature-worship, may well be abbreviated, but cannot wholly be cut out of the programme of our moral growth without detriment to the race.

The elimination of mystery: what has it not done for modern Italy? Whether the disfigurement of the landscape has not reflected itself upon the race? Whether the listlessness of so many Italian townspeople, and the evil precocity of their children, be not the nymphs' revenge for Eresichthon's crime? The old Greeks felt differently and so do their modern descendants; their humblest mechanic loves the country, and has therefore preserved a far nobler curiosity upon the things of life. The boy of the streets, who sees nothing of the protean witchery of flowers and living waters, is not a veritable boy at any time, since his youth is ended ere it began. We are not yet ripe for growing up in the streets; they stimulate the social instincts of the adult, but stunt the adolescent who craves for solitude and surroundings habitual to earlier periods of human history. We know what is said of the second generation of city-dwellers, even of high social standing; and has any good ever come out of that foul-clustering town-proletariat, beloved of humanitarians? Nothing—never; they are only waiting for a leader, some "inspired idiot", to rend to pieces our poor civilization. Whereas out of the very dregs of the country-folk has often arisen, by the operation of that dark law which regulates the meteoric appearance of "sports", a Lincoln, a Winckelmann, to guide men's footsteps in the path.

On these Siren heights—*Montes Sireniani*, they used to be called— the human element is lacking; there is no sound save the chirping of the cicadas among the olive branches; an azure calm, a calm of life, streams down from on high, permeating every sense with tremulous scintillations of vitality. It is always difficult to analyse sensations—imponderable moods; and in such moments of breath- less summer radiance every one will have feelings commensurate to the bent of his mind and habitual associations. Here, in spite of the solitude, it seems to me that no genii of earth or heaven are waiting to hold communion with mankind. I have felt the awe- inspiring midday hush in many wilds and wolds, and often enough the mind, surrounded by the unfamiliar, is prone to conjure up phantoms from inanimate nature. Here it is merely aglow with life; self-centred in the circumambient calm and stimulated to attention by the sun's rays, it is yet at rest. The landscape, therefore, and not only the hour and the man, plays a part when gods are to be created. Perhaps this helps us to understand the enigma of universal Pan. From being an Arcadian forest-god he became, as culture advanced, diffused and impalpable. The forest lost its noonday mystery and its Embodiment was no longer seen of men; he was merged into the brooding meridian stillness of all earth which no clearings, no cornfields, no sparkling cities could impair; his weaker comrades, the fauns and dryads, unable to endure this searching light, took refuge in yet shadier groves, or pined away.

Nor do immortal gods look down from cloudy pavilions, for the sky here is a vast dome, and not a plane. Wherever thunder-clouds touch mountain summits this quaint belief will arise, and Zeus, whatever his origin, found a congenial home in Greece, where the exhalations, formerly more abundant, even now repose upon the hill-tops. In Siren land they do not; they sail overhead in summer- time, a painted argosy that seldom anchors to spill its dewy freight against the mountain-sides, though the *Cloud-gatherer*—when the south wind blows—is busy as at Ægina, collecting out of a sunny sea invisible wreaths of vapour which he spins into a crown about the grey head of Capri. The community of this two-storey-world idea in Scandinavia and Greece is hardly a proof of the boreal descent of some Hellenic gods (we might as well trace it to old Australia, where a Walhalla was fabled among the interlacing boughs of lofty eucalypti); nor yet their violence and unruliness, for in early stages divinity naturally reflects the turbulence of human environment. Wotan, had he survived to this day, would doubtless have become an orderly fellow, even as Zeus did. Altogether, some little nonsense has been written concerning the anthropomorphism of the gods of Greece. As if any deity could afford to dispense with these traits! The Jahveh of the Jews was sufficiently human in his vindictiveness and jealousy; later on, when he became etherealized, the humanity of his son refreshed our interest in him. And what lends the devil his charm? His quasi-human attributes; his bargainings, his ill-treatment at the hands of heaven. Beings wholly divine are inevitably endowed with qualities of good and evil identical with our own: they are mere caricatures of good or bad men. The profoundly divine therefore is, and ever has been, profoundly uninteresting. These Greek gods are extra-human rather than super-human; they are interpenetrations of human motives with new and unaccountable elements. Much might also be said in favour of the view that their absurdities and excesses were deliberately contrived as a foil to the moderation-ideal of the Greeks themselves. Yet, polish away all excrescences and subtilize them to the vanishing point of purity—their pedigrees cannot be wholly expunged; some Lucian will always be there to rake up old scandals; to remind Jupiter Optimus Maximus of certain Cretan meadows and Venus, the *alma mater*, of that affair of the net.

Here, on these odorous Siren heights, far removed from duty's sacred call—for duty has become the Moloch of modern life—it may not be amiss to build a summer hut wherein to undergo a brief period of *katharsis*, of purgation and readjustment. For we do get sadly out of perspective with our environment in the fevered North, out of touch with elemental and permanent things; we are for ever looking up-stream. It is well, now and then, to glance backwards adown that flowing river and to note, before they fade from sight, the strange, half-forgotten landscapes one has traversed. Is it I, one wonders, who thought and felt thus? How one changes! And one's friends—how they change! And even public opinion, that exemplary biped which stands, nose in air and uttering incomprehensible grunts, with one leg in the illusions of the past and the other in those of the future—how it changes!

An old Hebrew, who taught the pleasures of a virtuous life after exhausting those of a voluptuous one, said: Go to the ant; he forgot

2

to remember that the ant sleeps for half the year. Man alone is a perennial drudge. Yet many of us would do well to *mediterraneanize* ourselves for a season, to quicken those ethic roots from which has sprung so much of what is best in our natures. To dream in Siren land, pursuing the moods and memories as they shift in labyrinthine mazes, like shadows on a woodland path in June; to stroll among the hills and fill the mind with new images upon which to browse at leisure, casting off outworn weeds of thought with the painless ease of a serpent and unperplexing, incidentally, some of those "questions of the day" of which the daily papers nevertheless know nothing—this is an antidote for many ills. There is repose in Siren land; there is none of that delirious massing-together in which certain mortals, unable to stand alone, can lean up against one another and so gain, for a moment, a precarious condition of equipoise.

To dream—yes; but, as de Quincey observed, *he whose talk is of oxen will dream of oxen*, and I am not attempting to prescribe for the uncivilized, particularly as they are in loving hands just now: is not the whole trend of our legislation a sustained effort to pamper the unfit at the expense of the fit, to foster the moral delusions of the crowd—of those whose spiritual activities are in abeyance? May they prosper! There will ever remain one badge of distinction to mark them from those of another fibre—their imperviousness to the meaning of certain old Siren voices—

O stay, oh pride of Greece! Ulysses stay!
O cease thy course, and listen to our lay!
Blest is the man our song ordain'd to hear,
The song instructs the soul, and charms the ear,
Approach! Thy soul shall into rapture rise!
Approach! And learn new wisdom from the wise!
We know whate'er the kings of mighty name
Achieved at Ilium in the field of fame;
Whate'er beneath the sun's bright journey lies.
O stay and learn new wisdom from the wise. . . .

for I perceive in this lay no promise of any of those things which they covet, of gold and diamonds and fair women and long life and earthly honours and the joys of Heaven; but only of enlightenment.

And whoso hears these voices, says Homer, nevermore returns to his home and family, which may be taken to mean that certain persons have rated wisdom higher than domestic bliss; doubtless a poetic exaggeration.

III

THE SIREN ISLETS

OF the five Siren rocks only three lie close together, and these are the so-called Galli. The old name Sirenusæ gradually died out; no earlier reference to them under their present one occurs, I believe, than that contained in the chronicle of the Abbot of Telese (1133), who records their capture by Roger of Sicily. He speaks of them as "Guallo"—evidently, therefore, a patronymic from the family of Guallo or Gallo on the mainland—and, what is more singular, he calls them "a little town placed *infra mare*". Now there is a spot called Guallo on the peninsula, but wise men will have it that he meant these islands, and I am not for arguing the point.

It is not absolutely clear, from this and other old documents, whether in those days the three rocks had the same configuration as now; presumably, yes; at the same time, they were certainly spoken of as one and single, and the Amalfitan doge, who lived awhile in exile here, might have found it a more tolerable residence if they had all been joined together. But he had been blinded, and they, whose hands are their eyes, may as well grope about on a rock as on a continent.

How fond they were of blindings and mutilations at this period— the straightforward killing of the Romans was too harsh for these Byzantines, who, like all squeamish people, were proportionately cruel.

Perhaps, too, he was confined in a dungeon, although there is no mention of any buildings on the islands when, in 1330, King Robert reared a brave tower there, whose cistern is still resorted to by fishermen and quail-hunters, for the protection of seafaring men against pirates. In fact, the island, or islands, are expressly called "uncultivated" in the deed which confers the guardianship of this keep to his trusty and well-beloved Pasquale Celentano, who established himself there with four soldiers, and seems to have liked it, for it was he who had applied for the post. His family is still extant.

And so they are at this present moment; uncultivated, treeless and, in summer, aflame with heat; struck by the sun's first beams, they glister through the livelong day and remain fiercely glowing, like incandescent rubies, long after the coast-line is drowned in the shades of evening. Yet there are wandering breezes and a harmonious wave-lapping suggestive of coolness. They lie in a rough circle, and anyone but a geologist familiar with the inevitable "quaquaversal dip" would take them to be the relics of a submerged crater, an illusion which is strengthened by the outward slope and half-moon shape of the greater islet, and by the riven pinnacles of stone gnawed by the waves into bizarre shapes and painted, wherever the spray can reach them, to a murky brown. And this is exactly what one old traveller called them—a mistake for which he was sternly rebuked by Breislack. So Dumas talks of the "granitic ramparts" of Capri, and a Swiss, writing only three years ago, praises its "*parois verticales de porphyre et basalte*". A deplorable lack of general intelligence, seeing that the principal charm of all Italian scenery, its graceful outlines and much of its delicate aerial tints, are exclusively due to a peculiar natural formation. Limestone, and no other rock, is able to produce them.

The Galli, again, are nothing but Apennine limestone—wrecks of the neighbouring peninsula which used to slope southward with a gentle incline so as to include them in its body, even as on the other side it still descends gradually seawards: they were torn off in some terrific prehistoric convulsion. In one spot the laminated strata are broken to form a melodious sea-cave—each cave in Siren land sings its own peculiar melody—the haunt of countless sly-twittering* swifts who rear their families in the shelving rock.

Were I writing a guide-book or historical account of this region, I would endeavour to give a systematic description of these legendary islets, supplemented with measurements and hints for travellers. But I am doing nothing of the kind; I am only dreaming through the summer months to the music of the cicadas, and dreams are irresponsible things that flit about aimlessly, dwelling with absurd gravity upon unconsidered trifles and never quoting statistics.

I sail across to the neighbouring rock of La Rotonda and find— nothing, save a peregrine that dashes off the cliff at my approach.

---

* The epithet applies only to the Alpine species, *C. melba*.

"Ah, if I had brought my gun!" exclaims my companion, with unfeigned anguish. Does he eat peregrines? To be sure he does, and finds them "better than pigeons". Of all the hawk tribe, they are only surpassed by the lesser kestrel, which is *squisitissimo*.

Long ago, the Anjou sovereigns caused the peregrines "in the territory of Capri and Sorrento" to be caught and trained for purposes of falconry.

The third islet, called "Castelletto" from its castellated appearance, is known to sailors as *Punta da Vuccacia* = Boccaccia = a piece of ordnance which, at some period, was placed there to command the straits. A broad rock-cut path, worthy of the Romans, and probably built to allow ships to be drawn on land, ascends part of the way: the rest is rather a dangerous climb. A precipitous crag, inaccessible to invaders; all the summit built over and the limestone chiselled smooth in certain tracts where a sentinel may have paced. I suspect that this fortress dates from 1532, for in that year a native of Sorrento received the grant of all three islets on the condition that one of them should be fortified. It looks as if no inspector had been sent down from head-quarters to see that the work was properly done: a jerry-built affair—King Robert's tower will long outlast it.

Treeless they are, the Siren rocks; but not flowerless. Now that the riot of vegetation has been allowed to grow for the last year or two, one can form some idea of what it would become if left undisturbed for longer periods. Capri, I believe, holds a record for variety of plants on a small space—

> *La Flore est de telle richesse*
> *Que dans ce réduit limité*
> *A huit cents arrive l'espèce,*
> *A trois cents, la variété. . . .*

sings the truthful bard, but nowhere on Capri do flowering plants rush into such reckless overgrowth as here. In the winter months the narcissus dominates; its scent is heavy upon the air and the glossy brown bulbs thrust each other out of the earth; in May the ground is hidden under a radiant tangle of many-hued blossoms that must be seen to be believed. Every flower of Campania seems to have taken refuge on this lonely rock. The rapid evaporation of sea-air no doubt contributes to this luxuriance, and also the rich soil of the outer slope.

I once attempted to draw up a list of the Galli flowers, but abandoned the idea; they shift with every month. Let him, whose mind is at peace, sojourn awhile on these rocks, and there elaborate a catalogue of all of them, great and small, with a shepherd's calendar setting forth their seasons of flowering and decay. Or better still if, detached from sordid cares, he buys the islets outright and replants them with ten thousand shade-giving trees, marrying the rough exhalations of briny sun-scorched rock with the fragrance of rose and cedar. What joy to watch their rapid growth in the deep, warm soil! In these days, when life is so complicated as to lose all homogeneity and unity of purpose, when our fine edges are worn off by never-ending trivialities and meannesses, I often think that planting trees and reclaiming the waste places of earth are among the few occupations that still commend themselves to gentler natures—pleasure and instruction for oneself, health and profit to posterity. . . .

According to Strabo, the Siren islets were "three stony and *desert* little rocks". His words are plain enough, and he uses them twice over.

Were they true, when he wrote?

For whoever, climbing up the usual path from the sea, arrives at the summit of the larger island, will perceive that the rocky surface here has been artificially levelled down for a length of some fifty yards, and, jutting out of the soil, will be seen the substructures of two thick parallel walls of the first century—Strabo's lifetime. Here, then, stood a grandiose edifice, slightly curved so as to follow the natural crescent of the island, with its larger façades fronting east and west. The nameless Siren-worshipper who designed this lordly pleasure-house had studied local conditions of landscape and ventilation; the site could not have been more happily chosen. In the hottest days of midsummer a sea-breeze rustled through those ample halls, and his view was superb, whether, in early morning, he let his eye wander over leagues of violet sea-calm towards Pæstum and the shapely peak of Alburno that fades into mist as the sun gains strength, or glanced westwards into the chaos of rocks and many-hued waters at his feet, with Capri and Ierate in the background, shutting out the world beyond.

The marbles are gone—gone into the mortar of King Robert's tower. Yet, searching among the debris on the hill-side, I found some fragments of white penthelic and *giallo antico* slabs for a pavement, and a systematic hunt might yield brick-stamps which would help to decide the age of the building. The ground sounds hollow in certain places, as if there were chambers beneath.

The foundations of this structure are massive enough to have supported a temple, but I question whether they ever did so, because we should probably possess some record of an ancient divinity worshipped here, and also because, at the water's edge on the inner side of the islet, are the remains of a bathing-house or harbour, or both combined, without which such a large establishment as that above could hardly have been considered complete. Its flooring, of irregular shape, is surrounded by formidable walls of reticulated Posilipo tufa leaning against the hill-side: in the centre stands a modern lime-kiln. Rocks have tumbled upon it and into the sea beyond, but I can detect no traces of its continuation below the waves. At the promontory of Marciano near Massa, on the contrary—a highly interesting point—there is another (contemporary) Roman villa with its little *dépendence* at sea-level, and here the masonry descends into the deep. These are the sites which ought to be examined by those who wish to settle the debated question of the former water-level.

Altogether, it would be well if some trained archæologist were to investigate this and other remains upon the southern shore of the peninsula, of whose existence no one seems to be aware.* No great outlay would be required to lay bare what is left of this building on the Galli-rock, and nothing more enjoyable or interesting could be imagined than this kind of work. Crusades are gone out of fashion for the moment and the only warfare at present worthy of the name is the bloodless crusade against fools ("The Warfare of the Future?")—can any nobler participation in it be imagined than that of unearthing those monuments of bygone ages in whose presence the veriest hind must perforce pause and bethink himself?

The ethics of ruins—their educational value: what has it not done for Italy of the Renaissance? Petrarca already, and Sannazaro and Boccaccio, have drawn deep draughts of enthusiasm from this source. And all this quite apart from the possibility that these deformed heaps of rubbish may hide some marble head, soiled with

* So there is the contorted ruin of a Roman building on the beach at Cantone, below the large tower, not far from a spring which gushed into the sea. The bricks, unfortunately, bear no stamp.

the dust of ages, from under whose stony brow there gleams a look of rare wisdom or sweetness; a revelation—inspiring, compelling.

Meanwhile, what of Strabo and his *desert* Siren islets? This: either the villa here and that on the islet of Isca, of which I will speak later, were only built after his death or, if during his lifetime, he had no knowledge of them. Supposing Mommsen to be correct in surmising that his *Geography* was written as late as the reign of Tiberius, there is still much to be said for the hypothesis of another scholar that it was composed in a distant region of Asia Minor, where it is not likely that the latest information was to be procured.

Be this as it may, one thing is interesting: he says that there were *three* Siren islets. Now if Isca be omitted from this group, as lying too near the land, there is still the large rock of Vetara close to the Galli which cannot be overlooked and which raises their number to four. Can this mean that the three (true) Galli rocks were at that time united into one single block making, together with Isca and Vetara, the three of Strabo? It almost looks like it. Far be it from one who has grown up under the shadow of Lyell to advocate cataclysms: in comparison with other catastrophes which have occurred in these regions the disruption of the Galli rocks from each other would be the merest trifle. We have some historical account of the havoc wrought here during the last thousand years by gales and landslides (ice and earthquakes have done little damage), and it stands to reason that the preceding ten centuries must have been equally fertile in disasters; all the time, too, majestic earth-contortions, they say, have tilted the country up and down, disquieting the works of man.

Where is the house of the poet Tasso, the convent of Revigliano, the town of Marcina, the harbour and arsenals of Amalfi, or the ancient Conca, whose picturesque horn juts into the waves opposite the Siren rocks, and where Richard Cœur-de-Lion halted on his way to Palestine? Engulfed, all of them. A complex study, bristling with difficulties, but full of geological and historical interest. Concerning the "Serapis" temple alone a voluminous literature has sprung up; whether the marshy situation of Pæstum be due to some such subsidence may still be questioned—the deforestation of the mountain slopes, which filled the plains with alluvial soil and damned up the river beds, might also be suggested as an explanation. So the islet of the Siren Ligeia has lately become joined to the mainland through the deposits of the Calabrian streams.

The Greek period over, ancient life on these eastern shores of the Parthenopean Bay resolves itself into one word—Tiberius. His predecessor, it is true, *discovered* Capri, for no earlier Roman, not even the diffuse Cicero, so much as mentions the island; it was as unknown to the aristocracy of his day as it is to the modern *Romani di Roma*, who would as soon think of sailing to the stillvex'd Bermoothes as to Capri: Augustus it was who landed here time after time, charmed with the convival Greek natives and the mild climate; who built those twelve Imperial palaces. But the court remained nominally in the capital. Of Tiberius we know that he *"insederat"*, concerning which cryptic word enough has been written, and that he lived here for ten consecutive years (Plutarch, who sometimes blunders in his dates, says seven); and what this entails may be observed when some sovereign of to-day establishes a temporary residence among the mountains, while country-houses of officials and snobs grow up like mushrooms all around. The Sirens always called Augustus back to them: Tiberius they held fast for good.

This island—Capri—was too small to contain the swarm of nobles and administrators who helped to conduct the affairs of the world; they overflowed and brought life to the mainland, and their names survive to this day in Ceserano, Marcigliano, Mitigliano, and so forth. To this inundation there is the testimony of Sorrentine inscriptions, of works of art like the Aphrodisius statue, and, above all, of the actual existing masonry.

No doubt there was a revival on these shores under Marcus Aurelius and another under Hadrian, but these were men of a different stamp; they were not true Siren-worshippers; they knew what *Weltschmerz* meant. The world had aged frightfully in those few intervening years. Marcus was a conscientious valetudinarian whom the world has agreed to take at his own valuation (that correspondence with Fronto has a sick-room air—the querulous note of expiring antiquity); in Hadrian were summed up all the romanticism and disordered curiosity of a soap-bubble renaissance.

The builder of this sumptuous villa on the Siren rock was no freedman, nor yet a mere worldling. I can conceive such persons establishing themselves in the fat fields of Sorrento, where there was "society" and some business to be done in wine or oil, or among the reeking baths at Baiæ; but it is contary to what one knows of human nature to suppose that an islet like this should appeal to them. No,

2*

he was a civilized man, and it is to be imagined that, unlike Tiberius, who could create his own society, bidding men come and go as he pleased, this one returned city-wards in the winter months to stimulate himself with the din of the Forum and the conversation of his town friends, and to test anew the capabilities of his digestion. The hermit's motto, *vixit qui latuit*, was not altogether his, since the man that has the true feeling for seclusion among these scenes will be the last to prolong his stay, though he may well return year after year, as the Sirens call him back. Nearly all the Roman villas on Capri and the opposite mainland face to the north, which proves that they viewed this country as a summer resort. Who can live here in the winter? Only "foreigners" come at that season. From November to April the whole wind-bag of Æolus is let loose; when there is no hurricane, it rains in torrents; Capri, even with modern appliances (such as they are) is often inaccessible, while the Galli rocks are surrounded for weeks by a weltering waste of foam. No sensible person, unprovided with the comforts—as well as the disillusions—of Tiberius could stand the uproar for three or four months on end; it is like being on board a boat, and when men come to like that kind of life they are, as Johnson remarked, "not fit to live on land. . . ."

Unavoidably one learns to take an interest in the winds hereabouts, seeing that these Siren regions are fanned by every breath of Heaven. In summer it is a simple matter; sea-breeze by day and land-breeze by night, stepping into each other's shoes with praiseworthy regularity; but later on things become complicated, and the catalogue of local winds swells to a formidable size. The northern *tramontana* which closes the pores (speak not of love to these folk when the *tramontana* blows), and the scirocco that relaxes them, are the best known, but not the most popular; the latter may well have increased since ancient times, perhaps on account of the deforestation of northern Africa, else the Romans, who had absurdly sensitive skins and nerves, would have execrated it even more than they did.

Blue-black tints and crisp waves prevail during the *tramontana;* an "honest" wind, because, blowing off the land, it is debarred from becoming dishonest so near the shore. The scirocco's tints are green and yellow, and it has no pretensions to honesty—its wintry convulsions are sometimes so violent that the salty spray is carried far inland, and can be tasted in secluded orchards on the last remaining figs. But perhaps this is cloud-work, for when the delirium is at its height, the clouds often descend and join the fun, tempting the waves to meet them half-way. When these water-spouts, careering distractedly over the waste, break, the clouds cling to what they can of the nether element and bear it away with them on their aerial voyages.

The great storm of 1343, described by Neapolitan chroniclers and in one of Petrarca's letters, blew from this quarter; it destroyed shipping and villages, swallowing what little was left of Amalfi (for that town had been reduced to a fragment before Mola da Tramonti wrote his chronicle in 1149), obliterating landmarks all along this coast, and thrusting even rivers, like the Sebeto, from their courses. Intense darkness fell over the land during those awful days, and turned men's minds to thought of prayer.

I can remember a scirocco phenomenon equally unearthly, perhaps, in appearance. At that time, too, our hearts were somewhat perturbed; things had happened; there had been wars and assassinations of kings, and it was feared, by the simpler sort, that retribution was due. A sultry afternoon was drawing to its close, and I had been observing a small cloud that emerged above the sky-line. It was round as a disc, of ruddy hue, and in texture so compact and un-ethereal as to appear solid. Slowly it grew, and never changed its shape; an hour passed; it gradually expanded into a monstrous peony upon the firmament and, instead of drifting as clouds do, seemed rather to be pushed forwards mechanically from behind the scenes. Its uncommon shape and colour, its spasmodic growth, began to attract attention; we herded together and found ourselves watching its movements not without uneasiness. Suddenly, after an unusually vigorous jerk, the cheering sun was effaced, blotted out behind the curtain, leaving the world in a dim roseate fog. The change was disquieting, and there fell upon us the hush of an eclipse. Then it rained in big, warm drops. I looked at my hand—blood!

"*Male pioggia, signore,*" said an old man, hurrying past me. *Male:* that was the word—an evil rain.

Next morning trees and flowers were smeared over with an incrustation of mud, and sprightly white-stuccoed houses splotched with brown. And presently wise men came with microscopes and chemical paraphernalia; they analysed a speck of the deposit of

the blood-rain and found in it plant-spores from the Sahara and
animalcules of a thousand kinds—a whole world in miniature,
fallen in a raindrop from the sky. . . .

It is rather puzzling when one comes to think of it, to conceive
how the old Sirens passed their time on days of wintry storm.
Modern ones would call for cigarettes, Grand Marnier, and a pack
of cards, and bid the gale howl itself out. But those ancient feathered
fowls—did they peck at each other viciously, or content themselves
with shivering in silence among their crags? So have I seen, during
a blizzard, the bedraggled vultures perched among the bleak hills
of Asia Minor. They sat round the corpse of a camel, one of the
unhappiest of its race, that had dragged huge carpets over the
mountain tracks and expired in the performance of a task for which
it seemed peculiarly unfitted. The vultures craned their necks, but
not one of them moved from its stone. They were plainly hungry.
But they preferred it dry.

No; summer is the time to pasture in Siren land. Even Mrs.
Shelley, for whom I entertain no profound respect, could not but
feel the charm of this season. "It seems", she writes from Sorrento
in summer, "as if I had not before visited Italy." The heat is too
considerable for violent exertion, but time passes quickly doing
even nothing, if one does it well. And for studious persons who
desire local information, there is literature galore—histories and
chronicles of the rich city of Massa in the olden days. They read
pleasantly under some vine-clad arbour.

Rich and populous it must have been, for older authors give
glowing accounts of its palaces and industries and great men.
How, then, came it to sink to its present level? The sages will refer
you to corsair raids or to the plague of 1656, quite forgetting that
the writers who describe such a flourishing state of things lived
exactly at the time of these events. I rather think it was another
kind of plague, the plague of a century of Bourbonism, which
reduced these regions to a condition of misery whence they are now,
thanks to a better government and to Argentina, slowly emerging.
For ordinary pestilences and famines and earthquakes are mere
amateurs in destruction whose effects are healed in briefest time:
there may even be witnessed, after occasions when the plough of
affliction has violently disrupted the soil, a strange quickening of
growth. But misrule strikes at the root of things, since the humane

strivings in a people, those of its elements that actively make for good, are so sporadic that their annihilation is wholly different from a haphazard calamity. And there was a sinister thoroughness in the Bourbon system which ensured success. The effects of such a conscientious selection of badness must necessarily endure; it takes longer to rear up that which is humane than its opposite, seeing that there are a thousand wrongs for one right. "There is no town and there is no country", says a Neapolitan historian, "which would not inevitably be impoverished by the loss of so many and such distinguished men." It is this same elimination of progressive elements which has done so much harm to Spain and Russia, and which paved the way, according to Professor Seeck, for the fall of ancient Rome. Medical men are beginning to estimate, with something approaching accuracy, the effect of wear and tear upon the individual organism; experiments on the lines laid down by Mosso and de Fleury may soon enable us to express it in mathematical terms; but its effect upon the organic system of communities—upon their arts, commerce, industry, and all the finer fibres of their social being—who shall compute it? Who shall estimate the vital strain of a century of terrorism?

Those Englishmen, therefore, who complain of certain unpleasant characteristics of modern Neapolitans, might do well to remember that the Bourbons had been incapacitated from further mischief when their saviours from over the sea appeared on the scene and allowed them to continue for another half-century that rule of brigands, monks, *lazzari*, and other vermin which was responsible for this deplorable state of affairs. There had been tyrannies before in Naples, odious tyrannies; but despots, secular and religious, had been powerless to smother the grand traditions of Hellenic culture, the envy and delight of ancient and mediæval Europe. A glance into early literature will show what Naples has done in the domain of philosophy—it was ever the first city of Italy for speculative thought; a glance into the works of pre-Bourbon travellers will afford a description of the inhabitants of Naples, and of the provinces, as *they* saw them. The Neapolitan Academy for the Study of Nature was the first to be founded in the world: it preceded the English Royal Society by nearly a century. One of the brightest pages in human history is the successful struggle of the Neapolitans against the inquisition. This, and much else, might be said in praise of pre-Bourbon Naples. But where philosophical books may not even be

imported into a country, much less printed; where the reading of
Voltaire is punished with three years' galley-slavery, and that of
the Florence newspapers with six months' imprisonment—how
incredible it seems, nowadays!—the flower of civilization withers
and fades away. Despotism, priestcraft, and proletariat have ever
been good friends; a kind of freemasonry, unintelligible to simple
folks, has conjoined them from time immemorial against the
honest and educated classes. Unable to stand alone, they lean
against one another for mutual support, and thus in the mephitic
calm of ignorance, the structure remains upright, a marvel of equipoise: like a child's house built of cards, a breath of enlightenment—
and it collapses.

We find natives of Siren land involved in all the movements of
the capital. Capri, for instance, distinguished itself in the inquisition-
frays—a certain Costanzo of that town was one of the three chiefs
of the *fuorasciti* who, while numbers of the Neapolitans fled into the
country to escape the bloodshed, purposely came to Naples with
their adherents in order to support the city against Don Pietro di
Toledo and his proposed inquisition. The contest was no laughing
matter. It lasted for months; the streets ran with blood; sparks,
they say, flew from the eyes of the terrible viceroy, and the notary
Grassi, who had been deputed to read the city's protest to him, was
so overcome by the ordeal that he took to his bed afterwards and
died in three days. As a pendant to this liberalism, the pious
Monsignor Apuzzo, Bishop of Sorrento, perpetrated the official
Bourbon "philosophical catechism"—an exquisite monument of
bigotry. And foreign residents, too, have sometimes come forward
with honour. There died at Capri, in 1892, the Englishman Wreford
who for nearly half a century, as *Times* correspondent, waged
unceasing warfare against Bourbonism and whose report on the ill-
treatment of political martyrs furnished the material for Gladstone's letter to Lord Aberdeen of 1851. It is fitting that a man like
this, who "did a knight's service for Italy and the world", should
not be forgotten, and the municipality of Capri will do well to erect
a tablet to his memory.* He came to the island, originally, for an
afternoon, and stayed there over thirty years.

The Sirens, says Hyginus, were fated to live so long as they could
detain passers-by. Can they be still alive?

And he who really finds time heavy on his hands might do worse

* They have since done so.

than compile a literary *catalogue raisonné* of this region.* By Janus! A little while ago I found myself recommending the planting of trees and the unearthing of Roman remains, but now it seems to me that the compiling of bibliographies is a more respectable occupation, for in tree-planting there are degrading collisions to be anticipated with thievish gardeners and workmen, as well as the painful reflection that posterity will turn into cash the fragrant groves, chuckling at the old fellow's sentimentalism ("he blundered into a good thing, now and then"); while the excavation of antiques runs perilously near the bric-à-brac business, a demoralizing form of commercialism. How one changes! But *malheur*, says Renan, *à qui ne se contredit pas une fois par jour!* Around the bibliographer's table there lies a passionless calm, unruffled by politics or sex-problems; we all become tender-hearted towards the innocuous enthusiast who writes for the delectation of one odd lunatic-scholar in every hundred years. The thing has been done, of course, by various writers—but in a perfunctory fashion; the ideal catalogue of a region like this must be compiled *con amore*. . . .

Here meanwhile, is a curious item touching a shipwreck on the Galli rocks which will be referred to therein. I translate it from a manuscript entitled *Dies brumales* in the convent of Sant' Anna del Pertuso. So far as I can discern, the *Dies brumales* seems to be the product of some monkish pedant-poet who aimed at inculcating, under the cloak of adventures, moral maxims to youths preparing for a religious life; somewhat after the fashion of the Jesuit Daniele Bartoli who published, in the seventeenth century, an edifying but wholly unreadable "Geography Transported into Morals".

"When Anselmus had done, the Prior told us that this about the Arimaspians was only an old fable contrived to show the folly of gold-seeking. For gold and love to aught save God, said he, are

* An unmistakably wholesome sign of the times in Southern Italy is the revival of local historical studies. Societies are formed, libraries collected, and every little spot has its champion biographer—often busy professional men, who sacrifice their leisure to patriotic researches. Siren land is no exception; much has been written of late concerning Sorrento and Capri; Filangieri's new account of Massa is scholarly and exhaustive and the bibliography of Doria promises well. Works which used to be picked up for a few sous are now worth as many francs, and the chief second-hand bookseller in Naples tells me that for the last three years not one of the rarer writings on Capri has passed through his hands; old monographs like that of Persico on Massa, Secondo on Capri, or Molegnano on Sorrento have clean vanished from the market: when found, they can be weighed against gold. Such facts are as convincing as a good Treasury budget.

the mainsprings of wrong action, and few evils that afflict mankind cannot be traced to one or the other. And he said that long before regular trafficke with the Orient was established by the Vessel of Cava, certain mariners of Amalfi went forth in ships and were often killed by barbarians or shipwrecked for their greed.

"And now a rare tale, quoth he, comes to my mind anent a vessel which foundered in a siroc not far from the Siren rocks, where all hands were drowned save only the captain's son, who was reserved for a worse fate. Him the waves bore to a pebbly beach, as far as might tire a little child to run, whereon sat a maiden singing, who looked up with eyes of friendship. Being a grave lad, he walked aside and, stumbling among the stones, happened upon a heap of decaying human bones, a loathly thing. Yet she followed with endearing words, till he lost reason for her sake. Fair to see was this maiden, and to bespeak—fair beyond all imagining to those she had fooled, and he deemed himself favoured above the angels. A brief infatuation, for soon a change came over her, and while he cherished her more than before, the light of love faded out of her eyes, and there stole into them the look of an hundred generations of tigers. Then ever and anon he would bethink himself of what he had seen among the rocks, and would fear for his life. For he had given his heart, but she had sharpened her teeth.

"And Anselmus said:

"'I conjecture that this was some Siren's mischief.'

"But the Prior held that Sirens are fables of the pagans, and that belike this was an earthly maiden, and what befell between the two is called earthly love."

IV

TIBERIUS

Let us examine this Siren-loving monster, Tiberius, a little nearer.

Broad-shouldered, stooping, and tall above the common measure, slow in his movements and speech, with great glittering eyes and hair falling over the nape of his neck, wrapped in a ceremonious and almost awkward reserve—such is the external impression we gain of him. And if, forgetting awhile his character as ruler of the world, we survey him in a private life, we soon discover what manner of man he was—a specimen of what the French call *la vieille roche*. Courteous and formal, a strenuous cultivator of the "grand manner", a conservative in speech, detesting all slipshod expressions, slang, and Gallicisms (Hellenisms); economical, conscientious, methodical; a scorner of luxury and dissipation and an outspoken enemy of the irregularities of fashionable married life. this old man—he was old, before he became emperor—possessed many of the virtues which, if we are to believe our grandfathers, were far commoner in their days than in ours. Of course his frugality was interpreted as avarice, while a certain invincible shyness, peculiar to many great men, was put down to pride—that celebrated pride of the Claudian house, whose true significance, like that of the democratic Gracchi, it has taken the world twenty centuries to understand. The younger generation of his day hardly appreciated traits like that recorded of him when, one day, only half a boar being served up at table—the other half having been eaten previously—he observed to the embarrassed company that "the half boar has just the same taste as the whole". A particularly fine fish was brought to him; he sent it out to be sold, remarking that some rich fellow like Apicius or Octavius would be sure to buy it. He was right; after some bidding, it fell to Octavius for 5000 sesterces. The profligate youngster Caligula, we are told, was kept very strictly "under the simple and wholesome mode of life" of Tiberius on Capri; whenever he went out for a spree, he disguised himself in a wig and muffler so as to escape unobserved. . . .

Of the military genius of Tiberius, his political sagacity, his assiduity in work: of his wonderful ability for finance and administration, there has never been a question. If the Roman world was able to withstand the shocks of the madmen who succeeded him on the throne, it was due to the stability and prosperity in which he left it. And wherein lies the secret of his intellectual superiority and successes? In this, I think: that he had a conspicuous preference for the able and honest common man. He knew the rottenness of the aristocrats of his day and treated them accordingly. "He was always unwilling to admit them to authority, and it is unquestionably true that, taking them as a class, they were during his long and prosperous reign treated with unusual disrespect. . . . Although he evinced the greatest anxiety to surround the throne with men of ability, he cared little for those conventional distinctions by which the minds of ordinary sovereigns are greatly moved. He made no account of dignity of rank, he did not even care for purity of blood. He valued men neither for the splendour of their pedigree, nor for the grandeur of their titles. . . . His large and powerful intellect, cultivated to its highest point by reflection and study, taught him the true measure of affairs and enabled him to see that to make a government flourish its councillors must be men of ability and virtue; but that if these two conditions are fulfilled, the nobles may be left to repose in the enjoyment of their leisure, unoppressed by those cares for the state for which, with a few brilliant exceptions, they are naturally disqualified by the number of their prejudices and by the frivolity of their pursuits."

Is not this an exceedingly truthful account of the aims and methods of Tiberius? Yet it is extracted out of no biography of that emperor; convert the "he" into "she", and the words will be found in Buckle's description of Queen Elizabeth.

Both sovereigns correctly judged that the nobles of their time had played their part—idle, intriguing, and discontented, they were now merely a menace to the peace of the empire. Among the self-made men whom the Roman emperor drew to his court was the senator Lucilius Longus, who clung to Tiberius "in good and evil days" and whose death, we are told, afflicted him as much as that of his only son. Another was the knight Curtius Rufus. To those who reminded Tiberius of this man's lack of pedigree, he was wont to reply: "Rufus, it seems to me, is his own ancestor". The minister Sejanus was also one of these *new men*, as the Romans disparagingly called some of the ablest of their time. The persons who witnessed the testament of Tiberius were "quite ordinary people". He married his grand-daughter to a man whose grandfather, Tacitus regrets to say, "everybody had known as a common knight in Tibur". Like Elizabeth, too, he had little respect for the senate, whose undignified flunkeyism made him sick. "O generation fit for slavery!" he exclaimed to them. And simultaneously he detested —an ancestral trait and one that he possesses in common with refined persons of all ages—the grossness of the proletariat. He never encouraged their cravings for gladiatorial shows. He gave few games. That sufficed to damn him in their eyes and to make them forget all he had done for the maintenance of public order, and all his munificence towards them in moments of public distress. "Into the Tiber with Tiberius!" may well have been sincere, for the common herd of ancient Rome was the same ignoble beast, governed only by its appetites, and as incapable of any generous or even consecutive thought, as that of our day.

The events of his life, a series of sharp disappointments, brought out more clearly with increasing age the characteristic of the Claudian house: cynical aloofness. Embittered in his family and marital relations, thwarted by the intelligent plebeian (Sejanus) in whom he had placed his confidence, he felt all the loneliness of his position.

He felt also—his power.

Modern Europe, grown wise with age, has muzzled its sovereigns. Thus has arisen a race of constitutional marionettes, whose chief occupation—to judge by the newspapers, at least—consists in "swopping" uniforms, rushing about the continent in special trains, and hanging ribbons and decorations round each other's necks. This is all as it should be, and it is well to remember that the muzzling has been done by the class of men whom Tiberius respected and sought to bring to honour. It is also well, now and then, to ask ourselves this question: how many of those who now "govern" Europe would display the magnanimity of Tiberius if they possessed a tithe of his power—how many would follow his example in refusing all external honours, or exercise his clemency towards religious dissentients, caricaturists, and political adversaries? The mind shudders to think of the pandemonium that would break loose if these were allowed, only for a day, the freedom of Tiberius. On that day, there would be more prosecutions for *lèse majesté* in Germany than in the immense Roman world under the whole reign of Tiberius; Austria and Russia would be aflame with the fires of *autos-da-fé*. There is recorded, on this last matter of religious persecution, a remark illustrating the fundamental sanity of Tiberius which cannot be too often repeated. A man was about to be put on his trial for insulting the divinity of the deceased Augustus, but the emperor stopped the proceedings by saying that "gods could avenge their own wrongs"; *deorum iniurias deis curæ—* a genial, golden pronouncement, which deserves to be graven over the portals of every church on earth.

The fact is, he had learned worldly wisdom where our present rulers can never hope to learn it—in the rough school of life. And he had the courage of his convictions. How many men and women of to-day, the slaves of contradictory conventionalities, might take to heart that saying of his: "Let them hate me, so long as they approve my actions." This is monumental. We may place it beside that sentence which Stahr, with great propriety, has cited at the end of his volume of Tiberius, and which shows his real feelings in regard to public opinion. After repeating the words of Tacitus to the effect that "it was not so much that he cared to gratify the present generation, as that he was desirous of standing well with posterity", Stahr quotes the final passages from a speech in which Tiberius deprecates the erection of a temple to himself and his mother: "For myself, conscript fathers, I am a mortal man; I am confined to the functions of human nature; and if I well supply the principal place amongst you, it suffices me, I solemnly assure you; and I would have posterity remember it. They will render enough to my memory, if they believe me to have been worthy of my ancestors; watchful of your interests; unmoved in perils and, in defence of the public weal, fearless of private enmities. These are the temples I would raise in your breasts; these are the fairest effigies and such as will endure. As for those of stone, if the judgment of posterity changes from favour to dislike, they are despised as no better than sepulchres. Hence it is I here invoke the gods, that to the end of my life they would grant me a spirit undisturbed, and discerning in duties human and divine: and hence, too, I implore our citizens and allies that, whenever my dissolution comes, they would celebrate my actions and the odour of my name with praises

and benevolent testimonies of remembrance." "And thenceforward", Tacitus adds—I cannot resist quoting this characteristic
touch—"thenceforward he persevered in slighting upon all occasions, and even in private conversation, this worship of himself; a
conduct which was by some ascribed to modesty; by many to
distrust of his merit; by others to degeneracy of spirit"—and by
none, it seems (certainly not by Tacitus), to its most natural cause,
common sense.

Common sense—that is the mark of Tiberius, and no wonder it
was a feature offensive, almost unintelligible, to dreamers who
yearned for things that are not, for things to come or things that
have been. A destructive flood had overswept some districts of
Rome, and there was an outcry that the goblins overhead must
be appeased and the Sibylline Books consulted with that object.
Tiberius thought it more profitable to appoint a commission to
enquire into the causes of the disaster and report upon the measures
to be taken for avoiding it in future. Sober talk like this will never
win a crowd.* Towards the end of his life he allowed senate and
nobles, both equally worthless and effete, to seize each other by the
throat; anticipating, probably, that the most impulsive and incapable on both sides would be the first to succumb, leaving the
men of moderation to survive. A rugged method, the method of
nature; yet a cynical and civilized modern aristocrat like the late
Lord Salisbury would have acted in precisely the same manner.
Brutality and common sense are not rarely different names for the
same thing. There are men who call surgeons brutal, because they
amputate limbs.

This firm grasp of general principles never degenerated with
Tiberius into coldness. On the contrary, there ran through his
nature an opposing current: a strong vein of kindliness and consideration for others which alone can explain many of the enigmas,
as they are called, of his life. He was capable both of feeling, and of
inspiring in others, deep attachment. He might even be called an
idealist in the sense that he seems to have expected more of the
world than he found it could, or would, perform; and, as such, his

---

* When it was announced to him that the skeleton of a giant had been unearthed and his views were asked as to what should be done with it, he replied
that "they had better leave the giant lying where he was". How different from
Augustus, who possessed something of the curious spirit of Sir John Soane and
founded the first palæontological museum in the world, containing "giants' bones
and weapons of heroes", which were zealously collected for him on Capri.

sufferings at the blows of fortune were proportionately the more intense. For the calculating individual changes little during life; from the cradle to the grave he pursues the even and not always lovely tenor of his way: the man of heart, as we say, has only to live long enough in order to become something of a cynic. And Tiberius lived to the age of seventy-eight.

Of his kindliness many instances are on record. Such was that little incident at Rhodes. "One morning, in settling the course of his daily excursion, he happened to say that he should visit all the sick people in the town. This being not rightly understood by those about him, the sick were brought into a public portico, and ranged in order, according to their several distempers. Being extremely embarrassed by this unexpected occurrence, he was for some time irresolute how he should act; but at last determined to go round them all, and make an apology for the mistake even to the meanest among them, and such as were entirely unknown to him." By what an accident of history has this charming episode been preserved! When his brother, whom he loved sincerely, died, Tiberius accompanied the funeral cortège, on foot, all the way from the forests of Germany to Rome. Paterculus, speaking from personal experience, has recorded how thoughtful he was, during his campaigns, for the health and comfort of his troops. When any officer was ill, Tiberius saw that everything was done for his well-being and recovery; "for all, who required it, a carriage was in waiting; the use of his sedan-chair was free to all, and I myself, among others, have profited by it." When at last his dissolute second wife Julia, the cause of endless trouble and pain to Tiberius, had been divorced from him by decree of her father Augustus, he "interposed by frequent letters to Augustus on her behalf, that he would allow her to retain the presents he had made her, notwithstanding the little regard she merited from him". His affection for his first wife Vipsania, whom Augustus obliged him to divorce for political reasons "not without great anguish of mind", is recorded by various ancient writers. A chance meeting of the two that took place after this event is thus described: "At divorcing Vipsania he felt the deepest regret: and upon meeting her afterwards, he looked after her with eyes so passionately expressive of affection that care was taken she should never again come in his sight". Observe, now, how so simple and natural a story can be misconstrued. After referring to this passage, Beulé says: *"Peu de mots peignent beaucoup de choses: ce ne sont point des larmes qui jaillissent des yeux de Tibère à la vue de la compagne de sa jeunesse; il n'éprouve ni douleur ni regret; ses yeux s'enflent, se tendent, s'enflamment. Les sens parlent donc seuls, c'est le cheval qui hennit devant une belle cavale."* Truly, the *dernier mot* of Beulé's *odium republicanum.*

Although such flagrant defamations are scarce, there are various passages where a misinterpretation of some authority, now lost, has led to far more serious errors. Here is an interesting example from the classics which I do not remember having seen recorded among the thirty-odd monographs on Tiberius that have come under my notice. On the one hand, we have the careful tables drawn up by Sievers, Freytag, and others, analysing the criminal cases under his reign, from which it can be seen how frequently he intervened to mitigate the sentence of the condemned. We have seen the testimony of Tacitus, who records a senator saying: "I have often heard our prince (Tiberius) bewail the event, when, by suicide, a criminal has prevented the exercise of his mercy". On the other hand, we are told that the emperor was so bloodthirsty that he lamented whenever a criminal "escaped" him by killing himself. "For he thought death so slight a punishment", says Suetonius, "that upon hearing that Carnulius, one of the accused who was under prosecution, had killed himself, he exclaimed: 'Carnulius has escaped me!'" The accounts both of Suetonius and of Tacitus may well have been drawn from the same original source. Now: this preventing—this escaping: what shall we make of it? Does the suicide escape his cruelty or his clemency? We may decide for the latter version by throwing into the balance the fine trait recorded of him to the effect that, although slow in his usual speech and almost wrestling, as it were, with the utterance of his words, "his language flowed freely and rapidly whenever he had occasion to succour (*quotiens subveniret*)".

Can anything definite as to the character of Tiberius be read out of his busts? I think not. I think we are not yet in a position to deduce a single mental quality from the features of any human being, alive or in effigy. Grossly asymmetrical lines will of course suggest a flawed physical structure and consequent disharmony of mind; but phrenology, the theory of Gall, and physiognomy, as expounded by Lavater and his disciples, are still on a plane with astrology; the modern historian or critic, who builds a hypothesis of character upon the evidence furnished by such vague speculations, is no less of a quack than Nostradamus. Like many inexact arts, to be sure, these tend to become more scientific every day; various currents are converging in that direction; but nothing exemplifies better the worthlessness of present-day authority in these matters than the conflicting characteristics which writers, according to their several passions or prepossessions, succeed in discovering in the busts of the Roman Cæsars. When one remembers with what slavish fidelity the artists of ancient Rome reproduced the original features in these works, it would stand to reason that the character to be read out of any single one of them would be constant. Yet it is no exaggeration to say that a portrait of one of the Cæsars is capable of as many interpretations as a contested passage in Holy Scripture. There is no vice, and there is no virtue, that has not been plainly read out of the busts of Tiberius. His mouth, according to one writer, betrays "indecision"; another discovers that "about the delicate mouth plays a smile of superiority"; a third writes, "probably at no time has nature formed such a perfect diplomatic mouth. Firmly closed, it illustrates Talleyrand's saying that speech was given us to conceal our thought"; while a fourth shudders at "the horrible grimace, which one cannot drive from one's remembrance". And so on, with every other item of the face.

In regard to the bust as a whole, a similar uncertainty prevails. In the Paris sardonyx cameo, Beulé recognizes, admirably portrayed, all the vicious qualities that form his idea of Tiberius, "*la bouche, le menton, sont gras, sensuels, épais, et tournent au type de Vitellius. Le cou est énorme, enflé par le vin, la bonne chère, et comme par un venin secret*, etc. etc." According to Bernoulli there is no reason for supposing this cameo to represent Tiberius at all! The "veiled head" sold to the British Museum by Castellani is rejected by some of the best authorities as not representing Tiberius, while many persons consider it one of the most life-like busts. As in most of them, the nose, the telling feature of the face, has been restored, and in the present instance by an unusually inferior artist, so as to change its whole expression. The nose of Tiberius was probably moulded after the aquiline pattern of his mother's, with whom he had many points of character and physiognomy in common. The restorer of this "veiled head" has given it a nose of a peculiarly London cast, so that the portrait at a distance looks less like Tiberius than like his family butler. The ears are also restored in conventional fashion —altogether, the bust is a good instance of the unwarrantable liberties that are taken with ancient works of art. And yet if this

London head were placed side by side with that in the Naples museum, the resemblance would appear in a flash, in spite of the disfiguring "repairs". The London portrait represents him fifteen or twenty years older than the other; there are lines of age about the face, and the eyes are more sunk under the prominent orbitals, but there can be no doubt as to the identity of the person. To compare photographs of these marbles is misleading; they must be examined on the spot, for a slight change in the position or height of the camera may affect the entire physiognomy; nor must it be forgotten that the profile differs on the two sides of the face. But what type of man these busts figure forth can only be deciphered by those who have made up their minds on the subject beforehand. Long years will elapse before serious psychological deductions can be drawn from the data of iconography.

After a youth of exemplary virtue, and half a century more of public life, during which the manners and morals of Tiberius were an honour to his age, he retired in his sixty-ninth year to the island of Capri, in order at last to be able to indulge his latent proclivities for cruelty and lust. So, at least, the wisest of us believed for twenty centuries. We have all heard of the reformed rake; Tiberius was the reverse: from being an Admirable Crichton, he became the prototype of the Marquis de Sade. But it is needless to go into this *res adiudicata;* historians like Duruy, Merivale, and Ferrero, however much they may disagree upon other questions, are at one upon this: that no scholar of to-day, with a reputation to lose, should stake it upon the veracity of Tacitus and Suetonius. That is a great step forward. Napoleon called Tacitus a "detractor of humanity": he seems to have arrived at this opinion upon purely *à priori* reasoning, but critical researches have borne it out. The Roman historian has been tumbled from his pinnacle, and there is poetic justice in the fact that Tiberius, whose memory he succeeded in disparaging for nearly two thousand years, has been the cause of this revision of judgment. Nor need we call this stately writer hard names; it suffices to say, what no one will deny, that he suffered from a constitutional dislike of the obvious; his mind was involuted; he worked with a fixed idea, and that fixed idea was diametrically opposed to the fixed ideal of Tiberius.

We often observe that an individual who is not fully bred exaggerates all the peculiarities of the race to which he desires to belong. Thus a German Jew, domiciled in London, will eat his plover not only putrid, like the rest of us, but putrid and raw. Even so Tacitus, as an aristocrat of the lower order, was extreme in his aristocratic tendencies, he was *plus royaliste que le roi;* for no one save really great people, like the Claudians of Rome, can afford to treat their class at its true value. According to Boissier, Tacitus "resigned himself" to the empire; it seems to me that he resigned himself with sufficiently bad grace, and if, like Tacitus himself, I could claim the gift of knowing the inmost thoughts of men, I should say that the anti-oligarchical leanings of Tiberius appeared reprehensible to this reactionary who yearned, in his heart of hearts, for turbulent days of immature political development, which every Roman of sense rejoiced not to have witnessed.

He took his pen in hand and wrote. All ancient literature of this class is what the Germans call a *Tendenzschrift:* we must ever remember that such a thing as truth is neither what authors endeavoured to write, nor what readers cared to read; the extent to which the whole world was tainted with the rhetorical spirit is not easily appreciated nowadays. And beside this love of simple veracity, another recent product of human growth is that of scientific psychology. The "great psychologist" Tacitus, who imposed upon ancient and mediæval Europe with his childlike and subjective method of approaching these problems, with his sublimely artful manner of reading imaginary characteristics into historical personages in order to draw puritanical conclusions therefrom, will find himself ill at ease among men who have outgrown scholastic morality, and think themselves quite moral enough when they try to discover a plain answer to this plain question: Is it true, or is it false?

The shrewd Montaigne seems to have been the first to doubt the sincerity of Tacitus; Schedlbauer cites a German pamphlet of 1646 in favour of Tiberius; but it was reserved for the French sceptic movement to shatter eternally the faith hitherto reposed upon Tacitus and Suetonius. As with other authoritative writings, it was little suspected how rotten—once touched—they would prove to be. Previous to that time, these tales were blindly believed. So Gilles de Raïs, who was executed in 1440 after having murdered eight hundred children, confessed in his defence that he was led into these excesses through reading Suetonius' life of Tiberius. Strange to think that, but for Suetonius—are we never to have an annotated modern translation of him?—we might not have heard of Blue-beard.

Then followed the inevitable reaction, a wave of sentimentalism and general obfuscation from which we are, at this moment, emerging. During this long and dark period, Tiberius again put on his old character; he was a "deified beast"; his court was composed of "pale and trembling slaves, dissolute women, and executioners". In this exhilarating company the old gentleman is supposed to have lived from the age of sixty-eight up to his death ten years later. That sane people could be found to listen to such nonsense, proves what a systematic education in "believing the impossible" can accomplish. What would they now say of Monsieur Bacha, the last of a succession of conscientious scholars who have dissected the fables of Tacitus, who consistently refers to the once revered historian as "*le poète*"? "*Dans l'invention de ses contes, Tacite s'est incessamment préoccupé d'intéresser le lecteur.*" I suspect that the chief reason why it pleased us to dislike Tiberius arose from the fact that Christ was crucified during his reign; the culpability of the emperor in this matter is not obvious, but when religious feelings come into play, the mind ceases to trouble itself with cause and effect. The logic of the emotions, says Ribot, does not acknowledge the fundamental principles of the logic of the intellect. One point is noteworthy: with this recent revival of rationalism has gone, hand in hand, an increased feeling of decency. The obscenities which charmed our pious forefathers of the Grand Tours, who would muse for hours over the *Sellaria* of Capri, and sell their last shirt to buy a sham sphinctrian medal, have ceased to absorb a generation fed upon healthier mental fare.

If we knew exactly why Tiberius, as a young man, shut himself up in Rhodes, we might understand the reason of his retirement to Capri. This departure for Rhodes may be regarded as the key to his character, and a great diversity of motives—fear, disgust, cunning, hatred of Julia, ambition, self-abnegation, disappointment, pride, general moroseness—have been assigned by various writers for this step. Family reasons, the eternal intrigues of the women of the Julian and Claudian houses, and his own mother's behaviour towards him, probably weighed heavily in the case of Capri; but, as Mr. Baring-Gould points out: "Throughout life that passion to be away from the stir of life, and to be alone with his thoughts and with his books, manifested itself spasmodically."

It is quite likely, too, that, convinced of the impracticability of republican and despotic systems of government, his friends and helpers all dead, he attempted the experiment of constitutional rule, interfering as little as possible in the machinery of the state, while reserving to himself the last word upon all graver matters. Above all, he was weary after a public life of nearly sixty years of incessant toil.

The idea of retiring from the cares of government may seem absurd to us. But we must consider the kind of work which confronted Tiberius. Modern sovereigns, whose most violent physical exercise takes the form of shooting tame pheasants or leading a drowsy state-ball quadrille, would be killed outright by a single one of his many campaigns: the economic problems with which he grappled day after day would permanently liquefy their brains. The labour of government is taken out of their hands by persons who are fitted to perform it; not one of them could say, with Tiberius, that "he found in work his only refuge from cares". Unlike him, therefore, they remain ever delightfully young, and it is hardly to be expected of them that they should bid good-bye to the world in this heyday of perennial youth. Our rulers never tire from the cares of government: they never feel them. Tiberius, at the age of sixty-eight, felt them, and this retirement to the rock-islet of Capri is of grave significance in the world's history, inasmuch as then, for the first time, the centre of the world was displaced, the spell of the Eternal City broken and, in the words of J. R. Green, "never thoroughly restored. If Milan, Ravenna, Nicomedia, Constantinople, became afterwards her rivals or supplanters as the seat of empire, it was because Capri had led the way." And small wonder if these closing years of the tyrant have appealed to the imagination of poets from early times, for he looms grandly in his majestic and mysterious isolation; there is pathos, too, in that ruined family life, and a tragic note in his hopeless endeavour to stem the rising flood of irrationalism and slave-spirit that were soon to overwhelm the great Roman world.

Where did all these Tiberius-legends arise? I question whether they were actually manufactured in Rome; they were probably a local product that found its way into the memoirs of the younger Agrippina. To the Greek population of Capri the personality and habits of this emperor were hardly sympathetic; no doubt his presence made them feel uncomfortable, especially when contrasted with the easy-going conviviality of Augustus. A certain sycophantic spirit of ancient lineage (the Romans would have associated it with their conception of *græculus*)—a certain hellen-istico-political tendency to anonymous letters and misrepresentations, may have laid the foundations upon which Tacitus and the others erected their surprising fabrics. Dion Cassius, who ought to have known better, since he warns his readers of the general untrustworthiness of all Augustan history, was yet too much of a Greek not to enjoy a little gossip of this kind. We all know that *les absents ont toujours tort* and that, as Bacon says, "mankind is possessed of a natural though corrupt love of the lie itself"—particularly when it is told of the moral shortcomings of great people. Some escapades of Caligula or other youngsters may be responsible for the origin of a few of these tales, all of which, if related of Tiberius, are improbable, and some impossible—a fact which did not strike his biographers, who, like our own earlier historians and painters, were less anxious about veracity than about making as fine a picture as possible. As Mr. Huidekoper justly observes, the persons whom Tiberius selected to accompany him to Capri were all good men, and the last to condone any form of vice. But the strongest evidence lies not in the praises of Paterculus. It lies in the silence of Seneca, who is outspoken enough as regards the irregularities of other emperors. "What necessity", asks G. M. Secondo, the contemporary of Voltaire, "drove Tiberius to indulge his lusts on Capri, when nothing hindered him from doing so at Rome?"

Among the many explanations of these Capri orgies that of Wiedermeister must not be omitted. He seriously suggests that the thoughtful entourage of the old man merely carried out the precepts of the contemporary physician Celsus as to the stimulating effects of sensuous pleasures upon the declining health of Tiberius. The tortures of prisoners and the nautch-dances were only nerve-tonics, scientifically applied. Perhaps the *gerocomic* method, not unknown among the ancients, was also attempted. Celsus probably drew his knowledge of it from the Orientals who still practise it; a certain old king in the Bible derived strength from it; as late as 1700 the great physician Boerhaave (according to Hufeland) was in the habit of recommending it for the infirmities of old age, and I am told that it is not yet altogether out of fashion in good society.

Wiedermeister is a good illustration of the evils of writing history on the *Leitmotif* system. Even as Pasch—to my thinking—perverts some evidence and omits the rest in order to show that "ambition" is the mainspring of every action of Tiberius, so this writer finds everything to agree with his preconceived theory of "insanity". Tiberius at Capri is supposed to have suffered from the mania of persecution, ending in senile dementia. In proof of his madness is adduced the fact that *he complained of the debauched habits of his (adopted) grandson Nero*. As if Tiberius had not been making complaints of this kind, and with perfect justice, all his life! We can understand Tacitus considering that a man who lives outside *la ville* must be a lunatic or a desperate person; the Emperor may well have been an enigma to republican bourgeois, but a modern writer, surveying this period of Roman history, might have noticed that the gift of self-control and sanity is precisely what distinguished Tiberius in a world that was rapidly losing the faculty of dominating its reflexes. The empire was breaking up from psychical disorders. Hysterical and otherwise mentally deranged individuals are apt to distrust the saneness of those who are placed in charge of them, and this, I think, accounts for most of the "madness" of Tiberius. In retiring at the close of an arduous life to enjoy the beauties of nature on fabled Siren shores, he was only doing what any civilized person might be expected to do.

Even at this distance of time it seems not easy to write of this man, as Tacitus claims to have done, without passion or partiality. Of the prodigious literature which has sprung up around his name, one of the best surveys will be found in Professor Gentile's interesting monograph. Happily it cannot be said of this controversy, as of many others, that it has produced more heat than light. I would express the opinion that the Tiberius question has been practically settled; nothing more, at least, can be learned out of books; the material at our disposal has been sifted in a perfectly satisfactory manner. Yet the record is far too incomplete to allow us to form a final judgment. To do this, we require the memoirs which he wrote himself, as well as the lost historical works of Pliny the Elder, Cremutius Corda, Paterculus, Seneca, and others. Of this ancient literature, which would complete our picture of Tiberius, a great portion is lost for all eternity; some of it remains, in all probability, within a few feet of our reach.

Whoever wishes to consult it must wait till a generation, which really possesses the civilization it vaunts, shall rescue it from the lava of Herculaneum.

V

THE PHILOSOPHY OF THE BLUE GROTTO

TO-DAY the north wind, the *tramontana*, is blowing. A glance out of the window suffices: the sea is deep blue, with ruffled face; mountains and villages are standing out in clear-cut sunshiny reality. And yonder goes the steamer conveying six hundred foreigners for their day's visit to Capri and its celebrated Blue Grotto. Unhappy mortals! They are packed like sheep, although they have paid untold sums for their tickets.

But—in parenthesis—if the foreigners were not constrained to travel first class and at exorbitant rates how could the steam-boat company pay its expenses? For the natives of the country are divided into two great sections: those who travel with third-class tickets, and those who travel with no tickets at all. And of these two sections the latter is by far the most numerous, comprising, as it does, every one who claims to be a friend or patron of the company, such as: all persons connected with marine service in any part of Italy; stationmasters, engineers, signalmen, soldiers, and so forth, as "colleagues"; hotel proprietors and their families and servants, because, if there were no hotels, there would be no foreigners for the steamers to carry; village fishermen, because they can handle an oar, and their wives and sisters who cook fish which comes out of the sea; certain privileged shopkeepers who once sold a piece of soap or a cigar to a patron; greengrocers, because the captain is fond of vegetables; pastry-cooks and confectioners, because the second stoker has a large family of children—in fact, almost the entire population of the country is exempted, for one reason or another, from purchasing tickets. Eight days ago a grimy house-painter, travelling in the "foreigners'" steamer, informed me that he always voyaged gratis because he lived in the same street as the captain.

Only the poorest of the poor, those who command no respect from either captain, crew, or agents, are obliged to buy third-class fares.

On board, however, the company makes no invidious distinction between these two great sections of natives: they are all accommodated with seats in the first cabin.

And occasionally it arranges for a public example *in terrorem*. Only a short time ago I listened to a stately old gentleman protesting, with tears in his eyes, that he was a prince of the blood besides being mayor of ——. But on that day the official was obdurate. It was "tickets or stay behind". Loudly grumbling, the venerable one extracted a few sous out of his pocket for a third-class fare, and presently I found him seated at my side, explaining to a sympathetic audience that the company had lost what little reputation for honesty it ever possessed. . . .

The *tramontana* generally blows for three days, and is followed by a spell of halcyon calm. Then is the time to visit the Blue Grotto, as an English poet of the thirties has very correctly pointed out—

> The day must cloudless be to visit it,
> The brilliant skies of Italy should pour
> A flood of radiance o'er the tranquil deep,
> And zephyrs even should be hushed and still, etc.

But not in the tourist crowd, although Augustus Hare tells us that the magical effect is enhanced by the rush of boats, the general confusion, and impassioned shrieks that burst forth on all sides. Nor yet in the morning hours, whatever the guide-books may say to the contrary, for it is only later in the day that the roof and sides of the cavern begin to clothe themselves with that quivering violet sheen due to the low position of the sun. This fairy-like bloom more than compensates for some lack of intensity in the blue of the water.

Dear Ouida! Is there really nothing to be said for the full-blooded generosity, for the passionate blend of realism and idealism of her earlier work? However that may be, it was these afternoon hours which her heroine Idalia, with her usual good taste, selected upon a memorable occasion for a visit to this "temple not built of men".

"Passion was stilled here; love was silenced; the chastened solemnity, the purity of its mysterious divinity, had no affinity with the fevered dreams and sensuous sweetness of mortal desires.

. . . The boat paused in the midst of the still violet lake-like water. Where he lay at her feet he looked upwards at her through the ethereal light that floated round them, and seemed to sever them from earth. . . . Would to God I could die now!"

This was the Blue Grotto of the last generation.

"When I entered it," says Gregorovius, somewhat more articulately, "I felt myself transported into one of those fairy-tales so real to childhood. The world and daylight have disappeared suddenly, and one finds oneself in the over-arching earth and in the blue twilight of electric fire. Gently the waves lap and the bubbles rise sparkling, as though flashing emeralds, ruddy rubies, and countless carbuncles were shooting up through the depths. The walls are of phantom-like blue and mysterious as the palaces of fairies. It is a glamour of strange nature and strange effects, quite marvellous, at the same time weird and familiar."

Plainly, the Blue Grotto must be one of the wonders of the world. Yet I question whether, if it were discovered to-day, it would attract the attention it once did. For it appeared on the crest of an immense wave of cavern and ruin worship that overswept Northern Europe—the reaction after the hard and brilliant sceptic movement of the preceding century. It was part of the return to nature; of the revolt from reason. Mankind was weary, for the moment, of straight thinking. Shelley warbled of odorous caves so tunefully that men were almost tempted to become troglodytes again; Rousseau raved of noble savages: he showed us how to discover beauty in Switzerland—the beauty of a coloured photograph. Yes; and long may Switzerland with its sham honey, sham wine, sham coffee, sham cigars, and sham Wilhelm Tell—with its inhabitants whose manners and faces reflect their sombre and craggy mountains—long may it continue to attract, and wholly absorb, the superbly virile energies of our own upper-better-middle classes! Thanks, Rousseau; thanks for not living in Italy.

Others did. Flaxen-haired dreamers, like Hans Christian Andersen, began to sing the praises of the Blue Grotto to a generation reeling with emotionalism. Says Speckter, another sentimentalist: "A melancholy, dreamy effulgence irradiates all things, and in this Blue Wonder are blended Love, Art and Nature. The Blue Grotto is the full, the over-full, nectar-goblet of Phantasy." They who wish to know to what depths of inanity this kind of talk can be carried, should read *Fiormona*.

3

The South Italian, constitutionally more sober and familiar with things of beauty, cannot wind himself up to this pitch of rapture over natural objects, besides being quite deficient in that pathetic fallacy which sets up a bond of communion between ourselves and the inanimate world. There are wondrous tints of earth, sky and sea in these regions—flaring sunsets and moons of melodramatic amplitude that roll upon the hill-tops or swim exultingly through the æther; amber-hued gorges where the shadows sleep through the glittering days of June, and the mad summer riot of vines careering in green frenzy over olives and elms and figs; there are tremulous violet flames hovering about the sun-scorched limestone, sea-mists that climb in wreathed stateliness among wet clefts, and the sulphurous gleams of a scirocco dawn when fishing-boats hang like pallid spectres upon the sky-line: there are a thousand joys like these, but the natives do not see them, although, to please foreigners, they sometimes pretend to.

The Blue Grotto belongs to that multitudinous class of objects whose connotation is uselessness and whose full charm is not to be perceived by the bodily eye alone. If the beauty, even of landscape, were to be perceived solely through the medium of the optic nerve, the myopic Hearn would assuredly not be the best describer of things Japanese. This is clear from the way Northerners used to write about this cave; it is not only intensely blue, but it also reminds them of things quite immaterial—of the fairies of their childhood, of the fabled blue flower of romance, of the legend of Glaucus and Elysian skies. Its beauty, therefore, lies partly in suggestion; there is something behind the blue—the mystic's spiritual associations. To a delightful Frenchman, on the other hand, its colour suggested a very material object: a candle held at the back of a bowl of sulphate of copper.

The old theory that the Greeks were insensible to the romance of scenery is exploded; apart from the testimony of the anthology and other literature, a single building, like the temple of Bassæ, proves that they were a-tremble in sympathy with the milder voices of nature. And what we may call the indifferent attitude of the South Italian in such matters results, I think, from two causes: the influence of the Romans, whose chief idea of beauty was some snug villa remote from politics and bores; and of mediæval movements, that destroyed certain finer emotional fibres and sundered the connection with the mythopœic lore and nature-gods of olden days.

The coils of muscle about the shoulders of some stripling as he strains himself to raise a heavy limestone block; a young girl whose swelling form gives promise of fruitful maternity; a waving corn-field, a shower in May, a dish of fat roasted quails—all this is still legitimately *bello:* but mountains are mere hindrances to agriculture, unsightly protuberances upon the fair face of earth, as the pre-romantic Englishman Burnet also called them (no ancient trait of ours, this fellow-feeling with nature: the very word "romantic", as applied to scenery, occurs for the first time in Addison)*; land-caves are useful for storing hay; sea-caves, blue or green, for sheltering boats in rain; the sea itself, with all its choral harmonies, is merely a place where fishes are caught. The war of elemental forces, stimulating to complex modern minds, has never laid aside for them the terrible and anti-human character with which Greek poets and artists long ago invested it, and which seems to have exceeded their limit of romantic beauty because of its destructiveness to man's life or handiwork. But while the native is beginning to understand, though not to share, the Northerner's passion for storms and cliffs and solitude, he still remains hopelessly at a loss to comprehend those recondite ideas of the beauty of pathological states, of suffering and disease which, creeping in from the East, have affected even us, the children of Goths. In short, it seems to me that the South Italian's notion of beauty is never disassociated from that of actual or potential well-being.

It is therefore hardly surprising that the Blue Grotto appealed so slightly to the inhabitants of Capri that they never succeeded in discovering what there was to discover in it. More than three-quarters of them, at this present moment, have not entered it. Those who have been there express no desire to behold its marvels a second time.

And are we not coming round once more to this old pre-romantic point of view? To the romanticists who flocked hitherward in such shoals that their writings and engravings still flood the market, Italy—her landscape, literature and art-relics—was a teacher, *the* teacher, the very crown of life. What is Italy now? I open a catalogue of travel publications and find, on three consecutive pages, a list of sixty-eight new books describing every corner of the globe, three of which deal with Italy: three out of sixty-eight,

* Addison in 1705, but John Evelyn in 1654.

and one of them a belated translation of old de Brosses' gossip (1739).

If we now go to Italy at all, we go not to learn, but to compare. Horizons undreamed-of, intellectual and geographical, have recently dawned upon us. Greece was discovered; then Egypt and Babylonia and the Sanscrit regions, and—to take only the case of antiquarians—men whose sole idea of research has been to excavate statues for decorative purposes and who, if they ventured to theorize at all, confined themselves to searching for ordered designs of Providence among disordered accidents of history—these men are now engaged in building up, out of mounds of Asiatic kitchen-refuse and such-like trash, a plan of man's early existence upon earth which their ancestors would have deemed the height of folly and blasphemy. Everything has shifted since *homo sapiens* himself shifted and ceased to be hinge of the universe; life, once the gift of a jealous god, has become a mere series of readjustments, and "nature" the summary of our experience of them; it is hopelessly old-fashioned, nowadays, to read benevolent intentions out of, or into, a movement of things of which we ourselves, together with all the gods and devils we ever created, are only an aspect—an emanation; and which, though it displays neither good nor evil, has yet taught us an entirely new code of morality: the code of truthfulness. We are no longer men of a book, like the Turk with his Koran or the ancients who ended in being hypnotized by their Homer—things that may be a strength in early stages but that lead to ossification; if we now die of a kind of national arteriosclerosis, it will not be the fault of our teachers.

The attitude of a present-day visitor to spots like the Blue Grotto is unintelligible unless one remembers this change in the world-spirit—unintelligible often to himself. I have heard people lamenting that they cannot feel its beauties as acutely as they think they ought. And yet there is nothing to grieve ourselves about; we receive as much sensuous stimulation from the landscape as is good for us and, to atone for lack of sentimentality, we are probably interested in many things of which our grandfathers never dreamt. A sincere zest in diverse facts of life—an opening of moral pores: this is the result of the new departure. Man's field of inquiry used to be limited, while his credulity was unlimited: it is now the reverse in both cases.

Who of us nowadays writes in language like that of Speckter?

Alas, we are tired of dreaming; we have become materialistic once more, like those horrid Frenchmen; we will read our Haeckel over and over again, but none of us—no, not one—visits the Blue Grotto twice. And yet it has made Capri. It has slowly but surely routed the rivals of this island, Ischia, Sorrento, and Amalfi, who are bursting with envy; it has created hotels, steam-boats, and driving-roads; it has stuffed the pockets of the gentle islanders with gold, transforming shoeless and hatless goatherds into high-collared Parisian cavaliers; it has altered their characters and faces, given them comfortable homes and a wondrous fine opinion of themselves. *Viva la Grotta Azzurra!* It has lately built the funicular railway; it has dappled the island with the villas of eccentric strangers; it has studded the lonely sea-shore with caves fancy-tinted like Joseph's coat. For hardly was the Blue Grotto discovered and the meaning of the word "blue" explained to these children of nature before other gorgeous caverns, hitherto unnoticed, claimed attention. The foreigners liked colour in caves. The foreigners brought money. Colour in caves is cheap. Let them have it! Therefore, in a twinkling, the two-mouthed Grotta del Turco became the Green Grotto; the venerable Grotta Ruofolo put on a roseate hue sufficient to justify the poetic title of Red Grotto, and the Grotta Monacone (*vide* the relation of Kopisch) was discovered to be white—actually quite white! The stranger had his wilful way, and the metamorphosis had cost the Capriotes not a *soldo*. It was a blessed time: every one beamed with joy. But what will the future bring? The gentle islanders have grown rich, rich beyond the dreams of avarice, and almost turn up their noses at *soldi;* while travellers are beginning to turn up their noses at Capri caverns, whose odours, to tell the truth, are not always of violets.

If the Green and other grottos had ancient names, what was that of the Blue? It used to be called Grotta Gradola: a pleonasm, inasmuch as Gradola, or Gratula, is merely a corruption of Grottola (grottola, gruptula, grupta, crypta), and the district overhead bears the old name to this day. I know no earlier proof to show that the Italians were acquainted with the Blue Grotto than that contained in Coronelli's *Atlante Veneto*, which includes an interesting map of Capri, whereon it is marked as "Grotta Gradola". Coronelli was cosmographer to the Venetian Republic, and his work is dated 1696. In the face of a document like this, how absurd it is to say that the cave was unknown to the natives and discovered by a foreigner! It was Landor, I believe, who said that people who talk loudest are always in the right. This was exemplified only the other day when some Germans once more "discovered" a new cave above the Grotta Bianca and filled the newspapers with reports of their achievement, which consisted in using the rope left there by a previous party and effacing an inscription by which they had recorded their visit. The true facts are preserved in the *Geographical Journal*.

The poet Kopisch took a swim in the Blue Grotto in August, 1826—it was not "inaccessible", for he entered it, a few days later, in a boat—but to Andersen belongs the merit of drawing the attention of Europe to its beauties. If *The Improvisatore* had not created such a sensation—who can read it nowadays?—Kopisch would not have thought it worth while publishing, at a later period (in 1838), his well-known account of this exploit, which he calls a discovery, though he admits that the grotto was known to the islanders at the time. The fame of the Blue Grotto was the cause, not the result, of this publication. And another proof of Andersen's moral claim has just come to light in the recently printed diaries of the poet Platen, who spent a few days on Capri in 1827 with Kopisch, sailing all about the island, and not so much as mentioning the marvellous grotto found by his friend in the preceding year. These two romanticists—Kopisch and Andersen—beat the drum. And it strikes me as characteristic of the Northerner that he should suppose that "superstitious dread" prevented fishermen, during long centuries, from visiting this particular cave. Little they know these folk who imagine that superstitious dread plays any part in their daily lives or that supernatural beings, devils or saints, are allowed to interfere in the main objects of existence! Every nook of the shore had been searched by them from time immemorial, and Beelzebub himself could never keep a Capri fisherman out of a sea-cave if there were half a franc's worth of crabs inside it.

Nor was Kopisch the first person to disport himself in this enchanted pool. Long ago, as the islanders will tell you, the Emperor Tiberius and the fair nymphs of his harem did the same, as is plainly proved by ancient masonry about the cave; indeed, seeing that nearly every sea-cave on Capri bears traces of old walls, all of which were built by Tiberius for bathing purposes, it may be imagined what a clean old gentleman he must have been. The only question

that remains to be solved is how he entered the cavern; volumes
have been written to show that the sea-level is not what it used to be
in his time, and it is therefore hotly disputed whether he walked,
dived, swam, drove, or flew into it. There is even something to be
said for the hypothesis that he crawled on all fours. For at the back
of the grotto is a mysterious and narrow passage opening westwards
into the bowels of the earth, which certain sages, who have assuredly
never explored it, declare to be an artificial tunnel leading from
the imperial villa at Damecuta to the cool waters of the grotto.
Tiberius and his frail cortège, after scrambling on their stomachs
for half a league through this dank and dismal drain, certainly
deserved, and perhaps needed, a bath. Let the sages decide these
matters: if we do not arrive at the truth, it will not be for lack of
theories. Like every one else, I have my own views on the subject,
but nothing would induce me to set them down here, for I dread
controversy, and there is no more fearful wild-fowl living than your
historico-physico-geologist. Another of these tunnels, near at hand,
is said to connect the *Palazzo a Mare* with the villa of Jupiter, about
three miles distant! It is nothing but an ancient cloaca, even as
that at the Blue Grotto is a natural crevice supplying in former days
the water which helped to erode the cavern.

There was a confusion at one time between the Blue Grotto and a
huge sea-cave called the Grotta Oscura, which lay on the south side
of Capri underneath the Certosa convent. This Grotta Oscura
used to be one of the sights of the island, and many writers have left
us descriptions of its magical twilight effects and drippings of water.
The locality is now covered by earth and rocks, a landslip having
taken place there in 1808 which closed it up and carried down two
donkeys who happened to be grazing overhead at the critical
moment, as well as a stout martello tower which the monks had
built as a refuge from pirates. The hour was well chosen for this
catastrophe, for the days were at hand when the corsairs ceased to
threaten these shores, and when a rival cave was to become world-
famous which would have eclipsed the beauties of the old. New
institutions, new attractions, had made them superfluous; they were
swept away at the right moment, and no trace of them remains save
the still fresh scar on the hill-side which affronts the traveller's eye
as he sails past under the shadow of *l' Unghia Marina*.

The shade of Tiberius, which used to haunt the Grotta Oscura,
forthwith emigrated to the new cave, where it has since resided.

This is one of the many myths invented by the *Cicerones* of past days, who understood the value of quoting historical authorities and of showing pseudo-historical sites to the credulous traveller of the Grand Tours. Thus there is also a "Grotto of Polyphemus" both at Sorrento and at Capri, and at the latter place an appropriately chosen "Point of the Sirens" which, seeing that it is not mentioned in any old deeds, maps, or books of travel, must be taken to be of modern manufacture. At a certain period, Neapolitans began to take a keen interest in their Siren origin; a large literature sprang up on the subject and the name *La Sirena* has been popular ever since: witness the ill-omened palace on the Posilipo.

On Capri the greater part of these legends are woven round the name of Tiberius. When one remembers that no serious antiquarian researches have been carried out on this island for the last hundred years, during which the science of excavating and interpreting ancient relics has been not so much revolutionized as created, one can understand the prevalence of this Cicerone-archæology. The "Villa of Jupiter" itself, which every tourist visits, is a purely modern fiction; old writers never describe it by that name; and so is the "Salto di Tiberio", where he threw objectionable people over the cliff, and the *Sellaria*, where other things occurred which are best left in the obscurity of a learned tongue. Yet to what outpourings of virtuous indignation have they not given rise on the part of our travelling forefathers, who were hugely interested in the misdeeds of Tiberius.

"May the memory of the monster vanish in the presence of this *wunderschöne Naturscene!*" exclaims the pious Stollberg, who became still more pious later on. "*Quoi!*" echoes a Frenchman, "*cette terre souillée n'est pas devenue stérile?*" An English author improves upon the Salto-legend by causing the spot to be artificially levelled "in order that the condemned might be made to take clean and flying jumps in his presence", while an Italian laments the "rocky promontory from which he was wont to cast his poor, innocent girl-victims". Such are the fruits of Cicerone-archæology.

It is a mistake, I think, to suppose that the various legends of Tiberius which now form part of the mental equipment of the Capriotes and constitute a profitable source of revenue have remained vivid in their memory ever since his day. This is the common belief: but I would hazard the statement that for more than a thousand years—before Italy began to be visited by tourists—

every reminiscence of the old Roman had faded out of the popular mind. Be this as it may, from Ben Jonson onwards a long succession of imaginative writers have chosen this theme. Byron meditated a play on the subject. Some of these stories are good, but many are sad drivel—there is whispered talk of grottos and weird abominations;* artless Anacapri maidens, Oriental slaves, Caligula, and other familiar figures enliven the scene, with an occasional *pas de caractère* (decidedly so) by the ladies of the ballet.

Meanwhile, it is really fitting that the inhabitants of this island, who owe to Tiberius more than to all the saints in the calendar, should put up a memorial to their benefactor. For *Timberio* is still a name to conjure with: to conjure things out of the foreigner's pockets. He is no dim memory, but a clear-cut personality who becomes more distinct and tangible in proportion as these gentle folk conceive themselves of his commercial uses. Several of the former generation knew him quite intimately, and found him most condescending and amiable—*un vero galantuomo*, one old man used to describe him. It is curious, too, to observe that the bloodthirsty aspect of the tyrant is becoming effaced, the popular mind having always a sneaking fondness for a genuine devil or Don Juan, who is never so black as he is painted. Even Timberio, every one knows, had his little traits of gentlemanliness. He was rather too fond of a pretty face, but Lord! so are our priests and a good many others as well. And then he was a real *Signore*, not like the people who come to the island nowadays and who are worse than any Neapolitan for haggling about small change; he paid for everything just what we liked to ask, he built deuced fine cisterns, and he was the only man who could afford a carriage and pair on Capri before there were driving roads. Fine sprees in the Blue Grotto: Ha, ha! As for that Salto of his—why, if that were put into working order again, it would be the best thing possible for the place; Timberio knew what he was doing, he knew! . . . Has His Excellency perchance a cigar about him? Ah! . . . And he had electric light in his bathroom, the scoundrel! Yes, signore, it is a pity Timberio died so young—those infernal women. . . .

* Old Ausonius evidently had something of this kind on his mind when he wrote that third tetrastych—

> Frustra dehinc solo Caprearum clausus in antro
> Quae prodit vitiis, credit aperta locis.

VI

BY THE SHORE

IT was on a cloudy morning in the days when I still suffered under the delusion that one could come to South Italy in winter-time, that I made my first acquaintance with the shores of the Sorrentine peninsula in Ciro's fragile barque. His surviving parent, a stalwart peasant woman, a veritable mother of the Gracchi, forcefully pressed his claims; he was the chief support of a large family, the perfection of qualities, and strong to handle an oar. He did not even smoke "like these vagabonds here", pointing to her other four male off-spring, "who smoked before they were born"; in short, a *figlio di giudizio*, meaning that he possessed tact and politeness combined with attention to personal advantage, a Homeric quality which calls for high praise among a people who admire a man in proportion as he thinks for himself.

I looked at the lowering sky and demurred on the ground of his inexperience. His age, yes; who could tell what his age was? Soon enough they would pounce down on him for military service, and then we would find out all about it. A blessed country, where women never know their ages, and men only for a brief month or so. For why keep track of one's years? Is it not like remembering one's infirmities? Wise men have enough to do, remembering those of their friends.

"Very well, then," she said. "You shall have the little Matilda as well. She is *appassionata* for her brother."

It was more than I had bargained for to take a squalling brat of four in a small boat as a guarantee that the weather would be fine, and I was casting about for an objection that should be unanswerable and yet not offensive to maternal feelings, when Ciro settled the matter by seizing the child with one arm and rowing off with the other. There was nothing more to be said. He quieted its fears with the tenderness of a mother and the resourcefulness of an experienced grand-aunt, and I must confess that, as infants go, she behaved with exemplary tact. They like babies, these boys. On subsequent occasions the little Matilda was left at home.

I asked him, as I have asked many others since, about the Sirens who sang among these rocks. But Ciro's only Siren was an imaginary *innamorata* who still loomed far ahead, though he would have me believe she was waiting for him round the next corner. And the other Siren stories I have heard all bear a modern stamp, thus: that there are three Sirens, young girls, but accursed (*maladette*); that there is one Siren, whom nobody has ever seen and who lives on the Galli islands, where she "calls the weather"; and lastly, that "the English caught the Siren and took her away with them". I am not sure to what this may refer. The English surveyed the coast in Bourbon times and drew up an excellent map of it; they left certain diabolical marks upon the cliffs which are still pointed out with awed respect. The rape of the Siren may date from those days.

Nor could he, or anyone else, give me information about the legend recorded by K. A. Mayer to the effect that "about the Siren islets a huge spectral ship, called *nave di Papa Lucerna*, sails by night; it dates from Roman times and is manned by Roman sailors. It blocks up the straits from Cape Campanella to Capri." This story seems to have faded out of the popular mind.

He knew all about quail-catching and how to snare the red-legged partridges on Mount San Costanzo, which are now, perhaps for that reason, as rare as the dodo; he had also killed some of the wild rock-doves that haunt the *Grotta delle Palumbe*, a yawning sea-cave which throbs with an emerald light-reflection not unlike that of the celebrated Green Grotto at Capri. You will do well to pay it a visit. It lies between Recomone and Isca, close to the rock-needle of Scopolo (locally pronounced Scrofolo)—a word of ancient Pelasgic origin, signifying cliffs in or near the sea, and recurring on Capri and on Ischia.

It is something of a coincidence that two out of the five Siren rocks should bear the names of Isca and Vivara, like the larger islands of Ischia—it used also to be called Isca—and Vivara on the other side of the Bay of Naples. The derivation of Isca is not quite certain; there are Iscas all along the coast; the other means a vivarium (of rabbits). Yet the Siren islet Vivara, though spelt thus on maps, is pronounced Vetara, and I cannot help thinking that this is a corruption of its mediæval name Avetaria. On Vetara there are quails and grass which are rented for about thirty francs a year;

a few ancient bricks, probably imported in post-Roman times; an open cistern; and a race of lizards darker than those on the sister-rocks and approaching in colour the well-known Faraglione breed of Capri.

Isca, which lies like some brooding, round-backed sea-monster within a hundred yards of the shore between Crapolla and Reco-mone, is a far more interesting place. For here are the remains of two Roman buildings, one at either extremity; the best preserved facing eastwards with a couple of rooms still intact, and marbles and fragments of pottery lying around; the other at the sunset end. At both points are rock-cut steps climbing up from the sea; those at the western corner wind past a roofless Roman chamber clinging to the hill-side which the fishermen—by way of giving it an expia-tory name, at least—call the chapel of Saint Anthony, though it clearly never served that purpose.

The most suggestive relic of paganism on Isca is a small grotto which Ciro showed me, and which lies about a yard above sea-level beneath this "chapel". Its entrance has been artificially heightened by chiselwork; within, is a dim and irregular rock-chamber, lined with Posilipo tufa. The builder or proprietor seems to have been dissatisfied with his original design, for new walls of the same period have been constructed across some of its angles, hiding the old ones and making the grotto smaller but more pleasing in shape. The masonry is still covered, in patches, with a fanciful incrusta-tion of limestone pebbles, presumably to heighten the quaint effect. Perhaps it was painted within, or partially inlaid with shining *tesseræ* of blue glass, like some of the caves on Capri.

What deity dwelt here? The water that now oozes from above, fashioning bosses and ridges of translucent opaline stalagmite upon the old flooring, may well have been collected in those days into a shapely marble basin which now serves, for aught we know, as font in some village church. Fully to enjoy this chill retreat one must escape into it, as I have sometimes done, on a breathless July after-noon and listen to the water dripping musically in the twilight and look back, through the narrow opening, upon the burning world beyond; then indeed one feels that its Haunter, whoever he was, deserved worship, and deserves it still. Ciro suggested that the "gentiles" used it *per pranzare*—for dining purposes, which is likely enough; they were fond of taking their pleasure in cool grottos, as we know from that accident at Spelunca where Tiberius nearly lost his life. At the water's edge is a diminutive harbour with what looks like an artificial entrance for a skiff; it reminds me of the Grotta Arsenale at Capri, which has also a small rock-hewn basin of ancient origin at water-level for the convenience of visitors: all of which would go to prove that the sea-level was approximately the same then as now.

Not far away is another semicircular cave with Roman walls and pavement. It lies about ten metres above the sea.

Did these two villas on Isca belong to different families? I like to think otherwise: Isca is too small for two families; too small, almost, for one. I like to think of some solitary Siren-worshipper here, spending a brief summer month amid his vines and books and flute-girls, and flitting from one end to the other of his microscopic domain according to the posture of the planets or his own ephemeral moods; or perhaps a pair of them who, in moments of misunderstanding, would separate awhile, each wending to his own abode, there to meditate upon words and actions misconstrued and the frailty of all human concerns, and how the thing called friendship, once that blithe communion of boyhood is past, is but the gossamer bond of the disillusioned or a frankly utilitarian speculation, seeing that most of us, but chiefly the noblest, are shaggy solitaries growling distrustfully, each in his own cave.

In Roman times the two villas may well have been embowered in trees and connected by a shady arbour. The islet at this moment is utterly bare, and it is hard to believe that only a few years ago it was partly covered with vines, potatoes, and melon-plantations, and partly with timber: six thousand bundles of firewood were taken from it. It is at present on the market; two or three thousand francs are asked, and I would be glad to think that it fell into the hands of one who would renew its forgotten charms. It has the great advantage of being easily rendered inaccessible, for the cliffs, though not high, are nearly unbroken all round the island.

A ship was wrecked here not long ago in a wintry storm; the sailors were cast ashore, where they lived for four days on grass and lizards till the gale subsided and they could be taken off. Such disasters are not invariably accidental. There was one on the south coast of Capri lately; the crew escaped as usual, but the boat was shattered to pieces and the sea covered for miles with its floating cargo of corn. The vessel was old and heavily insured, and the captain received the congratulations of all sensible folks. . . .

There are spots on this southern shore, as at Ierate, where the
precipices are wondrously beautiful, descending into the waves,
with mysteriously shaped openings in their smooth walls. One of
these fissures, under the lighthouse at Campanella, passes clean
athwart the rock and out at the other side, the sky looking through
the rift like a passionless eye of blue. Clouds of swifts emerge from
these rents and oval recesses, skimming the water with rapid wings.

Cliffs, sunny and bird-haunted. . . . How true is this old language? If a man took thought for never so long, could he devise two
happier epithets for these sheets of southern sea-rock, flashing in the
sunshine and enlivened by wild cries and flutterings?

What are these Æschylean birds? The grey swift and its harsh-
screaming northern companion; swallows of more than one kind;
the two kestrels. These are ubiquitous. Then: peregrines and
other falcons; rock-doves; the Mediterranean herring-gull with its
jocular laughing-note, and the azure-tinted thrush, whose cunning
brings tears to the eyes of the native sportsmen. It contributes little
towards the general commotion, but its loud and tuneful song
re-echoes among the clefts. In the breeding season it makes a long
roundabout to approach its nest, with counter-marches and
stealthy diversions, a piece of *malizia* which extorts the fisherman's
approbation. Sometimes, too, you may see the exotic wall-creeper
hovering among the ledges with jerky butterfly-movements, or the
kingfisher picking its way southward from rock to rock, when the
streams in the north have begun to freeze over. They call it *uccello
di San Martino*, because it generally appears on that saint's day in
November. It is strange to see this bird, which we associate with
dim forest pools and reedy streamlets, darting like a blue meteor
along the open salt-water beaches. Eagles and ravens, sea-fowl in
Greece, have deserted Siren land; the latter used to be so common
in Anacapri that one of the reproaches levelled in olden days at its
inhabitants was to the effect that they had learnt their harsh dialect
from the raven's croak. No doubt an ornithologist would find much
to interest him here during the spring and autumn migrations, for
a number of rare birds alight at these seasons. But the country will
wait long for its Gaedke, since every feathered thing is shot and
eaten, irrespective of size or species.

It is not good to be a bird in Siren land.

On the mainland opposite Isca is situated a miniature Blue
Grotto, which can be entered at low water or viewed from above

through a hole in the rock—whence its name *grotta perciata* (cloven). It is a favourite abode of the *bove marino* or hooded seal, an amiable monster which used to frequent the caverns of the Tyrrhenian but will soon be extinct. In severe storms this huge creature sometimes takes refuge among the rocks, emerging with half its body above the breakers: the face and cowl-markings are human enough to be mistaken by simple folks for those of a monk, and wherever there is a cave or promontory along these shores called Monaco or Mona-cone, it refers to the apparition of this sea-monk in days of old. The *monstrum marinum monachi forma* was a ceaseless source of marvel to the learned Aldrovandus, Olaus Magnus, Pontoppidan, Maiolus, and other sages; in 1531 there was even captured, in his full vest-ments, a sea-bishop, *vir marinus episcopi forma*—he was presented to King Sigismund. Of this race must have been the triton sounding a conch in a cave, concerning whose discovery ambassadors were specially despatched from Portugal to the Emperor Tiberius, and that other one, six cubits long, which was caught in the waters of Posilipo in 1660, with a trumpet in his mouth and a crown on his head. Like the Sirens, these male sea-dignitaries became so common in the Middle Ages as to lose much of their consequence. And, like them, they were generally mute: De Maillet reports that one who was kept alive at Sestri used to sit in a chair all day long, sobbing and refusing food, and could not be induced to utter a syllable.

Ciro told me how the *bove marino* lives here and at the point of Campanella, and now and then, on moonlight nights, swims over to the Galli rocks to eat the celebrated *frutta di mare* there, or to the Red Grotto at Capri to visit "certain relations"; which visits, he added, were always scrupulously returned. I imagined that these animals, familiar to me from the Ægean, had nearly vanished here-abouts. Not a bit of it, says Ciro. They are only sly—infernally sly.

"Why, only two years ago," he told me, "I caught one myself on this beach. I heard its voice: it was calling for its mother. And soon enough the old woman came up, but—! you should have seen how she made off when she saw me. It had no teeth and was as gentle as a little puppy-dog, a most delectable beast."

"What did you give it to eat?"

"Bread and beans. But it died all the same. One day they killed a very, very old one. He was the grandfather of the whole family, and he had a tremendous moustache as white as the sky. We all had compassion on him—he was so like the old general at Sant'

Agata. But the fish he had eaten! And sometimes they climb into
the vineyards at night to steal the grapes, just like a confounded
cristiano. Many people have had their grapes stolen that way. And
when they have had enough, they fold themselves into a sort of
ball, like an orange, and roll back into the water, and drink, and
drink. . . ."

"Don't you think someone else might steal the grapes?"

"Boys' tricks," he replied scornfully.

You will not hear folklore from the girls of Siren land. They are
not going to be caught talking nonsense, like their brothers. They
are quicker than boys in perceiving why a foreigner asks after such
things, and can cast off old memories of the race more easily, having
worked on them, I suppose, less thoroughly. Besides, for a stranger
to converse for any length of time with peasant girls or married
women is one of those things which are tolerated (foreigners are
queer people, anyhow) but not viewed with pleasure, and he will
be respected in proportion as he avoids the familiar tone with
women. Old cronies, of course, who have concluded their duties
towards society, are to be considered as outside this convention.
They are often perfect mines of animistic lore.

Wandering among the people here are also certain fairy tales,
conti di fata, reminiscences of Bidpai and *The Arabian Nights*—the
Hashish Eater, Sindbad, and about twenty others—some dull,
others humorous, many of phenomenal indecency. But when they
are told with an open, frank countenance, amid hearty peals of
laughter, they go forth naked and unashamed, like Adam and Eve;
and far more amusing. Hard to catch, these Milesian ghosts—the
men have no time for such trivialities, the boys are growing sophisti-
cated and self-conscious, and old women of the right sort are
becoming rarer every day. I have sometimes thought of collecting
them for scholars and doing them into monkish Latin, a sonorous
tongue allowing of tergiversations and *double entendres* and a mock
dignity peculiarly adapted to this kind of literature; not omitting,
in certain parts, some of those magnificent verses which are chiefly
associated with church music, but would serve a worldly purpose
equally well, such as—

> *O iuvamen oppressorum*
> *O solamen miserorum*
> *Da contemptum supernorum*
> *Dixit custos rotulorum.* . . .

The Romans may have invented Latin and the Moors rhyme, but it was reserved for Christians to contrive this happy blend of both, these full-blooded cadences that crash through the thin troubadourish squeakings of mediævalism like some purple-nosed abbot elbowing his way to the refectorium.

Projects!

Some of the men are good raconteurs, but they are apt to know too much; they are overlaid with recent experiences, and so they overlay their tales. Even as the young blackbird best displays the ancestral thrush-like markings of the race which become over-coloured in the adult, so here the younger generation portrays most clearly some of the traits and feelings of the past—of that incomprehensible, lawless, and terror-stricken past of which the individual child-mind is no mirror, but only a distorted reflection. For children begin by being older than their parents, and end in being younger, and the recesses of their minds are inaccessible as that Hercynian forest of old.

Compared with that of northerners, the mental outlook of these boys is restricted, and a narrow frame will hold the picture of their hopes and fears. But this picture has all the directness, the *naïveté*, of what is called the youth of the world; a very ancient youth, since it already bears the impress of uncounted generations of anti-lawlessness. It is not praising them unduly to say that their minds, like their limbs, grow straight without schooling, and that they possess an inborn sobriety which would be sought in vain among the corresponding class in the North. It is the quality which the Greeks called σωφροσύνη. Inured to patriarchal discipline from earliest childhood and familiar with every phenomenon of life from birth to death, they view their surroundings objectively and glide through adolescence without any of the periodical convulsions and catastrophes of more introspective races. Their entire vocabulary consists, I should think, of scarce three hundred words, many of which would bring a blush to the cheek of Rabelais; yet their conversation among themselves is refreshingly healthy, and many subjects, popular enough elsewhere, are tacitly ignored or tabooed. Not Puritans, by any means, nor yet the reverse; they will bend either way, but, the strain relaxed, they forthwith straighten like a willow wand: if this be not virtue, according to Aristotle's definition, what is? Emigration is unfortunately producing a very different crop of youths; gamblers, wine-bibbers, and flashily dressed *mezzo-signori*.

The environment, to be sure, to which these people are so well adapted, is one of archaic simplicity, and every one of its social and ethical problems has long ago been solved and codified; amid the wilderness of our ever-changing worldly circumstances they would be hopelessly lost; indeed, they regard our whole civilization as a vast perambulating lunatic asylum.

Small wonder, considering the exemplars of septentrional culture which occasionally stray hither: elderly females that wander by the sad sea-waves, distributing Protestant tracts to illiterate pagan fishermen; beetle-collectors; pale youths who fix up a hammock in which they live night and day, declaring that such was the way of the Christian Fathers, then suddenly vanish, leaving their bills unpaid; or downright lunatics like that batch of men and women who arrived the other day *vom lieben Schwabenlande* in apostolic garments, which they proceeded to doff in the market-place, till the population rose up against them. (They said it was the newest fashion in religion, which is quite a mistake, because it is the oldest— that of the pre-Adamites and gymnosophists. Francis of Assisi endeavoured to revive this sunshiny method of adoring the Almighty, to which Krafft-Ebing has given a new name.) To minds accustomed to militarism and the "Thing In Itself", there is something intoxicating in the purity of the atmosphere and the comparative freedom from police inspection—your Teuton loves being supervised—to be enjoyed here: it prompts them to improbable deeds. . . .

"Do you see that old house over there?" Ciro once asked me, pointing to a ruined tenement. "A *male sito*—a bad place, signore. Strange things come flying out of that window; bricks, and pieces of cloth, and lightnings, and God knows what. And sometimes— sometimes one can see a light burning inside. Ugly things."

"Would you be afraid of living there?"

"Afraid? Not likely! But they carried away everything years and years ago. Why, the carpenter alone said he would not do his part of the job for less than three hundred francs."

"The *munaciello*?" I suggested.

"Who believes in the *munaciello*!"

A good many people, apparently. Or perhaps they only pretend to; it is hard to say. He is quite a useful domestic spirit, if you know how to deal with him; he gives lucky numbers for the lottery and shows where money is buried. But you must keep the information to yourself, and not imitate the foolish woman whose oil jar he filled up day after day till she confided the secret to a neighbour, which spoilt everything. Sometimes he guards the house in the shape of a snake, or appears to the terrified wayfarer as a ghoul—a bodiless head.

More often he is simply spiteful; he throws people about. They re-furnished a certain resort of his, a decayed tower, thinking to drive him out: on the very first evening, he tumbled the proprietor out of bed. If you look up from the sea at Cantone you will observe to the westward, under the cliff of San Costanzo hill, a yellow* house, solitary, among olives; it is called "Grale"—a name I cannot explain—or *casa degli spiriti*, and it used to be a summer residence of the monks who lived below: its subsequent history is also curious but not edifying. This "house of the spirits", then, is a chosen abode of the *munaciello*—he threw a woman off the roof and a child out of bed; disguised as a pig, he actually tempted a man to cast himself over the precipice and so perish.

I lived in it for two months, but never caught sight of him.

A volume could be filled with the local legends of the *munaciello*, who is sometimes accompanied by one or more cats. It is the malicious and sly monk, with one foot in hell; but what makes him interesting is that around this rather plump modern contrivance have grouped themselves many fragments of ancient and mediæval beliefs, floating dispersedly adown the stream of time: the witch-element, Sabazius, Queen Mab, Poltergeist, the Familiar, Proteus, and so forth. A heterogeneous accretion; like those wanton islands of the South that are formed of multifarious river-debris lingering around some insignificant nucleus.

The Mammone, though he only frightens children, has a far purer pedigree, being the lineal descendant, they say, of Mormo, the terror of little Greeks and Romans. But perhaps this is a mistake; perhaps he is Mammon, one of the many heathen idols who become a demon. There is something of the *beetle* in Mammone which is not clear to me: beetles, great and small, are often called by this name, and if you ask why, the answer will be: "Because they are so ugly." It stands to reason that gnosticism and suchlike observances were more hateful than downright paganism to the early church, and I sometimes ask myself whether this *mammone*, this god of the heathen, was not identified in a manner with these cults and with

* Now painted pink. This is the house where *Siren Land* was begun in May 1908, at the section (p. 177) "The summer is fast drawing . . ."

the scarabs which poured into Italy during the later Empire, or were found among its ruins and worn, here as elsewhere, as amulets for their occult virtues. If you show a scarab to a child he will always call it "Mammone". However that may be, the beetle-charm, which differs from the ancient scarab shape, still survives and is credited with great efficacity: the Neapolitan murderer Erricone, when arrested recently in New York, was wearing one of them round his neck.

It is a singular parallelism, by the way, that the Mammone, a beetle, should be useful for frightening purposes, even as we talk of a bug-bear: bug signifying both a beetle and a fright. . . .

Many other caves and inlets we explored together in that craft of Ciro's, and much he told me of their wondrous lore: far-off memories now, flashing like sunny gleams across the intervening gulf. . . .

What Ciro's ambitions were, I never learned. Or perhaps I have forgotten. Doubtless they were modest and well within range of realization, for the improbable had no place in his worldly calcu-lations. On him Athene had set her seal of temperance; that want of self-knowledge, the greatest sin of the Greeks, could never be laid to his charge. Maybe he dreamed of some white-domed cottage among vines and olives, not far from the sea, with a boat near at hand, and five or six children as amiable and simple-minded as himself. His dreams, whatever they were, remained unfulfilled, for he lies buried in an alien land, under a flaming sun. So his mother told me some years ago, merely adding, with antique resignation, that he was a good son.

Requiescat.

VII

THE COVE OF CRAPOLLA

ONE of the quaintest spots in Siren land is the inlet of
Crapolla on the south coast. A rugged path, frequented
by fishermen who bring their produce over the ridge to
Sorrento and by a few bathing enthusiasts of Sant' Agata, leads
down the incline, becoming more precipitous as it breaks away,
perforce, from the stream which flows alongside, and which ends in
a cascade at the back of the inlet. This is no walk for a summer
morning when the glare from the shadeless limestone rock is terrific,
and one wonders how those old monks who lived in the abbey of
San Pietro di Crapolla close by the sea were able to endure it.
Likely enough, the road was shaded in those days by oaks, single
groups of which may still be seen along this slope in isolated spots
where it has been found too troublesome to cut them down. These
Theocritean vales are fast disappearing, since oaken timber is in
great request for shipbuilding at Piano di Sorrento and Castella-
mare—though not for purposes of furniture, as it grows too fast
to be solid; the chestnut takes its place in this respect.

The monks were of the Basilian order, and documents relating to
the abbey go back to the twelfth century: in fact, all along these
shores, at Nerano, Sant' Elia, Capri, and elsewhere, were small
monastic establishments, generally of Franciscans or Benedictines,
who spent calm and godlike days in these abodes of peace, content
with what vineyards and houses and ducats the pious inhabitants
gave them in exchange for spiritual consolations. No doubt the
corsairs are responsible for the abandonment of some of these convents. This one at Crapolla must have remained fairly intact till the
thirties, except that it was unroofed, for Marianna Stark describes
the mural paintings and the interior of the church, which was
separated into three aisles by a double row of columns, eight in
number; six being of Parian marble, the others of granite. It is an
utter ruin now. Some of the columns are supposed to have been

taken from the great Minerva temple at the promontory of Campanella—Donnorso, who wrote in 1744, is one of the first to make this assertion, which may well be true. The grey granite ones are still there, lying among the debris, and undoubtedly antique; the others, the white ones, were carried away from Crapolla about thirty years ago and sawn up, I was told, into window-sills, mortars for pounding sugar, and other domestic implements. *Sic transit!* At the entrance of the so-called Abbazia in Sant' Agata are two small marble columns* which are said to come from Crapolla— they are grooved in a spiral whose centre depression may have been overlaid with mosaic.

A hermit lived among the ruins of the ancient abbey so long as visitors went there to supply him with donations, solving the problem which ever confronts these holy men: how to *mangiare franco* (eat gratis).

Everyone knows who took away the wealth of Crapolla and other sacred buildings all over Italy. It was Napoleon.

"Come here, Don Gioacchino," he said one day to one of his scoundrel friends, "and let me see what advice you have to offer. Listen: I must make war with Moscow, a paltry half-year's job, and—well, I have no money. Now?"

"Half a year, your Majesty?"

"Not a day more."

"Make money with the church plate of these Italians and buy cannons with it. That will suffice for exactly six months."

"An excellent suggestion, *caro mio.* And you shall be general in my army."

And so it came about that the convents were raided and a new sort of money, called Napoleons, coined with their proceeds. But the war lasted seven months instead of six, and everybody was killed except Napoleon and his friend, who had sewn themselves up in the belly of a horse. Even that did not humble Don Gioacchino, for he afterwards tried to be governor of Naples, and the king was obliged to have him shot at Pizzo in Calabria.

Some say that the ship which took the wealth of Crapolla was so laden with gold that it foundered just outside the islet of Isca. *Chi lo sà!* If so, it will be fished up again when the blessed Bourbons return to power.

There was one thing which Napoleon overlooked when he sacked

* Now carried away.

this abbey : its *tesoro*, or buried treasure. It was a hen and six chickens of pure gold, and it was raised not so very long ago. A boat arrived late one evening with three men, who stepped out and walked up to the ruin; the first man carried a sack, the second a pick-axe, and the third—*the book*. That looked suspicious. . . . They hammered all night long, and when the sun rose they were gone. How it was found out? Why, a short time afterwards a small boy went to look at the excavation they had made and picked up a golden chicken which they must have lost or forgotten—he took it to the tax-collector at Sorrento, who gave him a few sous for it. (Lucky tax-collector! It was worth many hundred thousand francs.) Then other people looked more carefully, and soon discovered the exact spot where the hen had been sitting in the earth, with three chickens on each side of her.

The country is full of these treasure-legends, but the natives are not prone to supply information on the subject, fearing that the stranger may be versed in *l'arte* (magic) and thereby enabled to unseal the enchantment for his own benefit. This same "chicken-motif" occurs in many parts of Italy. It all depends upon the proper use of "the book"; few people, naturally, understand it, else the hoards would all have been raised long ago. At Campanella there is a golden lamb hidden in some crevice; at Pastena, too, in the subterranean passage of San Paolo, lies a fabulous treasure. A man crept in one day and filled his pockets with precious things, but on turning to go home he found, to his surprise, the tunnel barred with an iron gate. Then a Voice said—

"Disgorge your gold!"

He did so and the gate vanished. But he had shrewdly kept back a few coins and was creeping away well pleased with himself when, suddenly, the passage was blocked again.

"Out with the rest of it!" thundered the Voice; whereupon he reluctantly emptied his pockets and was allowed to escape into daylight again.

I, too, once crawled into this tunnel, but discovered nothing more valuable than the skeleton of a goat. . . .

And the legend of Campanella is interesting because, instead of the magic volume of Virgil or what not, the explorers entered the caves armed with a talismanic ring (Oriental influence). There, a monstrous figure on horseback issued from the darkness, saying that unless they succeeded in raising the treasure by the third attempt their lives would be sacrificed. They failed; and an immense wave of the sea rose up to drown them, which they appeased, in the nick of time, by casting the ring into the foaming gulf.

From Crapolla you can be rowed eastwards to Sant' Elia, the Ultima Thule of Siren land, where another treasure lies buried. It can also be reached by walking down from Torco, along a stony path skirting the cliff, with incomparable views over the Salernitan Bay and the Galli rocks; or again—an easier route—from the Colli di Sorrento past the once famous limestone arch, *Arco di Sant' Elia*, a portentous freak of nature. It is a sad wreck now, this one majestic portal opening upon the blue wonderland of sky and sea; the wind, which fashions the arches and pinnacles and melon-shaped grottos and all the bizarre accoutrements of these coasts, gnawed at the keystone till the span yielded. Richard Burton climbed over it in 1835—in 1843 it is described as "shattered".

There used to be a theory, still popular, that all these natural features had been eroded by the sea, a curious delusion, which postulated a frequent rising and sinking of the land and took no account of the fact that similar structures exist in limestone regions hundreds of miles inland. Subterranean threads of water, and rain, and wind, are responsible for them. The water filters through the rock in minute channels, disintegrating it by chemical action and, later on, by sheer mechanical force; where it issues, a cave is formed, with the help of winds and rain. This is the origin of nearly all the land-caves of the district such as the *grotta dell' Arco* and *del Castello* at Capri; in some, like that below the "Villa Jovis", the old water-course, now dried up, can still be plainly seen. Where the elements attack a rock which is softest in the centre, a natural arch is formed: a pinnacle, where it yields at the sides. The force of the wind is incalculable; even on apparently calm days, a terrific current may be rushing upwards from the sea, as on that fateful occasion in September, 1902, when some wood gatherers on Monte Lauro at Capri, throwing away a lighted match, suddenly found themselves enveloped in a conflagration and perished miserably all but one. The accident was witnessed by many fishermen from their boats, but nothing could be done for them; one by one they dropped down the awful six hundred feet of cliff into the sea, whence the charred bodies were afterwards recovered—their shrieks could be heard as far as the opposite mainland. Which, by the way, is not as wonderful as it seems; in this air, persons can sometimes carry on a conversation across half a mile of land or a mile of water.

THE COVE OF CRAPOLLA

I often find my way to Sant' Elia. It is a steep olive-covered slope trending seawards, and in former times may well have supported a few families that fled away when a cataract of rocks descended from above, among the debris of which their ruined houses are still discernible. Two shattered gateways against corsair-surprises, built at precipitous points on the paths leading east and west, also testify to the existence of a population at this remote spot, as do the mouldering remains of a once fair chapel by the water's edge. The place is sufficiently venerable, as its Byzantine name indicates; and a few fragments of antique marbles among the masonry of this sanctuary show that, in still earlier ages, some Roman villa may have stood near this site. An ancient land. . . .

The jewel of Sant' Elia is an old farm-house which lies out of the track of descending stones and, though uninhabited, is still in use. It is a sturdy little building and simplicity itself as regards architectural ornament and inner arrangement; a genial simplicity, born of rustic needs and corrected, and re-corrected, by ages of steady thought, which discarded all superfluities and culminated, at last, upon a note dignifying the lowliest things: fitness. There is a beauty in fitness which no art can enhance. This structure displays nothing of the prettiness, the mazy irregularity, of many Southern peasants' houses—much less the Giulio-Romano stateliness of sleek Lombardy farms: you enter into a rectangular loggia opening, in bungalow fashion, upon a row of rooms that shelter animals and implements and a ponderous oil-press and piles of glowing lemons; then, climbing up to the next floor, where the *famiglia* once lived, you find exactly the same pattern repeated. What more simple? But the site has been correctly chosen; the exposure duly calculated; the arches of the loggia are well proportioned, so are those of the rooms, whose vaulted ceilings are solid and high: in short, of ten thousand chances of wrong-doing, every one has been avoided and, like some smooth river at the end of its course, it now displays no trace of the torments and struggles which accompanied earlier stages. Such a dwelling marks the survival of the fittest—the coincidence of efficiency with economy *thus, and not otherwise*: the justification of yonder falcon floating, a speck of gold, in the empyrean; or, for that matter, of some humble beast that, trusting to immobility and a mottled pelt, even now evades his eye.

This *masseria* is utterly deficient, of course, in the comforts of civilization: it was built for no such purpose. Yet I have memories of certain impromptu luncheons—quails and cream cheeses and succulent raisins preserved in vine leaves—on that upper loggia with a civilized and charming companion; memories of blue sea shimmering through a silvery network of olive branches, with talks, over coffee, of far-away things. . . .

Less innocent conversations have also echoed within these walls. Here was a favourite meeting-place of the brigands who infested the peninsula up to the seventies—here they caroused and discussed their plans of operations, climbing up afterwards, by break-neck paths, to the heights of Marecoccola, where they separated. The great Pillone was the most celebrated of them—you can read about him in Bergsoe's *Italian Novels*.

An old woman, who witnessed their last stand against the *carabinieri*, told me how it befell. They were bivouacking on a hillock below Termini called *La Chiunca*, which in those days was covered with immense oaks; their enemies silently encompassed them and demanded a surrender. They refused, and a sanguinary fray began—the brigands shooting from behind the trees with deadly precision upon their unprotected assailants. But their ammunition was soon exhausted and they all fell fighting, save a few who managed to escape. Not a man of them was taken alive; a wounded one crawled away as far as Monte Faito, where he was afterwards found dead, with a crucifix (probably stolen) upon his breast. Such deeds of daring are over, for the present, in this country; the brigands of modern Italy have deserted their ancient fastnesses; they recline in the Chamber of Deputies, where no one molests them.

When I first heard this story the Germans were engaged in testing their new bullets upon the natives of Samoa, who thought themselves safe behind trees, and I imprudently told the venerable dame that her brigands would stand a poor chance against modern weapons such as these: bullets that pierce an oak. She said nothing—she was far too polite to contradict; but she thought a good deal, and I saw that I had sunk considerably in her estimation, not so much for trying to foist a fairy-tale upon her, as for believing it myself.

And the treasure of Sant' Elia? It lies buried under a tower near the sea. A workman's spade one day encountered an underground marble slab which bore the lettering: BEATO CHI SCAVA (Blessed who digs). Wild with excitement, the man delved lower and presently struck another one inscribed "Blessed who digs deeper", and after some hours of frenzied toil the third tablet was at last revealed. It was inscribed——. No, I cannot possibly pen that inscription; suffice to say, it was not very explicit as to the whereabouts of the treasure. Whoever is interested in the matter, must make a pilgrimage to the spot; the peasant who works the land is called *figlio del malpensiero* and will doubtless supply the desired information. It was his own father to whom the adventure happened, which proves that it must be true.

On Capri, at Veterino and in other parts of the island, there are a variety of treasure-legends; perhaps the best known is that of the equestrian statue of Tiberius, which a boy is said to have seen in a chink of the rock—the *motif* recurs in that of the Suabian Barbarossa, of Gyges as narrated by Herodotus, in Plato's *Republic*, and no doubt elsewhere.

All these hoards are guarded by spirits of the gentiles (Romans)— evil genii that have sought a refuge underground from the effulgence of Christianity. So it is all the world over: Minos creeps into the earth, into the universal Venusberg, and when the time is accomplished, great Jove, at Demogorgon's call, will descend and follow him down the abyss. Each deity becomes a demon in his turn, and his adherents pagans or provincials; to argue a common origin for those religions which possess an underworld is surely a mistake, for if the rulers of the moment are overhead, and the man on earth, whither shall the devils betake themselves save down below?

The Sirens, too, have suffered a sea-change; once earth-powers, they have now retired into the dim purple depths of ocean—a transmigration which necessitated some structural changes in their anatomy. Euripides already spoke of them as dwelling in Hades with Persephone. So gods and demi-gods go the way of men— *eodem cogimur.*

Strange, by the way, this startling metamorphosis of the Sirens in mediæval days. How came it about? According to Schrader, the first mention of the fish-tailed ones occurs in the *Liber monstrorum* which was written towards the end of the sixth century. He calls them a "Frankish invention". It seems to me more likely that fish-tailed mermaids existed from time immemorial all over the North, and that the compiler of this early work, being naturally puzzled what to make of the classic Sirens, brought them into the category of shapes familiar to him. Saint Isidore, a contemporary of the *Liber monstrorum*, and the Byzantines all invest them with the ancient bird-attributes.

Below the old abbey is the cove of Crapolla, a tiny beach dotted with fishing-boats and hemmed in by mighty walls of orange-tawny limestone. A colony of Roman fishermen lived here; their ruined abodes cling like bee-cells to the rock, and the conduit they built to regulate the cataract still serves its purpose. This is a lively place in summer-time, at sunrise when the fish are brought in, or in the late afternoon when you may contemplate the preparations for the coming night's work and watch the boats as they glide off severally, like sea-gulls taking flight from their nests, till the last one has vanished round the rocks, and you suddenly find yourself alone, quite alone, on the smooth, warm pebbles. Then is the time to dream awhile.

In winter Crapolla is uninhabited; the boats are drawn up out of reach of the waves which thunder in between the encircling precipices. Only one white-bearded fisherman, with a face like Father Christmas, lives here throughout this wild season. His name is Giuseppe Garibaldi,* and no one knows better how to catch the wary *cernia* as it lies hidden among the rocks; if he wished, he could be as rich as a king. But money slips like sea-water through his fingers and, when he makes a good catch, he prefers to treat his friends. For forty years he has known no other life than this, though he can tell of stirring times when he lived at Naples before turning his back on the world and carving out a quiet existence for himself in this secluded nook, where he now potters about, blithe and loquacious, in his leaky black tub. So he lives, this *cigale* of seventy summers, reckless of to-morrow and often gaily fasting for days together when his purse is empty. All too soon, I fear, he will be found lying lifeless upon the stone floor of his hut (his bed was pawned thirty years ago and never redeemed) and there will be one gentleman less on earth.

Several deaths have occurred at Crapolla owing to the rapacity of the country folk who lose their lives in scrambling upon the face of the cliff in search of firewood. Not long ago, the spirit of the last of these victims began to be troublesome by haunting the place, but the priests compromised matters by erecting a wooden cross on the spot where he fell, which satisfied everyone. Near at hand, at

* His real name was Persico, like that of the old historian of Massa. He died September 6, 1914.

Recomone, something of the same kind ought to be done, for it is a *male sito* in spite of all its natural charm. A shingly beach, solitary, overgrown with slender rushes and the strangely beautiful sea-thistle and other uncommon plants which have clambered down the hot gully overhead, Recomone is the chosen abode of a spectre, an *ombra* which does an infinity of mischief, such as throwing down stones and loosening the ropes of boats moored to the shore. The fisher-folk *fanno l'indiano*, they play the Indian—feign complete ignorance of the matter.

"How, signore?" they will say, "you believe in ghosts?"

The peasants are more communicative. There are two or three variants of the story, but the most generally accepted version is that, some years ago, a certain woman who had made much money by adulterating wine, died, and the sin preyed so much upon her spirit after death that it left her no peace. She used to wander dolefully about her former home, scaring old and young. At last it became such a scandal that they got a "strong" priest to talk to her. It was on this wise—

PRIEST. Now then, what is this they tell me? Prowling about the village, eh?

SPECTRE. I can't help it; I watered the wine.

PRIEST. You ought to have thought of that sooner.

SPECTRE. I did. But I always forgot again.

PRIEST. *Peggio per te*. I shall now banish you to some lonely spot, where you may do what you please.

SPECTRE. Oh, oh. . . .

PRIEST. Let me see—there is Fossa di Papa.

SPECTRE. Not there—not there! Rather to Recomone.

PRIEST. To Recomone then, and off with you!

This story is interesting, as an *ex post facto* explanation of some forgotten incident: this beach was in bad repute long before the present ghost was born. So the traveller Swinburne writes, in 1780, that "Nerano is famous among mariners for being haunted by evil spirits". Whether they really believe these tales is quite another matter. I think they merely derive from them a certain emotional shiver, an echo out of their own past, such as some persons obtain from a spiritualistic séance or from a creepy story well told.

These spirit conjurations are not invariably successful, and a

priest of questionable reputation should never attempt the task, for
spectres see things invisible to mortal eye and are notoriously
recalcitrant and plain-spoken. "And who the devil are *you*?" said
one of them the other day to a fat *canonico* who was threatening him.
"I know! A drunkard and a thief! You doctored your father's will;
you had four and a half litres of wine yesterday, and last Wednesday
you cheated sixteen francs out of your uncle. And what are you doing
to-day? Looking for a new cook, as usual. And why? Because——"
But the *canonico* suddenly remembered another engagement.

It is chiefly the young priests who are chosen to constrain these
rebellious spirits; chastity, and chastity alone, can rivet their
obedience, and the people are hopelessly sceptical as to the asceticism
of the older ones. . . .

The name Crapolla has been derived from "akron Apollinis",
as though a temple of Apollo had stood here. But this is pure
Cicerone-etymology—the origin of the word is the same as that of
Capri, and in old deeds it is actually called Capreola. What Capri
means is not quite certain; it is neither Greek nor Phœnician; there
are places with similar names all over Italy and half a dozen
Capri's and Caprile's within a few miles of here. Quaranta deduces
it from a Tyrrhenian root signifying rocky or stony. Why not?
When, nearly two centuries ago, Greek etymology could no longer
explain all local names and traditions, the enlightened took refuge
in Semiticism, and thus there grew up the ponderous Shem-Ham-
and-Japheth literature of Martorelli and his disciples, which we
have outgrown in its turn. Nowadays, the conveniently obscure
Tyrrhenian language helps to solve old difficulties. But it makes
new ones.

This Cicerone-etymology which has infected the whole of this
region—the whole of Italy, in fact—is a legacy left us by the *à priori*
scholarship of past generations which worked with fixed ideas:
it was pleasant to make learned assertions, and to believe is always
easier than to doubt or to deny. There is Nerano, for instance,
which has become fancifully connected with Nero—*Re Nerone* they
call him—who plays approximately the same part here as Tiberius
does at Capri. These are his baths; yonder, in those caverns, were
celebrated the orgies of which we have all heard. There are three
of these caverns under the crag of Mount San Costanzo; the largest,
a noble grot, distils limpid water which is collected into a small

reservoir. In one of these three lies the treasure, a golden statue of a child, but only one man had the *book*, and that was the old hermit of Capri who promised over and over again to come and perform the necessary adjurations, but somehow or other never kept his word; and now he is dead. He was the last person whom the Capriotes would have suspected of being versed in necromancy, an ex-shoemaker and a great simpleton, but the men of Nerano knew better: a prophet is of no account in his own country.

And how curious is the Cicerone-etymology which derives Citarella, the breezy hermitage upon Monte Solaro on Capri, from Venus Cytherea. Ever since it was wrongly reported that an antique pavement had been found here, learned local writers had elaborated visions of a snowy temple on this height, Eryx-fashion, with roses and doves and grave youthful priests—wisely omitting, however, the chief part of such temple equipment. The medical baths of Citara on Ischia—which is the same name—have also been brought into connection with this Venus and are therefore recommended as a cure for sterility. Here we have an instance of a serious custom growing out of wrongly derived etymology. These baths, which Iasolini also recommended for baldness and elephantiasis, are no longer taken by women. Perhaps waters with a contrary effect would not have lost their popularity so soon.*

I do not know the meaning of Nerano (it is also called Anarano, Donerano, Inerano, and Inderano in old deeds), but Citarella is one of the many names on Capri which wandered over during the Amalfitan domination—the result, I suppose, of overcrowding in the days before the Republic received its death-blow in the war with Pisa, when the Pandects were carried off. Says Edrisius: "The island of Capri is inhabited by men of Amalfi who keep flocks there." The family of Citarella is a well-known one; they were nobles of Ravello and patricians of Amalfi, and no doubt drew their name from the town of Cetara (Cetarelli) on that coast. Now what does Cetara mean? I cannot say. All kinds of origins have been suggested for the names of such places in Italy; perhaps it also means *rocky*, for Hecatæus has a "Kyterion polis", which is now Cirisano, on a

---

* The strangest of all these derivations are those invented solely *for the sake of symmetry*—the above-mentioned Veterino is derived from Vitellius because near at hand lies a "Timberino"; the islet of Vervece, near Massa, signifies a *sheep* (vervex) because Capri, just across the water, means a *goat*. The real origin of Vervece is *verruca*, a wart, an isolated protuberance; it is the same root as that of Eryx.

rocky height; Cetraro in Calabria is similarly situated; citarella, the rock-haunting bird, is the same as our kestrel; Bérard derives it from a Hebrew word signifying high spot, mount of sacrifice. The islet of Kythairon, whence Venus took her epithet of Cytherea, is notoriously stony and bare; Phœnicians founded her temple there, and her cult spread thence over Cyprus and Greece to Campania. And so we arrive, as the result of this philological disquisition, at a most unexpected conclusion: the name Citara (Citarella) is not derived from Venus Cytherea, but *vice versa.*

Let us never visit Capri without climbing up to Citrella, for it is a fair spot. It was a Dominican foundation and up to a short time ago a hermit used to dwell here, but the hermit business has decayed all over Western Europe, and of the six or more devotees who used to haunt the rocks and ruins of Capri only one has survived—the successor of that over-talkative Consalvo who, in 1528, as Gregorio Rossi relates, was in large part responsible for the defeat of the Spanish fleet and the death of the viceroy at the hands of Doria in the sea-fight near Conca. This cloudy abode used to be surrounded by a grove of wild Aleppo pines, but they have now been cut down as fuel and to supply the newly imported craving for Christmas trees: an amazing custom, when one thinks of it—to load a tree with lighted candles and other incongrous trumpery—which might well have remained in the land of its birth.

Here, at Citrella, were buried the victims of the cholera of the thirties, many foreigners among them, and it would be hard to find a pleasanter resting-place for all eternity, unless it be the crater-meadow of Monte Rotaro on Ischia where, simultaneously, the cholera victims of that island were interred. What a contrast between the two! On Rotaro the volcanic earth with its hoary mantle of vegetation and, within the deep funnel, a green woodland calm, as though seas and storms no longer existed upon earth: Citrella, poised like a swallow's nest upon its windswept limestone crag; far below, the Titanic grandeur of South Capri and the dimpled ocean, strewn with submarine boulders that make it look, from such aerial heights, like a map of the moon enamelled in the matchless blues and greens of a Damascus vase.

Citrella, of course, has its treasure. Some men saw a heap of gold and silver lying in a cleft of the rock, but a tremendous thunder-storm broke in upon their operations, the torch they carried was blown out three times, and . . . certain other things occurred; one of them died the same evening; all of which did not prevent the others from resuming the search next day. It is truly astonishing to hear educated natives, who have visited the university, speaking of these things in a hushed whisper. An occasional discovery of real value may have fostered the growth of these legends; in Campania, as in parts of the Orient, the ruins of an ancient civilization, with its subterraneous passages and marks of vanished pomp, gave them verisimilitude and a *locus standi;* Naples is half-way to Baghdad, and no one quite understands the native character who has not lived in the East.

This Oriental trait, if such it be, is only one of many that have been gradually superimposed upon one another. Whoever rightly deciphers the human palimpsest of the Parthenopean region will perceive how faint are the traces of Greco-Roman schooling, how skin-deep—as regards primitive tracts of feeling—the scars of mediæval tyranny and bestiality. And Christianity has only left a translucent veneer, like a slug's track, upon the surface; below, can be read the simple desire for sunshine and family life, and a pantheism vague and charming, the impress of nature in her mildest moods upon the responsive human phantasy. Our Gothic gloom and the sand-wastes of the East beget fearful gods and demons; those of Campania, though equally well accredited, are all in a manner sunny and humane, for the atmosphere is too limpid to permit the formation of terrifying spectres like those of Nurcia or even Beneventum.

There are witches hereabouts, *giannare* (from Diana, now queen of witches), but they are rather like ordinary women; there is nothing mysterious or malefic about them. As for the devil—did I tell you of the man who saw the devil last week? He was walking up this very road, about sunset, and there was the devil sitting on a stone in front of him. What he looked like? Oh, horns and hoofs and all the rest of it—nothing out of the way—just the devil, you know. The people will tell stories of the devil, popularly known as Saint Pantaleone, because foreigners like to hear such things, foreigners being rather simple folks in some respects; but though they speak with fervour and conviction, they do not take him seriously. Dozens of houses are haunted by him and his imps but, unlike many in our civilized England, the rents do not fall, and *cristiani* live in them all the year round.

4

How came the revered Saint Pantaleone to be identified with the Prince of Darkness? Because he gives lucky numbers for the lottery; therefore he must be in league with him; therefore he is the devil himself—an example of the rhetorical figure we learnt at school: "the part for the whole".

It is the same with the saints. Every one of the heavenly host may be cheated at a bargain; the Virgin and her infant Son—the adult Jesus is practically unknown here—are adored with feasts and flowers; they are *tanto belli;* but to endeavour to imitate either of them would be deemed a most unprofitable speculation. A Greek fashion of regarding the gods.

Saint John alone is an exception to the rule—he is positively vindictive in seeing his bargains carried out to the letter and has become quite unpopular for that reason. I cannot help thinking that this is because he represents to the common mind some ancient and ferocious heathen shape, whose midsummer fires are lighted to this day in many places: inexorability being the proud attribute of all the older deities. "'Tis hard to reach the heart of Zeus."

I picked up a curious local legend which amalgamates this ancient shape with the more recent Adonis and the still later Christian saint. Here it is:

They say that Saint John had a purse of money. And there was a mother and a daughter. Said the daughter: "How shall we manage to take away his purse?" Then the mother answers: "We must cut off his head." They say that the daughter took a sword and cut off Saint John's head and took the purse. When the *festa* of Saint John comes round (midsummer) he sleeps the whole time, because, if he were to wake up, the world would come to an end. On that day, the mother and daughter are always running across the sky, the mother with a beam of fire in her hand, to burn the daughter for having cut off Saint John's head. When Saint John wakes up, he always asks Saint Peter: "I say, when is my *festa* coming round?" And Saint Peter answers: "That's past long ago!" The old men say that if one puts a plateful of water outside the balcony and looks into it, one can see in the sky the mother with the beam of fire in her hand and the daughter running before her. Says the daughter: "Mother, Mother, why did you say it?" Says the mother: "Daughter, daughter, why did you do it?" And all that day long they are running across the sky.

That German divine who lately traced, with some little exacerbation, Catholic institutions to their pagan origins, forgot to discover, or perhaps to mention, that his own pseudo-rationalistic creed is far more deadly, since it infects those who lead the march of culture. If Italians are ever to have that reformation of which they talk so much, it is to be hoped that they will go a step further than the Germans, who pulled up at the first *Wirtshaus*. Even now, Neapolitans shrug their shoulders at Saint Januarius, whose periodical liquefaction is a fine pretext for fireworks and military music, and while the world is astonished at the nuptials between the lord of a great *Kulturstaat* and the Antique Fraud, Catholicism in Naples, ever serene and infantile, is gracefully expiring; its venerable frame suffused, dolphin-like, with all the myriad hues of the rainbow-tinted paganism whence it sprang. All this must be a matter of climate. New names will supplant old names, but so long as the climate of Campania does not change, its religious beliefs— ceremonies, rather—will always cluster round radiant elemental powers of sun and ocean.

We have wandered far, too far, from Crapolla. But there is nothing to hinder us from returning when the mood fits. And let us choose the sea-route on a night of full moon, for all discords dissolve in the mellow sheen of a Southern night and blossom forth, if you care to look, into new and ghostly harmonies. Peasants and bourgeois may sleep in their beds; your Siren-worshipper has this in common with Arabs and other primitive folk, that he knows the uses of night. (How often do the sensuous needs and pleasures of civilization coincide with those of wilder stages!) At such an hour the twin rocks guarding the entrance to Crapolla might well be mistaken for the portal of some Ossianic realm—the representation of it, rather; for stereoscopic vision being annulled, all depth and distance, rents and ravines, are merely indicated by mauve shadows upon a plain surface.

Have you never sailed under one of these precipices by moonlight? It is a picture that you see, not a palpable cliff of limestone; a picture that floats past you; some enormous, silver-tinted cartoon conceived by William Blake, in the mad moments betwixt sleep and waking. Those ancient, seared rocks, so familiar at noontide, have put on strange faces since the moon rose. Their complexion has waned to a livid splendour, and their wrinkles and bosses resolve themselves into unsuspected designs—designs of spears and shields and bastions and all the pomp of heraldry that melt away, under incessant showers of gentle light from above, into other combinations of form, ever new and so convincing, that at last the mind, weary of riddles, surrenders to the stony enchantment and drifts along in a calm disdain of reality.

Such, maybe, was the spirit that swayed those blameless seekers of the Holy Grail.

VIII

RAIN ON THE HILLS

AMOST unusual occurrence, this steady summer rain. The sky is thickly overcast; it pours in sheets. A month ago, it might at least have done good to the country. But what is the country to me, weather-bound in a small village far from my base, with every prospect of spending the night half-supperless among strange folks and in a strange bed? What demon guided my steps this morning?

There is this at least to be said in favour of a region denuded of trees, that a summer rain cools the air. England, with its dense vegetation, exhales a steamy heat after a shower at this season, and the sodden fields, with their sleek round trees, make the wanderer feel more than ever as though he were some caterpillar crawling about an interminable bed of lettuces. Yes, English nature is too green, and that green too monotonous in shade and outline; it is (*entre nous*) a salad landscape; you may find pretty vignettes of the sugar-water type, but London alone is picturesque in the large sense of the word—London and Newcastle-on-Tyne.

This rain will produce a short-lived crop of grass, to be scorched again in a few days. The year of Siren land has only three seasons: the cloudless summer of brown fields, cicada-days; the green spell of rain and storms; three months of flowery spring. Summer melts into winter by bland transition, without hectic tints of death and castings of leaves, and when, in May, the grass begins to wither, the vines take up the joyous refrain. One fact must have struck all who have spent a summer here—the difference in temperature between the cultivated and barren lands. The latter are perceptibly warmer. The coolness of Sant' Agata is due not so much to its height above sea-level or to its exposure to the refreshing mistral as to the fact that it lies in an ocean of fruit-trees and leafy walnuts and hazels; nor is it their shade, but rather what Professor Marsh calls the "frigoric effect of leafy structure" which brings about the chill.

To step from sunshine into shadow is naturally cooling, but whoever enters this cultivated zone even at midnight will shiver involuntarily.

A few hectic tints there are, but one must know where to look for them. If, in the early days of December, you happen to glance down some of the gullies clothed in ilex, you will be surprised to see the uniform green surface flecked with alien markings. This is the flowering ash, companion of the ilex, about to cast its leaves; each tree has a particular tint which it reproduces year after year at this season; some are spectral grey, others straw-coloured, but the most beautiful are the deep crimson whose effect, among the sombre holm-oaks, is exactly that of the red spots upon a blood-stone.

A month before the cicada strikes up, the last firefly has already extinguished its candle. Ischia is as full of fireflies as the Sorrentine peninsula, but there is not one on Capri; too little verdure, perhaps, or too much wind. I have never watched the brilliant tropical night-luminaries with greater pleasure than these humble ones, for there are sounds in the jungle at all hours of the night, but here the attention is unconsciously riveted by what seems an anomaly in nature—the noiselessness of so much commotion. They call them *fuochi morti*, with reference to their flickering lights; other nations connect them with Saint John, the midsummer saint, which would be inappropriate here, as they are all gone by that time. On the other hand, the common wood-louse (*oniscus*) goes by the name of *porcello di San Giovanni*, and the naturalist Latreille seems also to have been struck by its resemblance to a little pig, for he dubbed another kind *porcellio*. How this diminutive beast came to be connected with the great saint is past my finding out; in point of pedigree, at least, it is not unworthy of him, for if Saint John goes back to Attis and Adonis, the "little pig's" ancestors were already great people in Siluria.

And still it rains. . . .

Wild and exhilarating perfumes will arise as soon as the clouds disperse. As volatile oils, they start from the ground; afterwards, when the sun has warmed the withered plants, each one begins to breathe out its characteristic odour. It is rather hard to analyse this fragrant multi-herbal emanation: I suspect that the dried fennel-stalks are the *Leitmotif* in the symphony. The cistus bushes, whose frail purple and white roses would enchant a Japanese artist, give forth a pungent aroma when the sun beats upon them; other spots are dominated by the honey-sweet savour of scorched thistles,

of the wild juniper which, nowadays, can be seen to full perfection
only on the inaccessible crags of Montalto, or the common fig.
Those persons who are so curiously insensible to this last odour
should go to a certain mossy court-yard overshadowed by gnarled
fig trees and heavily permeated by their cloying scent: pleasant
were the November hours spent here long years ago when nothing to
the purpose was said, and every now and then a dry leaf, falling
upon the pavement with a metallic clang, startled the tongue-tied
ones into a full consciousness of their own thoughts. . . .

And far away can be descried, on clear days, a tall building,
firm-seated upon a rocky eminence above Amalfi: the Torre di
Orlando. This place is associated in my mind with the scent of wild
thyme, for its terrace is, or was, overgrown with it. General Avita-
bile, an Italian adventurer and vice-governor of the Punjaub
during the Indian Mutiny, whose life has lately been written by an
Englishman, built this noble palace, intending to end his days there
with a young wife whom he adored. Hardly had they settled down
before she murdered him. 'Tis wonderful—to paraphrase a saying
of Thackeray's—'tis wonderful what a woman may do, and a man
yet think her an angel. But the general appears, from all accounts,
to have been also something of a scoundrel. The house is at present
to be sold; the bidders are many, but I am told there are sixty-two
heirs to the property, and as soon as sixty-one have agreed on the
terms of sale the odd man raises objections. So it crumbles to pieces,
day by day.

And what more? Shall I tell of certain plants abhorred by the
peasants? There is the asphodel, the flower of the Elysian fields,
which became the English "daffodil", and whose derivation from
a-sphodelos (unburied) may be fanciful, but is none the less appropriate, as can be perceived by anyone who tries to keep the stately
roseate blossoms in a room. They call it *borro* or *cefalia*. Harmful to
cattle, it multiplies incredibly and the roots insinuate themselves
into the rocks with such demoniac tenacity that only dynamite will
dislodge them permanently. "*Assai terribile, questa figlia di putana,*"
I overheard a farmer saying the other day as, with pick-axe and
crowbar, he endeavoured to clear a patch of ground of them for
cultivation. Next comes the bitter sea-quill, known as *cipollana*,
from its immense onion-shaped bulb. In winter a bunch of juicy
green leaves crowns the root and nothing would be easier than to
extirpate it at this season. But the peasant has other things to do

just then; besides, he is waiting for the flower to appear in spring. Spring comes, but no flower; on the contrary, the leaves die away and the *cipollana* sinks into the earth and is forgotten. But in the heat of summer, when every other plant is withered and mankind walks as little as possible about the parched fields, detached spires of silvery blossom start in breathless haste from the ground. These are the flowers of the squill, beloved of Egyptian she-mummies as symbols of generation; the seeds are scattered broadcast in the nick of time to catch the first rain and the mischief is done. A sly plant. By the time the tell-tale leaves again sprout forth, the flowers have vanished; the peasant once more waits for the spring; and so on, *in sæcula sæculorum*. Unscrupulous Neapolitans import cart-loads of the leafless bulbs into the city, where the plant is unknown, and hawk them about the streets as "Californian lilies".

The ivy-leaved smilax is another pest; its inconspicuous blossoms smell sweetly for a few days and the red berries are pretty enough to see, but it is armed with poisonous claws and, once established among trees or walls, there is no ejecting it. They call it *raie* from its white roots (*radici*), which are sometimes boiled into a medicinal broth and which travel underground in all directions and at any depth, coming up to the surface whenever they feel inclined to make a fresh tangle of thorns for the discomfiture of optimistic cultivators. A friend of mine employed a man for a few months in eradicating them out of a small piece of land, paying him for the roots by weight; after an absence of two years, the smilax returned smiling from Tartarus.

Detested also by man and beast is the tree-euphorbia; even the goats sniff at its venomous secretion. But it is worth while strolling over these hills at the end of May to observe this plant before it sheds its leaves. Green all through the winter, it now takes on every shade of colour in its annual death-agony. No two bushes are tinted alike, not even when their roots are intertwined; earthy and ghostly white, orange and brown and vermilion, from coral pink to a rich burnished copper, from palest saffron to tawny gold. The red kinds are visible from afar and often shine with a lustrous iridescence, a rare freak of coquetry, like the *reflet métallique* of Oriental pottery. Ten days—and all is over; the gaunt stalks only begin to clothe themselves anew in autumn. Its acrid milk was formerly put to a singular use—the boys, in order to escape military service, injected a drop into their eyes, provoking inflammation and greatly puzzling the good doctors, till the trick became too popular.

Whereas the asphodel, owing to shallow soil, never attains any great size here, the "totomaglia" (euphorbia) seems to fatten on air and sun-scorched rock; one, a perfect monster of about sixteen feet in height, was lately cut down near Campanella: it yielded three faggots of wood, weighing, approximately, fifty kilograms apiece. Such giants are becoming scarce.

Other plants, rare and beautiful, grow in abundance on these limestone hills. The flora of Siren land has been better studied than other departments of natural history, particularly that of Capri; old Paolo Boccone already, in the seventeenth century, named certain plants peculiar to this island; others were engraved by the wise and lovable Cirillo, whose work remained incomplete (the first volume is dedicated to Sir Joseph Banks) because he was strangled by the Bourbons in 1799; Capri flowers have also been collected or described by Giraldi, Graeffer, Tenore, Gussone, and such a large number of recent botanists that a respectable literature exists on the subject. No one can fail to notice the red lily on the higher grounds, the gentian-hued lithospermum which fills up the crannies of the rocks, the wild stock, the brilliant vetch, the large purple anemone, and the blue thistle* (not so blue, however, as its representative on the African hills). It is astonishing that this plant, so common on the mainland of Italy, has not found its way to Capri. But the orchid tribe is particularly numerous there, twenty-eight species having been found. There is the sweetly smelling kind which is the last to blossom; bee orchids and butterfly orchids and birds'-nest orchids; the weird *homme pendu* orchid from which dangles the effigy of a man; others with monks' faces peering from under dusky cowls.

The little rock-islet of Monacone has a species of narcissus all to itself.†

And still it rains. . . .

It will be some time before the picture of this room is effaced from my memory. It is vaulted in the old style and the white walls are adorned with American calendars and advertisements; under foot, a richly tinted pavement of Vietri tiles, broken yellows and

---

* It is not a true thistle.
† Now considered problematical.

4*

blues, dating from the days ere the modern Neapolitan ware, with its undignified patterns and anæmic coloration, was exported hitherward. The massive furniture gives an air of well-being to the place; upon a commodious wardrobe stands the inevitable *lar familiaris*—the infant Jesus—under a glass case, and a fine selection of *caccio-cavallo* cheeses, suspended from iron hooks in the ceiling, reminds me of the dinner awaiting me at home.

Patienza!

The good folks have retired into the kitchen region, leaving me in sole possession here; the rain seems to have chilled their wonted communicativeness; an uncle, too, has lately arrived from over the sea and certain family questions, I understand, are likely to become acute. Every ten minutes a polite young girl thrusts her head within the doorway to ask if I am comfortable. Incomparably more comfortable, I reply, than out of doors. Perhaps the signore would prefer to write with a *calamaio*? No, the signore will continue to use his pencil, having learned long ago that neither pens, ink, nor blotting-paper can be procured in the kingdom of Italy.

"A long letter," she ventures to remark.

"To my *sposa*—at Naples."

"My bridegroom," she informs me, "is twenty-two and has been twice to New York. The last time he returned with three thousand francs, and the next time we go together."

"Is that your engagement ring?"

"Yes; it cost him thirty-five francs. And this watch and chain, a hundred and fifteen francs. And now he has bought me twenty pairs of silk stockings and says I must put them on, all twenty, when we go through the American Custom-house, else the officials will steal them. I think it will be difficult."

"The *sposo* might wear half of them."

"Oh, he! He could wear forty, but he won't."

Of course she will marry him; they all do; the old maid, so familiar to lovers of English landscape, is practically unknown in Siren land. But the husbands seldom take them to America, contenting themselves with sending money home and returning every now and then. Like the women of Lemnos, these sit manless among their rocks, doing a little laundry work and an infinity of chattering.

The Italian field-labourers wash their clothes but never their bodies; the Russian, their bodies but never their clothes; ours—neither. . . .

Dirty clothes, says Saint Jerome, are a sign of a clean mind. Saint Bernard, if I remember rightly, lays down a contrary maxim. . . . "Perhaps the signore would like to read? I have brought a book." Ariosto!

God forgive me; I cannot read Ariosto on a rainy day, and when the sun shines, he always contrives to make himself invisible. A very retiring disposition these heroic poets have.

Such modesty would ill become the present generation, and accordingly I find, in my very pocket, a modern trade circular—not always the worst kind of literature—Felix Alcan's catalogue. A pleasant sound, that name of Alcan; it smacks of—I know not what; of alcoves—alcohol. . . . It seems to me that the Jew is now doing more towards civilizing the West than he ever did in the past; he spends as liberally as we do, but more wisely, having a saner conception of charity: in short, he has learnt his lesson. And when the day of reckoning comes, the services rendered to the cause of enlightenment by Hebrew publishers and journalists will also not be forgotten. A nation fed upon Monsieur Alcan's pap has grown out of its infancy; it may well smile at bogies like *Jupiter tonans*, or *Vaticanus fulminans* with his attendant swarm of tonsured anachronisms. How we change! Here is a nation of Christians thanking Jews for their enfranchisement from the most odious tyranny on earth, that of the mind, engendered by a creed in defence of which they once persecuted them with fire and sword. The irony of history, with a vengeance.

What firm can show a list like this? Even if one wished to learn about things English, one could hardly do better than consult all these works on English trade unions, logic, psychology, free trade, ethics, and so forth. And our Anglo-American writers are represented in translations: Bagehot, Bain, Balfour Stewart, and all the rest of them. Have we anything approaching this widespread desire for knowledge; does our public ever hear of corresponding French authors, like Féré, Fouillée, Guyau? Would they care, moreover, to read abstruse works on *Éducation de la volonté* or *Solidarité morale*, many of which are here in their tenth, their twentieth, editions? And our publishers would not swoon away at the suggestion of bringing out those translations from foreign monumental works that figure here—at half the original cost? A poor student lamented to me some time ago that he was charged eighteen shillings for Shipley's *Invertebrata* and thirty-two shillings for Weismann's last

book. "Young man," I said, "learn French—you are never too old
to learn—and buy all your books, even those by English authors,
in French translations; the balance saved, send home to your aged
mother." "By jove," he replied, "I never heard of anyone teaching
French. The very thing! And as for that balance——"

Altogether—Alcan's catalogue: what a text for a lay sermon, if
the preacher were not rather in the mood for edibles than ethics.
Such, however, being the case, farewell, good monsieur! On some
later occasion, perchance, I shall desire you of more acquaintance.
Meanwhile, *Felix esto*. May your shadow, the *bulletin annuel*, never
grow less! May it outlast the Bo-tree's in miasmic Anurajpura;
may it outspread that of world-ash Ygdrasil, whose boughs encircle
heaven and earth and in whose branch-charmed twilight the
deathless gods revolve our fates.

"Can you supply me with something to eat, fair Costanza?"
"How not? Whatever you command."

Whatever you command. Fairy-like bubbles of Southern politeness which, when pricked, evaporate—as a friend of mine used to
say—into indifferent macaroni. Yes; not even macaroni can be
correctly prepared here; what goes by the name of parmesan being
a compound containing ninety per cent of potato flour, while of
butter, edible butter, not an ounce is made in all Siren land;
statistics reveal a disquieting importation of margarine. Were those
early authors, the Swiss Rehfues, the *junger Deutsche* of the *Fragmente*,
De Blainville, Portarelli, William Russell, and a dozen others—to
say nothing of Boccaccio—were they dreaming when they praised
the cow-products of Sorrento and Massa and Capri? No. But the
vineyards have hunted grass out of the land; the timber-cutting has
dried up all the hill-sides and watersprings. Fifty years ago the
slopes of Monte Solaro on Capri were so thickly overgrown that the
cows which pastured there used to wear bells round their necks in
order that they could be traced in the dense shrubbery; three
hundred head of cattle were exported yearly; nowadays, a single
dyspeptic calf could engulf the whole island in a day, so far as
normal fodder is concerned. May I never live far from a cow! A
real cow, I mean—not a tottering, scrofulous phantom that skulks
in dank cellars; a cow that eats grass and not bitter walnut twigs
and sulphate-of-copper-bespattered vine leaves; a cow whose
natural functions culminate in butter, not in lard. Oh that I had

the framing of the laws! How I would broil certain respected merchants in their own margarine tubs—ay, and their wives and children—how I would broil them!

"We have a fish soup; *guarracini* and *scorfani* and *aguglie* and *toteri* and———"

Take breath, gentle maiden; the while I explain to the patient reader the ingredients of the diabolical preparation known as *zuppa di pesce*. The *guarracino*, for instance, is a pitch-black marine monstrosity, one to two *inches* long, a mere blot, with an Old Red Sandstone profile and insufferable manners,* whose sole recommendation is that its name is derived from *korakinos* (korax = a raven; but who can live on Greek roots?). As to the *scorfano*, its name is unquestionably onomatopoetic, to suggest the spitting-out of bones; the only difference from a culinary point of view, between the *scorfano* and a toad being that the latter has twice as much meat on it. The *aguglia*, again, is all tail and proboscis; the very nightmare of a fish—as thin as a lead pencil. Who would believe that for this miserable sea-worm with verdigris-tinted spine, which an ordinary person would thank you for not setting on his table, the inhabitants of Siren land fought like fiends; the blood of their noblest was shed in defence of privileges artfully wheedled out of Anjou and Aragonese kings defining the *ius quoddam pescandi vulgariter dictum sopra le aguglia;* that a certain tract of sea was known as the "aguglie water" and owned, up to the days of Murat, by a single family who defended it with guns and mantraps? And everybody knows the *totero* or squid, an animated ink-bag of perverse leanings, which swims backwards because all other creatures go forwards and whose india-rubber flesh might be useful for deluding hunger on desert islands, since, like American gum, you can chew it for months, but never get it down.

These, and such as they, float about in a lukewarm brew of rancid oil and garlic, together with a few of last week's bread-crusts, decaying sea-shells and onion-peels, to give it an air of consistency.

---

* Its ridiculous airs and graces have struck even the unobservant natives, and small boys may be heard singing, among other *guarracino*-songs, the following ditty which I will transcribe phonetically for the benefit of the Ollendorff student:

> *Guarracino che ghieva per mar*
> *Ieva trattando di s'insudar*
> *Belle scarp' e ben pulit'*
> *Nu capiello a cannonat'*
> *E Nannina lo porta al lat'.*

This is the stuff for which Neapolitans sell their female relatives. But copious libations will do wonders with a *zuppa di pesce*.

"Wine of Marciano, signore."

"Then it must be good. It grows on the mineral."

"Ah, you foreigners know everything."

We do; we know, for example, that nothing short of a new creation of the world will ever put an end to that legend about the "mineral".

How unfavourably this hotch-potch compares with the Marseillese bouillabaisse! But what can be expected, considering its ingredients? Green and golden scales, and dorsal fins embellished with elaborate rococo designs, will satisfy neither a hungry man nor an epicure, and if Neapolitans pay untold sums for the showy Mediterranean sea-spawn, it only proves that they eat with their eyes, like children who prefer tawdry sweets to good ones. They have colour and shape, these fish of the inland sea, but not taste; their flesh is either flabby and slimy and full of bones in unauthorized places, or else they have no flesh at all—heads like Burmese dragons but no bodies attached to them; or bodies of flattened construction on the *magnum in parvo* principle, allowing of barely room for a sheet of paper between their skin and ribs; or a finless serpentine framework, with long-slit eyes that leer at you while you endeavour to scratch a morsel off the reptilian anatomy.

There is not a cod, or turbot, or whiting, or salmon, or herring in the two thousand miles between Gibraltar and Jerusalem; or if there is, it never comes out; its haddocks (haddocks, indeed!) taste as if they had fed on mouldy sea-weed and died from the effects of it; its lobsters have no claws; its oysters are bearded like pards; and as for its soles—I have yet to see one that measures more than five inches round the waist. The fact is, there is hardly a fish in the Mediterranean worth eating and therefore: *ex nihilo nihil fit*. Bouillabaisse is only good because cooked by the French, who, if they cared to try, could produce an excellent and nutritious substitute out of cigar-stumps and empty matchboxes. But even as a Turk is furious with a tender chicken because it cheats him out of the pleasure of masticating, so the Neapolitan would throw a boneless *zuppa di pesce* out of the window: the spitting and sputtering is half the fun.

"There is a fine *palamide*, too, from Mortella, brought in this morning. . . ."

It is the misfortune of Siren land to have been celebrated, since centuries, for these noble-looking fish, which are exported in thousands to the epicures of Naples and whose flesh tastes like shoe-leather soaked in paraffin. The natives, and not the foreigners, keep up the price of fish hereabouts; they are all icthyophagous, like the Athenians of old, and it is nothing short of a miracle that any kind of swimming or crawling creature continues to frequent these coasts, considering the way they are persecuted.

It is not good to be a fish in Siren land.

Hundreds of fry, which in a month or two would have weighed half a pound a piece, are caught to make a single dish; dynamite is also used, as well as the juice of the euphorbia and the roots of the cyclamen—locally termed *spaccapiatti*: split-plate—which poison the water and bring the fish to the surface. How admirable are the Italian fishery laws and how admirable it would be, for the little fishes at least, if they were obeyed, now and then! Latterly, too, acetylene has been substituted for the old-fashioned pine-torches at night, and with tremendous effect: the startled creatures collecting from far and near and thrusting their noses out of the waves to see the grand illumination. I have counted two hundred and eighty of these lights gleaming upon the dark waste of waters—they look like stars fallen upon the deep.

At this same Mortella (it lies near Cantone on the south side of the peninsula and the name derives from its myrtle-thickets) a tunny fishery was formerly established, which paid a yearly rent of four hundred ducats, and another one further along the coast at Sant' Elia; but the municipality, they say, taxed them so disproportionately to their gains that they emigrated to Conca. In these *tonnare* everything is caught except the tunny, which has wisely ceased to visit these regions. There was another establishment of the same kind on Capri, near the Palazzo a Mare, long ago.

From the summit of Mortella, too, you can often watch the dolphins playing, this stretch of sea being one of their favourite resorts. It is easy to conceive a liking for this sportive and classical beast, even if one disbelieves both the theory of Professor Schubert of Munich, who, in the nineteenth century (A.D.), wrote a treatise to prove that the human race was descended from a dolphin, as well as those old fables concerning his affection for mankind—how he helps them to catch fish, how he loves their arts and music, and has often saved the noblest of them from a watery grave. . . .

And still it rains.

The window where I sit would afford a fair view upon vineyards and distant sea, if the panes were not streaming with the downpour, which can be heard rushing like a cataract into the cistern at the back of the house. It has converted the roadway beside the door into a water-course—sticks and straws and nondescript objects careering downhill on its yellow flood. . . .

That is a humane conceit, too, of the dolphin's piercing the armour of the crafty crocodile as it lies hidden in the muddy African river, enticing to death the compassionate traveller with mock groans and tearful complaint; and a pretty story is told by Aulus Gellius or another of the ancients about a friendship between a boy and a dolphin. Let me see if I can remember it.

Hermias lived with his father, a fisherman, and of all the boys who learned letters at the gymnasium none was blither of heart or comelier of limb, and none excelled him in those manly sports which were so highly commended in those days. Swimming was his chief delight, and so it came about that one day when he was far from land, having outstripped all his fellows in a race, he was hardly surprised to see a dolphin plunging alongside of him. It played about him in fondest fashion, hiding its deadly fin as in a sheath—for the smallest wound from a dolphin's fin is death to man—and, as soon as the boy grew tired, took him gently on its back and bore him to the shallow water. It was plain that the sea-beast had conceived an attachment for him, for the next day and on all the following days, when work was over and the lads ran down to bathe, Hermias found the dolphin waiting for him. Whenever he wished to play with his new companion, he used to call out, "Simo, Simo!" and the dolphin instantly swam to the shore to meet him, vaulting in glad wheels over the surface of the water. Why did he call him Simo? He never thought about it; it seemed to be his natural name.

The news of this friendship soon spread about the town, and crowds of folk used to collect on the beach to see the fun. Stranger things were done in those times than nowadays; nevertheless, it was so remarkable that even Octavius Avitus, a mighty great lord and governor of the province, came down to see the boy and ask him questions. The old fisherman alone hated Simo, for he knew that the merest scratch from the dolphin's fin would be fatal to his son.

"That fish-friend of yours", he used to say, "mislikes me.

Beware, my boy, of his terrible fin." Sooner or later, he feared, some mischief would happen.

Even so it fell out.

"Ah, Simo, you have hurt me!" Hermias suddenly cried out. He had jumped too heavily on the dolphin's back and scratched his breast on the sharp point. Then he laughed again and thought it a small matter.

Simo saw the waves stained with blood and guessed the truth. He carried him to the beach and watched him slowly limping homewards; he even tried to rise out of the water, so as to follow his boy-companion, but could only struggle a few paces up the dusty path. And there he lay, panting on the hot earth. He could hear the waves behind him, lapping on the sandy shore and inviting him to glide back into his cool home, but he only thought of Hermias. Great tears dropped from his lidless eyes.

"I am hurt, father," cried the boy, as he fainted on the doorstep. The fisherman laid him on the couch and looked at the wound.

"That is the dolphin's work!" he exclaimed with anguish. "My poor child—my poor child!" Hermias never spoke again.

Then the father took down a brave axe that was hanging over the couch, and nets and other implements, and a lusty pair of oars, and strode seawards to reach his boat, determined to battle with the murderer of his son. Suddenly he staggered backwards and the axe dropped from his hand: his enemy, the sea-beast, was stretched across the sunlit path before his eyes.

The old man stared in wonderment at this prodigy.

Simo lay in the agony of death. His eye was glazed, and colours of every imaginable hue chased each other over his smooth body, while now and again the flanks heaved, as though a sigh had escaped his heart. All at once his skin became wrinkled and ashen grey. The dolphin had died out of love for his lost playmate.

The townsfolk, when the heard the news, took counsel how best to honour the memory of this strange and strong attachment. They laid the two friends in one tomb, and over it they reared a marble statue of a fair lad astride upon a dolphin, in order that all who passed that way might learn that loving affection is still in repute upon earth. And Octavius Avitus, the governor, was not content even with this, but caused medals to be struck, with an effigy of the two comrades upon them, and therein showed not only his kindliness but also his understanding, for the tomb and the statue have long since crumbled away, but these coins are still scattered all over the world, bearing into distant ages the report of their happy friendship and unhappy fate. . . .

No tales of this kind are in circulation among the people here; still, they certainly regard the dolphin with no hostile feelings, probably because they have observed its reckless, death-scorning love for its offspring, which appeals to their own hearts. Regarding the fabled play of colours before death, I have also inquired: they know nothing. This may be due to lack of observation, for they have little eye for such things. But, so far as it goes, it coincides with my own experience, which I cannot claim to be extensive, since I only once had an opportunity of watching a dying dolphin. It had been harpooned and dragged on board, where it lay shivering and breathing hard. A youth was then seen to sharpen a long knife: he was a student of physiology. Turning up his sleeve, he plunged the blade swiftly into the dolphin's breast, whence he drew forth a quivering something, which he examined carefully. There was no iridescence—not the faintest trace of it; perhaps the death-stroke had been too rapid.

The fishermen here have elaborated what seems to be a myth for excusing this animal's ravages among the fish. It is not the common dolphin, they say, which is responsible, but a rarer kind called *ferone*. The *ferone* never travels in schools, but by himself; he destroys the nets out of sheer spite and makes a point of killing more fish than he can eat. When the *ferone* appears on the scene, all the common ones, the *fere*, take to flight. In short, he lords it over the others, he is guileful and malicious, and no death is bad enough for him. This reminds me of "bull-elephant" stories in India, and may possibly have the same foundation in fact.

A much more mysterious monster is the *gatta marina*, or sea-cat. It raises its head above water to see where the nets are, and then dives in that direction to eat the fish in the meshes. It has four feet with prodigiously long claws and only comes at certain seasons, and then not always. Its colour is black—that is, not altogether black; and it weighs less than a hundredweight, but often more. It is covered with a sort of fur, rather like the dolphin, but a little different. Nobody eats the sea-cat except some people, who do. . . .

Inexhaustible is the fish-lore of Siren land; they have a firm belief that everything which creeps and flies on earth has its counterpart under the waves. Shall I tell you of the sea-turtle and how, every now and then, a "marine flea" crawls under its flapper, which makes it very angry, because at such times, it can only swim sideways in an absurd fashion, and all the other fishes laugh at it and pull its tail, till at last——

"Perhaps the signore would prefer a hen?"

No, thank you. I know those hens and how they are caught. This is the manner of it. The careful housewife singles out the scraggiest of her fowls, which forthwith stops eating and watches her steadily with one eye, doubtless aware of her intentions. The preliminary coaxing being of no avail (it is merely done for form's sake), five small boys are despatched in pursuit with sticks and stones. They begin by liking the job, for their prey, sure of victory, marches straight in front of them without deigning to look round, an easy mark for projectiles. One stone grazing its tail, it takes flight and settles in the vineyards on the hill-side, amid howls of execration from the boys. Other pursuers are roused and join in the chase; a cloud of missiles envelopes the bird as it gallops and flutters over stones and up trees, into gullies and thickets; the rabble vanishes from sight—you can hear them shouting a mile off.

An hour or so having elapsed, the hen is seen, a speck on the horizon, flying down from the mountains in a straight line, pressed hard by an undaunted knot of pursuers. *Sant' Antonio!* It is going into the water like last year! And, sure enough, it glides into the waves about three hundred yards from the shore and begins to preen its remaining feathers. May its mother be barren! May its children die unblest! The boat—the boat! It is launched, and at the very moment when the oar is about to descend with a crash upon the muscular frame of the victim, it rises like a lark and perches upon the roof of the church. *A chi t'è morto!* Out with the ladder! All work ceases in the village, the school is closed for the day; the priest and the tobacconist, mortal enemies, are observed to exchange a few breathless words. Bedridden hags crawl into the piazza and ask whether there is an earthquake. No, the hen! The church! The signore! The foreign signore wants the hen—the hen on the church! Just as the nimble *figlio di Luisella* has placed his foot upon that last rung of the ladder—*Ah, Santo Dio!* It has flown away, away into the brushwood, where none but the swiftest and surest-footed can hope to follow.

Towards Ave Maria it is carried in, vanquished. The conqueror, streaming with perspiration and attended by the entire populace, proudly holds it up for your inspection by one leg—the other is missing. A small boy, reluctantly, produces it from his pocket.

Is this a hen?

There is not a vestige of feathers on its body; the head, too, seems to have come off in the heat of the fray. The conqueror tells you that he could have shot it, but was afraid of spoiling its plumage. The careful housewife asks whether you will have it boiled or *al cacciatore*?

What is left of the bird looks as if it were already half cooked. . . .

IX

THE LIFE OF SISTER SERAFINA

A<small>N</small> authoritative, religious biography of Sister Serafina di Dio, the Christian ornament of these regions, was published at Naples in 1723, and further details concerning her can be gleaned from certain *Positiones super Dubio*—ecclesiastical writings printed at various times with a view to procuring her beatification and containing statements as to her life and habits made by eye-witnesses under oath. From these sources, and from them alone, I cull the following facts, so far as they concern her. And inasmuch as these documents prove her to have modelled the incidents of her birth, life, and death in a truly amazing manner upon those of the more celebrated Spanish nun, Saint Teresa di Dio (born nearly a century earlier), I will occasionally refer—for a reason which will become apparent later on—to the latter saint, whose biographies are in the hands of all scholars. . . .

This remarkable woman, foundress of seven convents of the Carmelite order, whose influence extended beyond the limits of Siren land, was born, the third in a family of six children, at Naples on October 24, 1621. Her father was a Neapolitan man of business, and her mother—she was the man's second wife—belonged to the noble family of Strina, which is conspicuous in the mediæval records of Capri. She was baptized, on the day of her birth, in the church of Saint John at Naples, receiving the worldly name of Prudentia; and it was observed with surprise that the infant did not weep during the ceremony, but kept her eyes gravely fixed upon the officiating priest.

Saint Teresa's mother was of nobler stock, too, than her father. She was, moreover, the mother's third child, and likewise the offspring of her father's second marriage. And furthermore she was baptized on the day of her birth, in a church dedicated to Saint John.

At an early age, the child Prudentia was taken to Capri, where

she lived with her parents at the foot of the Castiglione hill, and at
a remote house which is still pointed out in the district Moneta as
the "house of Sister Serafina". In this rural solitude, as it must have
been in those days, she soon began to read the *Lives of the Martyrs*,
and to brood over their past torments and present bliss—fervent
dreamings, which were strenuously fostered by her mother, as well
as by her maternal uncle, who, as her confessor and parish priest,
had been able to discern in the infant all the elements of future
holiness. Doubtless this compilation, that has produced many saints
and ascetics, profoundly influenced the unfolding of her childish
mind, but her mother had simultaneously hit upon a second and
equally effective device for working upon little Prudentia's emotions :
she used to take the child into churches and chapels* and allow her
to gaze, wonder-struck, upon the marvels within. Flickering lights,
odours of incense, sternly resplendent images, grave and wondrously
clad priests, swaying censers, and rapid torrents of exultation from
the organ overhead : all these contrivances, so strange, so purposeful,
so different from the green and sunshiny fields of Moneta; and all
of them moving to the glory of Something still more wonderful,
still more mysterious, that hovered around and above the altar—
how indelible an impression must they have made upon the fabric
of her young senses ! When adults, with fairly developed reasoning
powers, cannot withstand these sensual allurements, what shall be
expected of a child? Without understanding a jot of the meaning
of all this golden pantomime, her thirsty youth drank it in, and with
such effect that in later years Sister Serafina could never retain full
control over herself at the sight of a holy object; her trances were
of so peculiarly an automatic form that at the sight of a crucifix,

---

* Among these, the hermit chapel on the summit of the "Villa Jovis" is
particularly mentioned, and the picture of Madonna del Soccorso which she there
worshipped exists to this day; it is the oldest of its kind on Capri; the type is semi-
Byzantine and of that dark tint (*bruna, nera, schiavona: nigra sum, sed formosa*) which
is credited with peculiar efficacity. Many of these miraculous pictures, like that
of Monte Vergine or the "brown mother" which was imported to Naples from
Mount Carmel, were painted by Saint Luke, but some are unquestionably of later
date. So the managers of the Pompeii sanctuary have wisely acquired a genuine
"black" madonna, which was manufactured not long ago by a Neapolitan artist.
Black idols are also adored in Russia and Greece—the idea goes back to Pessinus
and the Kaaba, to lingams, meteorites, and what not. This chapel, by the way,
used to be dedicated to Saint Leonard, one of the many saints of Siren land who
have faded away before the effulgent humanity of the Mother of God, whose
picture was then appropriately "discovered under a mass of old masonry": a
common motif all over Italy.

for instance, she would at once fall into an ecstasy, thus learning to believe implicitly and devoutly what most of her fellow-Christians can but dimly hope to understand : the Real Presence. The crucifix which *spoke to her* (like that of Saint Thomas Aquinas) is still preserved at Massa.

Saint Teresa was very remarkable for her crucifix worship.

The penances which this infant imposed upon herself reached the number of twenty a day. In order to cleanse her tongue for the reception of the Eucharist, to which she had been accustomed since the age of eight, she would lick the ground; she disciplined herself with chains, poured hot wax upon her skin, and was advancing fast, by these and similar outrages upon her body, in the favour of God, when the devil was permitted to make use of certain light-hearted girlish friends in order to bring about, as he thought, her destruction. She was then a lively and beautiful girl of fourteen, and the following avowal to her confessor reads rather seriously : "To put it shortly, plainly, and truthfully, I have committed all the sins that can be committed in this world." In point of fact, her earthly cravings had merely manifested themselves in a reprehensible desire to see the carnival like her friends; a desire that was providentially not gratified because, finding in her pocket a copy of the *Legends of the Holy Virgins,* she glanced into the book and was led to see the error of her ways before the masks appeared on the scene. A severe reaction followed upon this irregularity, and further diabolical attempts by seductive or terrifying images were victoriously repulsed.

A more important matter, and one that marks an epoch in her development, was the determination of her father to have her married to a Neapolitan acquaintance. This father, although pious enough (two of his brothers were Jesuits), strongly disapproved of what he called his daughter's religious excesses and, judging a rich and happy marriage to be a sound counter-irritant, pressed the matter forcefully, and would doubtless have gained his point but for the wiles of the uncle, the parish priest, and of a certain Sister Ippolita, a Dominican nun, who played, at this period, the rôle of spiritual intermediary between Prudentia and Jesus, her Elected Spouse. Sister Ippolita, a shrewd woman, understood that this was no time for half-measures. She cut off Prudentia's long and beautiful hair, dressed her in some of her own oldest clothes that were absurdly too big for the girl, and induced her to present herself in this garb before her enraged father, whose exact words the biographer, perhaps wisely, fails to report, though their sense may be inferred from the statement that he heaped threats and maledictions upon his disobedient child. After this defeat the father yielded, like a sensible man, to the importunities of his household, and was thenceforward left in peace. He had done his best, and failed. We are told that throughout life he had been little more than an instrument in the hands of the devil, so far as Prudentia was concerned, and it was not without significance that he should die early, confessing his errors and imploring the pardon of his virtuous daughter who was now left, at the age of twenty-four, to indulge her genius without fear of contradiction.

Saint Teresa, it will be remembered, was also led into an excess of childish piety by the *Lives of the Martyrs*. She too, as a comely girl of fourteen, was tempted by the devil, who made use of certain youthful friends to compass his end. And, exactly like Sister Serafina, she was re-converted through the instrumentality of a nun and a pious uncle.

What that genius was, may be read in the life of Saint Catherine or any of her innumerable prototypes in mediæval or still earlier Christianity. It was an uninterrupted rhapsody of love to Jesus, her Spouse. She was "consumed, burned, maddened, suffocated, intoxicated, liquefied" with Love; she "desired to turn to ashes by reason of the Fire of Love, and then arise in order to become ashes once more out of Love". Her voluminous writings (an enumeration of their titles and contents fills nearly five printed folio pages) breathe an atmosphere of intensest passion—of love, warm and palpitating; they are essentially non-theological, personal lucubrations. For she had all the mystic's impatience of dogma; when touching, at the suggestion of her confessors, upon themes like the Procession of the Holy Spirit or the Incarnation of the Word, her speech at once becomes obscure; how indeed—as Professor Maudsley asks—how speak ineffable things save in unintelligible language? Like Teresa, she merely coquetted, if I may decently so express myself, with the mysteries of the Trinity, that tremendous doctrine which exerts, from its very incredibility, a magnetic attraction upon this class of persons, affording the simplest test of what constitutes religious mystic, whose mind, attuned to improbabilities, discovers to be plain, necessary and beautiful, what others describe as—somewhat puzzling.

Saint Teresa's epigram on this subject, "the greater the absurdity, the more I believe", finds an echo in Sister Serafina's pious exclamation: "O luminous obscurity, so clear to all who love you!"

And what may be called the Gothic or Hell-fire sub-species of Christianity, with its charnels and skeletons, inspired her with peculiar and proper disgust. She could not bring herself to think upon these gloomy aspects of her faith, the bottomless pit, the wailings, fiery torments, and gnashings of teeth; convinced, like many other charitable Christians, that the threat-and-bribe system was incompatible with a pure and spontaneous love to God. "A strange thing," she says, "that one should love God out of interest or out of fear." For this reason, she "wished to abolish Hell and Paradise alike".

Even so, Saint Teresa desired to "blot out both Heaven and Hell".

Nor did her religion lack that typical roseate complexion which demonstrates that *naturam expellas furca, tamen usque recurret*. Her numerous letters and poems to her Divine Lover would shock the ears of Northern Puritans; they resemble the languishing Celestial Amours of Saint Gertrude—amorous plaints, couched in language that might be addressed with equal propriety by some terrestrial Juliet to her Romeo. The very name of Jesus was of so sweet a taste in her mouth that on uttering it she frequently swooned away, and was therefore obliged to deprive herself of this joy in the presence of others "till she was given sufficient robustness of spirit to repress these external movements". In this respect she resembled a certain bishop of Saluzzo who, according to Saint Alfonso di Ligurio, perceived such a pleasant aroma in his mouth each time he pronounced the sacred word *Maria*, that he invariably licked his lips afterwards.

She had been subject to ecstatic conditions ever since the age of eight. She distinguished, during these trances, four principal modes of perceiving the presence of Jesus: the student of psychology will find them highly interesting, as they are defined with the pseudo-scientific precision of the Spanish nun.

Saint Teresa also speaks of four modes, though later on, in the "Castello Interior", she raised the number to seven.

This is how her trances appeared to others:

"One evening she retired into her cell so liquefied with love that she seemed actually to die, and she began to say: Do you not see

Jesus Christ? making signs towards the altar, which was visible from her cell; and became so liquefied that she fainted away, so that we could hardly hear the words she was saying. Sometimes she said: "*Dio bello, quanto è bello Dio!*" and whilst uttering these words she seemed to die, and then suddenly laughed aloud, and cried almost at the same time, and seemed deprived of all strength. . . ."*

It was not long before her Divine Spouse gave token of His particular affection for her. He told her, in visions, "Thou art my bride—I wish to remain ever with thee"; indeed, He loved her, we are told, more than she Him, and thus spake He to the angels: "Behold how fair is My bride, how she resembleth Me; yea, she is altogether My image"; and she, on her part, would remain convulsed with joy on hearing the word *Amami* (love Me) softly uttered as she partook of the Celestial Food. In order to render herself more worthy of His affection she indulged in an orgy of mortifications such as would have killed a more grossly constituted individual. Her very chastity became a form of voluptuousness; never was maidenly modesty carried to a more frenzied pitch. As an infant at the breast she had already felt uneasiness when a man entered the room, and never ceased crying till he left, and such was her sensitiveness in later years that on discovering that one of her pupils secretly cherished a portrait of her brother, a male, she fainted with grief and surprise, and would have died outright "had not Christ, compassionately appearing to His bride, fortified her soul". She refused to sit in chairs that men, even priests, had previously occupied; suckling infants of the male sex were not tolerated within the precincts of her convents, and her eyes were so well trained in a downcast look that, walking one day in the streets of Naples, she accidentally collided with her head against the feet of a criminal who was hanging from a gallows in front of her, to the intense astonishment of passengers.

Earthly womanhood was even more distasteful to her, for while she regarded men, exclusive of priests, as a necessary evil, a beast by nature, whose only *raison d'être* in this world—Saint Jerome held the same view—was the procreation of female children for conventual purposes, women were grievously to blame, if they chose the wrong path. After an unavoidable visit to her convent of the wife of the governor of Capri, who came in somewhat fashionable

---

* Whoever wishes to understand the true nature of these seizures will find ample materials in the works of Havelock Ellis and other modern scholars.

attire, she addressed her pupils on the appalling example of vanity displayed before their eyes and, as a humiliation, set the example of taking a skull and licking it with her tongue in every part. Her infectious zeal fired them to cut off their hair and torture their bodies with a variety of instruments which the biographer describes as "horrible to behold", in spite of the protests of the parents, who reminded Sister Serafina that hers was an educational establishment, a *conservatorio*, and not a nunnery—claustral confinement was not inaugurated here till nearly a century after her death—all this, "in order that they might render themselves more attractive in the eyes of God", whose taste, on the subject of female beauty, would seem to differ considerably from ours.

More repulsive to her than all was any manifestation, or even hint, of the natural functions of womanhood. The *Life* speaks relatively little of her love to the Mother of God, and, reading between the lines, one gains the conviction that even the motherhood of the Madonna, so touching and sublime to many, was hardly congenial to her ultra-virginal mind. Thus, when the Virgin and Son appeared to her simultaneously, she was always in a dilemma whom to adore, and finally she prayed the Virgin not to bring the Son, as He attracted her so strongly that she feared to be wanting in due reverence towards her. "She was so ravished by the incomparable beauties of the Divine Son that she reverently prayed the Virgin Mother to excuse her if in His presence she lacked due respect for her"—a frame of mind which the Mother of God, we are told, benignly appreciated. This is what we should expect, for even holy men cannot escape from the toils of their organic nature. So male saints, in all times and places, prefer the milder charms of female divinities, and the greatest panegyrists of the Madonna have always been of that sex.

Nothing but the ideal youth, spotless and eternal, of Jesus or Saint Michael appealed to her heart. This may be purity. But it is the purity neither of Nausikaa nor of the sage ("The purity which proceedeth from knowledge is the best."—*Mahabharatha*).

The same comparative lack of veneration for the Mother of God was a marked trait in the Spanish nun, who, like Sister Serafina, wrote innumerable love poems and letters to Jesus and was finally adopted by Him as bride.

I will not weary the reader with a list of the torments which

Sister Serafina underwent in order to please her Spouse: the catalogue of her cilices and other machinery for self-torture is a truly
formidable one. She would pray for hours, extended in the attitude
of crucifixion on the stone flags of her cell; she starved herself, and
her girdle, to prevent her from satisfying hunger, was so tightly
drawn that it was found at her death imbedded in the flesh; being
forced by the physician to eat meat, to which she had been unaccustomed, she experienced a double joy—the joy of swallowing
what was pre-eminently unpleasant to her palate, and the joy of
immediately vomiting what her stomach refused to contain. Her
modesty forbade her to take a bath, but when this became urgently
necessary on account of her health "she discovered a manner of
enjoying an heroical suffrance by sitting in it when too hot, so that
all the skin came off her body". Many of her penances are devised
in apparent emulation of Elizabeth of Hungary and far too nause-
ating to be printed; disorganized, indeed, must be the mind that
thinks to please its Maker by such refinements of nastiness that even
an enthusiastic religious eye-witness, beholding these things, is
obliged to confess: "Which when I saw, I grew sick, and reverently
vomited." Instead of ordinary food, she lived on the Eucharist. Its
Mysteries had become Realities and she saw through the veil of its
earthly allegory into the bright realms of truth beyond. Her confessors were perpetually forced to interpose their authority to
restrain this luxury of self-maceration, and her implicit obedience
to them is all the more remarkable in one who, by her hourly
personal communication with the Powers of Heaven, could well,
one might suppose, have dispensed with any mediation on the part
of man. Can obedience go higher than this?

"One day having been forbidden to approach the Sacred Table,
she perceived Jesus coming towards her after the consecration of the
Host and kindly inviting her to partake of it; Whom nevertheless
this child of perfect obedience repelled. . . ."

The confessors of Saint Teresa were likewise obliged frequently to
moderate her excessive love of penances. Like Serafina, she worshipped obedience, regarding it as the greatest of the virtues.

One result of this godly mode of life was the inevitable impair-
ment of health. Sister Serafina was infirm throughout life; one ill-
ness alone lasted for ten years and brought her to death's door. She
suffered from chronic feeling of heat, while hallucinations of all the
five senses were everyday occurrences; she was declared to be

"hectic" and inwardly consumed to cinders, though free from all organic disease.

Even so, Saint Teresa was delicate throughout life and near death's door at one time; she had the same hallucinations and feelings of heat; she was likewise declared to be "hectic" and inwardly consumed to cinders, though of a naturally vigorous constitution.*

Yes; they were all "burnt", these spouses who approached so near to the Most Highest; for God is a consuming fire. . . .

But another result was an increase of favours showered down upon her by the Divine Lover, who now openly avowed His predilection for her. The stigmata appeared on her hands; her heart was wounded with a dart borne by an angelic child of about twelve years of age, "presumably Jesus Christ"; she enjoyed ecstatic raptures of Heaven and Hell, and wrote, under spiritual guidance, upon the different methods of prayer.

How miraculously parallel is the career of Saint Teresa! She had the same visions of Heaven and Hell and wrote similar treatises upon methods of prayer; the stigmata likewise appeared on her hands, while an angelic child, belonging to the highest order of cherubim, transverberated her heart with God's spear. (See Bernini's monument in the church of S. M. della Vittoria in Rome.)

Sometimes Sister Serafina wrote at the inspiration of Jesus, and it is with surprised regret that the reader of the *Life* learns that a dissertation on Divine Love, *taken down at the immediate dictation of Our Lord*, has been deliberately discarded from this work. Why has the author neglected to publish this treatise? "On account of its length!" Surely this, in a book of seven hundred and forty printed octavo pages in double columns, filled with so many irrelevant details and repetitions, is an unpardonable oversight! Her influence in celestial spheres was such that the patron saint of Capri used her as a vehicle of communication with the Pope, and the Pope, in his turn, besought her intermediation with Heaven. She was furnished with the services of two guardian angels (Saint Teresa had but one), and with what amounts to almost the same thing, namely, the enviable gift, common to many pious persons, of a vision which decides on all occasions of doubt what is to be done. This comfortable faculty, indeed, if the matter be regarded aright, does

---

* A recent author, A. Marie (*Mysticisme et Folie*, Paris, 1907), discovers traces of constitutional hysteria in the Spanish nun.

constitute the piety of pious people and contradistinguishes them from ordinary mortals, who have only judgment and experience to go upon; for how shall they whose every action, down to the most trivial of life, is regulated by divine orders—how *can* they go far wrong? She performed many miracles, such as appearing in two places at once, foretelling the deaths of friends and others, curing diseases by touch, and instinctively detecting priests who had led immoral lives.

These are among the very miracles of Saint Teresa.

The laws of nature were frequently "suspended"—to use a phrase popular both with Gibbon and the late Duke of Argyll—at the request of Sister Serafina; she allays a storm at sea; quiets an eruption of Vesuvius; like Saint Anthony of Padua, she preaches to animals who understand; like Apollonius of Tyana or the *flying monk* Saint Joseph of Copertino, she is levitated and suspended in air with her head almost touching the ceiling; like Sixtus V and General Manhes, but unlike anyone else in ancient or modern times, she succeeded in extirpating brigandage in the kingdom of Naples; she is useful for childless families, and undergoes a variety of flaming transformations: all of which things are seen and vouched for by devout persons, whose testimony needs must fortify those who possess any belief in the value of witness to the miraculous. But, in my opinion, the most useful wonder that she performed was by liberating in September, 1683, through her intercession with Saint Michael, the beleaguered town of Vienna, the bulwark of Faith, from the Turks. Little did the inhabitants of that city think that they, and thousands of their fellow-religionists, were saved from a fate too awful to contemplate through the supplications—more effectual than those of all Christianity combined—of the humble nun of Siren land. This act alone, if her biographer is indeed not mistaken, might be thought to entitle her to that honour of beatification which fell to the lot of Saint Teresa.

These peculiar graces provoked not only the envy of man, who is ever ready to persecute with his calumnies all that emerge above the common herd, but also of the devil. Throughout life Sister Serafina had frequent visitations of the prince of darkness, and her behaviour in these embarrassing moments may be commended to all who undergo similar experiences; for instead of proceeding to Luther's lengths of undignified personal rudeness, she tried rather conciliatory methods, and once actually induced him to pray and adore

the Saviour. For the rest, his insinuations were not always character-
ized by the astuteness with which he is commonly credited. One
day she observed a young man seated in the corridor of the convent,
guitar in hand, who informed her that he was tempting the nuns—
a transparent device, which she had no difficulty in confounding
("The Devil as Troubadour" is a common apparition all over
Christianity—cf. Lermontoff's *Demon*.) Such was her reputation in
the infernal regions that the devils were heard complaining angrily
that she would not let them settle even upon the roof of the monastery.

Saint Teresa, too, had life-long conflicts with devils.

Altogether, there is an astonishing uniformity in the lives, miracles,
penances, temptations, and deaths of the ten thousand saints that
have sprung up from the fertile soil of the South. Many of their holy
idiosyncrasies, such as self-mutilations, devil-visitations, odour of
sanctity, etc., will be found to be already the property of pagan
predecessors in every part of the world. Is this due to wilful plagiar-
ism? Surely not. It is due to the small range of their mentalities,
for in proportion as materials are limited, so will their permu-
tations and combinations be limited. Like some great writer on
human affairs, who fails to express his rich and varied thoughts in
the restricted medium of a provincial dialect through sheer de-
ficiency of adequate words and phrases, even so the Great Contriver
of all things, harping, for His or our pleasure, on the same few
strings of these His poor defective instruments, can coax forth no
fresh sound, but ekes out lack of novelty by reiteration of monotony.
Nor let it be forgotten that the merit of Catholic saintship belongs
by one half, at least, to the confessor, to whom these willing creatures have surrendered body and soul for the glorification of himself, his Order, or his God.

With the approach of the seventh climacteric an immense change
comes over Sister Serafina: it is nothing less than a psychic revolution. From being an ascetic dreamer, a trembling Spouse of
Christ, a writer of visionary colloquies and poems, she is transformed into a practical woman. There are convents to be founded.
Her friends and relations fostered the scheme; the apostolic injunction *virgines castas exhibere Christo*—what anguish would have been
avoided if that phrase had never been written!—was interpreted
as implying a command, and a timely vision in a Neapolitan church,
during which the Virgin and her Son gave minute instructions

as to the order of the monastery to be founded, and the colour and cut of the clothes of its inmates, naturally left her no further choice in the matter. She at once went to Capri with seven Neapolitan girls who were to become the first inmates of a convent which was dedicated to the Saviour, but is generally known as Saint Teresa. We are told that the building of this establishment cost about 150,000 ducats; this will give some idea of the energy and resources of its foundress. Where had she found the money?

The fearful plague of 1656, which crept over from the mainland, they say, in a lock of hair sent by a maiden to her lover on Capri, had claimed among its victims Sister Serafina's mother, as well as her pious maternal uncle and confessor, the parish priest, who made a will on his death-bed leaving his wealth to his niece on condition that it should be employed in the erection of a convent. This was a very humble start, but a divine vision promised further help, which presently arrived, contributions flowing in from her new confessor, from the Archbishop of Amalfi, the Viceroy of Naples, and other devout friends and relatives. The convent was completed in 1678 and festively inaugurated by Cardinal Orsini, afterwards Pope Benedict XIII, who was Sister Serafina's firm friend throughout life. (It was about this time that she permanently discarded her worldly name of Prudentia.)

It had been a fierce struggle. So much local opposition had been raised by the clergy and populace of the island that the work was nearly abandoned at one time, though it proceeded rapidly towards the end. The devil, too, with characteristic malice, endeavoured to raise an obstacle at the very moment of inauguration: he delayed, up to the day preceding the ceremony, the despatch from Naples of a large slab of marble destined for the high altar, and as it arrived nevertheless in time, he caused it to break in two pieces during its transport; but the crafty cardinal, determined not to be outdone, discovered a block of antique travertine, which served the purpose equally well.

Saint Teresa, too, underwent a complete revulsion of character at the approach of the seventh climacteric; a new epoch begins; the mystic is transmuted into a shrewd and active woman. She had a divine vision in church which commanded the foundation of her first monastery. The work began like that of Sister Serafina, in humblest fashion; but another vision promised help, which presently arrived. Yet she had to combat so much local opposition that the building was nearly abandoned: later on, it proceeded rapidly, though the devil took a personal interest in the matter and contrived a variety of obstacles.

Meanwhile other convents were being built by Sister Serafina; one at Massa Lubrense in 1673; another one, two years later, at Vico Equense. A fourth grew up at Nocera in 1680, while the large one in Anacapri was constructed, in 1683, in accordance with a vow made during the Turkish siege of Vienna to the Archangel Michael, who, having performed his share of the bargain, insisted politely, but firmly, upon the fulfilment of hers. Next, a convent was reorganized at Torre del Greco in 1685, while the seventh and last was consecrated at Fischiano near Salerno in 1691. Thus, in a remarkably short space of time, these establishments were begun and ended.

One of the chief peculiarities in their internal organization was that they were nearly always recruited from the first convent of Saint Teresa on Capri. This, in its turn, was filled by girls from Naples, as the islanders, acting probably under orders from their bishop and clergy, looked askance at her schemes from the outset. The inmates were all of good families, and in Anacapri most of them had two rooms and a servant. From Capri, where they learned the rules from the lips of the foundress, they were transplanted, as occasion arose, to her other institutions, and such was their discipline that even after her death the nuns of Capri were held in great request for reforming convents. It is not reported in full how far those rules differed from those of similar houses; they are described as "veritable distillation of the finest perfection of Christianity", and elsewhere as "those of Saint Teresa, but accommodated to various circumstances of time and place, some things modified, others added, whenever she thought them necessary for the improvement of souls".

It may be well to enquire what gifts enabled Sister Serafina to carry forward these great works. She possessed a dominating personality, a wholeheartedness and zeal, the vehemence of which swept all opposition before it. What persons animated by one single idea, and that grounded on pure emotionalism, can do, may be seen in the life of Mahomet or Joan of Arc or, for that matter, of Saint Teresa. She would have allowed herself to be hewn in pieces rather than yield in her conviction, and all who came under her influence—children, paupers, bishops, workmen, sinners, politicians

—were swayed to think as she did. Of her power over the female mind, a pathetic example occurred when a young girl, who loved her home and had long resisted all temptations to be won over to a more saintly life, yielded at last to the torrent of Sister Serafina's golden eloquence and confessed that "the *disordered love to her parents*, by which she had been previously blinded, had left her heart". Another instance of this hateful destruction of the most sacred ties of humanity is afforded by the history of a nun of Saint Teresa convent. As a vain young girl, she had been persuaded to kneel down before a crucifix by Sister Serafina who then, with great fervour of spirit and in a loud voice, exclaimed to the Symbol: "God of Abraham, God of Isaac, God of Jacob, illumine this creature", and hardly had the girl heard this terrific invocation (for the strange-sounding Semitic names must have been less familiar to her than to Protestant Bible-readers) than "she saw five rays of light issuing from the five wounds of the Crucified, which, uniting together, formed as it were a dart which came towards her and perceptibly wounded her heart, making her feel as though she had entered from a great darkness into the Light", whereupon Sister Serafina joyfully called the others to embrace the new nun. This account is curious, as it illustrates the artificial production of an illusion under the contagious influence of what Murisier calls *expectant attention*: doubtless the identical form of deranged vision that manifested itself to Sister Serafina upon every provocation.

Pious eloquence alone will not build convents. Unlike many enthusiasts, this one, in her worldly relations, kept well within the bounds of sanity, and her calm self-restraint and business capacity in the presence of man affords a striking contrast to her self-abandonment towards God. The analogy with Saint Teresa instantly occurs to the mind. How useful this gift must have been during the construction of her various convents, in reconciling the conflicting interests of workmen, architects, and landowners, in steering her path through the inevitable social intrigues of priests and private families that are connected with all such undertakings, may easily be imagined. It was these practical talents, inherited, no doubt, from her much-despised father, that commended her to the notice of the high ecclesiastical dignitaries who employed her for these various tasks, and in this respect she may not inaptly be compared to Swedenborg, who had likewise inherited from his father a judgment in earthly affairs that was often surprisingly sane. But here the likeness ends. The Scandinavian dreamer speaks from celestial heights as the friend, nay, the instructor, of angels, and his hysterical utterances, that reflect the violent climatic changes of his home, are always expected to contain some hidden allegory which his disciples must unravel if they wish to save their souls: Sister Serafina is only an occasional visitor to Heaven, not an *habituée;* she is humble in the presence of the heavenly hosts, and there is no misinterpreting her central, narrow, but intense creed of love, for it glows as the bland and steady sun "under the roof of blue Ionian weather".

In her own department she was a born administrator. She would take no child over the age of thirteen years, and preferred them still younger, even four years old. This surprised others, but she knew, from personal experience, the importance of perverting the senses ere reason awakes; to seduce the enemy's outposts while the main body of his troops is yet distant—what general will not admire these tactics? She was particularly severe in not allowing intimacies between girls, well aware of the truth that it is evil communications, and not evil examples, that corrupt good manners. She disapproved of their undue affection for confessors; their love should be all for God. Widows and others who had been in contact with the world were not encouraged to enter her convents, and this, again, is true wisdom—of its kind. . . .

No significance need be attached to the fact that the rules of Serafina resemble those of Teresa, as she deliberately set herself to copy them, which can hardly be said of involuntary things, such as hallucinations, visits from celestial personages, and miracles performed after death. Yet the reader of Teresa's life cannot but be struck by her surprising similarity in traits of character to the other: she had the same passion for making nuns; she was equally severe in not allowing friendships; like Serafina, she did the humblest menial work in her capacity of prioress; she made the discipline harsher than many nuns could bear, etc. etc.

A life so active was not without tribulations. Her independence, her originality, and, in one word, her success were provocative of no small ferment on the island of Capri, for a woman enjoying familiar converse not only with cardinals and other exalted members of the Church, but also with supernatural powers, exposed herself to much friction with the local clergy who could claim no such distinctions, and who resented her influence upon the family life

and general social condition of Capri. This lurking grudge sometimes broke into open conflict; she was often on the worst of terms
with the bishops who, for the rest, were not always distinguished
by appropriate pastoral virtues. Thus, in 1652, Saint Costanzo
was obliged to appear in a vision to Sister Serafina, requesting her
to draw the attention of the Vatican to the unsatisfactory conduct
of the bishop, in consequence of which the offending ecclesiastic
was suspended from his functions and an apostolic vicar appointed.
Nor was she the only person who had difficulties with these prelates:
the prior of the Carthusian monastery on Capri obtained an order
from Gregory XV "that the monastery may not be molested by the
Bishop of Capri", and, at an earlier period, a papal injunction had
been issued against the local secular clergy "who, with armed
hands, robbed the farms and live stock of that monastery at the
instigation of their bishop". Stirring times. . . .

She had also her competitors, if such a word can be used. A small
island like Capri, which contained at that time only two thousand
inhabitants, would seem to have had its spiritual needs sufficiently
supplied by a saint like Sister Serafina, two monkeries and two
nunneries, a bishop and a staff of about fifty priests, to say nothing
of innumerable errant religious teachers of various denominations,
two archbishops and half a dozen bishops within a few miles,
and at least six permanent resident hermits as examples of holy
life.

And yet we learn that about 1695 "the islanders had little assistance in spiritual affairs" and that it had therefore been deemed
advisable to send out for their guidance and consolation the Father
Bonaventura da Potenza, then a young man. The biography of
Sister Serafina makes no more mention of this incident than the
biography of the male saint makes of her. He lived in the ancient
monastery of San Francesco, and though he performed miracles and
penitences after the manner of his kind, yet he seems to have lacked
the *éclat* of the mystic nun, and his stay on the island—doubtless
merely an anti-Oratorian demonstration—was cut short. He left,
after three months, for Ischia; convinced, probably, that Capri
was not large enough for two saints at a time.

There were more serious matters. She was accused in her younger
days of immoral relations with her uncle and confessor, the parish
priest, an affair that gave rise to a "horrible scandal", and the
Bishop of Capri, without inquiring into the matter, punished both

severely, but afterwards relented. There is no reference in her biography to this story, which I refuse to believe, though the Devil's Advocate (whose duty it was to reply to the above-named *Positiones super Dubio*) doubtless made good use of it by designating the priest's legacy for the construction of the convent as an "expiatory" one.

She was called a hypocrite, witch, drunkard, liar, lunatic, thief: all of which things she bore with Christian meekness. She was accused of consulting twelve books of necromancy and, strangest of all, or adorning herself with lace undergarments. Here we see the foolish lengths to which human malevolence will go. Lace underwear! Will calumniators never learn that there are limits to what can be believed? And yet, according to Lea, this was a favourite accusation on the part of the Spanish Inquisition.

She was inveigled into the controversy concerning Molinos the quietist, whose insinuating doctrines spread rapidly and had wrought much mischief among the faithful before they were discovered to be heretical, although she wrote a treatise condemning the views of the subtle Aragonian monk, a treatise which was the fruit of a vision during which Jesus expressed to her His horror that "these persons" would do away with His humanity. This vision is interesting on account of its self-evident genesis; it was generated by her own strong preconceptions upon this subject, for if Christ were to lose His humanity, love for Him, as she conceived it, would lose its flavour.

Saint Teresa was also particularly sensitive regarding the humanity of the Saviour.

So long as she remained superior of Saint Teresa convent all went well, but on resigning the post she was often ill-treated by her successors and subjected to every kind of malignity and petty annoyance.

The most painful episode in her life was her imprisonment in her cell, without the consolation of the Eucharist, for two years and a half, by order of the Inquisition—a humiliation that redounded in the end to her glory, for by decree of the holy office she was liberated in 1691 and declared to be "most innocent of the charges laid against her". I do not know what these charges were; the *Life* hints at the matter obscurely, to the effect that the "holy office was desirous of trying her spirit". It is pretty certain that she would not have been treated so well but for the intercession of her friend the powerful Cardinal Orsini; and the true cause of this violent seclusion is doubtless to be sought in the old rivalry between Jesuits and Oratorians—Sister Serafina was largely under the influence of the latter order—that broke out at this period in recrudescence of a peculiarly petulant character. She had been frequently confessed by Jesuits, who helped her at times but, as is seen in this matter, could also become her bitterest enemies.

Even so, Saint Teresa was frequently confessed by Jesuits, who assisted her on some occasions and turned ferociously against her on others.

Excess of piety and impiety alike aroused the hatred of this infamous band of man-demons, whose repeated discomfiture in the kingdom of Naples does eternal honour to its inhabitants. What, after all, can possibly be the explanations of an institution so anti-human in its aims and methods? Is it not a form of Sadism? The movement towards enforcing sacerdotal chastity which began soon after Hildebrand, and the rise of Orders like Dominicans and Franciscans who strove to make the ascetic principle a reality in life, produced a mania intelligible enough to a modern alienist: a mania for the infliction of cruelty. These flesh-subduing tendencies on the part of the religiously earnest crystallized themselves in the person of the mediæval inquisitor, whose office, ostensibly designed for promoting orthodox notions, was in reality a contrivance for the relief of lust by the infliction of torture. *Usque recurret!* The procedure itself, carefully framed so as to afford the judges every opportunity of tormenting the accused who, by the same rules, was deprived of all chances of explaining himself, proves this sufficiently clearly: a form of Sadism. . . .

I linger upon the personality of this energetic single-minded woman, for she is the embodiment of what the Hellenic spirit was *not:* its very antithesis. Earthly existence she held to be an illusion; the world was death; the body a sinful load which must be tortured and vexed in preparation for the real life—the life beyond the grave. To those Greeks, the human frame was a subtle instrument to be kept lovingly in tune with the loud-voiced melodies of earth and sky and sea; these were the realities; as for a life beyond, let the gods see to it—a shadowy, half-hearted business, at best.

Is it not a suggestive coincidence that her convent at Massa should have been built upon the presumable site of that old

Siren temple, perhaps with its very stones? Here, upon this spot, these two ideals confront one another, threatening, irreconcilable. . . .

And now what of this religion of Sister Serafina?

To pronounce upon it, is to pronounce upon the Christianity of which she is an exponent or, at least, a representative. She was a nun, an enemy of normally constituted human society, and in so far to be highly extolled among her fellow-religionists, since "the true monk"—to quote the words of Professor Harnack—"is the true and most perfect Christian". But the monasticism of the seventeenth century, though it still professed the ideals and conformed to the three fundamental rules of earlier days, could not fail to be profoundly modified in form and method by the events of fourteen centuries.

The Christianity of Sister Serafina is that of Saint Teresa. It appeals to primitive, but not always noble, impulses in human nature. Too indolent to scale the heights of doubt or dogmatic speculation, it avoids those fruitful sources of dissension and finds contentment in phlegmatic submission to authority; too selfish to expend its energies in altruistic schemes, it silently disregards, while professing loudly, the perilous and irksome doctrine of neighbourly love; too sensual to desire or conceive an impersonal deity, it throws the impetus of its misguided sexual yearnings into a sub-carnal passion for the Son of God who, by a presumption unique and degrading, is supposed to appreciate and actually to reciprocate such sentiments: the whole edifice, if it deserve that name, being interpenetrated and enlivened by mysticism, the convenient refuge of all who can feel, but not reason. No wonder its adherents declare themselves ready to die for so comfortable a creed; but martyrdom, whatever Dr. Johnson may say to the contrary, is a test neither of truth nor of usefulness.

And yet, as a religion, it lacks not vitality—the vitality of the tortoise, a living fossil, uncouth, rigid of structure, tenacious of life. For unlike most things upon earth, Christianity cannot be improved. The many "modernized" varieties of that cult which invite criticism with inevitable and fatal results—how unfavourably do they compare with that of Saint Teresa, which not only ignores critical methods but actually thrives on ridicule and turns so-called disproof to its own nourishment. This is its strength, and in this sense, and because it fosters the emotions and leaves reason severely alone, it may truly be called a Christianity after the heart of its founder. *Let him become a fool, that he may be wise.*

This is assuredly not the best that can be said of the faith of Sister Serafina, but it is the truth; and when it is added that hers was a somewhat grim and uncompromising personality—she had all the *adamantine hardness* of Saint Teresa—it may well be asked wherein lies the attraction which she exercises even upon those who differ fundamentally from her in their whole conception of life. Simply in this: that she was a sincere, homogeneous entity. What she believed to be true she sought with all her heart, and this alone entitles her to respect in a world that is only too full of composite, disharmonious characters, where sincerity and saintliness do not always blossom on one tree, where each wears a different face according to the occasion, and the few religiously minded are either sunk in drowsy pragmatism* or distracted by frantic endeavours to reconcile ancient folk-lore and modern science.

The twofold aspects of her Christianity are admirably epitomized by herself in a letter to a confessor: "O that I could shed a thousand times my blood for the saving of souls; I weep for the Turks, heretics, and other infidels, and for Christian sinners", but then follow immediately the words: "O that I could steal all the daughters from their mothers and lock them in a monastery."

She lived in an atmosphere of cowardice, intrigue, and hypocrisy;

---

* Pragmatism: the last ditch in the metaphysico-sentimental steeplechase; a bastard Buddhism which the artistic Professor James has conjured up, like an enchantment, out of the rubbish-heaps of Koenigsberg and Athens. And yet, watching the antics of a certain disciple, he must sometimes experience sensations akin to those of a domestic fowl which has hatched a duckling. "The only certain and ultimate test of reality is the absence of internal friction." What is this but Newman's *illative sense*? I like a thing, therefore it is true: pleasure the test of truth! Rather let us ask: what reality has ever been established without internal friction? Or again: "The Beatific Vision as the ideal of knowledge." What is this but the "divine frenzy" of Plato or Saint Teresa? Under such auspices, conscientious intellectual labour may well take a back seat; after pragmatism—the new Messiah. I have not followed recent phases beyond noting that Mr. Hobhouse, in the *Aristotelian Proceedings*, has made short work of these mystic, creative-feminine dreamings, while Mr. Peirce, the inventor of the word pragmatism, has been obliged to coin a new one "pragmaticism", in order to explain what he originally meant: an ominous symptom which reminds one of Goethe's "*wo der Gedanke fehlt, da stellt das Wort sich ein*". What is the whole of pragmatism but a systemization of those disordered flashes of intelligence that animate the savage or child, who create realities to coincide with emotional states? Its votaries yearn for the non-real, for consolation from the bewildering stress of phenomena: the *horror of a fact* underlies all such conciliatory, "*demi-vierge*" systems of philosophy.

she saw mankind in some of its worst aspects and suffered experiences that might well embitter a saint; but her faith remained childlike and mild. There are, to be sure, occasional spasms in her writings that savour more of the ferocious vindictiveness of the Old Testament than the unwholesome slave-morality of the New; yet, on the general score of tolerance, she may be held up as an example to Christians of all colours. Our intelligence, our humanity, turns with loathing from the unspeakable cult that thirsted for the blood of the noblest, and would gladly furbish anew its rusty engines of horror: had its adherents thought and felt as Serafina did, there would have been no burnings and thumb-screwings, no hagglings as to probabiliorism, *filioque*, or Gadarene pigs—unlovely phenomena, calculated to make the world-reformer despair of uplifting a race that can wallow in such abysses of criminality and absurdity.

We may unhesitatingly condemn the compulsory seclusion in convents of sane and well-behaved individuals, but it is well to suspend judgment on certain other aspects of her life. She cultivated fasting "in order to have the mind more free to think of God". What, in itself, more laudable? And if early training and natural disposition had caused her exalted tendencies to run in one particular direction, are therefore similar mortifications wholly to be eschewed, or is it not rather true that, mischievous if carried to excess, they constitute nevertheless a veritable means of procuring enlightenment? No advancement in learning will come from gross feeders; whoso seeketh knowledge must mortify the flesh; the wisdom of all ages is proof of this. Many who are paid to preach continence to others would be listened to with greater respect if they practised it themselves, and some of Sister Serafina's "spiritual exercises" would assuredly have no harmful influence upon the pampered prelates of our own Church.

But the majority of those who divine this truth fail to grasp it entirely, and thus it has come about that the splendid ideal of self-discipline, which has given to humanity so much of beauty and of use, has likewise created monstrosities of the type of Macarius or Simon Stylites; for the machinery of the mind is artfully balanced and the penances must be precisely such that the nerve-centres respond to the finest impulses—beyond that point lies the dream-region, where the ravings of an ill-nourished brain are mistaken for divine truths.

Self-macerations can be defended only on hedonistic principles.

5*

Arguing on these lines, it may clearly be contended that neither the philosopher nor yet the Christian dare disapprove of the maxim that each may do as he likes with his own body (*If thine eye offend thee, cut it out:* contrary texts, as usual, are at hand), and that pleasure, which entails no harm on others, may be sought where it can be found by every one, according to his varying tastes and temperament, let the manner of it be condemned by the physician, derided by the worldling, and imitated only by the fool. Such practices bring their own reward, for saints who despise the flesh will necessarily leave no children to inherit this idiosyncrasy, which perhaps accounts for the extinction of the saintly species in these later days.

Above all things, she must be judged in relation to her times. Devil-beatings were commoner then than now, but sane thinking is still at a discount; *incubi* have merely been replaced by "Christian Science". . . .

And lastly, it is important to remember that the appearance in these regions of types like Sister Serafina is of an episodic character; they are not an indigenous growth, but a fruit of that graft of Spaniardism which—if we are to believe modern Neapolitans—is the greatest evil that has ever afflicted their province. Spaniardism is responsible for the cloud of monks and confessors that settled like locusts upon the land and of whose deadly works the reader may form some opinion from the pages of Giannone—himself their victim; for the shattering of political life and of wholesome domestic ideals by spy-systems, Jesuit-horrors, and the enforced seclusion of women in inner chambers, of children in convents; Spaniardism brutalized the Neapolitans by beast-shows, dazed them with ultra-Oriental ceremonials, maddened them by outrageous exactions, bad faith, by the gallows, the rack, and the wheel; Spaniardism filled the provinces with the fierce unrest of brigandage, shackled in ruffs and grandiloquent buffooneries the old native freedom of costumes and of speech; it smothered letters, music, arts, and science in the sandy deserts of theology and infected decent Catholic observances by an alien ascetic taint, by gloomy absurdities of the Saint-Teresa type,* and by a hideous and still-persisting realism

---

* The viceroys introduced her cult, and one may speculate to what an extent such a tissue of puerile fictions, forcefully disseminated by confessor and civil magistrate, sapped the well-springs of common sense and of common morality. "It was a curse of the Spanish administration, to make the present unendurable

such as when, on Good Friday, the head of the Crucified is orna-
mented with real human hair, while His body and the snowy
winding sheet are bespattered with fresh cow's blood, in order to
make the effect more "life-like". There have been unceasing protests on the part of Neapolitans of all classes, priests and laymen,
against these abominations which the viceroys imported from their
savage and sombre Spain, the least Christian of all Catholic
countries. Thus, Signor Manfredi Fasulo has discovered at Sorrento
the declaration of two young girls of noble family, aged twelve and
sixteen respectively, who in 1555 went before a notary and publicly
avowed that "they did not wish to become nuns, being, on the
contrary, somewhat in favour of the married state". Great must have
been the abuses ere timid children could be driven to take a step
of this kind. Indeed the history of Siren land during this period is
one long wail of suffering; it will be long ere the Spanish virus is
eliminated.

Her end was full of griefs.

For many years she had suffered ill-health and a variety of
calamities. A rebellious faction sprang up in the convent of Saint
Teresa; the superior lost no opportunity of ill-treating her; the
nuns were at discord among themselves; a slip of paper with a
variety of improper words on it, was found pinned to the door of
her cell. Her own niece drowned herself in the cistern of the convent,
a sad and mysterious affair that "caused much gossip"; some spoke
of incurable melancholy, others, in whispers, of harsh treatment.
Powerless to help, she saw a rapid decline going on under her very
eyes. Meat, which she had contrived to eliminate from the bill of
fare (Saint Teresa had done the same), was plentifully eaten; the
nuns refused to rise at early hours for prayers; the spirit of chastity
abated; a friendship between a priest and a *conversa* gave her much
pain, and the dismissal to Naples of a young doctor to whom many
inmates of the convent had shown themselves more attached than
may have been needful, was attributed to her machinations and
gave the signal for open rebellion.

During her last days all was trouble and confusion. She was
hated and avoided by the whole establishment, and some of the

and to sow no seed for the future . . . a pattern of what a government should not
be"; so says Von Reumont, in his *Carafa von Maddaloni*, a carefully documented
study of this period, which deserves to be brought up to date. (An English translation in Bohn's Edition.)

nuns insisted upon leaving it, although they were warned that they would lose one half of their dowries. Simultaneously with these inner convulsions there arose such a mighty tempest at sea that no doctor could come from Naples, and her ordinary confessor, who had been apprised of the approaching end, was unable to console her dying moments. She had to content herself with the ministrations of two Capuchin monks who happened to be on the island, as she seems at this time to have been on bad terms with all the local secular clergy.

Nor was this all. For the devil, driven to desperation by his repeated failures to undermine her saintliness, took violent measures and was heard beating her in her cell. How the nuns were able to distinguish these diabolical flagellations from those which Sister Serafina habitually inflicted upon herself—sometimes a thousand strokes without interruption—we are not told; but we may rest assured that this somewhat brusque method of persuasion, not unknown in the histories of other saints, met with as little success as it deserved.

Sister Serafina viewed all these tribulations as a particular favour of Heaven, for she had always prayed that she might depart this life purified in the crucible of griefs, in torments, and alone.

Even so it fell out.

After lying for some days in an ecstatic condition, and in the attitude of crucifixion, she expired on March 17, 1699, in the seventy-eighth year of her age. And immediately there followed a general reconciliation in the convent; all were united in such love and perfect charity "as had never been her lot, during life, to witness". She passed away in a trance of love and with paralysed tongue. Her corpse, assuming a roseate hue, remained incorruptible and flexible for a long time and exhaled an ineffably sweet perfume; her blood flowed as freely after death as in life. . . .

Thus went to her rest, in the *odour of sanctity*, the venerable Sister Serafina di Dio, and as to her present state no Christian can be in doubt, for if Paradise be reserved for those who practise poverty, chastity, and obedience with all the sincerity of a simple heart, then assuredly she is sitting there now. She performed miracles three years after death and gave advice as ghost; her picture sweats and speaks, the oil that burns before it being medicinally useful; pieces of her clothing are efficacious as talismans, and pilgrimages to her tomb have been known to produce cures for various ailments, though I have been unable to obtain authentic records of any recent cases.

She was buried, amid an incredible concourse of people, in the church of S. Salvatore on Capri; but in 1813 her coffin was taken out and reverently entombed in the parochial church of that island, and, in 1820, once more reverently changed to another part of that church, whence, in 1856, it was again shifted, reverently opened and closed again, and deposited in a different locality, whence, in 1893, her remains were once more removed, examined by the chief medical officer and other notabilities, sealed up again, and laid to rest elsewhere, with a lengthy inscription to record these reverend exhumations and peregrinations.

May she now rest, if possible, in peace!

Before her burial, however, a number of pious experiments had been made with her corporeal parts, in order to justify a claim to saintliness. A death-mask was taken thirty-four hours after her demise, but the plaster of Paris became warm from the heat of her corpse, the cause of which was soon seen to be the heart, which exhibited miraculous signs and, like that of Saint Teresa, maintained heat throughout her body. The lungs, the liver, the kidneys were all taken out and found to bear tokens of a holy life; the bowels were likewise removed and examined, and on the fourth day after death her veins were again opened and blood flowed freely, proclaiming her miraculous state. Five days later her scattered remains were collected in a coffin, and crowds of men and women came to satisfy their *pious curiosity* by gazing upon the decomposing organs of this venerable ascetic. To their hallucinated senses these poor shreds of mortality appeared more lovely and fragrant than ever. Truly an edifying spectacle! The pagans, for superstitious purposes, scrutinized the entrails of beasts: the Christians, those of saints. . . .

The concordance with the Spanish nun, in these latter events, is so amazingly close that, were not similar parallelisms observable in the life-histories of many other saints, a critical reader might almost be tempted to suspect the biographer's *bona fides*. Without dilating upon these extraordinary coincidences, it will suffice to report that Saint Teresa, too, died in a trance of love and with paralysed tongue; that her corpse, assuming a roseate hue, remained incorruptible and flexible for a long time and exhaled an ineffably sweet perfume; that the blood from her dead body flowed as freely as during life; that her coffin was frequently shifted about, while her soul performed miracles and gave advice as ghost.

Nevertheless a medical practitioner, who was called to view the remains of Sister Serafina, refused to depose that they were *in statu miraculoso*, whereas the physician who examined those of Saint Teresa had no hesitation in giving a certificate to that effect.

I cannot say how far this conduct on the Italian doctor's part proved a hindrance to the beatification of Sister Serafina, or to what an extent his Spanish colleague's certificate weighed favourably in the balance when the case of the Spanish nun was considered. Save in this one microscopic detail, the saintly lives and works of these two mystics are so alike that it would seem hardly just to refuse the highest honour to one of them merely by reason of the pronouncement of a worldly professional, who may well have been mistaken, prejudiced, or even bribed to conceal the truth. Nor will I endeavour to solve the enigma of the quasi-miraculous concordance in the lives and deaths of these two women, but my reason for referring so frequently to Saint Teresa will now be clear: namely, that the reader should observe what apparently trifling circumstances can influence the decisions of the Vatican. A carnal doctor's certificate *seems* to dispose of Sister Serafina's claims to the honour of beatification; outweighing a lifetime of saintliness, of miracles and Christian propaganda in which—to judge by the official biographies sanctioned and approved by the Pope—she differed not a jot from the more fortunate Spanish ascetic. In view of the issue at stake, such a respect for the pronouncement of a nameless man of science would be regarded, even in lay circles, as a kind of rationalistic bigotry.

Her contemporaries, at least, judged well of her merits; hardly was she in the grave before the project was set afoot to procure her beatification; among the number of these early promoters I find the name of "Jacobus Tertius Magnæ Britanniæ Rex". The attempt has been repeated up to the days of Leo XIII without success; and thus she, who deserves the title of Beata as well as many another one, must content herself, meanwhile, with that of Venerabile. A Carmelite Pope would doubtless entertain the project if the necessary gold were forthcoming, and Monsignor Canale, the religious historian of Capri, naively but correctly laments the poverty of the island as the cause of its failure. Yet saints have often waited long for their final honours—Saint Elizabeth, for instance, three hundred years; Saint Leopold, three hundred and fifty. These regions have also grown richer of late, while the price of canonization, according to Silvagni, has now been reduced to 200,000 francs. Thus the hope of many may still be realized, if the stream of wordly prosperity at present flowing into Siren land from Argentina, can be diverted into channels of unworldly zeal.

X
OUR LADY OF THE SNOW

How strange is that process of mental association, and how a mood, the most volatile of things upon earth, will often persist and grow into a suggestion and become attached to some locality, twining itself inextricably among houses and fields and pathways! Can anything be more unlike these many-folded radiant coast-lands than the interminable plains of Russia, with their pale skies and weary humanity? Yet the first time I came here I fell in with a Russian gentleman and his daughter, and memories of that ephemeral acquaintance have tinged the country for me. He was not even a true Siren worshipper, such as I have met many since that day; he came here on account of his health, and she, either to be near him or to think out certain problems for herself. Parthenope was Greek to both of them.

Still there are Sirens, too, in the chilly waters of the Baltic, and the name of one of them, Roussalka, was soon to have a mournful sound in many Russian ears.*

Although I never met them after that winter, the septentrional mood is apt to return, like the subtle odour of birch trees clinging to the olives and myrtles of an alien shore. No harm in this, for things are best perceived by contrasts; the Englishman, who never submerges his identity, is a good describer of foreign lands, and the image of the South is not seen so clearly on the spot as when it rises like an exhalation before the mind's eye amid hyperborean gloom. That was a sage remark of him who said "the material furnished by the tropics can only be utilized in a Northern atmosphere".

The good Ivan Nicolaevitch was probably a professor of philosophy or geology at some public institution, but I never had the curiosity to inquire; I like to taste my friends, but not to eat them.

* *Roussalka* (Mermaid) was the name of a training-ship which went down in the Gulf of Finland.

He can hardly be alive at this day. As for the daughter, she may well be sojourning in Siberia, for she was a liberal of the type which Russia needs and therefore banishes. As I remember her now, she seems to have been one of the million good-humoured Northern girls with barbaric splendour of complexion and eyes of intense velvety blue, eyes like twin mountain lakes lying deep down in fringe of fir, calm and mysterious. The father was of another type, pale with a straggling beard—meekness graven into every line of his face; full of perplexing and suggestive theories, one of them—based, he said, on "statistics"—to the effect that the next Messiah would be a Russian pauper, and another, that parents ought to be forbidden by law to argue with their children (he detested Locke). His ideal was state management in everything, a delusion which crops up in the "anticipations" of many modern writers who would complicate life instead of simplifying it.

Forcibly were those times recalled to me when I revisited the Cimentaro, where we had been together. The Cimentaro is a bank of volcanic tufa which lies in a valley above Massa; they hew tunnels into the soft material and extract it as a building stone. You can cut it with a knife. It becomes more valuable—that is less spongy—the deeper you excavate, and the rock is not blasted, but artfully split away from the cliff with wooden wedges and then chopped up into blocks of convenient size. Walls built of such friable stone must necessarily be thick and coated with plaster against the damp, but it is none the less cheaper than limestone in the long run.

My friend was hugely interested in the operation. At last he said:

"We have no stones in our country. Before a house can be built, a road must be laid down to bring the stones for the house. And before the road can be built, a railway must be laid down to bring the stones for the road from God knows where—Finland, perhaps. The railway? It is laid, at first, on wood."

It struck me as an extraordinary statement. But I found it sufficiently true when I visited his country some eight years later.

The tufa of Naples is of yellow tint and harder in texture than this, which changes, in proportion as its moisture evaporates, from a rich purple-brown through mouse colour and hyacinthine shades to a bluish grey. They tell me it costs four centimes a brick at the quarries, but the price is doubled and even trebled by the time it reaches its destination, for it must be transported on the backs of mules who can only carry about seven bricks apiece. These volcanic deposits probably date from the times of the grand Phlegræan eruptions.

Days of the Titans! Like a section of an Emmenthaler cheese is the map of that smoking Cimmerian region west of Naples with its craters, great and small, many of them now submerged beneath the waves but still traceable with the sounding-line, that belched forth in prehistoric ages a fiery deluge; the sea must have turned solid, for its caves and inlets are chocked up with cinders; the air likewise, since deep deposits, like this one, are everywhere. At Villa Nova, on Capri, you can see bombs of pumice over a metre in circumference: conceive the height to which they must have flown in order to reach this spot in their parabolic descent! Vesuvius, whose last column of ashes rose eighteen kilometres into the firmament, is a child's popgun when compared with these engines of primeval wrath. And the sport went on for centuries. No wonder the firm-seated limestone was "dislocated" in these earth-convulsing battles of the giants, and Capri and the Siren rocks shook themselves free from the mainland.

The church of Pastena, higher up the stream which flows past the Cimentaro, reposes on a bed of this material, and here and there along the sides of the valley, at various elevations, can be seen patches of tufa resting upon its limestone ledges. They tell a curious story, namely that the river-bed was already fashioned by water at the time of the catastrophe: the stream was temporarily choked up and obliged to do the work of erosion over again. Whence I conclude that the Cimentaro is an aerial formation—that it fell from the sky to where it now is. And if this be the correct way to account for these upland deposits, it would surely be more logical to extend this explanation to the immense contemporary layer on which Sorrento stands, rather than to postulate an aqueous origin of which we have no proofs.

From here we walked, I remember, through the village of Monticchio up to the summit of Monte Arso, the burnt mountain, which Maldacea described as an extinct volcano—so easily are legends formed from names. It was *burnt* only because unproductive in his day and has now ceased to merit this designation, being crowned with a house and green vineyards. The rock of the Tore is a soft Tertiary sandstone called *macigno*, which overlies the limestone in many places; all the lanes are paved with it, and often have

I thanked Providence for causing Massa to be built in the neighbourhood of its quarries, for it is never slippery in summer and never
wet in winter, whereas the limestone is objectionable at all seasons
unless one goes barefoot or wears the corded shoes called *paragatti*
which were introduced from Spanish South America. The peasant,
with characteristic anthropomorphism, calls this sandstone *pietra
morta*, dead stone; as opposed to the *pietra viva* or limestone.

It is hard work, at first, bringing such recalcitrant stuff into a
fit state for cultivation; the stones must be crushed and mixed with
earth and the trenches for the vines excavated to a depth of six
feet. But the trouble is amply repaid, and green oases, like this one,
are now springing up in various parts of the Tore. I have tried to
obtain data of revenue and expenditure, but in vain, as the cultivators are shy of giving information which might lead, they think,
to an increase of taxes. Certain it is, after the vines have begun to
thrive, that the produce of a single season will often exceed the entire
initial outlay including the cost of the land—not a bad speculation,
therefore, for those who can afford to wait a few years.

This peasant on Monte Arso has also had the luck to strike water,
if luck it can be called which is the inevitable result of digging. The
Tore are saturated with springs which dry up, for the most part, in
summer, but there must be a permanent supply of liquid between
the porous *pietra morta* and the impenetrable limestone. To Ivan
Nicolaevitch it seemed a simple matter to tap this reservoir by
means of artesian wells sunk through a few feet of sandstone, and a
profitable one, seeing that the villages are largely dependent on
rain water collected in cisterns which is apt to fail or to become
tainted, although living eels are kept in them for purposes of
"purification". But I should like to see the faces of the gentlemen
of the *municipio* if his proposal were submitted to them. No doubt
the water of clean cisterns is purer and cooler than this surface-
flow, but they are not always kept as they should be; many hundred
people draw their supply from one not far from here which was
recently found to contain 1440 micro-organisms to the cubic centi-
metre.

Here, beside the "burnt mountain", stands the burial ground of
seven villages; it is called Santa Maria della Neve—Our Lady of
the Snow. A depressing place. Nature is cheerful all around, but
within—an ill-kept square of earth, immense and bare, surrounded
by high walls and overgrown with weeds. Are these people so poor

that they cannot do anything for its appearance? It is hard to believe; money is pouring in from America.

No Sirens will sing dirges on a spot like this. Yet that was their charge in olden days; they were divinities of death, symbols of funeral chant and lamentation, and this one attribute of their many was reverentially clung to by the Athenians.

Upon the grave of Sophocles was sculptured a Siren, bewailing the loss of the master whose golden voice was to be heard no more, "and even now", says Pausanias, "the Athenians are wont to compare the persuasiveness of his poetry and discourses to a Siren's song".

Siren-vases, such as that formerly in the Pourtalès collection, have been discovered at Sorrento, but no Greek tombs with these elaborate ornaments. Those that have been unearthed seem to have belonged to the lower classes; they are simply inscribed; FAREWELL. It is touching, this simple word, though our modern conscience might well be disquieted with such eloquent and candid brevity. And yet—after the conventional sepulchres of our ancestors, with their paraphernalia of skulls and cross-bones, their laboured lies in barbarous Gothic Latinity or worse English, setting forth virtues which the dead never exercised and hopes of Heaven he may well have derided—how true is the pathos of this last greeting; how it speaks of a time when men looked serenely into the eye of death and found in their hearts, not in their heads, the feelings they would utter! Some ancient funeral inscriptions are as untrustworthy as our own, and the Roman *vale* had doubtless grown to be a mere formality; but the men who first of all carved this salute on sepulchres meant what they said: farewell!

Hither—to Our Lady of the Snow—they bring the dead for burial from various villages. The road is a mere track in many places and the discomfort must be considerable for all who take part in these scrambling processions, especially during the many wintry days of rain and storm. I have often asked why these communities do not buy a burial ground nearer home, and have received a variety of explanations—none convincing. The truth seems to be that irksomeness is counterbalanced by cheapness, for a plot of land near a village costs money, while the waste of time counts as nothing. Orientals! At Tramonti, further inland, the cemetery is at the head of the valley and on the summit of a truly formidable hill—a funeral there must mean half a day's loss of time for those who attend it from beginning to end. One would think that the expense of conveying the coffin up these rough tracks would alone swallow up a considerable sum. But this is avoided by the system of confraternities, each member of whom pays a small yearly contribution which entitles him to a free burial when his time comes. No wonder everybody belongs to these societies, for they make interments enticingly cheap.

But will they sleep in peace?

Ay, there's the rub. Soon enough their bodies will be ousted to make room for others, even as in old England men were "knav'd out of their graves" in the same callous fashion. Surely this disrespect for those who have gone before is a sinister feature of catholicism, and a sensitive person, haunted perpetually with the spectre of Unrest after Death before his eyes, may well become predisposed in favour of the fiery resolution. Poor men's bones are cast to the winds, for an avaricious progeny denies them even a few square feet of earth wherein to repose; the skeletons of their betters are periodically resuscitated and examined, put into new coffins, and reverently moved about: lucky the saint or warrior whose anatomy is complete after all these posthumous perambulations. The ancients displayed more piety in this matter. The Romans, it is true, had their Esquilinus, their *ager informis*, but their respectable dead were respectably dealt with and left in peace. Yet even the present system is an improvement upon that which was in vogue up to a short time ago, whereby the poorer dead were simply pitched, uncoffined and head foremost, into a black hole, *fossa carnaria*, which lay below the church. In this pit of abominations they lay undisturbed, until some newcomer, sliding down, jolted them into another position. The *fossa carnaria* at Massa is closed with a marble slab inscribed "The Way of all Flesh"; others bear the familiar but wholly untruthful legend "Return whence Ye came".

Can these bones live? If so, great will be the confusion in such caverns when the last trumpet sounds. The Italian government abolished these horrors under vehement protests on the part of the Vatican; but it will be long ere the priests can bring themselves to countenance cremation, which would cut off one of their chief sources of revenue. Religions should stand on their merits, no doubt. Yet there is something to be said, even for a State-paid clergy. . . .

Not all the cemeteries of Siren land are in this sad case. The two burial-grounds on Capri are decent and harmonious spots, and a picturesque one crowns the summit of Santa Maria above Massa, where the scarlet geraniums grow to gigantic clusters. It is forlorn but still fair, this ancient citadel; they fought furiously here in the fifteenth century—Ferdinand of Aragon besieging it for two years to oust the obstinate Anjou adherents. When at last it yielded, the citizens were emptied out of the contumacious rock and made to settle at its foot. Their devotion to the Anjou cause had been constant and not unrequited. There has lately been printed, from a manuscript in the Paris National Library, a really interesting book —the diary of Jean Le Fèvre, who died in 1390, after being Bishop of Chartres and chancellor to the Anjou kings Louis I and Louis II. Reading this honest old-world journal, one might think that the inhabitants of Siren land were an exceptional order of beings to be favoured out of all proportion to the rest of mankind—honours and benefits of every kind being showered upon them by the Court. A positive infatuation: on one day alone—July 2, 1387—the queen wrote over twenty-five letters to private citizens of Capri. Where are these letters now? *Muribus corrosæ*, no doubt; eaten by the mice, which already fattened on Capri documents in old Le Fèvre's day.

And a charming site is the new cemetery at Capo Corno near Massa, where the ordered cypresses, flame-like children of Zoroaster, overhang the sea and sway to its breezes. Here one can realize how greatly the appearance of the country would be improved if there were more of these queenly growths punctuating the landscape, as in Tuscany. The natives will not have them, on account of their funereal associations: a puerile prejudice, which gives to churchyards the monopoly of a beautiful and useful tree.

Resting, the other day, outside the walls of the desolate cemetery on the Tore, I found at my feet an unusual object—a pebble of flint. How came it here? Soon enough I discovered others; a mine, a vein of it. Is this, then, the place whence the prehistoric cannibals who lived in Siren land drew their supply for their weapons? No; the quality was not good enough for these fastidious creatures who, nor content with flints of the first water, imported obsidian from the distant island of Palmarola, or rather Lipari, and jade, or rather jadeite, from the Alps. The Tore are utterly barren in useful minerals; there is nothing worthy of exploitation to be found on these hills; no salt or iron or petroleum or coal. Perhaps we ought to thank God for this.

Perhaps not. For are these things really the curses which dreamers like Ruskin would have us believe? I thought of pre-commercial Scotland, a land of brigands and bigots. And now? A swarthy mineral, hidden in the bowels of the earth, has woke up latent possibilities in human minds, transforming uncouth savages into thoughtful citizens; giving to England some of her best adminis- trators and to the world a number of glowing writers and of thinkers, deep and daring, who have overturned pernicious maxims of con- duct and set up sound ones in their stead. Many a single county in Scotland has produced more men of original genius than tracts twice as large in the more favoured climates of Europe. Coal! For if you reckon it out, it will be seen that most of the great men of that country have been born within a remarkably small radius of time and an equally restricted one of space; the commercial rise of the central plain, conditioned by the discovery of coal, has led to this unprecedented intellectual rise. True, the pristine beauty of Edinburgh is now shrouded in coal-dust and smoke—but there! you will never satisfy an artist.

Would a similar quickening effect, I wonder, be produced by the discovery of coal on these hills?

At this awkward question my musings were interrupted by the arrival of a funeral procession; a young man had died; he was preparing for some notarial post to enable him to help his large family with occasional contributions and had succumbed to a brain fever from over-work. He seemed to have been a general favourite, yet no one was here to testify affection or esteem on his last journey. Besides the two priests who received three and five francs respectively and who walked about a hundred yards in front of the coffin chatting and laughing, there was only the carpenter, the confraternity in their white frocks, and the youth's two brothers, whom custom compelled to attend; no comrades, no unpaid priests, no teachers, not a single woman, not one of his fifty relatives— every one is related hereabouts—not a soul, in fact, but went under compulsion. They had not even the questionable pretext of bad weather for avoiding the ceremony, as it was a lovely day; but that, perhaps, afforded an even better one. And the service was of barbarous brevity—a Toda would have been ashamed of it. Then the confraternity and priests dashed their vestments into a box and tripped back over the hills in work-a-day clothes, a merry group. Only the carpenter, a serious-looking man of middle age, paced along apart from the others in solitary and sombre abstraction, smoking a black pipe. I inquired why he did not join the rest of them, and received the enigmatical reply: "It is ever thus." He had driven a harder bargain than usual on this occasion—eighty-five francs.

"Walnut?" I queried.

"All imitation! Assassin of the poor! . . ."

"I know a cemetery in my country," Ivan Nicolaevitch once said to me, "which is liquid mud. The dead are lowered into it, but soon enough they rise and float on the surface."

There is no end to these unnecessary horrors.

At Capri they excavated, a good many years ago, an urn of blue cameo glass reposing in a leaden casket. It contained ashes and a coin and was of such fine workmanship that its price quickly rose to £100. These fair and fragile vessels, of which the Portland vase is the best example, were used both for festive and funereal purposes, and so dignified ancient life in two of its aspects—the cinerary purpose, to preserve intact the ashes of the dead, which we allow to rot, in an imperishable envelope; the festive one, inasmuch as their conviviality was a less trivial function than ours, almost a rite, in the performance of which nothing was considered too good, however precious or liable to be broken on such occasions. But these choice urns lead up to the glass sarcophagus of Alexander the Great, to the mummies and exquisite tomfooleries of Egypt, where Death tyrannized over Life. So the treatment of the dead, taken by itself, is hardly an index of a people's intelligence or kindliness; the clever and humane Parsees have a custom which appals us, and the Eskimos, warm-hearted folk, are as callous as beasts in this respect. . . .

After the stragglers of the procession had vanished round the hill, I retraced my steps and conversed awhile with the guardian or grave-digger, who was amiable enough, but rather common-place for a man of this absorbing occupation. "This," he said, "is the chapel of Monticchio; this, of Sant' Agata; this, of Termini—and life is short, signore, and we must all manage somehow to eat." *Dobbiamo tutti mangiare:* that was the extent of his worldly philosophy.

In the last of these burial chapels I was struck by the frequent recurrence of an historical name upon the tombstones, that of

Amitrano. According to Capecelatro, an abbot of this name was beheaded by Masaniello, and his brother also killed in that tumult. In those days many conspicuous men in Naples came from this peninsula, which was populated more numerously, and by better classes, than it is nowadays. This clan presumably draws its name from the spot called Metrano or Mitrano near Termini, which now consists of only five houses, but seems to have been larger formerly, for Persico reports that sixteen captives were taken from here in the corsair raid of 1558. Perhaps it overflowed into Termini, which is of comparatively modern growth, having only become a parish in 1615, and where the name Amitrano is very common. A-Mitrano —from Mitrano. On the same principle, Amalfi has been derived (wrongly, they say) from A-Melfi, as though originally a colony from the town of Melfi.

Another member of this family wrote a description of that same corsair raid, and yet another one was a celebrated local brigand who died not so long ago and who had hit upon a singular method of impressing the country-folk. He gave it to be understood that he had sewn a consecrated wafer into his body, with the consequence that however much blood he might lose in encounters with the police, his wounds immediately healed again. His pursuers were taken in like the others, for, to corroborate this fraud, he used to carry a skinful of animal blood about with him and spill large quantities of it wherever he had exchanged shots with them, turning up safe and sound a few days later. The theory of his charmed life is still believed by some of the old people.

And the derivation of Mitrano?

From Mithra, I think: the sun-god. He is known to have been worshipped at Naples, Pompeii, and Capri, and votive chapels sprang up in his honour all over Italy. Why not on these hills? The Oriental element was not lacking in the courts of Augustus and Tiberius; at later periods, too, when the cult of Mithra became more widely disseminated, these coastlands must have been the residence of Eastern merchants from their natural attractions or from convenience of situation near the great trade-routes; of freedmen, or retired military officers who had become attached to the cult of the Persian god which accompanied them on their campaigns into the remotest parts of earth.

Thus Siren land has contributed its mite towards unhinging the reason of the Western world. For Eastern religions lose their finest strains when transplanted out of their native soil, and that of Mithra, imported into Italy, efficiently carried on the work of undermining the common sense of Europe. Only the modern Scotchman, the Roman of the Republic, and a few other favoured races whose minds are constructed on the watertight-compartment system, can withstand the toxic effects of certain speculations which in no wise impair the sanity of those among whom they originated. We lack the light touch in spiritual matters. Our climate and racial development has made us strenuous and prone to turn words into deeds; of the many things that we take too seriously, none have wrought greater social havoc than the airy religious dreamings of the East.

Christianity has moulded our destinies; if the sun-god, to whose former worship these engraved tombstones on the Tore remotely testify, had supplanted Christ, what then? The answer is not difficult. They underwent a progressive convergent development; the world-spirit that presided over their birth (to use a now antiquated mode of speech) drew from both what its then bilious appetite craved for, and rejected the rest. It would have ended in a mere difference of name. And not even that: Mithra, like Christ, is the "Light of the World", and Cybele, his whilom associate, is the Madonna or *Gran Madre di Dio*, the Magna Mater of old, who was worshipped both at Capri and Sorrento. The *Monumentum Ancyranum* has shown that Augustus was not unfavourable to her cult—a fact which may have contributed to her popularity in this part of Campania which he visited so frequently.

Tertullian laments that the institutions of Christ and Mithra were alike from the beginning; thus December 25, the feast of Mithra, was the only occasion of the year when the king of the Persians was allowed to get drunk: a custom of this kind still lingers in parts of the Christian world. They grew up together and engaged awhile in fierce competition; like rival trading concerns, each copied what was successful in the other. But the religion of the sun-god was too rational to survive, for it solved the problem of sin and evil without recourse to predestination, and kept the door of hope ajar for the believer who, by personal endeavour, should purge away his guilt. That did not suit the hysterical spirit of an age which required faith and prearranged damnation for its enemies. It succumbed also because it seems to have excluded women from participation in the mysteries—a fatal error, if propaganda was its aim. Yet, before expiring, Mithraism had been permitted—"by an inspiration of the devil", says Saint Jerome—to leave many of its leading characteristics as a legacy to the younger cult.*

In these days, when humanity is infected with observances whose grotesqueness is their only claim to success, it is well to look backwards and to realize that there exists on earth no nearer approximation to verity than the original figure of Mithra the Mediator, the God of Light and Truth. He is the hypostasis of intelligent human effort adjusting itself to a non-moral environment. Ormuzd and Ahriman are dim cloudy shapes; none can tell us what they are about; Mithra, the Redeemer, is made man. In favour of dualistic religions it has been contended that a single god, knowing all things and responsible for all, is a profound immorality. The sun alone, passionless contriver, enemy of lies, is above reproach. He makes and unmakes the atoms in our brains which make and unmake Jehovahs; he is responsible for all things on earth, good and evil; yet his name is unsullied as his face. What divinity shall be compared to him? The wise man of all ages will not hesitate whom to adore when he beholds the Great Fire by whose operation all things derive their first breath of life and the faculty of continued living; when he remembers that the ruby is kindred not in colour only, but in substance, with the arterial life which flows through his veins—a kinship of blood binding the cosmos to himself, whose body contains the common properties of the earth, whose humours, they say, are swayed by her satellite, whose very thoughts are but expressions of solar virtues.

Our vistas on Mithraism and such themes have been widened by the labours of men like Rawlinson, Champollion, and Cumont. The myth of the sungod was a simple matter for our grandfathers. Now that we know a little more, we know a little less; and it is really worth contrasting the diffidence of a modern writer on this subject, like Reville, with the facile *ex cathedra* utterances of the great Dupuis and his school. We are confronted by an agglomeration of facts and ideas, by a complexity of geographical, psychological, and

---

* Original to Mithraism are: the idea of moral regeneration; draught from the mystic cup; sacramental rites; consecration of bread and water; confession of sins; the sacred flame on the altar; asceticism; veneration of the Sabbath; the last judgment; martyrdom; resurrection; hope of immortality; expiation of sins; baptism; lustration of neophytes; confirmation; penitences.

historical data, that staggers the intelligence. Who will now unravel the mysteries of Zeus, of Heracles? These protean phantoms, that figure forth every aspect of human thought and passion, elude our grasp. True it is that, modified almost beyond recognition, the old gods are still alive within us; antique ideals permeate our spiritual life; the blood of Apollo and Aphrodite flows through the veins of Christ and his Virgin Mother. Yet these venerable shapes, though vital, remain intangible. Their birth-places are beyond our ken. We pursue them, but they flit tantalizingly into wilds of Thrace and Tartary, past Memphis into regions of god-fearing Æthiopians where old Nile collects his waters—from Italy to Greece and over cloud-capped Aryan uplands they lead us on till, looming gigantic through the haze, they vanish in the twilight, in the limbo of Oriental tradition, Promethean workshop of the gods.

So I mused; but the radiance of Mithra did not avail to dispel a spectral image floating before my eyes, the *phantasma* of that funeral with its unseemly haste and callousness, which I finally decided to regard as a perversion of the ancient point of view—of that serenity in the face of death which was praised as distinctively Hellenic by men like Herder, whose enthusiasm for things Greek may sometimes have overshot the mark, based, as it was, upon the contrast between Periclean sunshine and the political and metaphysical fogs of their own country.

It was another of these enlightened Germans, Lessing, who remarked that without the help of revelation no intelligent man could ever have come to regard death as a punishment. He was alluding to Christianity; but the early Christians, to judge by the sepulchral monuments of the catacombs, did not hold this sad and wrong view. And although certain Romans like Seneca already began to dwell with luxurious introspection upon the terrors of the grave—a habit which grew into an obsession during the Middle Ages, when mankind was haunted by the fearfullest shapes of gloom—yet it was reserved for later ages to cast the full blight over reasonable men. We had not thrown aside our mirthfulness with our mail-shirts; our ancestors took themselves less seriously than we take them; the merry England of Chaucer, with its masks and mummeries, has many affinities with South Italy of to-day. For so long as indulgences can be cheaply purchased, the religious conscience cannot be troublesome: that unction *in extremis*—what a

glorious salve! But when the ghostly intermediary was taken away
and man found himself face to face with a god whose time was
occupied in noting down his inmost thoughts, then the reign of
haunting terror began; well might he dread the approach of death
and tremble for his chances hereafter.

Siren land has been affected by these mediæval fermentations,
but chiefly on the material side; on the moral, it seems to me that
the identical causes which have co-operated to form our Northern
sensibility in certain matters have here produced a clean contrary
effect: that spiritual blunting or anæsthesia of which this funeral was
an example.

And the Greeks? The idea that we entered into the world
tainted from birth, that feeling of duty unfulfilled which is rooted
in the doctrine of sin and has hindered millions from enjoying life
in a rational and plenary manner—all this was alien to their mode
of thought. A healthy man is naturally blithe, and the so-called joy
of life of the ancient Greek is simply the appropriate reaction of the
body to its surroundings. And if Greek life was heaving with a soft
undercurrent of melancholy, it was the melancholy not of psychic
constipation but rather of wistfulness; it was what Pater called a
"pagan melancholy". They did not brood; a sane mind broods
over nothing; it insists upon being distracted. The death of a com-
rade needs must convulse our organism, but, if sound, it resents the
intrusion and seeks to regain its equipoise; it must have certain
safety-valves of which our puritan conscience, speaking dimly of
something beyond the objective fact of death, does not approve.
Or is it not going too far to say of such calamities, as a well-known
American writer has done: "Every other wound we seek to heal—
every other affliction to forget; but this wound we consider it a
duty to keep open—this affliction we cherish and brood over in
solitude." We consider it a duty. Why a duty? The masochistic
note of modern life. . . .

Those men of old who carved upon sepulchres that single word
"farewell" struck the mean between our hyper-sensitiveness and
the indifference of the South.

It is easy to see that, in a general way, the inhabitants of the
Parthenopean region have deviated less than ourselves from the
standard of rightness as regards these tracts of primitive feeling,
the reason being that they received Jewish ascetics upon a foundation of classical culture, as men; we, "as a little child" whose

organism was susceptible like that of the Pacific islanders when catarrhs were introduced. They were never taught to disrespect the *encumbrance* of Oriental dreamers—the human body, that exquisite engine of delights; the antagonism of flesh and spirit, the most pernicious piece of crooked thinking which has ever oozed out of our poor deluded brain, has always been unintelligible to them. That is why they remained sober when the rest of us went crazy. There were no sour-faced Puritans in Naples, no witch-burnings, no inquisition—the Neapolitans never indulged in these fateful extravagances; they held that the promptings of nature were righteous and reasonable, and their priests, whatever they might profess to the contrary, still share this view and act accordingly; anti-asceticism is the key-note of their lives, and pruriency, offspring of asceticism, conspicuous by its absence in young and old, in literature and society. More than ourselves, they have kept in view the ancient Hellenic ideal of Nemesis, of that true temperance which avoids troubling the equilibrium between man and his environment.

The *ancient* Hellenic ideal: for Greeks themselves overthrew it; soon came Orphic mysteries, and Plato, and the rest of them, stuffed with Eastern lore, and men found it easier to babble charming nonsense about souls and essences than to investigate the facts of life. The old idea of sanity perished; ethics ceased to be a department of physiology; an ego-centric and introspective existence began. Men regulated their behaviour not according to nature, but according to the imaginary exigencies of an imaginary life beyond. From such incorrect premises it was impossible to draw correct conclusions. Would it be wrong, I wonder, to call Pythagoras, albeit he hit upon a few good things, one of the corner-stones of the temple of crooked thinking, or even to say that all mankind, from Socrates to Kant, had lost their bearings in the search after verity? Surely not, if the leaders are to be taken as representative of the rest.

Most of us have learned to distrust apothegms. You may cram a truth into an epigram: the truth, never. Did not the stoics and epicureans, for example, rebuild the old striving under the title of "virtue"; have not sane men lived sane lives from the beginning of the world, despite their teachers? Thus every epigram requires a foot-note.

Assuredly, this sentimental lingering in burial-places is unwholesome. For last night I had a dream, a horrible dream, one of those dreams that endure, that haunt us with their white faces through all the sunshine of the day.

It was evening, and the train had left me at some unknown spot. It might have been a town or village in the English "black country", for coal-dust had crept over houses and roads and trees, and a murky cloud hung in the sky as though some demon, with outstretched wings, were brooding over the land. Troubled in mind, I wandered about the streets. Uncouth buildings, with a thousand chimneys and projections, towered into the sky; everywhere lay, in chaotic confusion, mountains of black mineral wealth, and carts, and iron contrivances of menacing aspect, whose purport I could not fathom. Pallid men and women, straggling home from the pits, scowled at me. It was all very gloomy and evil; the fearsome exaggeration of dreams got hold upon me. Some catastrophe was about to happen. I began to run.

My steps took me to a squalid cemetery. It contained tombs without end—a wilderness of tombs. And there, suddenly, a tall grave-monument, leaning against the enclosure, beckoned to me as though to invite attention, and I found myself examining it carefully. It was in good taste and had evidently been reared by some person of means, but although scarcely ten years old, it already wore a look of dismal neglect, for the stone was encrusted with unclean lichens and, instead of bright flowers, a generation of rank summer weeds, black with soot, had thrown themselves over it and there decayed.

Ah, the cemetery on the Tore! And yet. . . .

What a spot, I thought, to lie in for all eternity! If this should be my lot! And—how soon are we forgotten! For this tombstone must have been built and tended by some loving heart not so long ago; but that friend had now died in his turn, and there was none left to cherish the loved one's grave. A world of tenderness and affection wiped out, as though it had never been . . . and only ten years: how soon, how soon! Certain events flashed through my consciousness, until an intensity of grief and compassion, such as only dreams can inspire, overwhelmed me at the thought of this unknown fellow-creature.

Then curiosity tempted me to see who lay beneath this stone, but it was too dark to read the inscription and, searching in my pockets,

I discovered that I must have lost or mislaid my matches. After all
the direful impressions of that evening, even this pleasure, this
harmless little caprice, was to be denied me. I felt like crying with
the peevish impotence of a child.

On the wall sat an old man, smoking a black pipe. The guardian!
And yet—he was changed somehow; his face wore a curious look.
Can he have guessed my very thoughts? With suspicious alacrity,
he jumped down and stood at my side. There was a lantern in his
hand: a stream of light poured from it.

"Now," I said, "we shall see."

The name on the tomb was plainly legible.

It was my own.

XI

ON LEISURE

COME, let us discourse beneath this knotty carob tree whose boughs have been bent earthward by a thousand gales for the over-shadowing of the Inspired Unemployed, and betwixt whose lustrous leaves the sea, far down below, is shining turquoise-blue in a dream of calm content—let *me* discourse, that is —for if other people are going to talk, as Whistler used to say, there can be no conversation—let me discourse of leisure, the Siren's gift to men. But, first of all, pass nearer those flasks. They contain the closest approximation to that "gold of Sant' Agata"—*oro stravvecchio, oro del padrone*—the formula of whose composition was peevishly thrown away, like any ordinary Great Seal of England, what time the inn became a menagerie. Its label alone may be read on some bottles which need not be uncorked. "Never," said an august personage long ago to me, "never give a man cigars, wine, or food above ten per cent better than what he gets at home. Never." The serpent's wisdom! On this principle these caravanserais are worked, and all we can do is to seek our "gold" elsewhere. Meanwhile: your health! Drink, my friend, and let me see that smile of yours; soon enough, I daresay, neither of us will smile any more, though we may grin for all ages to come, if the soil is dry. . . .

A sorry preamble, this; not exactly a "captation of benevolence" in the Ciceronian style. But what matters the exordium, if the *oro* is to our liking? Let us drown it in four inches, and begin again.

They had no *oro* in those times. Cicero's son, that ineffable drunkard and vagabond, knew this right well; if he had lived a little later, he might have found a substitute in the pages of Athenæus. But he was born before his time, like all great men. For where the *oro* now grows were forests; Pollio built his temple with their beams and the Amalfitans their fleets, and at their feet grew the wine of Sorrento, which Caligula called "a respectable vinegar". A

6

dangerous liquor, by Hercules: did not doctors recommend it to their patients? In those days, the boughs of the grapes at Sorrento waxed so high and mighty that labourers were wont to insure their lives before climbing up to gather them.

Be prepared, under such a mere boughing acquaintance, for indifferent wine; like that inky fluid of the Naples Campagna where the grapes likewise clamber up to heaven out of sight of the peasant, who periodically forgets their existence and plants hemp and maize in their earth. No vine will endure this treatment; personal contact is the first requisite for good results. Where is that "master's eye"? He would need a telescope to see his progeny. And the cultivator must also be a man of feeling, for there is a communion between the vine and him who tends it more subtle than between master and dog or lover and his beloved, and, bless you, more enduring. They end in resembling one another. Think of the priest-ridden Nieder-oesterreicher and his sour vintage! Then wander through golden Provence, wander to the Mainthal and Deidesheim of old romance, where the farmer loves his vines as children, and tell me if the liquor does not reflect the man? The taste of the wine depends upon the heart of the vintner.

And leisure is the *primum mobile* of the universe.

Without leisure, the sun, moon, and stars would not have been created, for it stands to reason that the Creator could not have carried out this idea if He had been busy at the time. Are not mankind and all the beasts of the field also products of leisure moments?

The wine of Capri used to be famed throughout Italy. It has now become a noisome sulphur-and-vinegar compound that will etch the bottom out of a copper cauldron; and though the natives still drink it by the gallon—what older travellers tell us of the sobriety of the Capriotes is hard to believe—yet, in the interests of public health, it would be better if the manufacturers of *vero vino di Capri* were confined to the distillers of the relatively harmless Neapolitan preparation which goes by that name. Montesquieu lodged with the Carthusians on Capri and praises their wine in his journal. This shows that the exigencies of French politeness are not necessarily at variance with truthfulness: no man of the world will sniff at monks' liquor. But the amiable monarch Ferdinand, whom the Capriote Arcucci used to entertain for weeks at his house with "Tears of Tiberius", a self-coined and self-manufactured native

wine of noble pedigree, hit upon a more original way of showing
gratitude, for he hanged his good host in 1799—hanged him, that
is, after the Christian Bourbon fashion, when white-haired patriots
and delicately nurtured women and mere lads of sixteen were
attached by the neck to tall gibbets, and while one fiend in human
shape, called *tira-piedi*, clung to their feet, the executioner climbed
up from behind and seated himself firmly, like the Old man of the
Sea, upon their shoulders, where he was swayed to and fro by the
victim's convulsions till at last the vertebræ were broken—all this,
amid the shrieks of ten thousand ruffians, applauding the wit and
wisdom of their lazzarone-king. It is well to bear these things in
mind when one hears so much, even at Naples, of the good old
times. Murat, the royal *tartarin*, had a finer conception of humanity;
instead of murdering his benefactors, he planted French cham-
pagne grapes upon the heights beyond Naples, out of which they
still extract a drinkable stuff called Asprigno. Try it, when you
have the chance.

Another bottle?

So be it.

Now, leisure should be spelt with a capital "L", otherwise it
runs the risk of becoming materialized, like many similar things
which have ceased to be abstractions. This is what they call "treat-
ing a concept as if it were an entity". *The Unknown*, for instance.
I have passed that stage: the *Hibbert Journal* stage. We create a
word for our convenience and forthwith, unless we are on the look
out, there comes over it a horrid change. The word was made man.
It puts on flesh and blood and begins to give itself airs. Soon
enough, it stares us in the face, as though we were total strangers.
"Know you?" it jeers. "Know you for a fool!" Many respectable
men have been eaten alive by the words of their own creation, for
their appetite exceeds that of Frankenstein's healthful monster,
and I have reasons for suspecting that, like the ferocious Scythians
of old, they only drink milk.

Milk! That explains everything.

Try, also that of Ischia. As a *vino da pasto*, it is surpassed by none
south of Rome; indeed, it is drunk all the world over (under other
names), and a pretty sight it is to see the many-shaped craft from
foreign ports jostling each other in the little circular harbour, one
of the few pleasing mementoes of Bourbonism. Try it, therefore,
through every degree of latitude on the island, from the golden

torrents of thousand-vatted Forio up to the pale primrose-hued
ichor, a drink for the gods, that oozes in unwilling drops out of the
dwarfed mountain grapes.

Large heart in small grape.

Try also the red kinds.

Try them all, over and over again. Such, at least, was the advice
of a Flemish gentleman whom I met, in bygone years, at Casa-
micciola. Like most of his countrymen, mynheer had little *chiar-
oscuro* in his composition; he was prone to call a spade, a spade;
but his "rational view of life", as he preferred to define it, was
transfigured and irradiated by a child-like love of nature. "Where
there is no landscape," he used to say, "there I sit (i.e. drink)
without pleasure. Only beasts sit indoors." Every morning he went
in search of new farm-houses in which to *sit* during the afternoon
and evening. And every night, with tremendous din, he was carried
to bed. He never apologized for this disturbance; it was his yearly
holiday, he explained. He must have possessed an enviable digestion,
for he was up with the lark and I used to hear him at his toilette,
singing strange ditties of Meuse or Scheldt. Breakfast over, he would
sally forth on his daily quest, thirsty and sentimental as ever. One
day, I remember, he discovered a cottage more seductive than all
the rest—"with a view over Vesuvius and the coastline—a view, I
assure you, of entrancing loveliness!" That evening he never came
home at all.

Everything which distinguishes man from animals is the result
of leisure.

There must have been moments, for instance, when reclining at
the entrance of his cave, with his head in the shade and his feet in
the sun, the progenitor of our race amused himself with scratching
cabalistic signs upon his grandmother's skull or wondering how to
propitiate the rain-demon that spoilt yesterday's dinner. Here we
have the *prima stamina* of art and religion accounted for—by leisure.
Or, to take a corporeal illustration: we still have muscles for flapping
our ears, but leisure has made them useless. A fly settling on our ear,
we soliloquize thus: "Ha! A teasing insect, as I conjecture. Let me
see if I can kill, capture, or at least disable it"; and, instead of an
automatic and beast-like ear-twitching, we execute a careful movement of hand and arm. Our godlike physiognomy is due to leisure
which has permitted of meditation, brain-changes, and consequent
skull-modification. How could we have become the cosmopolitans

we are without leisure, which has allowed of observation, deduction of conclusions, mathematics, astronomy, and navigation?

Unlike the beast, we walk upright because leisure has induced curiosity, tools, hand-specialization, and back-bone alteration. Our teeth and digestive system are different from those of the apes—leisure, forethought, seeds, settled habits, regular meals, changes in stomach and teeth.

Leisure first made man formidable on earth. And our virtue, so far as it differs from that of animals, is purely the result of leisure. What is virtue? The conduct which conduces to the actor's welfare; the line of least resistance along which the sage walks and the fool is driven or kicked. In this sense, a flea is exactly as virtuous as a man. But a difference arises, when man begins to argue on the subject. Can anyone argue without leisure?

No—not altogether; the taste of the wine does not wholly depend upon the heart of the cultivator; it also depends upon the heart of him who drinks it. Wine is like friendship: we must meet it half-way. But often this is impracticable; one cannot try all brands; two faces peering at one another through the windows of lighted railway carriages. . . . The world is full of untasted liquor, of inchoate friendships swallowed up in the murk of night. And even when possible, what would it profit if a man carved out his heart and laid it at your feet? The postman would return it next morning with an extra fee for overweight. So the wise man, like our great English philosopher, will slobber out his gruel if too hot; but not his heart, however ardent. We be solitaries, despite our leisure.

Who is this exquisitely arrayed shadow that shakes its hyacinthine locks in disapproval? Ah, I recognize you now, you precious creature, though your hair has grown longer than ever since the angels took you—quite absurdly long, in fact. No, you were never a solitary, I grant; you were sociable enough; you found your friends very useful. So young and so wise, you used to remind me of that grey-haired babe, the Etruscan god—with a difference. He never would drink wine, would this quintessential, Cinque-Cento Symbol; it disturbed his delicate thinking faculties and likewise, I doubt not, his complexion; he never would listen to good Monsieur Janet, who has proved, to every one's satisfaction, that "intolerance of alcohol is one of the stigmata of degeneration".

Another bottle?

. . . . . .

For this class of persons are built the hotels in the larger towns of South Italy, where, even when the food will pass, no wine can be procured at any price. Whoever wishes to taste good native vintages at Rome or Naples must gird his loins and crawl into the bowels of the earth, into dank tartarean caverns such as Rembrandt loved to paint, where a greasy oil-lamp, sputtering overhead, casts flickering lights upon a double row of Gargantuan vats receding into the gloom and strikes warm tints from the red noses of a group of coachmen, wood-porters, and birds of that feather who are perched on rickety chairs in the black gulf between, helping down their liquor with an occasional plateful of some dubious vermilion stew that simmers in a corner of the wine-soaked floor. These are the customers who get their money's worth; theirs the wine that never enters the big hotels, whose proprietor buys up falsified "Margaux" for the élite and, for the simple tourist, poisonous local mixtures by the shipload, which he sells at two francs fifty a bottle as *vin du pays*, making a profit of 350 per cent.

A Neapolitan costermonger would throw this stuff in his face: if we all did the same, we would soon be better served. But we come to this country armed with too much patience; the real "signore" pays gladly; he never complains, even when at death's door from the effects of our treatment; he would drink our ditch-water, if it did not cost us more than the wine we give him. No wonder that word *signore* has become synonymous, in the vernacular, with *simpleton*, for nothing amazes these people more than to see a man, apparently sane, meekly submitting to outrageous extortion. For the rest, there is little connoisseurship in the matter of Bacchus surviving in this country; centuries of misrule and starvation have blighted the delicate flower. The ancients, whatever may have been the real state of the case, at least talked as if they had judiciously filled cellars; they bragged in good style and in good cause. Their descendants have inherited echoing subterranean vaults, dim and cathedral-like, full of possibilities; but nothing more. And yet I have sometimes heard them saying that the Germans are—relatively to themselves—savages. Body of Bacchus! When D'Annunzio shall compose an ode equal in ethical significance to *Im tiefen Keller sitze ich*, I may be prepared to consider that proposition.

A nation without a cellar-lore can hardly be said to exist, save on the map.

Yet the lower classes occasionally display a pathetic reverence for good wine. I once intercepted a familiar acquaintance returning to Siren land from Gragnano, where he had been transacting some macaroni business. He informed me with a proud smile that he was bringing back a present to his family. What was it, I asked? A scarf for his wife—toys for the children? Nothing of the kind. It was a six-year-old bottle of that sparkling dry wine of Gragnano for which the devil, unless I am much mistaken, will sell his soul at any hour of the day or night; the poor fellow beamed all over in anticipation of the family treat. I was quite touched by his kindliness.

"Will they really like it?" I queried.

"Won't they!"

But they never got it, for I loved him so dearly that I drank it myself, then and there.

And those early Italian builder-monks, clearly, were connoisseurs of the right kind. That was an ultra-modern yearning which led them to dwell on lonely hill-tops and there to plant and ponder; depend upon it, they felt impulses which the common herd never feels: the poet's craving for solitude and rocks and clouds; the gourmet's stimulation of a wilderness without and good cheer within; the creative joy of the artist who covers the naked canvas with teeming life, of the god who bids waters flow in dry places. Such retirement necessarily took on the religious complexion of its age, but the cowl does not make the monk: they were Strindbergs and Huysmans who dwelt at La Cava. At Cassino the Benedictines built nobly and meditated, but here amid careering cloud-wisps and moist forest-gloom these cowled academicians junketed and entertained princes, caring nothing for external parade. Those thick, plain walls tell their story; they are not the faltering language of men who doubt; they have analogies, none too remote, with the solid luxury of a London club. And if you would taste the fruits of this mediæval epicureanism, go to the archives. Hither came, tottering with age and cares, the Wizard of the North, and knocked at the gate; then sadly turned to go. No magic key was found to open for him the world of glittering romance that slumbers within those parchments; his age of miracles was over. Walter Scott at the portals of La Cava—a fine subject for a picture. . . .

And another also came in later years in whom Italy lost a perfect lover. A Siren worshipper was Gissing, though his Sirens were not always of the right kind. That is surely a strange criticism which deplores the personal note in his *Ionian Sea;* as if the moods of such a

man were not as vital and veracious as the reasonings of others!
I am inclined to think that he died of congestion, for there was that
within him—some macrocosmic utterance—which vainly endeavoured to pierce the gathering mists of introspection; the Rycroft
litany, beloved of the weaker brethren, marks the parabola into the
enfolding gloom. The old, old story: inefficient equipment, not of
intellectuality but of outlook and attitude, and likewise of *bête
humaine;* of that tough, cheerful egotism which, sanely regarded, is
but sanity itself. When they asked the Leontine philosopher how he
managed to attain a hundred years with such glowing health and
jollity, the sage was wont to shake his hoary locks and roar out:
"BECAUSE I NEVER WENT A STEP OUT OF MY WAY TO PLEASE ANYBODY
BUT MYSELF!" With a spark of that spirit, Gissing might be alive to
this day. To allow one's body to be torn to pieces by harpies is a
freak of chivalry beyond the dreams of Amadis.

These convent-builders loved old wine and, on this account
alone, cannot be accused of wholly misusing their leisure. But what
chapters could be written on that subject! Diseases due to misuse
of leisure: toothache, baldness. Customs due to misused leisure:
tall hats, picnics. Thought-products due to misused leisure: envy,
fraud, the *evil eye.* Institutions due to misused leisure: codes of
honour among schoolboys, army officers, and other imperfectly
civilized associations; the *vendetta.* Modern examples of misused
leisure: German feudal barons (Sudermann's *Frau Sorge*), or those
Spaniards who can sustain life for a week on a glass of sugar-water,
while, if their conversation be stopped, they pine away and die.
The subject-matter of this endless debate? *Pesetas.*

Leisure is the curse of the poor in spirit.

What a mistake to say that complexity argues culture! Nobody
but savages, wasters of good leisure, could invent solemn, sense-
defying buffooneries like totemism, or the vendetta, as still practised hereabouts. It is in the blood—the whole *Iliad* is nothing but a
vendetta; it is the soul of the people, their all-in-all; not a man you
meet but has half a dozen on hand, of one kind and another, to
amuse his idle moments, and if you suggested expeditious English
methods of settling accounts he would laugh at you; he does not
want his accounts settled; the *brooding* is exactly what he likes. There
are vendettas of a thousand kinds, each with its regulations and
mode of procedure firm-fixed as the Polar star; the simplest are
those of the young men and boys who, when they have differences

to adjust, retire to the nearest wine-shop and dig knives into each
other; a kind of game, they will tell you; if five or six are wounded
on such occasions they call it *mezza-quistione*—half-a-dispute.

Which reminds me of a fine old-fashioned game they play in the
Caucasus. The Caucasian swells, like the Scotch, take great pride
in keeping up their time-honoured sports, and one of them is this:
In order to break the monotony of their interminable banquets
and drinking-bouts, the host, at a given moment, causes all the
lights in the room to be extinguished. This is the signal for the
ancestral game to begin. Forthwith each guest unbuckles his
revolver and fires six shots at random across or under the table.
It is done in perfect good humour, as the rules require. After that,
the lamps are re-lighted, the corpses counted and carried away,
and the bowl passes round once more. They call it "odd man out"
—in the Georgian tongue.

Or the Evil Eye, which we all learn to believe in, sooner or later.
At Capri there dwells a tottering hag known as Serafina who, sixty
or seventy years ago, was useful for carrying postal telegrams to
their destination. She can barely crawl now, but, in spite of protests
as to her inefficiency on the part of ignorant visitors, she retains her
official place undisputed. So the authorities have ordained; and
for the best of reasons.

She has the Evil Eye.

"What would you, signore? Supposing we turned her out, and
something afterwards happened to our wives and children? We
should have only ourselves to blame."

Whence it follows that the *fascino*, the evil eye, is something of a
commercial asset, if you know how to use it; it is as good as a fixed
income, as was demonstrated to me by a soft-voiced, lamb-like
individual with whom I happened to be conversing the other day,
and who told me the following, absolutely truthful.

TALE OF THE EVIL EYE

"There is a restaurant in Sorrento, the 'Ace of Spades'—you
have heard of it, signore?—which was successfully managed, long
ago, by the masterful Don Peppino until his wife died and old age
and infirmities began to creep upon him. Having no sons and only
one daughter, a great beauty, who was going to inherit all his

6*

money—every one was after her, but the old fellow never joked on that subject: quite the reverse, in fact—he looked about for some one to help him with serving the customers, and finally hit upon a penniless youngster nicknamed *cagnapezzo* (Autolycus, trash-collector)—a miserable person, whose real name was Pasquale.

"Imagine, signore, Don Peppino's amazement when, the first day after they had come to terms, this individual quietly observed—

"'I've been expecting this job for some time. And now, dear Peppino (the impudence!), I must ask you not to call me *cagnapezzo* any more, but Pasquale, *Don* Pasquale, see? Because, in a month or so, I think I'll marry your daughter.'

"'Out you go!' said Don Peppino, seizing him by the scruff of his neck.

"'Wait a bit, old man. A pretty girl, your daughter; re-markably pretty.'

"That same evening she was run over by a carriage and killed.

"In short, Don Pasquale, as he insisted upon being called, had the evil eye; he was a *iettatore;* there was no denying the fact. And there was no getting him out of the house again. That affair of the daughter had established his reputation; the whole town began to fawn upon him, and soon enough old Don Peppino died and the other appropriated all his worldly goods and presently married a rich wife and had a family of his own.

"The years went by, signore; and the lamented Don Peppino's business flourished so well under the control of the evil-eyed Pasquale and his three children that, his own wife having died, he too was obliged to find an outsider to help in the concern. This was a smart youth called Antonio; yes, signore, a very smart youth.

"'And mind,' said the landlord, after explaining to him his duties, 'mind I don't see any goings-on with my daughter Concetta. Because if I do, you know—well, *you know* . . .' hinting, signore, at his notorious capacities as *iettatore*.

"'No, I don't,' said the new waiter, quite calmly. 'Good-looking young fellows, those sons of yours.'

"'Say *benedico!*' shrieked Don Pasquale, threateningly.

"'Say it yourself. Uncommonly fine boys; both of them, I mean.'

"Within a week they caught smallpox and died.

"A pure accident, signore."

Don Pasquale had unwittingly engaged another *iettatore* as

waiter: at least, so he thought. Here was a mess; two evil eyes under one roof! People thought that the business would go to pieces, but, like sensible men, they arranged affairs between themselves in a kind of armed truce, exercising their peculiar *fascino*-functions on alternate days—so the priests said. But Antonio knew what he was after.

As soon as due mourning for the sons was accomplished, he observed, casual-like—

"'Pity they died. But Concetta would make a good manageress.'

"Don Pasquale pretended not to hear.

"'I was saying that Concetta would make a good manageress. *That was rather awkward about the boys, eh?*'

"'Take her and be damned,' growled Don Pasquale.

"This marriage, signore, was the beginning of an unbroken friendship in the family. The establishment is now thriving under their triangular supervision to an extent which would have made the lamented and masterful Don Peppino green with envy, green! Come and see for yourself, signore! Old Pasquale, I am sure, would be delighted to welcome you, and so would Concetta."

. . . Rather a queer story, I thought. Who ever heard of two Evil-Eyed Ones living together?

"How do you know all this?" I asked my lamb-like informant.

"How do I know it?" he echoed. "Because I am Antonio, Concetta's husband—at your service."

"Oh. Have a cigar, my friend! Here, take two of them. . . ."

Then there was the wine of ——. I recall the times when as much of this nectar as was good for any Christian could be drunk for a franc; nowadays, the widow only sells it as a favour to old clients, "in memory of her dear departed husband"—at four francs a bottle! It was insidious stuff, most insidious. Your head remained serene like the snowy peak of Olympus which reflects, above its misty girdle, the crimson rays of sunset; the tongue wagged with eloquence and discrimination: the rest was turned to marble. Even as that Indian plant whose bended twigs incline to the soil and presently sprout up around the parent stem, a goodly family of daughters—often the brown herdsman, faint with the noonday heat, seeks refuge in that pillared shade: even so your feet, hitherto free to move at your bidding, had noiselessly descended into the floor and there taken root. You rose to bid farewell—that is, tried to rise—and found yourself anchored to earth firmer than rocky Olympus. Then, indeed, that frank departing gesture crystallized into a strange phantasm of a grin; you smiled, like the suitors of Penelope, "with alien lips". In this petrifying, gorgonizing action it resembled the wine of the Glotterthal, the wine that Sybel loved. Not that he disparaged other vintages; he liked them all; he was "no monopole", as the kindly hostess often had occasion to observe.

A propos, are there any cases of women being held captive by the Sirens? I know of very few. Have they been too preoccupied with their own charms to take notice of any others? The Sirens themselves were women, you know; and probably dressed rather oddly. Also, they were idle fowls who kept men from their duty, whereas our wives and sisters used to be stern champions of male drudgery—for man must work and woman must dress—and this has led to a little bickering in the past. But woman is changing once more; she is becoming free as after Pericles or the Renaissance, and can therefore laugh herself out of that time-honoured privilege of saying foolish things in the grand manner which seems to have bewitched our gallant forefathers. She is beginning to realize what songs the Sirens sang.

Let me explain, my young friend—I am in the mood for indiscretions—how it happened. Man, the infatuated idealist, always on the look-out for something to adore, created, in one of his moments of mediæval vapours, the Madonna-woman. It was a benignantly grinning idol, inanely oracular, to be approached on bended knees. In those days, women had to acquiesce in all his unhealthy whimsies, and many of them began to take the thing seriously and to play his game. Now, they mean to have no more of it; they are sick, utterly sick, of the Madonna business. They mean to laugh again and to enjoy life like other beasts of the earth: like men, in fact. Whenever, therefore, you catch yourself thinking that women are saints and angels, be sure you take a blue pill. The whole epidemic would have been avoided if our ancestors had thought of that.

By the way, it was rather an unflattering definition of a "real lady" which I read not long ago, to the effect that *she alone knows how to wear diamonds*. However that may be, the real gentleman, I conceive, is he who knows how to employ rationally any amount of leisure that may fall to his lot. Every other of the ten thousand definitions of that word is lame beside this one, which Aristotle already formulated, or at least divined, when he bound up gentlemanliness with elegant leisure and contra-distinguished between ἡδονή and εὐδαιμονία. And well may we pause before condemning such Hellenic ideals, if we call to mind what Galton says of the average intellectual standard of the Athenian as compared with ours. These men wrought not only in marble; they were the master-critics of the art of life. What constitutes, I wonder, the real test of a refined state of society? The existence of a preponderating class of intelligent and good citizens, not actively engaged in self-defence or the pursuit of wealth. This is honourable leisure, the flower of human development. It may be said that such a condition resembles that of the mariners who have dropped their oars, spell-bound by Siren voices. Likely enough. But while it lasts, it represents civilization. Everything else, at its best, is only progress. If the flower wither not, how shall the seed prosper?

We called him Sybel, because he seemed to have stepped straight out of Auerbach's cellar. He liked it old and sweet and plentiful, no matter where it came from. He used to take a nap halfway through and then, waking refreshed, laugh at us youngsters for being already so far gone, which of course made us more uproarious than ever. But one evening he sobered us effectually. He had lain down with a beaming countenance as usual, and we were beginning to wonder when he would wake up again, for it was considered right never to disturb him, the sleep being good for his heart, as he explained (he was far too fat ever to mean what he said). Beside myself, only the theologian and an Æsculapius had remained articulate at that hour; the latter, I remember, was setting forth the symptoms of hydrophobia to the hostess, who listened with an air of abstraction, having heard the story before. A shred of conversation still lingers in my mind.

"I tell you, madam, the dog was a mad as could be. He was as mad—as mad—as mad——"

"Then how did you escape?"

"Why (confidentially), you know, of course. By pretending to be a mosquito."

But Sybel still slumbered and we began to discover that his behaviour was disrespectful to the company at large. It was resolved that energetic measures be taken. The theologian's eye wandered round the room and finally reposed upon a stick of sealing-wax;

but a hot liquid drop, falling upon Sybel's outstretched arm, produced no effect. He only beamed.

"Which goes to prove," said Æsculapius, gravely, "according to the precepts of Hippocrates and Peter of Bokhara, that life is extinct."

And so it was. Poor Sybel must have been dead for two hours at least. Yes, he sobered us effectually that evening.

Fear not, long-suffering friend; I am not yet in my anecdotage; I will speedily make an end on't, so far, at least, as you are concerned. As for me, I am only just beginning to enjoy myself, and I will not be put out of my humour—no, not for the treasures of Mogul or Montezuma. Say me, shall I explain how it came about that the Mexican nobles, while quaffing *chocolatl* at sunrise upon the summit of their vapour-belted *teocallis* to the martial chant of *itzli-putzli-popocodl*—how it came about that these warrior-chieftains were in so far not forgetful of their rank and pedigree as to wish that some other kind of beverage could at last be invented? *Chocolatl*, indeed! No wonder they were bloodthirsty ruffians, for all their feathers.

There shall be no *chocolatl* in the land, when I am king. A song, ho!

My mother bids me bind my hair
With Cinque-Cento ribbons rare,
But oh my daddy, won't he swear—

—What, another bottle?

We be creatures of habit, and it matters little what a man's habits are, so long as they are regular. Besides, what says this letter, just received? *All strains to be avoided.* To resist is ever a strain. I have been subject to temptations from earliest childhood, and always know beforehand whether I shall yield or not. I always yield—the line of least resistance. But it is time, methinks, to recapitulate the most salient points of the discourse. Let me see. . . .

A flea hath virtue.

Excellent fooling, i'faith! Why, what a flea has cannot be worth much. I'll have none of it.

Here is something better. Your health, my patient friend, and—as they say hereabouts—*cento figli maschi!*

One of the most noteworthy features of that ancient Mexican civilization was the prevalence of the snuff-taking habit. Regarded as an isolated phenomenon, there is not over-much to be said on the subject; but when viewed, as the historian should view it, in conjunction with the wonderful astronomical knowledge and other accomplishments of this tenebrous and sombre race, it assumes another import—quite another import. His Grace the Archbishop Lorenzana, in his account of New Spain. . . .

XII

CAVES OF SIREN LAND

WHAT shall we think of that immense homogeneous civilization which is said to have covered the shores of the Mediterranean basin from neolithic to Homeric times? Did it receive, in the course of ages, affluents from wiser East or sterner North, or was some spark enkindled in its midst—some skin-clad Gutenberg or Flavio Gioia or Roger Bacon—that lighted the way over the dim gulf of years? For if it laboriously worked itself upwards step by step, the mind grows dizzy at contemplating the abysm of time between the most cultured of these men and the still rude society of prehistoric Troy or Cnossos. But why a "homogeneous" civilization? Because their weapons and dwelling-places are similar? So are those of the Papuan and Swiss lake-dwellers. Necessity produces these things by analogous variation—even as certain snakes, nowise related, have in different parts of the world hit upon the identical method of defending themselves by poison. Their cranial capacity or configuration? Skull-measurements are laudable studies, but when a wise man begins to discuss their bearings upon race-problems, it is time, as the Persians say, to put one's trust in God. And if "homogeneous" implies contemporaneity, what is there to show that there may not be a lapse of a thousand years between a flint knife from Tunis and a similar one from Apulia? Sooner or later, I suspect, this homogeneous civilization will go the way of the Aryans, who probably never existed; being a kind of nebular hypothesis which, in our present state of ignorance, explains a small bundle of disconnected facts—not always correctly.

They tell me that prehistoric spear-heads have been found buried under the soil of what afterwards became Pæstum and Cumæ. If this is true, it shows that the Greeks were probably in contact with these people; or, at all events, that they were satisfied with the localities once chosen by them as settlements.

Previously to that they lived in wigwams or skin-shelters, for the supply of caverns, though considerable, cannot possibly have been equal to the demand. This is the first step in the direction of social habits; God created the cave: man the wigwam. To this period must be assigned the numberless fragments of hand-made pottery, red without and black within, that litter the slopes of Anacapri. Some of these pieces have a horizontal line of corded ornament in relief at the rim; it seems to have been done by affixing a raised band of clay to the vessel while unbaked and then modelling it with a turn of the thumb. Into what wonderful phantasies has not the art of ceramics blossomed since those days! And yet this prehistoric embellishment is identical with that on the modern earthenware washing-tubs that stand outside every cottage in Siren land. So pottery, universally distributed, slow-moving and serving easily ascertained purposes throughout the globe, is to the ethnologist what shells, despite their infinite variety, are to the geologist—Ariadne's thread.

Wherever caves have been explored in this region, as the Grotta Nicolucci at Sorrento or the Grotta delle Felci on Capri, interesting results have been obtained; stone celts, terra-cotta vases, remains of domestic animals, and knives of obsidian. Some seeds, too, seem to have grown, for hand-mills are among the relics. But the people were cannibals for all that; cracked human bones, mixed with those of pigs and sheep, suggest marrow-sucking propensities. Likely enough, these were the *Sirens* of early navigators—the women being sent out by their men-folk to lure sailormen ashore with their songs. And they actually had cosmetics, the minxes; a shell containing a mixture of red ochre and fat testifies to neolithic vanity. The skeleton of a rachitic child has also been found. Ointment boxes and scrofulous infants—here are some of the delights of modern life in embryo, to say nothing of "a little music", not the least of them.

I can name various caves in this region which might well contain relics of these anthropophagous Sirens. But such excavations, to be of value, must be carried out cautiously and systematically, in order to obtain some idea of the age of the embedded remains and of their age in relation to one another, which can only be done by means of sections and photographs showing their juxtaposition with the cave deposit. And this deposit is a study in itself, for it varies greatly; in some caves it is of extremely slow growth; in others, which are more accessible to wind-drifts, vegetable matter, or materials falling from above, it is relatively rapid. To excavate a cave on these scientific lines requires a greater outlay than may be thought, without which the remains are best left to repose where they are, in expectation of some future enlightened amateur.

Excavating accidentally some years ago I came across the charred remains of a fire, beside which lay a celt of jadeite, another of limestone, and two or three round pebbles to be used for slinging. The green celt is a rolled river-pebble, carefully worked up (it must be a rare pleasure when a scientist like A. B. Meyer, who has fought a lifetime for his pet theory of the European origin of these jade implements, once hopelessly discredited, at last sees it universally acknowledged). A certain pathos attaches to these objects, all lying close together as they had been left thousands of years ago, for they cannot have been lost, in the ordinary sense of that word, seeing that their owner would have remembered where he lit his fire and returned to seek them there, and they were far too precious to have been thrown away. No; the owner never returned because, for some reason, he could not—he was hindered by death or capture.

The introduction of a fine material like jade must have created something of a revolution in the social habits of these people, for its blades are as superior to the ordinary ones of siliceous limestone as a steel razor to one of obsidian.

What songs these Sirens sang, though a puzzling question, is not beyond all conjecture. We may be sure that these fierce wenches were not capable of modulating subtle strains. Their melodies may well have been the original of those primeval chants, the Linus-song, the *wailing in the vineyards* of Isaiah—autochthonous, sphinx-like, fraught with the hopes and fears of a forgotten race—that are still wafted upon the summer breezes of Siren land and defy the musician's art to record them, though Tosti has made the attempt in one of his Neapolitan songs. They call this mournful and veritably prehistoric wail the "peasant's song", *canzone di personale* (=parzionale = a metayer) : it can be heard at the time of harvest, vintage, or olive-gathering (some suppose that it was imported by the Moors). Or perhaps they resembled the yodler of the *homo alpinus* or of the London milkman—the most bestial of human cries. Life was simple in those days, and with a little imagination it is not difficult to construct a domestic scene of the period, after this fashion :—

WOMAN (*approaching*). I sang Hoio. Another sea-fool comes.
MAN. Who spoke to you? (*Enter a Greek sailor*). The new green one for *you*—white-faced, seal-eyed man-pig.

WOMAN. Hoiotoho-swar!

SAILOR. That song again! To what land of marvels have these good folks led me?

MAN. See this green stone. It cuts sharp: eia-weia! *You* know.

SAILOR. Opopoi! I do begin to fear mightily. How he rolls his eye under those cavernous brows; and she, with wolfish clashings of teeth—Ai, Ai! Papaiax—they seize me—attatai, papai, pai, io, moi, moi, omoi, otototototoi—

WOMAN. They sing wrong.

MAN. They eat right.

(Interval)

WOMAN. Righter than the last, wallawa-hupla!

MAN. Who spoke to you? See this stone.

WOMAN. I sing right. Ja, ja.

MAN. Atcha! You eat wrong. Fetch another man-pig.

This little scene thows a light not only on the importance of jade in the prehistoric household, but also on the theory of these savages regarding the inverse ratio of musical talents and edibility which alone explains how it came about that the Siren family did not end after the fashion of the Kilkenny cats—namely, because, like the modern inhabitants of Siren land, they devoured not each other but only strangers from over the sea. Note, likewise, certain resemblances between the neolithic, Teutonic, and Hindustani tongues, which may help to elucidate the Aryan question.

It must have been these decoying arts which induced Servius to think that "according to the truth" the Sirens were ladies of questionable reputation. This is going too far. You ungentlemanly old fellow, what maggot has got into your grammarian's brain? Those Sirens who strewed the shore with whitening bones were respectable mothers of families finding food for their husbands and little ones; but yours—what occupation would they have on lone Tyrrhenian rocks? Seek them, rather, in Memphis or Babylon.

This same Grotto delle Felci at Capri was afterwards transformed by the ancients into a sylvan sanctuary of Pan or Priapus—to judge, at least, by the remains of an altar and by three huge stalagmitic growths now broken off which may formerly have been of ceremonial significance. The influence of these caverns upon the religious life of olden days is easily underestimated. When one remembers with what reverence these mysterious openings into the fertilizing mother earth were regarded, it might have been expected that many of them would have been devoted to the worship of generative forces, even without the written testimony of Suetonius, who connects these very *antra et rupes* with sexual orgies. Apposite popular names, which will not be found on maps, have been given to some of those grottos and towering rock-needles. "*Le culte de la génération,*" says Lefèvre, "*a exercé une influence, vraiment énorme, sur la pensée humaine, sur la conception de l'univers, sur les institutions sociales*", and among a population with an historical record like that of this province, relics of ancient sex-worship can be found by whoever looks for them. Strange, for instance, in a land where every beast, however harmless, is doomed to death, is the serpent-worship which the Mosaic curse and Christianity alike have not succeeded in extirpating; it brings misfortune to kill those that establish themselves in the neighbourhood of houses, and a drug prepared by chemists out of others purposely caught on the hills imparts virility and long life—another instance showing how frequently the attributes of this animal as a priapic emblem and as one of eternity coincide (I presume the conception of health, Æsculapius, is to be regarded, philosophically at least, as intermediate between the two).

And not long ago I came across a striking relic of these unholy observances at Torco: the larger intestine of an ox inflated with air and affixed upright over the lintel of a private house, with a streamer of red cloth attached to it—*for good luck*, the proprietor told me (coalescence with horn-emblems against the evil eye). The fish is another of these phallic symbols that go back into hoariest antiquity; its Italian name has a very different colloquial signification—in this province only—from that which the piety of early Christians drew out of those mystic characters. And in the now removed flooring of the church at Positano was a large marble phallus—women knelt on it and maintained that prayers thus offered up were of peculiar efficacity. I might mention also the shape of amulets and, in certain localities, that of bread as baked at Easter-time, the procreative festival of spring; the "sexes" attributed to domestic objects like hinges, screws, bolts, mortars, hooks and eyes, etc.—indeed a volume could be written, though perhaps not published, on the subject.

The introduction of Attis, Cybele, Flora, Liber, and so forth must have helped to sustain these deeply rooted primitive cults which began in fetichism and, after a thousand elaborations, are once more relapsing into it. The church, meanwhile, unable to expel these lewd shapes from their cloven rock of ages, has changed their names, and Our Lady of Lourdes now occupies a cave on

Capri: some weeks ago was celebrated the tenth anniversary of her installation amid incredible pomp and circumstance. Simultaneously, it was thought well to purge the Blue Grotto of its Tiberian associations by the erection of a plaster-cast Madonna over the entrance, the passage of this image across the water being attended by certain childlike religious buffooneries which scandalized the more godly among the foreign spectators.

Numberless are the caves in Siren land. They vary from minute fissures to vast oval amphitheatres capable of sheltering a population, like that one at Capri wherein the natives took refuge during Saracen raids; some are dry, others distil water from invisible rifts or pendent beards; they were all moister in the days when there was timber overhead, as can be seen by the many distorted, discoloured, and perennially dry stalactites which hang from their roofs. Some of these caves, like that above Sant' Elia, are beautifully tinted in a pattern of orange stripes converging towards the centre; nearly all of them are decked out with fantastic pinnacles and niches, suggesting a fairy-scene on the stage. The maidenhair fern droops in clusters from the ledges; tufts of *campanula fragilis* dangle their porcelain bells of pale amethyst from the fretted vault overhead; here and there a leafy fig, emblem of fecundity, thrusts formidable roots into the crevices or writhes like an octopus over the stones. The flora of these caverns would be worth studying, since even common flowers that find their way into these rainless and dewless recesses begin to look a little different from their companions outside. In some of them, like that which lies opposite the islet of Isca—a spacious grot, divided into two chambers by a natural arch, with a fine southerly prospect, a right royal abode in prehistoric times—can be found the *mesembryanthemum nodiflorum* and other rarer plants. At their entrance, on the sun-scorched rock, grow the eglantine, the rosemary, thyme, and caper plant.

The materialistic peasant cuts down this fair vegetation and stores it within against the winter; other caves he converts into goat-shelters by a rude enclosure. Of the lore attached to these hollows, he remembers chiefly the plutonic legends of buried wealth with its guardian spirits.

In the narrower fissures, which often run into the bowels of the earth, foxes establish themselves, to his great annoyance. They and the wolves are the only wild beasts of the country. The latter descend during the cold months in all directions from the clefts and

beech-woods of Faito on Mount Sant' Angelo; they seldom attack
"Christians". Yet only two years ago a boy of fifteen was devoured
near Cava by one of these furies—nothing was found save his feet
encased in their thick boots; and a woman was lacerated by
another while cooking macaroni in her kitchen. The ravening she-
wolves are blamed for these desperate deeds. It was calculated that
during last winter over one hundred dogs had been eaten by them
in the district of Preazzano and Ticciano, which lies just outside
the gates of Siren land—these gates being the openings which lead
from the Sorrentine plain between walls of rock into higher regions,
the flying buttresses of the mighty Sant' Angelo.

The village of Sant' Agata, they say, owes its foundation to a wolf,
which carried off the daughter of a certain knight of Massa. The
father, having vowed to the virgin that if he rescued the child alive
he would then and there erect a church in her honour, found the
little one uninjured, and on that very spot built the church round
which the village of Sant' Agata subsequently grew up. If we laugh
at wolf-stories now, it is because we have forgotten what that grey
horror, with eyes aflame, meant to our ancestors—how for untold
ages it terrorized mankind, leaving a deep scar on lore and literature.

Few superstitions are more firmly rooted hereabouts—all over
the world, nearly—than that of the werewolf. The word *lupomanaro*
can be heard every day as a vituperative, and any child will tell
you that there are two kinds of wolves—dog-wolves and man-
wolves (*lupo-cane* and *lupo-cristiano*). Certain mortals and certain
animals are dowered with the gift of distinguishing the *versipellis* even
in daytime, when he appears in human garb; a sure test is this—if a
shrine or crucifix happen to be on the path along which he is going,
he cannot proceed, but must turn back. There lives a *lupomanaro*, a
poor peasant called *il lungo*, in a solitary cottage near Sant' Agata.
When the moon is full, he runs about exactly like a wolf, with his
hands resting on his knees; when he comes to a cross-way, he howls
fearfully.

"Does he change his skin?" I enquired.

"No."

"What do you call his disease?"

"*Male grande—male di luna.*"

Thus lycanthropy, with advancing civilization, is merged into
epilepsy. Other werewolves are men who work in hot bakeries at
night and suffer from *male piccolo* or convulsive asthma; they crawl

about the streets in the early hours of the morning, panting and groaning. Then is the time to cure them. If you can creep up from behind and stab them in the back with a piece of steel—a knife, for instance—they will exhale all their wolfishness in one wild howl.

Even to the very tail of the peninsula these marauders penetrate; not a year passes without some dogs or goats being killed at Termini, and last winter they forced an entrance into the so-called *grotte delle capre* or goats' caves on San Costanzo, and did a fearful massacre among its inmates.

The summer is fast drawing to its close. But it will not do to say farewell to Siren land without visiting this line of caves which lie on the southern flank of the mountain, one above the other, under a projecting wall of rock. Every morning some two hundred far-tinkling quadrupeds issue from these caverns to graze the coarse herbage on the slopes. A rough path leads past them up the steep incline, and I never walk that way without a feeling of reverential awe for these immemorial shelters whose stones are polished by the footsteps of bygone ages. They lie high up, in the solitude, among stones. The glittering Tyrrhenian rises into the firmament and its many-tongued laughter floats up to their threshold which, in olden days, may well have been shaded by holm-oaks and laurels and pines. There is a fine flavour in the wild landscape all around; but within, the atmosphere is rank and murky with the odours of a thousand generations of goats. For these grottos, remote as they are from human habitations, must have been useful from earliest times as a refuge for flocks. On the hill-side near at hand you may find fragments of the familiar black and red prehistoric pottery. These men, already, took shelter here.

Whether the goats have greatly changed since those primeval days, I cannot tell.

And the shepherds? The skin mantle was cast aside for a shapely tunic, and the tunic replaced by the blue cotton shirt of yesterday; popes and emperors have come and gone; the woodlands are swept away and the very mountains have put on new faces, but these goat-boys are the same dreamy, shy, sunburnt children as in the days when Phœnicians sailed in their black ships past yonder headland. They "think of nothing". Simpler than fisher folk or tillers of the soil who must ever revolve contingencies of weather and market, gentler towards their charges than keepers of horses and other beasts, they glide through youth watching the combats and loves of their flocks, rescuing the little ones from craggy ledges and tending the lame and weary, while day by day an intense feeling of endearment towards these warm and frolicsome comrades grows up in their breasts. This is their world—a goat-world; their very countenances reflect it.

Stumbling upon such primitive conditions, we seem suddenly to step outside and beyond the decent Hellenic civilization, with its ordered household, its sceptred kings, well-greaved warriors, and grave dames; its cornfields and broad-browed oxen. We seem to enter that outer world of hollow rocks where men neither sow nor reap; the monster-engendering cycle of Polyphemus and his goats.

To what pipings have these caverns listened, when Troy was yet unsung? To what mad, hot whisperings? The moon alone can tell, for she has looked straight into them time out of mind. But the moon is discreetly silent, having seen many things upon earth; she knows the ways of man and beast, and is not easily made to blush. Maybe some Daphnis, when the world was young, drove his flocks into them night after night and year after year, thinking of nothing. And one day there emerged, casting a wild glance about him, the progenitor of that troop of faun-like creatures, whose poignant truthfulness first appalled, then enslaved, our reluctant imagination.

Dreams?

Perhaps not altogether. I, too, have dwelt with shepherds in Arcadia. And saints of God, wandering in the stony wilderness, have encountered the fauns, face to face, ay, conversed with them; while Monsieur Hedelin, advocate, priest, and preacher, has demonstrated their existence beyond all possibility of doubt, if the facts in this book are true. The fauns *are*: they have been ever since Hellenic days. But the Greeks did not invent them—they only found them. Pathetic animalesque shapes, nymphs and fauns, titans and chimæras, the offspring of human intercourse with nature in her seductive and sterner moods, crept into Greek art and were made man. Sometimes, by an intuition of genius—how difficult the feat is, can be seen by those who would imitate it—a compound imaginary being was artistically fixed; the human element emprisoned in beast body (sphinx), or remorselessly welded upon it (centaurs). But not all these sub-human forms beloved of children and heralds express single-hearted strivings like Pegasus—strength wedded to heaven-soaring flight—or the winged Psyche.

The griffin is merely picturesque.

Yes; it was a feat of genius to arrest those composite phantoms in that precise moment when, trooping past the mind's eye, their grace outweighed their grotesqueness. An ingredient of strangeness, says the English sage, is requisite to full beauty, and doubtless there is no lack of strangeness in these conceptions. But what distinguishes Greek man-beasts from those of other nations is that this ingredient, though inevitably present, is forcefully subordinated to a human note of pathos or graciousness. If, as I think, Greek artists held that the grotesque, the horrible, may be a means, but rarely or never to an end, it is easy to understand why certain things were beyond their power or desire of expression. The man-wolf, for example, is recalcitrant to the chisel under such conditions. Not that there is any lack of foundation in fact; he is as well authenticated as the fauns and has been circumstantially described by eye-witnesses from early times; but short of falsifying the truth immeasurably—a sin— nothing could be done towards investing the beast with that ele- ment of graciousness which they deemed indispensable and which even their direst imaginings, the medusæ or furies, display. Also: he does not allow of the requisite vagueness of interpretation. Enviable fauns! In their happiest moments they were espied and eternalized by loving friends: how many of us mortals will share their fate?

In the Sirens too, in the old Sirens, the Greeks had a hard task before them. Gradually they moult; the feathers drop off their limbs and bosom; it is a downward process of purification, the nobler parts being the first to glow with the new light. Whatever Baudelaire may have thought to the contrary, there is nothing so incontestably anti-bestial as the naked human body, and this per- haps explains the startling fact that Greek gods and goddesses, in proportion as they become civilized, tend to discard garments and covering devices of all kinds. The brute may still lurk within fine clothing or feathers. But only the Etruscans despoiled the Sirens of all bird-like attributes.

Did the Greeks sometimes go too far in their rejuvenations? It was well that those bearded Sirens were done away with, but what are we to say of the old and new Bacchus, or that absurd Eros-baby, which had supplanted the fair and pensive youth, fraught with a burden beyond his years? Venus Urania, methinks, ought to have a beard.

One point strikes me as noteworthy. From whichever country

these creations entered Greece, and whatever may have been their original guise and import, they were quickly remodelled and stamped with the hall-mark. It may be a trifling matter, that of these mixed symbolic art-productions, but it serves to illustrate the whole trend of Hellenic thought. Nothing overmuch. . . . Two attributes, such as the Minotaur possesses, are sufficient for the mind to assimilate at a glance.

In Assyria they wrought man-headed winged bulls. A people nursed in Chaldæan modes of thought may have found no difficulty in rapidly grasping the inner coherence of so much allegory, but a simple, unprepared spectator is taken aback by this plethora of attributes and ponders as to their meaning; these Assyrian bulls, like Irish ones, seem to become valuable in proportion as they are pregnant.

The Greek sculptor thought otherwise; he demanded an instantaneous flash of comprehension, and therefore rejected them and their fellows. For Greek art remained objective long after philosophy had gone the way of Plato, as we know from late masterpieces like the Nike of Samothrace and the Venus of Milo, which speak, in clearest language, to the beholder. The artist feels: the philosopher reasons, and reasoning, the latest and most delicately etched pencilling on the mind's surface, is the first to become blurred. Clear feeling will outlast clear argument, because it is older: the drunkard, who strips off the various layers in the order in which he has put them on, is an admirable illustration of this. Gorgias might grow grey in discussing problems of immortality; he might interpret them this way and that and never solve the knot; but if the Greek citizen remained for a moment in doubt as to the significance of a work of art, its purport was missed.

And nowadays?

Nowadays we are become somewhat metaphysical and subjective to these matters. The meaning of a picture or statue may not thrust itself upon us in this crude, straightforward fashion; the morsel must be chewed before swallowed and relished only of the elect; prayer and fasting are requisite to initiate us into the mysteries which the master sought to express. It is all for the best, no doubt. Times are changed. The Greeks liked garlic.

As for the fauns and their fellows—these dream-creatures wander over flowery meads in the dim borderland between the monstrous and the sublime, and whoever seeks them will not seek in vain, for their existence is coeval with man and Hellenic art only discovered them in the sense that Vasco de Gama discovered the Indies or Volta electricity. Critics, meanwhile, shake their heads in sagest fashion; but whether they approve or not, who shall say? These conscientious gentlemen are puzzled and disquieted, having no clear preceding exemplar to guide them. They wish such things had never been invented. There are *pros* and *cons;* besides, there are fauns and fauns. . . .

"Not guilty, but don't do it again," they mumble at last; a reasonable verdict, when one comes to think of it, and one which might well be extended to certain faun-makers of later days.

POSTSCRIPT

Nobel says that the Slav religion was largely fashioned by forests. Even so, it seems to me that the *prima stamina* of what was afterwards known as Hellenism were originally hewn out, so to speak, under threats of a discordant and destructive environment.

Pelasgian immigrants, the stock of old Greece, the builders of bridges and canals, the sowers of seeds, were leagued against a common enemy—nature. Old Mother Earth was false and ferocious to them; she thwarted them at every turn; the land was peopled by things hostile to man and his ordered ways; there were torrents and gloomy forests and yawning clefts and swamps; the sea, unconquered, grim, or smiling only to destroy; shaggy men, acorn-devouring, who skulked in caves. So those early settlers learned to feel acutely on the subject of humanity, of man the regulator and restrainer of savagery; they held in horror the crude shapes and forces of the outer world, and the keynote of their spiritual strivings became an intense anti-bestiality—far intenser than it is easy for us to conceive nowadays. For times have changed, and we regard ourselves as a portion of nature, rather than her foe.

Long afterwards, when earth and ocean had put on a friendly or at least familiar demeanour, and when the infusion of fresh blood had given to these people their plasticity and versatility, we find persisting this venerable ideal, this humanizing tendency, product of forgotten struggles with the brute and sombre forest. It tinges to latest periods their conception of art and literature and conduct, cropping up in the most unexpected places.

I spoke of the Eros-baby, a late apparition, and one of their relatively few representations of the infant-type. And the odd thing is, that these infants in Greek art are not only few, but also of rather indifferent execution. The Plutus-infant, the baby Hercules, even the Dionysus-child in the arms of Hermes—they have all come in for a share of adverse comment, and Mr. John M. Robertson, who is not given to talking at random, merely voices the general opinion of critics when he says that "the Greek sculptors never learnt to model a tolerable infant".

Can it be that from ignorance of its true genesis this particular aspect of their creative genius has been misread? That the Greeks, rather, never *deigned* to model a tolerable infant?

I think they were quicker than ourselves to detect in the infant-type with its convulsive movements, eyes far apart, flattened nose, crooked legs, and prevailing animalesque characteristics of structure and locomotion, something abortive, incomplete; a caricature of that human body which was for them the full expression of what I have called anti-bestiality; particularly offensive, because it accentuated the features which we possess in common with the brute. This made their artists so niggardly and uncharitable towards babyhood that they never cared to figure it, unless conventional reasons obliged them to do so. Even we, who have outgrown such sensitiveness and become more robust than the Greeks in such matters, still discover in infants a resemblance to the ape, and in the ape the most odious distortion of ourselves.

As soon as—without violating that approximation to truth which canons of good art demand—the infantile traits could be made a subject for idealization; as soon as the child unveiled its heart and ambiguous simian lines dissolved into the soft-stirring smile of boyhood, giving promise of new beauties about to emerge triumphantly and drive the bestial strains back into the dusky caverns of the past, no one has treated the human form with more loving appreciation. But it is as if they hesitated to give their artistic imprimatur to what was not convincingly human, and in this one may be tempted to recognize an echo of those old struggles with the brute.

The change in family life and the new position of women have fostered greater intimacy between the father and his helpless offspring, and from this relation has grown an infant-type, and a mother-type, unknown to the Greeks. The Madonna, myrionymous like her prototype Isis, and the infant Jesus—Horus in the arms of Isis—have also contributed to the establishment of this new ideal.

If Greek art was stepmotherly towards babies, ours went too far in the other direction, for the Christian conception of this divine infant, which may justifiably be idealized in virtue of its unique character, disturbed our artistic treatment of ordinary ones. We over-idealized them, expunging the simian traits before they had shown any indication of fading away. Thus arose, by judicious modelling, a new infant, a composite being with the features and limbs of man, woman, or child *à discrétion*, and in whom the naturally vacant stare of dawning life was metamorphosed into a gaze of concentrated piety of world-wisdom, reflecting sentiments such as no infant ever possessed; sentiments such as those recorded of Saint Nicolas of Tolentino who, as a suckling babe, was already so convinced of the propriety of ascetism that he voluntarily abstained from partaking of his mother's milk on two fixed days of each week.

Whoever looks for such babies in Hellas will look in vain, for this is the anti-bestiality of an age which regards man himself as the brute, to be contrasted with a diaphanous angel-type hitherto unrevealed. The Renaissance, too, was not over-conscientious in its plastic representations of the infant-type: witness the "Cupid" of Donatello, whose *torso* might be mistaken for that of a Zeus or Neptune. Altogether, this delirious blossoming is to be appreciated for what it wrought upon the minds of men rather than for its artistic achievements, which are flawed with introspection and not for ever young. These men painted nature as they saw it, with seraphic simplicity; but their renderings of the human form lack the universal application of antiquity; they revived the form, without assimilating the spirit, of their masters.

A scholar might amuse himself by tracing back the whole Nemesis-conception of the Greeks to those old Pelasgian nightmares —to the violence of nature, the immoderation of the beast, teaching them their lesson of measure. He might speculate, too, upon the various shapes that floated through early Greece without being artistically adopted—upon the many creatures of earth and air and phantasy which were thrust aside as abhorrent to this rather narrow sense of what was good or fair. The primitive Sirens, I suspect, escaped this fate by a miracle, the miracle of Homer's adoption and transmutation of them; poets and writers of a more refined age would have been merely puzzled or repelled by such fearsome forms. These demons of putrefaction, but for the *Odyssey*, must have waited long centuries to be appreciated.

They must have waited till our day.

For, unlike those old farmers on jungle-clearings, we live on terms of sympathy with our natural environment. We can afford to do so, even as the Romans could afford to cherish conciliatory relations with their conquered enemies. Thus, nature becoming our hand-maid, new fountains of enjoyment have sprung up for us, such as the picturesqueness of the desert, of poverty and squalor, of decay; the weird and droll and uncouth, the sumptuous and exotic, have all found a place in our catholic estimation; we admire the extravagances of Egyptian carvings or Gothic skeletons, and gloat over grotesque *chinoiseries* which a Greek would have dismissed as abuses of man's higher faculties.

Humanity alone, as a subject for treatment, has expanded into a many-voiced organ when compared with that clear but thin reed of theirs. What did Hellenic art know of the humour of old age—of those kindly wrinkles? Of the haunting charm of youthful etiolation? Of barbarian strength and virtue? In the *Iliad*, again, we hear only of captains and kings—the common herd does not exist. But nowadays even vulgar persons, with vulgar hopes and fears, may be made interesting. We relish it at least on a level surface, in homely scenes, Delft-ware style; for when a tragic passion with heights and depths is to be sounded, none save a cunning master, who cheats us into giving them the feelings of their betters, can make the thing endurable; they *will* wallow, these good folk, having, as Schopenhauer observed, "no height from which to fall"; their griefs and toys are alike lowly, and oftentimes past comprehension.

All this, even without the intervention of the Jesus-Horus ideal, would have paved the way for a conception of beauty so extended as to include the simian features of the infant.

The outlook is widened—forest-gloom dispersed.

But those keen human notes, the wild cry of Hellas, are no longer heard: a choral symphony has drunk them up.

XIII

THE HEADLAND OF MINERVA

THERE is a project afoot to continue the driving-road from Sorrento, which now ends at Termini, as far as the point of Campanella. Italy is full of such designs of local patriotism. Often enough, after some thoughtful mayor has collected money during his term of office for an undertaking of this kind—roads, drainage, or water-supply—his successor will spend the whole sum in pyrotechnics in honour of the village saint: thousands of francs carefully hoarded up being thus thrown away in a wild orgy of a single night. Shoulders are shrugged; a new collection begun: *Italia farà da sè*—that charming mixture of enthusiasm and inefficiency! It will ever be thus under a communal system as established here; no public spirit can exist where the good intentions of a few are absorbed by the vices to which the institution lends itself; where each reacts upon the other by ties of relationship or business and by preordained obligations of love and hatred; where the caprice or envy of a single man will suffice to frustrate a project secretly approved by all. What they require, these villages, is an independent and benevolent tyrant after the pattern of the old *podestà*: the municipal system marks a theory of government which ill accords with their habits of life.

Not that the building of this road is a pressing need. There are too many roads in the country already and, were nothing else to be amended, I could wish that the inhabitants might long continue to waste their superfluous wealth in making noises and bad smells to the glory of God—for such are the local fireworks.

The time to take this walk is the early morning, before the sun has begun to beat down upon the western slope of Mount San Costanzo, along which the path runs. The road leads gradually downwards, at first through olives and then along the bare hill-side, fragments of Roman masonry and paving-stones proving that it follows the ancient track, till we reach the platform on which stand

the lighthouse and the tower of Campanella—so called from a
gong which used to be sounded there at the approach of pirates.
Here are abundant old remains, but no trace of Minerva's temple.
Holstenius, who wrote his annotations to Cluver in 1666, and who
seems to have visited the place, says that the temple (of the Sirens,
he calls it) stood upon the site of the present Campanella tower,
which was built with its materials; adding, however, "so the
inhabitants say"—which makes his testimony almost worthless.

And, favourable as the site is for a public building of this kind,
yet the Roman poet's description of the "Sorrentine peak" from
which the goddess looked down is somewhat inappropriate, seeing
that Campanella is only about thirty yards above sea-level; unless,
indeed, the whole mountain was identified by a figure of speech
with the deity herself, whose shrine lay at its foot. The cosmographer
of Ravenna has "Syrrentum, Minerva", and Guido, about whose
age there is some uncertainty, speaks of "Minervum, in which is
the temple of Minerva, where Anchises the father of Æneas first
saw a man feeding horses, as Virgil reports". No horses could
pasture here nowadays. He was alluding to the *castrum Minervæ* near
Otranto.

I do not know when the promontory ceased to bear the name of
the goddess: in the Golden Book of King Roger (1154) it is called
ras M.ntirah, which its latest editors consider a mistake for *ras
Manirbah* (Minerva); the tower was erected *in loco ubi dicitur Minerva*
in 1334, and is similar in shape to that on the Galli, which was built
at the same time, though in better repair. Many antiquities have
been found at this spot, but the traveller Borch, who landed here
in the eighteenth century to collect coins, was sadly disappointed,
for the natives whom he calls "*aussi fourbes que bêtes et méchans*"
brought him "*un petit écu de France usé et une pièce d'argent aragonaise,
disant que c'étaient deux antiques de grand prix*"—which annoyed him
considerably.

In the fourteenth century, too, the corals between *Capram et
Minervinum* were a royal monopoly: so says a document which has
been excavated by Monsieur Georges Yver in that vast post-tertiary
deposit known as the Archivio at Naples.

Among the stones to be picked up at the site are certain lumps of
red volcanic scoriæ. I regard them with interest, as proving that
some, if not all, of the buildings at Campanella date from the early

imperial epoch. For I have found this material, which was used by
the Romans for the modelling of vaults, and where lightness was to
be combined with strength, nowhere save in those ruins of Capri
which cannot have been built before Augustus. Now if this scoriæ,
as I strongly suspect, was brought from Vesuvius—like the "tufa
of Herculanum" concerning which there have been learned dis-
cussions—before that mountain was covered with ashes in 79, the
age of these buildings is determined pretty accurately within two
close-lying limits. Mason-bees now construct their houses in its
almond-shaped cavities, selecting it for the same reasons which
commended it to the architects of Roman palaces: because it is
dry, porous, and adhesive to plaster.

In winter the waves dash fiercely against this hoary promontory,
and even in the bluest days of midsummer there is an unquiet
heaving of the waters near the point. No wonder the Sirens chose
it for their seat, for once ships began to pass between here and
Capri, there can have been no lack of wrecks and victims. A part
of the fleet of Augustus was shattered against these very rocks in the
year 34. Gold and silver galore must be lying under the waves in
those narrow three miles; anchors and chains, too, and rusty
implements such as were used on one memorable occasion when the
great medical school of Salerno was flourishing; flourishing and
yet envious; envious of the fame of the mineral waters of Pozzuoli
which attracted travellers away from their own town—for the
waters, you perceive, cured patients gratis, while the Salerno
doctors used to send in heavy bills—so envious, that certain rich
and well-reputed physicians of that school, to wit, Sir Antoninus
Sulimella, Sir Philippus Capograssus, and Sir Hector de Prochyta,
after taking counsel how to remedy this vexatious state of affairs,
decided that it was no time for half-measures.

They therefore embarked in Salerno upon a small vessel carrying
certain iron instruments wherewith to deface the marble inscriptions
and figures at Pozzuoli which set forth the blessings of those healing
waters. That, they thought, would ruin the reputation of the sister-
town. But alas! on the return journey after this impious expedition
the boat was "miraculously submerged between Capri and
Minerva" and the iconoclastic physicians engulfed together with
their crow-bars, hammers, and chisels. The defiant letterings were
doubtless engraved anew, there being no lack of Roman marble
tablets at Pozzuoli; as for the waters, they flow on health-giving as

7

in times of yore, for have not their virtues been contrived, ere the beginning of the world, by Virgil, the archimage?

It was a frankly mediæval expedient of revenge, inconceivable nowadays; and yet—hearts do not change so quickly; we only weave new garments in which to clothe hopes and fears that are for ever old. And a relative or descendant of this same Hector de Prochyta was the most un-mediæval of Italy's sons—John of Procida. Often enough he sailed through these straits. If we could but read his diary! What perils by sea and wanderings in lonely places, momentous battle-councils, beggarly rags exchanged for the splendours of Byzantine court or Vatican, and as easily resumed again; what shifts and intrigues! How comes it, I wonder, that none of our scholars has written a monograph on him and the great Hohenstaufen, their aims and aspirations? Why does our reading public, so greedy of things Italian, know of him nothing save schoolboy recollections of Sicilian Vespers? If they would turn aside from their Cinque-Cento infatuation and forget, for a while, the squabbles of microscopic Tuscan princelings and the hallucinations of neurotic monks and carvers of saints, they would behold, in John of Procida, a MAN. They could watch how this man's character is drawn out by adversity, *educed*, till he towers like an Ifrit above his fellows and his age. More than this: they would be confronted by a phenomenon rare indeed in mediæval history—by a striving, an ideal, that would do honour to themselves in this twentieth century.

Vengeance is mine, said the Jewish god who liked to keep all the good things for himself; such was not the notion of *Dominus Iohannes*. He tumbled into a dishonoured grave the proudest prince in Christendom, and the tremors of his splendid, sanctified hatred were felt from London to Constantinople. His ambition was the unity of Italy—a portent, a dream undreamed in that night of barbarism, a cry that none save the prophetic voice of Dante echoed down the centuries to come. This doctor of Salerno was endowed with an astuteness and a tenacity that verge on the preternatural; he was no party conspirator, but an independent statesman of singularly modern cast, who drove popes and kings and emperors, with the precision of an automaton, the way he meant them to go. That transient gleam is the "wolf's tail" of our present political status; it prefigures the triumph of reason over its hereditary enemies, monkery and militarism. With a keen eye to the advantages of trade in an age of feudal putrefaction, he built the harbour of

Salerno and instituted an annual fair, which is still held in that town. And amid a life of breathless State activity, he calmly continued to practise medicine; he was *facile princeps* in the land; great men travelled hundreds of miles to consult him, and some of his recipes are printed in pharmacopœias of to-day. At his advice, no doubt, the Emperor Frederick actually permitted the dissection of dead bodies for anatomical purposes, a concession to common sense not rare, but unique, in mediæval times. It was John of Procida, too, who thought fit to adorn, at his own expense, the last resting-place of Hildebrand, Prince of Popes. This act alone would suffice to stamp the man: there was, without a doubt, an element of grandeur in him.

It is easy to be modern nowadays, though not all of us have discovered the secret; it was easy, maybe, at Rome or Cuzco or Nineveh; but to be modern under the sterilizing, paralysing blight of European mediævalism was reserved for a few prodigies—martyrs, rather, since most of them paid for this distinction with their blood. And even in the matter of dying, John of Procida was phenomenal. At a patriarchal age, he expired in his bed; almost forgotten, as one historian remarks. Likely enough he was "almost forgotten". Mont Blanc does not show to full advantage from the Grands Mulets, and it takes a far distance of time to see John of Procida in his true perspective.

In these waters, too, his friend Roger de Lauria, with a resourcefulness and audacity unparalleled up to that day, crushed the fleet of the Anjou king and captured his son. . . .

One is apt to forget that Athene was a *parvenue* in these lands of the Sirens; travelling westwards, she ousted them from their headland whose oldest name, Sirenusson, was then changed, in her honour, to Athenaion. In early days, before the temple of the Sirens was actually built at Massa, their residence was probably imagined to lie on the south side of the promontory and about its storm-tossed capes and islands; they gradually crept away from their homesteads, Athene following in their wake. It is quite intelligible, that these old but deathless maidens of the sea, in whose nature were elements incongruous and hard to expound, should yield before a wholly beneficent goddess with clearly marked sexual and mental attributes. For, previous to setting out on this voyage, she had passed through the crucible of Hellenic purification—it is as far a step from the astute companion of Odysseus or the Egyptian

Tritogeneia to her whom we know, as from the wooden xoanon of
Athene Polias to the idealizations of Periclean art. Man first
appeases, then worships, his devils. There was nothing left to
appease or disentangle in bright-eyed Athene; she is cast in one
mould and her ægis gleams with fine humanity, flashing the message
onward into furthest ages. The older Sirens were enigmatical, if not
hostile. They retreated before her and never turned to look back,
and when the sanctuary of Parthenope at Naples became celebrated,
that in Massa decayed—the familiar movement from East to West,
to which the township of Massa itself and of Sorrento, of Naples
and Paris and London, all bear witness.

This was explained somewhat differently in the Middle Ages.
Says the old Cronaca di Parthenope: "A virgin girl, unmarried
and called Parthenope, of surpassing beauty, daughter of the King
of Sicily, came with great number of ships to Chiaia (Naples). By
a chance she sickened there and died of that same distemper and
was buried. And here, on her grave, was the temple erected."

If you are in the mood for a scramble, you can be rowed from
Campanella a mile in the Massa direction as far as the Cala di
Mitigliano, and thence climb up the ravine to the summit of
Mount San Costanzo. It is rough walking till the farm of Mitigliano,
about half-way, is reached. In the vineyards here may be seen a
few Roman remains and four huge amphoræ, one of them still
intact and in its original position. This, then, is the ancient Metel-
lianum (there is another place of this name near Cava). And not
far from this site were unearthed, some six years ago, a "shepherd"
of gold and a metal helmet which were sold for fifty francs to a
Sorrento jeweller, though "who knows how many millions they
were really worth". It is impossible to obtain clear details of such
discoveries; not only are the natives incapable of describing what
they see with their eyes, but also, like the Irish, they hesitate to reply
until they know what one would be glad to hear; if one persists in
merely asking for the truth, they suspect hidden motives and become
evasive. The Oriental influence, I suppose—the same which always
prompts them to answer one question with another.

"Why do you invariably answer my questions with another
question?" I once enquired.

"Why shouldn't I?"

Above this farm stands the venerable chapel of Mitigliano with

a "miraculous" picture, and the ruins of a small convent whose
inmates, they say, were enslaved by the Turks. A furious nocturnal
treasure-hunt took place here not long ago in which cellars, walls,
and cisterns were demolished. "They found nothing," the farmer
told me; "at least (with a wink) so they said."

Mount San Costanzo has two summits divided by a saddle-
shaped depression—La Croce and the chapel itself. The mists of
Byzantium still cling to those grey rocks, for Saint Costanzo was
patriarch of Constantinople, whose body, carefully packed in a
barrel, floated from the Euxine into the Bay of Naples; it arrived
fresh and uninjured, nor is there anything profane in the conjecture
that the occupant of the barrel had been treated with bitumen,
large quantities of which must then have been stored at Byzance
for the manufacture of *Greek Fire*. His relics, what is left of them, are
now lying at Monte Vergine, that vast repository of bones which
were imported in ship-loads from the saintly East to the confiding
West; nearly every calendar saint is represented in the official
catalogue by a tooth or a knuckle, and among the items I observe,
to my astonishment, "the skeletons of Shadrac, Meshac, and
Abednego", which Frederick II, who could never resist a joke, is
supposed to have sent over from Jerusalem.

Now: how did this come about? For, if I remember rightly, the
patriarch Theophilus was also anxious to possess these anatomies
and despatched the monk Colobi on a boat of clouds to Babylon
for the purpose of fetching them, but the three saints stoutly
refused to quit their tombs, though promising to oblige the patriarch
in other matters. How did they come to reach Jerusalem, and to
change their minds on the subject of exportation?

It is all rather incredible nowadays; men like Trajan, Pericles, or
Sardanapalus are of yesterday, in comparison. Yet the bone trade
revived quite recently; not with the East, but with His Holiness
the Pope, who forwarded saints' skeletons from the Vatican to
Naples in exchange for castrated boys to warble the praises of God
in the Sistine Chapel. San Domingo and other travellers have
collected details of this interchange of commodities.

The Oriental notes lingered long in these regions: San Costanzo,
Santa Maria di Costantinopoli, Sant' Elia, Santa Sofia, and others
all date from the times when the shadowy exarch still reigned at
Ravenna. And mediæval Greek was spoken here up to remarkably
late days; the Suabian laws were promulgated in Greek and Latin;

Greek was in familiar and official usage up to 1450, and six Greek churches, says the learned Mazzocchi, survived in Naples up to the thirteenth century. But the Normans whose piety, or shrewdness, generally placed them on the side of the Roman pontiff, had meanwhile dealt an unexpected death-blow to the power of Byzantium in the West, by introducing the silk-worm into Sicily.

We are apt to be unfair to Byzantium. It must not be judged, I think, by what it created or wrought into fresh forms, but by what it preserved. As a period of repose and conservation—as a mere wedge of time and dominion interposed while the savage North was ripening for its legacy of antiquity—its services to mankind are past all reckoning.

In those centuries, when the inhabitants of this district may often have wondered to whom they owed allegiance, were laid the seeds of that opportunism and lack of living conviction in public affairs which now, after another thousand years of misgovernment, have borne such baleful fruits. It is good to read, now and then, in the old chronicles, of the deeds of those improbable creatures, of Sikard and Grimoald, Radelchis, Gaidelgrime and Sigelgaita, whose very names sound like a roll-call from the Niebelungen-lied; of the Greek dukes of Sorrento and other lordly phantoms that conjure up visions of Shakespeare's mellow geography.

A seething witches' cauldron was South Italy; dark and passionate shapes emerge from the brew, clash their weapons or mutter a prayer, and again sink down.

In those ages, too, when men really believed the unbelievable, they built sanctuaries upon the hill-tops—proximity to heaven being esteemed favourable for the exaudition of prayers; nowadays, mankind refusing to climb, the churches have descended into the valleys to suit the convenience of a lukewarm generation. An attractive site like San Costanzo hill must have been occupied from earliest times: Christianity in Siren land under Marcus Aurelius is no impossibility, if we are to trust Tertullian and Origen. Yet the arch-pagan Symmachus praises for its (heathen) religious zeal the town of Naples where they used to say, "it was easier to meet with a god than with a man". Hill-worship in the provinces gradually declined: the saint-bishop Antoninus of Sorrento was charged before the Pope, in the ninth century, with "celebrating mass on mountain summits against Christian usage, and thus propagating a new and most pernicious heresy". Why *new*—why this exacerbation? There is more than meets the eye in this indictment. The good man's heresy would be no heresy in these days when every Catholic bishop, according to a convenient fiction, is accompanied by a "portable altar" wherever he goes.

And the crucifix on the sister-summit also goes back, I suspect, to the days of Constantine the Great, being a repetition of one of those legendary crosses on which the archangel Michael, the Apollo and Lucifer of Christianity, who then winged his way westwards and settled upon cloudy peaks all over Europe, was wont to alight; the material emblem surviving while the Oriental tradition faded away before the western one of Calvary. Yet not all the crosses hereabouts can claim this venerable origin. That on the rock Vervece was erected only a few years ago in commemoration of some sailors who were shipwrecked there; two others, which do not improve the landscape, were placed on peaks behind Sorrento, in order that storm-tossed mariners "might have something to look at", by certain mighty landlords to whom much may be forgiven, for they have planted much.

There runs a legend at Termini to the effect that the chapel on San Costanzo hill was built by the saint himself, under protest. The elders of the village having determined to construct his shrine lower down, the saint sent several messages to say that he preferred the hill-top; and all in vain. The site of the new church, they told him, was already mapped out, and the sooner he acquiesced the better.

"You won't?" he said. "Well, then, I must build it myself."

So saying, he collected stones and mortar, and in a night the whole edifice was completed. That settled it. This, of course, took place hundreds of years ago, or even more; but what he did to the men of Nerano who refused to send their *figlie di Maria* to his feast at Termini, even under promises of payment, is a matter of yester-day. He simply "shook his chains"—is this a reminiscence of some Typhœus-legend?—and an avalanche of rocks poured down upon their village* from the heights overhead. Since that time, the *figlie di Maria* of Nerano are the first to put in an appearance at Termini on the festive 14th day of May, and the last to depart homewards—and gratis.

* The rock-strewn relics of this place can be seen about half-way up on the left side of the direct footpath connecting Nerano with Termini, and immediately under the hill. Or this may have been one of the villages destroyed by the Corsairs in 1558.

Then, two years ago, there was that affair of the grasshoppers. . . .

Sometimes, too, he fashions a boat out of a walnut with a tiny sail to it, and steps on board. In this cockle-shell he paddles out from among the rocks with the merest phantom of an oar; but the barque swells to a goodly size as he recedes from land, and lucky fishermen have sometimes met the saint cruising about in broad daylight: he likes to take his pleasure on the water, like any other *cristiano*.

A very mysterious transaction took place in the Middle Ages. The present patron of Massa is no longer San Costanzo but San Cataldo, an Irishman who terminated his mild mission in the seventh century at Taranto, where there used to be a wonderful wooden statue of him (now replaced by the usual metal abomination), and where his epitaph, which has a familiar sound, may still be read—

> *Me tulit Hibernae, Solimae traxere, Tarentum*
> *Nunc tenet: huic ritus, dogmata, iura dedi.*

In Capri, however, there is a deserted shrine of San Cataldo, and we are told that long ago the men of Capri "piously robbed the bones of San Costanzo from Massa, where he used to be protector, and made *him* their patron, which he still is". In short, it seems as if the two communities, with some little violence, had "swopped saints".

In those troubled days, San Costanzo was useful at Capri for scaring away the Saracens with his torch, and this is the attitude in which he used to be conventionally depicted. Now, inasmuch as it stands to reason that an ordinary torch would have been ineffectual for this purpose, we must assume that he was granted the power to brandish some more conspicuously effulgent meteor, probably a *fax ardens*; or perhaps a *capra saltans*, a *lancea*, a *trabs verticalis*, a *draco volans*, a *clypeus*, *stipula*, *pyramis*, *jaculum*, or some other of those fiery coruscations which Cardan*—or is it

---

* Correct as this particular proposition of Cardan's may be, it would be wrong to esteem him unassailable at all points, as has been done. He errs, to my thinking, in respect of the salamander. Your salamander is a cold lizard, hairless and poisonous by nature, and while all of this family have four legs and a head, yet none save the true salamander can withstand the action of fire. Though generated in the flames, as Aristotle in one passage affirms (he contradicts it in another), his cold is nevertheless held to be such as to extinguish them. Pliny, Galen, Aelian, Dioscorides and others of the ancients hold this view. Olympiodorus and Saint Augustine, with other Christian Fathers, likewise. Even so Nierembergius, who

Paracelsus?—conjectures to be the excrements of the stellar firmament.

Yes, I can well believe that THE INFINITE was the one original product of mediæval cogitations and their chief intellectual legacy to posterity; that word epitomizes the intellectual inertia and moral dyspepsia of those times.

Lucky the mortal who arrives on the summit of San Costanzo during one of those bewitching moments when the atmosphere is permeated with a glittering haze of floating particles, like powdered gold-dust. The view over the Gulf of Naples, at such times, with its contours framed in a luminous aureole rather than limned, is not easily forgotten. They are rare, and their glory of brief duration. On other occasions this fairy-like effect is atoned for by the clarity; not only Siren land, but half Campania, lies at our feet. Far away, the sinuous outlines of Tyrrhenian shores with the headland of Circe and the Ponza islets that call up grim memories of Roman banishments; the complex and serrated Apennines whose peaks are visible into the far Abruzzi country; nearer at hand, Elysian Fields, Tartarus and Cimmerian gloom, and the smoking head of Vesuvius decked with a coral necklace of towns and villages. Not an inch of all this landscape but has its associations. Capua and Hannibal; the Caudine Forks; Misenum and Virgil; Nisida, the retreat of a true Siren-worshipper, Lucullus; the venerable acropolis of Cumæ; Pompeii; yonder Puteoli, where the apostle of the gentiles touched land; here the Amalfitan coast, Pæstum, and the Calabrian hills.

And everywhere the unharvested sea. The sea, with its intense restfulness, is the dominant note of Siren land. There is no escaping from it. Incessant gleams of light flash from that mirror-like expanse; even when unperceived by the senses, among squalid tenements or leafy uplands, they will find you out and follow, like some

---

elucidates certain of the opinions of his predecessors touching the matter. And likewise, to my amazement, the illustrious Cardan. For is it not improbable, I ask, that so exiguous a creature should quench a fire however great, or even permanently live in it? Wherefore I submit as follows: That the salamander, by reason of his chilly humour, may well extinguish a small fire, but never a great one; and that, if placed in a combustion similar to the one which flickered about the above-mentioned Shadrac, Meshac and Abednego, he may, and does, survive for some days or even years, but not—like the pyrausta, Charistian Birds and other fire-loving creatures—for ever. *Profiteor me haud alio sensu hanc sententiam proferre, aut accipi ab omnibus velle quam quo ea solent, quae humana tantummodo auctoritate, etc. etc.*

all-pervading, inevitable melody. How the *Odyssey* throbs with those luminous vibrations! Forest voices are the music of Bach; we seem to wander in cool wooded glades with sunlight pouring through leaves overhead, to breathe the fragrance of dew-spangled moss and fern, to hear the caress of light winds playing among the crowns and the rustling of branches and streamlets and all those elfish woodland notes which the master himself, in his solitary wanderings, had heard and thenceforth emprisoned everlastingly—coaxing their echoes into those numbers whose enchantment none but chosen spirits, little less than angels, can unseal. Some are of multiple voice, like that god-gifted Tschaikovsky, whose melancholy is flecked by exotic passions such as Mozart or Beethoven never sang—for how shall that come out of a man which was never in him?—lilting, super-sensuous measures from old Samarkand where they loved with the love of dæmons; muffled pulsations, oft-repeated, doom-enforcing; or an ominous metallic quaver—the wail of the myriad Tartars who fell by the blood-stained waters of Tengis, or, it may be, some premonitory cry of his own tormented soul that fled from earth, all too soon.

Others may reflect the camp or court. But Homer voices the sea. . . .

There are many spots on earth as fair as the Parthenopean bay—equally fair at least to us moderns, whose appreciation of art and of nature has become less exclusively human. The steaming Amazonian forests and the ice-crags of Jan Mayen appeal since yesterday to our catholic taste; but whoever takes the antique point of view will still accord the palm to the Mediterranean. Here, true beauty resides with its harmony of form and hue—here the works of man stand out in just relation to those of nature, each supplementing the other. Elsewhere, she is apt to grow menacing—gloomy or monstrous. In the North, the sun refuses her aid and man struggles with the elements; he vegetates, an animated lump of blubber and dirt, or rushes frantically in starving hordes to overrun the bright places of earth; in the tropics his works shrink into insignificance, he is lost in a fierce tangle of greenery, sucked dry by the sun, whom he execrates as a demon—he dwindles into a stoic, a slave. Here, too, an ancient world, our ancient world, lies spread out in rare charm of colour and outline, and every footstep is fraught with memories. The lovely islands of the Pacific have a past, but their past is not our past, and men who strike deep notes in such alien soil are like those who forsake their families and traditions to live among gipsies. Niagara will astound the senses, but the ruins of Campania wake up sublimer and more enduring emotions.

No person of culture, however prosaic, will easily detach himself from such scenes and thoughts—is it not the prerogative of civilized man to pause and ponder before the relics of his own past?

It is time to depart. The swallows have flown overhead on their long journey, and the redbreast's plaintive whistle announces that the summer is ended.

And how much there is still to see—the remains of Pollio's temple with the baths of Queen Joan, and crumbling towers and sites innumerable! Yonder is Erche, for instance—a commanding plateau opposite Santa Maria surrounded by ravines on three sides and within a few hundred yards of which the old Roman road to Minerva's temple must have passed: how came the name of Hercules to wander so far inland? And only the other day I found my way to a solitary group of houses called Scuola, a singular appellation which reminds me of that *school* of poets and philosophers which was imagined to lie near the promontory of Athenæum; the Sirens' songs, according to Pontanus, being nothing but the irresistible seduction of eloquence and literary pursuits. "What has been said of the sweet voices and songs of the Sirens is a fable illustrating the attractions of eloquence, and the cult of knowledge of letters." Was it not good of the old humanist to associate the Sirens with lettered ease? At Scuola, too, there stands a decayed chapel with a pavement of hand-painted tiles that depict the expulsion of our first parents from Paradise. They shine with the lustre of eternal youth and, to judge by the date, the work may well have been executed by the hand of the celebrated Lionardo Chiaiese who, together with his two brothers, was a pioneer of majolica in Naples, and whose two other pavements, at Anacapri and in the Neapolitan nunnery of Suor Orsola Benincasa, are considered masterpieces impossible to reproduce with modern methods. The scene is drawn with great freedom and taste, and I have endeavoured, twice, to interest certain folks at Naples to safeguard it ere the crazy roof,* through which green plants are vigorously sprouting, shall crash

* It has since fallen in. See my *Looking Back*, p. 225.

down upon the stern young archangel and all the wondrous beasts of the garden.

It is the same everywhere. Go where you will, new discoveries and suggestions are lying in wait; impossible to avoid stumbling upon relics of Roman rule, of old Hellas, or mediæval romance that are crowded into these few miles. The memories start up at our feet, like the fabled dragon-brood of Cadmus. These are the delights of Siren land.

But the summer is ended, though there may well be another kind of Siren land where we can take our joy at all seasons, if so disposed. Not in the stars, however: nobody but Plato would have thought of making the Sirens live in those remote spheres. What you cannot find on earth is not worth seeking.

Yet there will still come days of sunlit splendour—Saint Martin's summer, they call them—when the sea uplifts an unruffled countenance to the crystalline dome overhead, which then looks so securely built as though it could never be broken up—days when it might be well to sail over to Capri once more or to examine the site of the old Siren temple at Fontanella near Massa (if such it was), whose marbles were hammered to pieces and scattered broadcast in the year of grace 1896. "It is best not to speak of these things," said my informant, who witnessed the desecration. Montorio, though he knew nothing of the temple buried beneath the soil, relates that a religious procession used to wend to this spot in former days and to salute it with cannon-shots, as if a spectral Siren-cult had persisted far into Christian times—— Enough! The half is better than the whole, and whoso hurries unduly will never catch the *genius loci* of these regions. Fontanella and the rest of them must wait for another season, since the scanty olives are gathered and vine leaves changing to yellow.

Cicadas no longer sing.

Green patches have sprung up on the burnt Tore yonder.

The summer is ended.

FOUNTAINS IN THE SAND

I
EN ROUTE

LIKELY enough, I would not have remained in Gafsa more than a couple of days. For it was my intention to go from England straight down to the oases of the Djerid, Tozeur and Nefta, a corner of Tunisia left unexplored during my last visit to that country—there, where the inland regions shelve down towards those mysterious depressions, the Chotts, dried-up oceans, they say, where in olden days the fleets of Atlantis rode at anchor. . . .

There fell into my hands, by the way, a volume that deals exclusively with Gafsa—Pierre Bordereau's *La Capsa ancienne: La Gafsa moderne*—and, glancing over its pages as the train wound southwards along sterile river-beds and across dusty highlands, I became interested in this place of Gafsa, which seems to have had such a long and eventful history. Even before arriving at the spot, I had come to the correct conclusion that it must be worth more than a two days' visit.

The book opens thus: *One must reach Gafsa by way of Sfax.* Undoubtedly, this was the right thing to do; all my fellow-travellers were agreed upon that point; leaving Sfax by a night train, you arrive at Gafsa in the early hours of the following morning.

One must reach Gafsa by way of Sfax. . . .

A fine spirit of northern independence prompted me to try an alternative route. The time-table marked a newly opened line of railway which runs directly inland from the port of Sousse; the distance to Gafsa seemed shorter; the country was no doubt new and interesting. There was the station of Feriana, for instance, celebrated for its Roman antiquities and well worth a visit; I looked at the map and saw a broad road connecting this place with Gafsa; visions of an evening ride across the desert arose before my delighted imagination; instead of passing the night in an uncomfortable train, I should be already ensconced at a luxurious table d'hôte, and so to bed.

The gods willed otherwise.

In pitch darkness, at the inhuman hour of 5.55 a.m., the train crept out of Sousse: sixteen miles an hour is its prescribed pace. The weather grew sensibly colder as we rose into the uplands, a stricken region, tree-less and water-less, with gaunt brown hills receding into the background; by midday, when Sbeitla was reached, it was blowing a hurricane. I had hoped to wander, for half an hour or so, among the ruins of this old city of Suffetula, but the cold, apart from their distance from the station, rendered this impossible; in order to reach the shed where luncheon was served, we were obliged to crawl backwards, crab-wise, to protect our faces from a storm which raised pebbles, the size of respectable peas, from the ground, and scattered them in a hail about us. I despair of giving any idea of that glacial blast: it was as if one stood deprived of clothing, of skin and flesh—a jabbering anatomy—upon some drear Caucasian pinnacle. And I thought upon the gentle rains of London, from which I had fled to these sunny regions, I remembered the fogs, moist and warm and caressing: greatly is the English winter maligned! Seeing that this part of Tunisia is covered with the for-saken cities of the Romans who were absurdly sensitive in the matter of heat and cold, one is driven to the conclusion that the climate must indeed have changed since their day.

And my fellow-traveller, who had slept throughout the morning (we were the only two Europeans in the train), told me that this weather was nothing out of the common; that at this season it blew in such fashion for weeks on end; Sbeitla, to be sure, lay at a high point of the line, but the cold was no better at the present terminus, Henchir Souatir, whither he was bound on some business connected with the big phosphate company. On such occasions the natives barricade their doors and cower within over a warming-pan filled with the glowing embers of desert shrubs; as for Europeans—a dog's life, he said; in winter we are shrivelled to mummies, in summer roasted alive.

I spoke of Feriana, and my projected evening ride across a few miles of desert.

"Gafsa . . . Gafsa," he began, in dreamy fashion, as though I had proposed a trip to Lake Tchad. And then, emphatically:

"*Gafsa?* Why on earth didn't you go over Sfax?"

"Ah, everybody has been suggesting that route."

"I can well believe it, Monsieur."

In short, my plan was out of the question; utterly out of the question. The road—a mere track—was over sixty kilometres in length and positively unsafe on a wintry night; besides, the land lay 800 metres in height, and a traveller would be frozen to death. I must go as far as Majen, a few stations beyond Feriana; sleep there in an Arab funduk (caravanserai), and thank my stars if I found any one willing to supply me with a beast for the journey onward next morning. There are practically no tourists along this line, he explained, and consequently no accommodation for them; the towns that one sees so beautifully marked on the map are railway stations—that and nothing more; and as to the broad highways crossing the southern parts of Tunisia in various directions—well, they simply don't exist, *voilà!*

"That's not very consoling," I said, as we took our seats in the compartment again. "It begins well."

And my meditations took on a sombre hue. I thought of a little overland trip I had once undertaken, in India, with the identical object of avoiding a long circuitous railway journey—from Udaipur to Mount Abu. I remembered those "few miles of desert".

Decidedly, things were beginning well.

"If you go to Gafsa," he resumed, "—if you really propose going to Gafsa, pray let me give you a card to a friend of mine, who lives there with his family and may be useful to you. No trouble, I assure you!"

He scribbled a few lines, addressed to "Monsieur Paul Dufresnoy, Engineer", for which I thanked him. "We all know each other in Africa," he said. "It's quite a small place—our Africa, I mean. You could squeeze the whole of it into the Place de la Concorde. . . . Nothing but minerals hereabouts," he went on. "They talk and dream of them, and sometimes their dreams come true. Did you observe the young proprietor of the restaurant at Sbeitla? Well, a short time ago some Arabs brought him a handful of stones from the mountains; he bought the site for two or three hundred francs, and a company has already offered him eight hundred thousand for the rights of exploitation. Zinc! He is waiting till they offer a million."

Majen. . . .

A solitary station upon the wintry plain—three or four shivering Arabs swathed in rags—desolation all around—the sun setting in an angry cloud. It was a strong impression; one realized, for the first time, one's distance from the life of civilized man. Night descended with the rush of a storm and, as the friendly train disappeared from my view, I seemed to have taken leave of everything human. This feeling was not lessened by my reception at the funduk, whose native manager sternly refused to give me that separate sleeping-room which, I had been assured, was awaiting me and which, as he truthfully informed me, was even then unoccupied. The prospect of passing the night with a crowd of Arabs was not pleasing.

Amiability being unavailing, I tried bribery, but found him adamantine.

I then produced a letter from the Resident of the Republic in Tunis, recommending me to all the *bureaux indigènes* of the country, my translation of it being confirmed and even improved upon, at the expense of veracity, by a spahi (native cavalryman) who happened to be present, and threatened the man with the torments of the damned if he failed to comply with the desires of his government.

"The Resident", was the reply, "is plainly a fine fellow. But he is not the *ponsechossi*."

"Ponsechossi. What's that?"

"This," he said, excavating from under a pile of miscellaneous rubbish a paper whereon was displayed the official stamp of the *Ponts et Chaussées*—the Department of Public Works for whose servants this choice apartment is—or rather ought to be—exclusively reserved: the rule is not always obeyed.

"Bring me THIS"—tapping the document proudly—"and you have the room."

"Could I at least find a horse in the morning—a mule—a donkey —a camel?"

"We shall see!" And he slouched away.

There was nothing to be done with the man. Your incorruptible Oriental is always disagreeable. Fortunately, he is rather uncommon.

The excellent spahi, whom my letter from headquarters had considerably impressed, busied himself meanwhile on my behalf, and at seven in the morning a springless, open, two-wheeled Arab cart, drawn by a moth-eaten old mule, was ready for my conveyance to Gafsa. In this instrument of torture were spent the hours from 7.30 a.m. to 4.30 p.m., memories of that ride being blurred by the physical discomfort endured. Over a vast plateau framed in distant mountains we were wending in the direction of a low gap which never came nearer; the road itself was full of deep ruts that caused exquisite agony as we jolted into them; the sun—a patch of dazzling light, cold and cheerless. At this hour, I reflected, the train from Sfax would already have set me down at Gafsa.

Save for a few stunted thorns in the moister places, the whole land, so far as the eye could reach, was covered with halfa-grass—leagues upon leagues of this sad grey-green desert reed. We passed a few nomad families whose children were tearing out the wiry stuff—it is never cut in Tunisia—which is then loaded on camels and conveyed to the nearest depot on the railway line, and thence to the seaboard. They were burning it here and there, to keep themselves warm; this is forbidden by law, but then—there is so much of it on these uplands, and the wind is so cold!

The last miles were easier travelling, as we had struck the track from Feriana on our left. Here, at an opening of the arid hills, where the road begins to descend in a broad, straight ribbon, there arose, suddenly, a distant glimpse of the oasis of Gafsa—a harmonious line of dark palm trees, with white houses and minarets in between. A familiar vision, and often described; yet one that never fails of its effect. A man may weary, after a while, of camels and bedouin maidens and all the picturesque paraphernalia of Arab life; or at least they end in becoming so trite that his eyes cease to take note of them; but there are two spectacles, ever new, elemental, that correspond to deeper impulses: this of palms in the waste—the miracle of water; and that of fire—the sun.

A low hill near the entrance of the town (it is marked Meda Hill on the map) had attracted my attention as promising a fine view. Thither, after settling my concerns at the hotel, I swiftly bent my steps; it was too late; the wintry sun had gone to rest. The oasis still lay visible, extended at my feet; on the other side I detected, some three miles away, a white spot—a house, no doubt—standing by a dusky patch of palms that rose solitary out of the stones. Some subsidiary oasis, probably; it looked an interesting place, all alone there, at the foot of those barren hills.

And still I lingered, my only companion being a dirty brown dog, of the jackal type, who walked round me suspiciously and barked, or rather whined, without ceasing. At last I took up a stone, and he ran away. But the stone remained in my hand; I glanced at it, and saw that it was an implement of worked flint. Here was a discovery! Who were these carvers of stones, the aboriginals of Gafsa? How lived they? A prolonged and melodious whistle from the distant railway station served to remind me of the gulf of ages that separates these prehistoric men from the life of our day.

As if to efface without delay that consoling impression, my downward path led past a dark cavern before which was lighted a fire that threw gleams into its recesses; there was a family crouching around it; they lived in the hollow rock. A high-piled heap of bones near at hand suggested cannibalistic practices.

These, then, are the primitives of Gafsa. And for how long, I wonder, has this convenient shelter been inhabited? From time immemorial, perhaps; ever since the days of those others. And, after all, how little have they changed in the intervening thousands of years! The wild-eyed young wench, with her dishevelled hair, ferocious bangle-ornaments, tattooings, and nondescript blue rags open at the side and revealing charms well fitted to disquiet some robust savage—what has such a creature in common with the rest of us? Not even certain raptures, misdeemed primeval; hardly more than what falls to man and beast alike. On my appearance, she rose up and eyed me unabashed; then sank to the ground again, amid her naked and uncouth cubs; the rock, she said, was warmer than the black tents; they paid no rent; for the rest, her man would return forthwith. And soon there was a clattering of stones, and a herd of goats scrambled up and vanished within the opening.

The partner was neither pleased nor displeased at seeing me there; every day he went to pasture his flock on the slopes of the opposite Jebel Guettor, returning at nightfall; he tried to be civil but failed, for want of vocabulary. I gave him the salutation, and passed on in the gloaming.

II

BY THE OUED BAIESH

THIS collecting of flint implements grows upon one at Gafsa; it is in the air. And I find that quite a number of persons have anticipated me in this amusement, and even written tomes upon the subject—it is ever thus, when one thinks to have made a scientific discovery. These stones are scattered all over the plain, and Monsieur Couillault has traced the site of several workshops—*ateliers*—of prehistoric weapons near Sidi Mansur, which lies within half a mile of Gafsa, whence he has extracted—or rather retrieved, for the flints merely lie upon the ground—quantities of instruments of every shape; among them, some saws and a miniature spade.

My collection of these relics, casually picked up here and there, already numbers two hundred pieces and illustrates every period of those early ages—uncouth battle-axes and spear-points; fine needles, apparently used for sewing skins together; the so-called laurel-leaves, as thin as cardboard; knife-blades; instruments for scraping beast-hides—all of flint. What interests me most, are certain round throwing-stones; a few are flat on both sides, but others, evidently the more popular shape, are flat below and rise to a cone above. Of these latter, I have a series of various sizes; the largest are for men's hands, but there are smaller ones, not more than eleven centimetres round, for the use of children: one thinks of the fierce little hands that wielded them, these many thousand years ago. Even now the natives will throw by preference with a stone of this disc-like shape—the cone pointing downwards. But, judging by the size of their implements, the hands of this prehistoric race can hardly have been as large as those of their modern descendants.

Then, as now, Gafsa must have been an important site; the number of these weapons is astonishing. Vast populations have drifted down the stream of time at this spot, leaving no name or mark behind them, save these relics fashioned, by the merest of chances, out of a practically imperishable material; steel and copper would have rotted away long ago, and the stoutest palaces crumbled to dust under the teeth of the desert air.

The bed of the Oued Baiesh, which flows past Gafsa and is nearly half a mile broad in some places, is rich in these worked flints which have been washed out of its steep banks by the floods. Walking here the other day with a miserable young Arab who, I verily believe, had attached himself to me out of sheer boredom (since he never asked for a sou), I observed, in the distance, a solitary individual, a European, pacing slowly along as though wrapped in meditation; every now and then he bent down to the ground.

"That's a French gentleman from Gafsa. He collects those stones of yours all day long."

Another amateur, I thought.

"But not like yourself," he went on. "He picks them up, bad and good, and when they don't look nice he works at them with iron things; I've seen them! He makes very pretty stones, much prettier than yours. Then he sends them away."

"How do you know this?"

"I've looked in at his window."

A modern "atelier" of flints—this was an amusing revelation. Maybe—who knows?—half the museums of Europe are stocked with these superior products.

Sages will be interested to learn that Professor Koken, of Tübingen, in a learned pamphlet, lays it down that these flints of Gafsa belong to the Mesvinian, Strepyan, Præchellean—to say nothing of the Mousterian, Aurignacian, Solutrean, Magdalenian, and other types. So be it. He further says, what is more intelligible to the uninitiated, that a bed of hard conglomerate which crops up at Gafsa on either side of the Oued Baiesh, has been raised in days of yore; it was raised so slowly that the river found time to carve itself a bed through it during the process of elevation; nevertheless, a certain class of these artificial implements, embedded since God knows when, already formed part of this natural conglomerate ere it began to uplift itself. This will give some idea of the abysm of time that lies between us and the skin-clad men that lived here in olden days.

An abysm of time. . . .

But I remembered the cave-wench of the Meda Hill. And my

companion to-day was of the same grade, a characteristic semi-nomad boy of the poorest class; an orphan, of course (they are nearly all orphans), and quite abandoned. His whole vocabulary could not have exceeded one hundred and fifty words; he had never heard of the Apostle of Allah or his sacred book; he could only run, and throw stones, and endure, like a beast, those ceaseless illnesses of which only death, an early death as a rule, is allowed to cure them. His clothing was an undershirt and the inevitable burnous, brown with dirt.

"What have you done to-day?" I asked hin.

"Nothing."

"And yesterday?"

"Nothing. Why should I do anything?"

"Don't you *ever* wash?"

"I have nobody to wash me."

Yet they appreciate the use of unguents. The other day a man accidentally poured a glassful of oil into the dusty street. Within a moment a crowd of boys were gathered around, dabbling their hands into it and then rubbing them on their hair; those that possessed boots began by ornamenting them, and thence conveyed the stuff to their heads—the ground was licked dry in a twinkling; their faces glistened with the greasy mixture. "That's good," they said.

Such, I daresay, were the pastimes of those prehistoric imps of the throwing discs, and their clothing must have been much the same.

For what is the burnous save a glorified aboriginal beast-skin? It has the same principle of construction; the major part covers the human back and sides; the beast's head forms the hood; where the forefeet meet, the thing is tied together across the breast, leaving a large open slit below, and a smaller one above, where the man's head emerges.

The character of the race is summed up in that hopeless garment, which unfits the wearer for every pleasure and every duty of modern life. An article of everyday clothing which prevents a man from using his upper limbs, which swathes them up, like a silkworm in its cocoon—can anything more insane be imagined? Wrapped therein for nearly all their lives, the whole race grows round-shouldered; the gastric region, which ought to be protected in this climate of extremes, is exposed; the heating of their heads, night

and day, with its hood, cannot but injure their brains; their hands
become weak as those of women, with claw-like movements of the
fingers and an inability to open the palm to the full.

No wonder it takes ten Arabs to fight one negro; no wonder their
spiritual life is apathetic, unfruitful, since the digits that explore
and design, following up the vagrant fancies of the imagination,
are practically atrophied. You will see beggars who find it too
troublesome, on cold days, to extricate their hands for the purpose
of demanding alms! Man has been described as a tool-making
animal, but the burnous effectually counteracts that wholesome
tendency; it is a mummifying vesture, a step in the direction of
fossilification. Will the natives ever realize that the abolition of this
sleeveless and buttonless anachronism is one of the conditions of
their betterment? Have *they* made the burnous, or vice-versa? No
matter. They came together somehow, and suited one another.

The burnous is the epitome of Arab inefficiency.

They call it simple, but like other things that go by that name, it
defeats its own objects of facilitating the common operations of life.
It is amusing to watch them at their laundry-work. Unless a man
stand still and upright, the end of this garment is continually
slipping down from his shoulders; one of the washerman's hands,
therefore, is employed in holding it in its place; the other grasps
a stick upon which he leans while stamping a war-dance with his
feet upon the linen. This is only half the performance, for a friend,
holding up *his* cloak with one hand, must bend over and ladle the
necessary water upon the linen with the other. Thus two men are
requisitioned to wash a shirt—a hand of one, two feet of the other.
No wonder they do not wash them often; the undertaking, thanks
to the burnous, is too complicated.

Yet there is no denying that it adds charm to the landscape; it is
highly decorative; its colour and shape and peculiar texture are
as pleasing to the beholder as must have been the toga of the old
Romans (which, by the way, was a purely ceremonial covering,
to be doffed during work: so Cincinnatus, when the senators
found him at the plough, went in to dress in his toga ere receiving
them).

Stalking along on their thin bare shanks, their glittering eyes and
hooked noses shaded within its hood, many adult Arabs assume a
strangely bird-like appearance; while the smooth-faced youths,
peering from under its coquettish folds, remind one of third-rate

actresses out for a spree. In motion, when some half-naked boy sits merrily upon a galloping stallion, his bare limbs and flying burnous take on the passionate grace of a panathenaic frieze; it befits equally well the repose of old age, crouching at some street-corner in hieratic immobility.

Yes, there is no denying that it looks artistic; the burnous is picturesque, like many antediluvian things. And of course, where nothing better can be procured, it will protect you from the cold and the stinging rays of the sun. But if a European wants a chill in the liver or any other portion of the culinary or postprandial department, he need only wear one for a few days on end; raise the hood, and you will have a headache in ten minutes.

Nevertheless I have bought one, and am wearing it at this very moment. But not as the poorer Arabs do. Beneath it there is a suit of ordinary winter clothing, as well as two English ulsters—and this *indoors*. Perhaps this will give some idea of the cold of Gafsa. There is no heating these bare rooms with their icy walls and floorings: out of doors a blizzard is raging that would flay a rhinoceros. And the wind of Gafsa has this peculiarity, that it is equally bitter from whichever point of the compass it blows. Let those who contemplate the supreme madness of coming to the sunny oasis at the present season of the year (January) bring not only Arctic vestment, eiderdowns, fur cloaks, carpets and foot-warmers, but also, and chiefly, efficient furnaces and fuel for them.

For such things seem to be unknown hereabouts.

III

THE TERMID

THE chief attractions of Gafsa, beside the oasis, are the tall minaret with its prospect over the town and plantations, and the Kasbah or fortress, a Byzantine construction covering a large expanse of ground and rebuilt by the French on theatrical lines, with bastions and crenellations and other warlike pomp; thousand of blocks of Roman masonry have been wrought into its old walls, which are now smothered under a modern layer of plaster divided into square fields, to imitate solid stonework. It looks best in the moonlight, when this childish cardboard effect is toned down.

One of the two hot springs of Gafsa is enclosed within this Kasbah, while the other rises near at hand and flows into the celebrated baths—the *termid*, as the natives, using the old Greek word, still call it. It is a large and deep stone basin, half full of warm water, in which small fishes, snakes and tortoises disport themselves; the massive engirdling walls demonstrate its Roman origin. Thick mists hang over the *termid* in the early mornings, when the air is chilly, but later on it becomes a lively place, full of laughter and splashings. Here, for a sou, you may get the boys to jump down from the parapet and wallow among the muddy ooze at the bottom; the liquid, though transparent, is not colourless, but rather of the blue-green tint of the aquamarine crystal; it flows rapidly, and all impurities are carried away.

There are always elderly folk idling about these premises, and youngsters with rods tempting the fish out of the water; day after day the game goes on, the foolish creatures nibble at the bait and are drawn up on high; their fellows see the beginning of the tragedy, but never the end, where, floundering in the street, the victims cover their silvery scales with a coating of dust and expire ignominiously, as unlike live fishes as if they came ready cooked out of the kitchen *panés et frits*.

Above this basin is another one, that of the women; and below it, at the foot of a lurid stairway, a suite of subterranean (Roman) chambers, a kind of Turkish bath for men, where the water hurries darkly through; the place is reeking with a steamy heat, and objectionable beyond words; it would not be easy to describe, in the language of polite society, those features in which it is most repulsive to Europeans.

How easily, as in former days, might now a health-giving wonder be created out of these waters of Gafsa, that well up in a river of warmth and purity, only to be hopelessly contaminated! The French tried the experiment, but the natives objected, and they gave way: these are the spots of the sunny ideal of "pacific penetration". Any other nationality—while allowing the Arabs a fair share of the element—would simply have rebuilt this *termid* and put it to a decent use, in the name of cleanliness and civilization; the natives acquiescing, as they always do when they recognize their masters. Or, if a display of force was considered inadvisable, why not try the *suaviter in modo*? Had a couple of local saints been judiciously approached, the population would soon have discovered that the *termid* waters are injurious to health and only fit for unbelievers. What is the use of a *marabout*, if he cannot be bribed?

I am all for keeping up local colour, even when it entails, as it generally does, a certain percentage of local smells; yet it seems a pity that such glorious hot springs, a gift of the gods in a climate like this, should be converted into a *cloaca maxima*, especially in Gafsa, which already boasts of a superfluity of open drains.

But my friend the magistrate showed me a special bathing-room which has lately been built for the use of Europeans. We tried the door and found it locked.

Where was the key?

At the *Ponts et Chaussées*.

Thither I went, and discovered an elderly official of ample proportions dozing in a trim apartment—the chief of the staff. Great was this gentleman's condescension; he bade me be seated, opened his eyes wide, and enquired after my wants.

The key? The key of the *piscine*? He regretted he could give me no information as to its whereabouts—no information whatever. He had never so much as seen the key in question; perhaps it had been lost, perhaps it never existed. Several tourists, he added, had already come on the same quest as myself; he also, on one occasion last year, thought he would like to take a bath, but—what would you? There was no key! If I liked to bathe, I might go to the tank at the gardens of Sidi Ahmed Zarroung.

I gently insisted, pointing out that I did not care for a walk across the wind-swept desert only to dip myself into a pool of luke-warm and pestilentially sulphureous water. But "the key" was evidently a sore subject.

"There is no key, Monsieur"; and he accompanied the words with a portentous negative nod that blended the resigned solicitude of an old and trusted friend with the firmness of a Bismarck. This closed the discussion; with expressions of undying gratitude, and a few remarks as to the palpable advantages to be derived from keeping a public bathing-room permanently locked, I left him to his well-earned slumbers. . . .

It is hard to understand what the guide-books mean when they call the market of Gafsa "rich and well-appointed": a five-pound note, I calculate, would buy the entire exhibition. The produce, though varied, is wretched; but the scenery fine. Over a dusty level, strewn with wares, you look upon a stretch of waving palms, with the distant summit of Jebel Orbata shining in the deep blue sky Here are a few butchers and open-air cooks who fry suspicious-looking bundles of animal intestines for the epicurean Arabs; a little saddlery; half a camel-load of corn; a broken cart-wheel and rickety furniture put up to auction; one or two halfa-mats of admirable workmanship; grinding-stones; musty pressed dates, onions, huge but insipid turnips and other green things, red peppers——

Those peppers! An adult Arab will eat two pounds of them a day. I have seen native women devouring, alternately, a pepper, then a date, then another pepper, then another date, and so on, for half an hour. An infant at the breast, when tired of its natural nourish-ment, is often given one of these fiery abominations to suck, as an appetizer, or by way of change and amusement. Their corroding juices are responsible for half the stomach troubles of the race; a milk diet would work wonders as a cure, if the people could be induced to do things by halves; but they cannot; it is "all peppers or all milk", and, the new diet disagreeing with them at first, they return to their peppers and a painful disease.

It is this lack of measure and reasonableness among them which accounts for what I believe to be a fact, namely, that there are more reclaimed drunkards among Arabs than among ourselves. They will break off the alcohol habit violently, and for ever. And this they do not out of principle, but from impulse or, as they prefer to call it, inspiration; indeed, they regard our men of fixed principles as weaklings and cowards, who stiffen themselves by artificial rules because they cannot trust their judgments to deal with events as they arise—(the Arab regards terrestrial life as a chain of accidents) —cowards and infidels, trying to forestall by human devices the unascertainable decrees of Allah.

Allah wills it! That is why they patiently bear the extremes of hunger, and why, if fortune smiles, they gorge like Eskimos, like boa-constrictors. I have seen them so distended with food as to be literally incapable of moving. Only yesterday, there swept past these doors a bright procession, going half-trot to a lively chant of music: the funeral of a woman. I enquired of a passer-by the cause of her death.

"She ate too much, and burst."

During the summer months, in the fruit-growing districts, quite a number of children will "burst" in this fashion every day.

Mektoub! the parents then exclaim. It was written.

And no doubt there is such a thing as a noble resignation; to defy fate, even if one cannot rule it. Many of us northerners would be the better for a little *mektoub*. But this doctrine of referring everything to the will of Allah takes away all stimulus to independent thought; it makes for apathy, improvidence, and mental fossilification. A creed of everyday use which hampers a man's reasoning in the most ordinary matters of life—is it not like a garment that fetters his hands?

Mektoub is the intellectual *burnous* of the Arabs. . . .

There is some movement, at least, in this market; often the familiar story-tellers, surrounded by a circle of charmed listeners; sometimes, again, a group of Soudanese from Khordofan or Bournu, who parade a black he-goat, bedizened with gaudy rags because devoted to death; they will slay him in due course at some shrine; but not just now, because there is still money to be made out of his ludicrous appearance, with an incidental dance or song on their own part. Vaguely perturbing, these negro melodies and thrummings; their reiteration of monotony awakens tremulous echoes on the human diaphragm and stirs up hazy, primeval mischiefs.

And this morning there arrived a blind singer, or bard; he was

led by two boys, who accompanied his extemporaneous verses—
one of them tapping with a pebble on an empty sardine-tin, while
the other belaboured a beer-bottle with a rusty nail: both solemn
as archangels; there was also a professional accompanist, who
screwed his mouth awry and blew sideways into a tall flute, his eyes
half-closed in ecstatic rapture. Arab gravity never looks better than
during inanely grotesque performances of this kind; in such moments one cannot help loving them, for these are the little episodes
that make life endurable.

The music was not altogether original; it reminded me, with its
mechanical punctuations, of a concerto by Paderewski which contains an exquisite movement between the piano and kettle-drum—
since the flute, which ought to have supported the voice, was
apparently dumb, although the artist puffed out his cheeks as if
his life depended upon it. Only after creeping quite close to the
performers could I discern certain wailful breathings; this brave
instrument, all splotched with variegated colours, gave forth a
succession of anguished and asthmatic whispers, the very phantom
of a song, like the wind sighing through the branches of trees.

IV

STONES OF GAFSA

THERE are interesting walks in the neighbourhood of Gafsa, but I can imagine nothing more curious than the town itself; a place of some five thousand inhabitants, about a thousand of whom are Jews, with a sprinkling of Italian tradespeople and French officials and soldiers. Beyond naming the streets and putting up a few lamps, the Government has left it in its Arab condition; the roadways are unpaved, hardly a single wall is plumb; the houses, mostly one-storeyed, lean this way and that, and, being built of earthen-tinted sun-dried brick, have an air of crumbling to pieces before one's very eyes.

A heavy and continuous shower would be the ruin of Gafsa; the structures would melt away, like that triple wall of defence, erected in mediæval times, of which not a vestige remains. Yet the dirt is not as remarkable as in many Eastern places, for every morning a band of minor offenders is marched out of prison by an overseer to sweep the streets. Sometimes an upper room is built to overlook, if possible, the roadway; it is supported on palm-rafters, forming a kind of tunnel underneath. Everywhere are immense blocks of chiselled stone worked into the ephemeral Arab clay as doorsteps or lintels, or lying about at random, or utilized as seats at the house entrance; they date from Roman or earlier times—columns, too, some of them adorned with lotus-pattern, the majority unpretentious and solid.

What do the natives think of these relics of past civilization? Do they ever wonder whence they came or who made them? "The stones are there," they will tell you. Yet the wiser among them will speak of *Ruman*; they have heard of *Ruman* moneys and antiquities.

Arabs have a saying that Gafsa was founded by Nimrod's armour-bearer; but a more reasonable legend, preserved by Orosius and others, attributes its creation to Melkarth, the Libyan and Tyrian Hercules, hero of colonization. He surrounded it with a wall pierced by a hundred gates, whence its presumable name, Hecatompylos, the city of a hundred gates. The Egyptians ruled it; then the Phœnicians, who called it Kafaz—the walled; and after the destruction of Carthage it became the retreat and treasure-house of Numidian kings. Greeks, too, exercised a powerful influence on the place, and all these civilized peoples had prepared Gafsa to appreciate the beneficent rule of the Romans.

Then came vandals and Byzantines, who gradually grew too weak to resist the floods of plundering Arab nomads; the rich merchants fled, their palaces fell to ruins; the town became a collection of mud huts inhabited by poor cultivators who lived in terror of the neighbouring Hammama tribe of true Arabs, that actually forbade them to walk beyond the limits of the Jebel Assalah —a couple of miles distant. So the French found them in 1881.

There are, however, a few decent houses, two-storeyed and spacious; in one of them, I am told, lives the family of Monsieur Dufresnoy, to whom my fellow-traveller at Sbeitla gave me a card. He is absent at Metlaoui mines just now, and his wife and children in Paris.

The cleansing of the streets by prisoners does not extend to the native houses and courtyards, which therefore survive in all their original, inconceivable squalor—squalor so uncompromising that it has long ago ceased to be picturesque. What glimpses into humble interiors, when native secretiveness has not raised a rampart of earthen bricks at the inside of the entrance! In the daytime it is like looking into vast, abandoned pigsties, fantastically encumbered with palm-logs, Roman building-blocks and rubbish-heaps which display the accumulated filth of generations—there is hardly a level yard of ground—rags and dust and decay! Here they live, the poorer sort, and no wonder they have as little sense of home as the wild creatures of the waste. But at night, when the most villainous objects take on mysterious shapes and meanings, these courtyards become grand; they assume an air of biblical desolation, as though the curse of Heaven had fallen upon the life they once witnessed; and even as you look into them, something stirs on the ground: it is an Arab sleeping uneasily in his burnous; he has felt, rather than heard your presence, and soon he unwinds his limbs and rises out of the dust, like a sheeted ghost.

It is an uncanny gift of these folks to come before you when least expected; to be ever-present, emerging, one might almost say, out of the earth. Go to the wildest corner of this thinly populated land, and you may be sure that there is an Arab, brooding among the rocks or in the sand, within a few yards of you.

The stones are there. This is another feature which they have in common with the beasts of the earth: never to pause before the memorials of their own past. Goethe says that where men are silent, stones will speak. If ever they spoke, it is among these crumbling, composite walls of Gafsa.

A Roman inscription of the age of Hadrian, which now forms the step of an Arab house, will arrest your glance and turn your thoughts awhile in the direction of this dim, romantic figure. How little we really know of the imperial wanderer, whose journeyings may still be traced by the monuments that sprang up in his footsteps! Never since the world began has there been a traveller in this grandiose style of Hadrian; he perambulated his world like a god, crowned with a halo of benevolence and omnipotence.

And it occurs to me that there must be other relics of antiquity still buried under the soil of Gafsa, which is raised on a mound, like an island, above the surrounding country; particularly in the vicinity of the *termid*, which we may suppose to have lain near the centre of the old town. And where are the paving-stones? The pains-taking John Leo says that the streets of Gafsa are "broad and paved, like those of Naples or Florence". Have they been slowly submerged under the debris of Arabism, or taken up and worked into the masonry of the Kasbah and other buildings? Not one is left: so much is certain.

I borrowed Sallust and tried to press some flavour out of his description of Marius' march to the capture of Gafsa. It was a fine military performance, without a doubt; he led his troops by un-suspected paths across the desert, fell upon the palace, sacked and burnt it, and divided the booty among his soldiers: all this without the loss of a single man. The natives needed a lesson, and they got it; to this day the name of Marius is whispered among the black tents as that of some fabulous hero. But what interests me most is the style of Sallust himself. How ultra-modern this historian reads! His outlook upon life, his choice of words, are the note of to-morrow; and when I compare with him certain writers of the Victorian epoch, I seem to be unrolling a papyrus from Pharaoh's tomb, or spelling out the elucubrations of some maudlin scribe of Prester John.

8

The stones are there. And the quarries whence the Romans drew them have also been found, by Guérin; they lie in the flanks of the Jebel Assalah, and are well worth a visit; legions of bats —*tirlils*, the Arabs call them—hang in noisome clusters from the roof.

Concerning these bats, the following story is told in Gafsa.

Not long ago a rich Englishman came here. He used to go out in the evenings and shoot bats; then he put them into bottles with spirits of wine—he was an amateur of bats. On the day of his departure from the place, he said to the polyglot Arab guide whom he had picked up somewhere on his wanderings:

"You will rejoin me in Tunis in ten days. Bring me more bats— tirlils: *comprenni?*—from this country. I will give you fifty centimes apiece."

"Bon, Monsieur," said the guide, and took counsel with the folks of Gafsa, who, after certain reservations and stipulations, showed him the way into these quarries.

On the day appointed he entered the rich tourist's hotel in Tunis, followed by ten porters, each carrying a large sack.

"Hallo!" said the Englishman, "what's all this?"

"Bats, Monsieur."

"Eh? How much?"

"Bats; *tirlils, chauve-souris, pipistrelli.* . . . They will need much bottles. Six hundred tirlils in each sack; ten sacks; six thousand tirlils. Much bottles! Three thousand francs, Monsieur. Shall I open him?"

The tourist cast a dismayed glance over the sacks, gently heaving with life.

"Look here," he said, "I'll give you fifty francs. . . ."

The Arab was surprised and grieved. He thought he was giving a pleasure to Monsieur, who had asked for bats. He had been obliged to borrow money from his aged mother to help to pay the nine hundred francs which he had already disbursed for assistance in catching the tirlils; he had risked his life; there were the transport expenses, too: very heavy. He had travelled with many Englishmen and had always found them to be men of honour—men who kept their word. And in this case there were witnesses to the bargain, who would be ready, if necessary, to go into the French tribunals and testify to what they had heard. . . .

"I see. Well, come to-morrow morning, but go away now, quick!

before I break your head. Take your damned tirlils to your damned funduk, and be off!—clear out!—*comprenni?*"

And he looked so very angry that the Arab, a prudent fellow, walked backwards out of the room, more surprised and grieved than ever.

Thanks to the disinterested and strenuous exertions of a Jewish international lawyer, the affair was settled out of court after all—fifteen hundred francs, plus expenses of transport.

V

SIDI AHMED ZARROUNG

SIDI AHMED ZARROUNG—that is the name of the miniature oasis visible from the Meda Hill, at the foot of those barren slopes. It is a pleasant afternoon's walk from Gafsa.

The intervening plain is encrusted with stones—stones great and small. Here and there are holes in the ground, where the natives have unearthed some desert shrub for the sake of its roots which, burnt as fuel, exhale a pungent odour of ammonia that almost suffocates you. Once the water-zone of Gafsa is passed, every trace of cultivation vanishes. And yet, to judge by the number of potsherds lying about, houses must have stood here in days of old. An Arab geographer of the eleventh century says that there are over two hundred flourishing villages in the neighbourhood of Gafsa; and Edrisius, writing a century later, extols its prosperous suburbs and pleasure-houses.

Where are they now?

One of these villages, surely, must have lain near this fountain of Sidi Ahmed Zarroung, which now irrigates a few palms and vegetables and then loses itself in the sand; a second spring, sulphureous and medicinal, but destructive to plants, rises near at hand. This is the one which the gentleman of the *Ponts et Chaussées* recommended me for bathing purposes.

I saw no trace of ancient life here; there is only a muddy pond, full of amorous frogs and tortoises, cold-blooded beasts, but fiery in their passions; and a few Arabs that live in the large white house, or camp on the plain around. They told me that the descendants of the holy man who gave his name to the place are still alive, but they knew nothing of his history beyond this, that he was very pious indeed.

If you do not mind a little scrambling, you can climb from here up to the last spur of the Jebel Guettor which overlooks the plain—it is crowned by a ruined building, once whitewashed, and easily visible from Gafsa. On its slopes I struck a vein of iron, another of those scientific discoveries, no doubt, like the flint implements, in which someone else will have anticipated me. And here I also found iron in a more civilized shape, a fragment of a shell—relic, perhaps, of the first French expedition against Gafsa, or of some more recent artillery practice.

From its summit one sees the configuration of the country as on a map; the high Jebel Orbata, 1170 metres, now covered with snow, coming forward to meet you on the other side of the wide valley. From this point it is easily to realize, as did the commander of that French expedition, the significance of this speck of culture, its strategic value: Gafsa is a veritable key to the Sahara. I daresay the abundant water-supply of the town is due to these two chains of hills which almost touch each other and so force the water to rise from its underground bed.

At this elevation you perceive that Gafsa is truly a hill-oasis, bleak mountains rising up on all sides save the south. There, where the two highest ranges converge from east and west, where the broad waterway of the Oued Baiesh has in olden days, when it wandered with less capricious flow, carved itself a channel through the opening—there, at the very narrowest point—sits the oasis. A tangle of palms that sweep southward in a radiant trail of green, the crenellated walls of the Kasbah gleaming through the interstices of the foliage—the whole vision swathed in an orange-tawny frame of desolation, of things non-human. . . .

I was tempted to think that the sunset view from the Meda eminence was the finest in the immediate neighbourhood of Gafsa. Not so; that from the low hills behind Sidi Mansur, with the stony ridge of Jebel Assalah at your back, surpasses it in some respects. Through a gap you look towards the distant green plantations, with a shimmering level in the foreground; on your other side lies the Oued Baiesh, crossed by the track to Kairouan, where strings of camels are for ever moving to and fro, laden with merchandise from the north or with desert products from the oases of Djerid and Souf. The dry bed of the torrent glows in hues of isabel and cream, while its perpendicular mud-banks, on the further side, gleam like precipices of amber; the soil at your feet is besprinkled with a profusion of fair and fragile flowerlets.

Here stand, like sentinels at the end of all things living, the three or four last, lonely palms—they and their fellows lower down are fed

by a silvery streamlet which is forced upwards, I suppose, by
contact with Professor Koken's conglomerate; above and below
this oasis-region the river-bed is generally dry. It must be a wonderful sight, however, when the place is in flood—a deluge of liquid
ooze careering madly southward towards the dismal Chotts amid
the crashing of stones and palm trees and the collapse of banks. For
the Oued Baiesh can be angry at times; in 1859 it submerged fifty
hectares of the Gafsa gardens.

Instead of returning by the main road from Sidi Mansur, one
can bend a little to the right and so pass the military hospital, a
large establishment which looks as if it could be converted into a
barrack in case of need. This is as it should be. Gafsa is a rallying-
point, and must be prepared for emergencies. Here, too, lie the
cemeteries: the Jewish, fronting the main road, with a decent
enclosure; that of the Christians, framed in a wire fence and containing a few wooden crosses, imitation broken columns and tinsel
wreaths; Arab tombs, scattered over a large undefined tract of
brown earth, and clustering thickly about some white-domed
maraboutic monument, whose saintly relics are desirable com-
panionship for the humbler dead.

The bare ground here is littered with pottery and other fragments
of ancient life testifying to its former populousness: flint implements,
among the rest. Of the interval between the latest of these stone-age
primevals and the first Egyptian invasion of Gafsa we know nothing;
they, the Egyptians, brought with them that plough which is figured
in the hieroglyphics, and has not yet changed its shape. You may
see the venerable instrument any day you like, being carried on a
man's back to his work in the oasis.

Athwart this region there runs an underground (excavated)
stream of water, led from Sidi Mansur to nourish the Gafsa plantations. Through holes in the ground one looks down upon the
element flowing mysteriously below; figs and other trees are set in
these hollows for the sake of the shade and moisture, and their
crowns barely reach the level of the soil. This is no place to wander
about at night—a false step in the darkness and a man would break
his neck. There was talk, at one time, of leading this brook, which
is sweet and non-mineral, into Gafsa for drinking purposes, but the
native garden proprietors raised their inevitable howl of objections,
and the project was abandoned.

If you ask a local white man as to the misdeeds of his adminis-

tration, be sure he will mention the affair of the railway station
which was built too far from the town, and this of the Sidi Mansur
water. And who, you ask, was to blame for these follies? Oh, the
controlleur, as usual; always the *controlleur*! It is no sinecure being an
official of this kind in Tunisia, with precise Goverment instructions
in one pocket, and in the other his countrymen's contrary lamen-
tations and suggestions, often reasonable enough. . . .

Loaded down with a choice selection of Sidi Mansur flints, which
are singular as having a white patina, I returned to Gafsa in the late
afternoon and entered my favourite Arab café. Here, at all events,
if you do not mind a little native *esprit de corps*, you will be able to
thaw your frozen limbs; all the other rooms of Gafsa, public and
private, are like ice-cellars. There are many of these coffee-houses
in the town, and this is one of the least fashionable of them. Never
a European darkens its door; seldom even a native soldier; it is not
good enough for them; they go to finer resorts.

At its entrance there lie, conveniently arranged as seats, some old
Roman blocks, overshadowed by a mulberry, now gaunt and bare.
It must be delightful, in the spring-time, to sit under its shade and
watch the street-life: the operations at the neighbouring dye-shop
where gaudy cloths of blue and red are hanging out to dry, or,
lower down, the movement at the wood-market—a large tract of
"boulevard" encumbered with the impedimenta of nomadism.
There is a ceaseless unloading of fuel here; bargains are struck about
sheep and goats, the hapless quadruped, that refuses to accompany
its new purchaser good-naturedly, being lifted up by the hind legs
and made to walk in undignified fashion on the remaining two.
Fires gleam brightly, each one surrounded by a knot of camels
couched in the dust, their noses converging towards the flame,
while old desert hags, bent double with a life of hardship, bustle
about the cooking-pots. There are brawls, too—Arabs seizing each
other by the throat, raising sticks and uttering wild imprecations. . . .

But within that windowless chamber, all is peace. Eternal twilight reigns, and your eyes must become accustomed to the gloom
ere you can perceive the cobwebby ceiling of palm-rafters, smoke-
begrimed and upheld by two stone columns that glisten with the
dirt of ages. Here is the hearth, overhung by a few ancient pots,
where the server, his head enveloped in a greasy towel, officiates
like some high priest at the altar. You may have milk, or the mixture
known as coffee or tea flavoured in Moroccan style with mint, or

with cinnamon, or pepper. The water-vessels stew everlastingly upon a slow fire fed with the residue of pressed olives. Or, if too poor, you may take a drink of water out of the large clay tub that stands by the door. Often a beggar will step within for that purpose, and then the chubby serving-lad gives a scowl of displeasure and makes pretence to take away the cup; but the mendicant will not be gainsaid—water is the gift of Allah! And, if so please you, you may drink nothing at all, but simply converse with your neighbour, or sit still and dream away the days, the weeks, the year, sleeping by night upon the floor.

A few of the customers are playing at cards or sedately chatting; others begin to prepare their favourite smoke of hashish. A board is called for and the hashish-powder spread out upon it. The operator chops it into still finer particles by means of a semicircular blade, deftly blowing away the dust—this brings out its strength. He is in no hurry; it is a ceremony rather than a task. Slowly he separates the coarser from the finer grains, his fingers moving with loving deliberation over the smooth board. Then the cutting process is repeated once more, and yet again. Maybe he will now add a little of the Soufi stuff, to improve the taste.

At last all is ready, and small pipes are extracted from the folds of the burnous and filled with half a thimbleful of the precious mixture. Two or three whiffs, deeply inhaled, stream out at mouth and nostrils; then the pipe is swiftly passed on to a friend, who drains the last drop of smoke and knocks out the ashes. Not a word is spoken.

Hand him your pipe, if you are wise, and let him fill it for you. This *kif*, they say, affects people differently; but I think that, as a general effect, you will discover a genial warmth stealing through your limbs, while the things of this world begin to reveal themselves in a more spiritual perspective.

I thought of the sunset this afternoon, as viewed from Sidi Mansur. They are fine, these moments of conflagration, of mineral incandescence, when the sober limestone rocks take on the tints of molten copper, their convulsed strata standing out like the ribs of some agonized Prometheus, while the plain, where every little stone casts an inordinate shadow behind it, clothes itself in demure shades of pearl. Fine, and all too brief. For even before the descending sun has touched the rim of the world the colours fade away; only overhead the play of blues and greens continues—freezing, at last, to pale indigo. Fine, but somewhat trite; a well-worn subject, these Oriental sunsets. Yet the man who can revel in such displays with a whole heart is to be envied of a talisman against many ills. I can conceive the subtlest and profoundest sage desiring nothing better than to retain, ever undiminished, a childlike capacity for these simple pleasures. . . .

A spirit of immemorial eld pervades this tavern. Silently the shrouded figures come and go. They have lighted the lamp yonder, and it glimmers through the haze like some distant star.

And I remembered London at this sunset hour, a medley of tender grey-in-grey, save where a glory of many-coloured light hovers about some street-lantern, or where a carriage, splashing through the river of mud, leaves a momentary track of silver in its rear. There are the nights, of course, with their bustle and flare, but nights in a city are apt to grow wearisome; they fall into two or three categories, whose novelty soon wears off. How different from the starlit ones of the south, each with its peculiar moods and aspirations!

Yet the Thames—odd how one's *kif*-reveries always lead to running water—the Thames, I know, will atone for much. It is even more impressive at this season than in its summer clarity, and as I walk, in imagination, along that rolling flood flecked with patches of unwholesome iridescence and crossed by steamers and barges that steer in ghostly fashion about the dusky waters, I marvel that so few of our poets have responded to its beauty and signification. They find it easier, doubtless, to warble a spring song or two. The fierce pulsations of industry, the shiftings of gold that make and mar human happiness—these are themes reserved for the bard of the future who shall strike, bravely, a new chord, extracting from the sombre facts of city life a throbbing, many-tinted romance, even as out of that foul coal-tar some, who know the secret, craftily distil most delicate perfumes and colours exquisite. The bard of the future . . . h'm! Will he ever appear? As an atavism, perhaps. Take away from modern poetry what appeals to primitive man— the jingle and pathetic fallacy—and the residue, if any, would be better expressed in prose.

My neighbour, a sensible person, has ceased to take interest in the proceedings. Perched upright at first, his head drooping within the folds of his cloak, he has slowly succumbed; he has kicked off his sandals, stretched himself out, and now slumbers. I, too, am beginning to feel weary, and no wonder. . . .

8*

Primitive man with those flints of his, that weigh me down at this moment. This stone-collecting, *par exemple!* I wonder what induced me to take up such a hobby. The German Professor, as usual. Ah, Mr. Koken, Mr. Koken—those light words of yours have borne a heavy fruit. I possess four hundred implements now, and they will double the weight of my luggage and ruin my starched shirts, especially those formidable "præchellean" skull-cleavers. And I know exactly what the customs officer at Marseilles will say, when he peeps into my bag:

" *Tiens, des cailloux! Monsieur est botaniste?* "

And then a crowd of people will assemble, to whom I must explain everything, with the result of being arrested for smuggling forbidden mining samples out of a colony and ending my days in some insanitary French prison.

VI

AMUSEMENTS BY THE WAY

MEANWHILE, to satiate myself with Gafsa impressions, I linger by the margin of the pool that lies below the fortress. Hither the camels are driven to slake their thirst, arriving sometimes in such crowds as almost to fill up the place. Donkeys and horses are scoured by half-naked lads; in the clearer parts, a number of tattooed Bedouin girls are everlastingly washing their household stuffs. Only on rare occasions is the liquid undisturbed, and then it shines with the steely-blue transparency of those diamonds that are a class by themselves, superior to "first-water" stones. At the slightest agitation all the accumulated ooze and filth of generations—rags and decomposing frogs and things unmentionable—rise to the surface in turbid clouds. The element wells out hot, from under the neighbouring Kasbah, with a pestiferous mineral aroma.

Hither comes, at fixed intervals, my friend Silenus, the water-carrier, on his philosophic donkey; nearly all Gafsa draws its supply of cooking and drinking water from this fetid and malodorous mere.

A fine example of French inefficiency, this "*abreuvoir*". Two hundred francs would suffice to tap the liquid a few yards higher up, by means of a common cast-iron pipe, whence it would rush out, pure and undefiled, to fill in a few moments those multitudinous water-skins that are now laboriously furnished, by hand, out of the often tainted pool below.

And of native inefficiency, likewise. Day after day, age after age, have these women done their laundry-work at this spot, and yet their clothing, for purposes of the work, is more hopelessly inadequate than the burnous of the males. They will arrive wrapped up in twenty rags that are always falling off their backs and shoulders (they possess no baskets). One by one these articles are removed, soaped with one little hand, stamped upon by two little feet, and laid aside. Nothing remains, at last, but a single covering garment—

a loose chemise full of artistic possibilities for the onlookers. It gives the poor girls endless trouble, for it is continually slipping off their bodies on one side or the other, and one hand is engaged, all the time, in counteracting these mischievous movements. Standing as they do up to their knees in the water, it is tucked up high and of course tumbles down again every minute. At the end of their washing they are as wet as drenched poodles.

No harm in this, in summer-time; but with the thermometer below freezing-point they would suffer considerably were they not inured, like other creatures of the desert, to every kind of discomfort.

The chief mental exercise of the Arab, they say, consists in thinking how to reduce his work to a minimum. Now this being precisely my own ideal of life, and a most rational one, I would prefer to put it thus: that of many kinds of simplification they practise only one—*omission*, which does not always pay. They are imaginative, but incredibly uninventive. How different from the wily Hindu or Chinaman, with his almost preternatural sagacity in small practical matters! Scorn of theories is one of their chief race-characteristics, and that is why they end in becoming stoics—stoics, that is, as the beasts are, who suffer without knowing why.

There was one of these girls in particular whom I noticed every day, and whom, at last, I compassionately supplied with a couple of safety-pins, after explaining their uses. She was decidedly ugly. But sometimes you may see others here, with neatly chiselled limbs and elfish eyes of a sultry, troubling charm into which, if sentimentally disposed, you can read an ocean of love; these need not be supplied with safety-pins. An enthusiastic Frenchman at Gabes actually married one of these sphinx-like creatures—a hazardous and quixotic experiment. As brides for a lifetime (slaves) they cost from a hundred to six hundred francs apiece, and even more; and you will do well to *abonner* yourself with the family beforehand, in order to be sure of obtaining a sound article, as with the Tartar girls in Russian Asia and elsewhere. As a general rule, those of the semi-nomads—the Gourbi people—cost more than those of the true wanderers. The price varies according to the season and a thousand other contingencies; it rises, inevitably, in the neighbourhood of settled places, where employment of one kind (olive-picking, etc.) or another—chiefly of another—can be found for them.

One of the prettiest I ever saw was offered me for three hundred francs. It was an uncommon bargain, due to a drought and certain family mishaps. These little wildlings are troublesome to carry about. They are less nimble and amiable than the boys, and often require more beating than a European has time to give them. You can always sell them again, of course; and sometimes (into the towns) at a good profit.

The Arab woman is the repository of all the accumulated nonsense of the race, and her influence upon the young brood is retrogressive and malign. It matters little what happens in the desert where men and women are necessarily animals, but it does among the middle and upper native classes of the larger places. Here the French have established their so-called Arab-French schools, excellent institutions which are largely attended, and would produce far better results but for the halo of sanctity with which boys in every country—but particularly in half-civilized ones—are apt to invest the most flagrantly empty-headed of mothers. In Tunisia, as soon as the youngsters return home, these women quickly undo all the good work, by teaching them that what they have learnt at school is dangerous untruth, and that the Koran and native mode of life are the only sources of happiness. Then, to keep the son at home, the mother will hasten to catch a bride for him who shall be, if possible, more incompetent than herself, in order that she, the mother, may retain her ascendancy over him. The father, meanwhile, shrugs his shoulders: *Mektoub!* There is no fighting against such heroic perseverance on a woman's part; besides, was he not brought up on the same lines?

The mischief is done, for Arabs relapse easily; even native officers, who have served for years in the French army, will, on returning home, don the burnous, sit at street corners, and become more *arabized* than ever. So it comes about that, if the eyes of the former generation were entirely averse from French rule, the present one is Janus-faced—looking both ways. Some day, presumably, there will be a further adaptation, and their eyes, like those of certain flatfish, will wander round and settle down definitely on the right side. . . .

This is a favourite month for native weddings. There was one going on last night. I looked into the courtyard of a ruinous building which was crammed with spectators. The Aissouyiahs were performing, in honour of the occasion.

These are the dervish fanatics whom everyone knows. They eat scorpions, glass, nails, and burning coals; they cut themselves with knives and other instruments—impostors, for the most part.

It is mere child's play to what you can see further East.

Yet, with the starry night overhead, and the flare of torches lighting up a seething mass of faces below, of bronzed limbs and bright-tinted rags dangling at every altitude from the palm rafters and decayed stairway, the scene was more weirdly fascinating than as one generally sees it—in mosques or in the open daylight. There were wild strains of music and song; a wave of disquietude, clearly, was passing over the beholders. These performances, at such a time, may originally have taken place for purposes of nuptial excitement or stimulation; but it requires rather an exotic mentality to be stimulated, otherwise than unpleasantly, by the spectacle of little boys writhing on the ground in simulated agony with a long iron skewer thrust through their cheeks. They catch them young; and these scholars, or aspirants, are indubitably frauds and often worse than frauds. Mixed with them are a certain proportion of unbalanced, half-crazy individuals, who really work themselves into a frenzy and give the semblance of veracity to the entertainment. A judge of native physiognomy can generally tell the two types apart. There are also a few sensible men—butchers, porters, and the like—who do not mind a little pain for the sake of the profit.

For the rest, the ceaseless mandarin-like head-wagglings and mutterings of the names of Allah would stupefy anyone's brain up to a point. It is not only Arabs who daze their understandings with godly ejaculations, oft repeated. The marabout leader, who is a kind of *maître de ballet*, enfolds each performer in his arms and makes a few passes round him, or kisses him. The uninitiated then reel off in a trance of hypnotic joy; the others do the same, in more theatrical fashion. At the end of each one's trick he demesmerizes him once more, and perhaps touches the wound with his hands. He passes the skewer or sword between his lips as a disinfectant—a wise precaution.

These lacerations heal quickly. I have spoken to men labouring in the fields on the day following such excesses, and found them ready to "work" again the same evening.

It ended up with a beast-dance—two fine negroes, all but naked, depicting the amorous rages of panthers or some other cat-like feral. This was really good, of its kind; and if, as regards the earlier part of the programme, it was still difficult to tell where religion ended and sensuality began (it sometimes is), there was no doubt about the last item, which was purely sadistic. Soon there issued the familiar trillings from the balcony, and the firing-off of guns, to announce that the drama was terminated.

It is we shrinkingly æsthetic creatures who conjure up by a mere effort of the imagination what these blunt folk cannot conceive without gross visual stimulants. That is because they have not enjoyed our advantages; they are not civilized. Among other things, they have not gone through a "reformation". Take a northern stock, sound in mind and body; infuse into it a perverse disrespect for the human frame and other anti-rational whimsies; muddle the whole, once more, by a condiment of Hellenistic renaissance and add, as crowning flavour, Puritan "conscience" and "sinfulness"— mix up, in a general way, good nourishment with ascetic principles —and you will attain to a capacity of luxuriance in certain matters that may well be the envy and despair of poor primitives like the Arabs.

Extremes meet. Performances such as these are beyond good and evil. They are for the wholly savage or the wholly civilized. We complain considerably just now of the swamping of class distinctions in our lands, but a man of culture has a prerogative to which the biliously moral middle classes can never aspire: to be an Arab, when it suits him.

VII

AT THE CAFÉ

WHETHER it be due to the incessant cold and dry winds, that parch the more genial humours, or to some other cause, there is certainly a tone of exacerbation, at this moment, among the European residents at Gafsa. I noticed it very clearly yesterday evening in the little French café—a soul-withering resort, furnished with a few cast-iron tables and uncomfortable chairs that repose on a flooring of chill cement tiles—where, in sheer desperation, two or three of us, muffled up to our ears, congregate before dinner to exchange gossip and imbibe the pre-prandial absinthe.

I announced my intention of leaving shortly for Tozeur.

"So you have not yet taken your fill of dirt and discomfort in Tunisia, Monsieur?" asked one of the clients. He is a wizened old nondescript with satyr-like beard, a kind of Thersites, who is understood to have established, from the days of Abdelkader and for "certain reasons", his headquarters at Gafsa, where he sips absinthes past all computation, exercising his wit upon everybody and everything with a fluent and rather diverting pessimism. "You will probably perish on the road to Tozeur, in a sand-storm."

"Ah, those sandstorms: they interest me. Have you ever been to Tozeur?"

"God forbid! Gafsa is quite bad enough for me. Or you may be strangled by the Arabs; such things occur every day. You smile? Read the papers! At some places, like Sfax, there are regular organized bands of assassins, the police being doubtless in their pay. Be sure to hold your revolver in readiness—better carry it in your jacket pocket, like this. . . . No revolver! (To the company at large) *He has no revolver!* In that case, don't dream of going out after sunset, here or anywhere else in this country. And read the papers."

It was always "read the papers".

I mentioned that I had walked home, at midnight on the previous evening, from the station.

"Then don't do it again, if you value your life. Not long ago a lieutenant was attacked on that very road, and almost beaten to death. He managed to crawl back to barracks, and is now a wreck, incapacitated from further service. By a miracle he was able to identify one of his assailants. They gave him—what do you think?— two years' imprisonment! Why not the *Légion d'Honneur* while we are about it? Then there was the Italian—a respectable Italian, for a wonder—who went out for a walk and was never heard of again. The country was scoured for two months, but not so much as a button was ever found—not a button! They had buried his body in the sand. That's their usual system, cheap and effective. And the guide-books say that Tunisia is as safe as the heart of France— ha, ha, ha! I wonder how much they are paid for making that statement, and who pays it?"

"The hotel proprietors, with an occasional subsidy from the Government." This from a bloodthirsty young extremist in gaiters and riding-breeches, who had once been a *colon*, a farmer, but had given it up in disgust. "We cherish these savages," he went on, "as if they were our uncles and aunts; everywhere, that is, save in those districts which are still under military rule. There you should see the natives stand up and salute you! I am anti-military myself; but I maintain that this salute should be kept up, as demonstrating the gulf that exists between ourselves and them. But the moment you leave the zone the gulf is systematically bridged over, to make it more pleasant for the poor, misused Arab. Let me tell you what I think. I think that the Sicilians would have managed things better than we have done. And I also think that our *controlleurs*, they are not Frenchmen, but Arabs."

"*Voyons, voyons!*" said a clear voice from another table—a new-comer, apparently. "These are the criticisms to which we are exposed, because we introduce an enlightened and progressive policy."

"Progressive policy be damned! We have held Gafsa for the last thirty years, and what have we done to improve the place? Nothing."

"Pardon me! We have planted twenty-seven pepper trees. Tunisia exists for needy people in search of work. If you can't make it pay, leave it alone. You have every facility for buying land, for importing this and that—why don't you settle down and make yourselves at home? A colony, my friend, is not an orchid."

"And as for those Sicilians," interposed the faun-like wooer of the Green Fairy, "I think you're all wrong. I admit that they are more flexible than we are, if you like to put it that way. They will do things that no Frenchman can do; they will establish themselves in places where no Frenchman could live; they will eat things which no Frenchman could swallow; they will oust the very Arabs out of the country in course of time, by sheer number of progeny and animal vitality. Oh, yes; it's clear the Sicilians can lower their standard to any extent. But they can never raise it. They are the cancer of Tunisia. Wherever they go, they bring their filth, their *mafia*, roguery and corruption. Every Sicilian is a potential Arab, the difference between them being merely external; the true African variety wears less clothes and keeps his house cleaner. I know them! A race of sinister buffoons and cut-throats, incapable of any ennobling thought, whose highest virtues are other men's vices, whose only method of reasoning is the knife. . . . Don't accuse me, Messieurs, of prejudice, when I am trying to state the case impartially."

You will often hear it put as baldly as that. The alien inhabitants of Tunisia are well hated by a certain type of Frenchmen. The country has been compared to a wine-bottle that bears some high-flown label indicative of fine stuff within—the French administration—but is filled, unfortunately, with a poisonous mixture from round the corner, the Jews, Sicilians, Maltese, and Corsicans.

It is as difficult for a tourist to arrive at a just opinion on this subject as for the average Frenchman. The traveller will not find it easy to acquire the necessary first-hand data, while the other is warped by his congenital xenophobia.

In 1900 there were 80,000 Italians, mostly Sicilians, in the Regency, as opposed to 20,000 Frenchmen, one-half of whom were Government servants. This great predominance of a foreign stock scared some good folks, and a *Comité du peuplement français* was organized, to study ways and means of populating Tunisia with French citizens.

If Sicilians could obtain grants of land under the same conditions as Frenchmen, large tracts, now waste, would be converted into gardens, to the profit of the exchequer. Is it worth while? No, thinks the Government; and with reason. French rule in Northern

Africa is a politico-moral experiment on a large scale, with what might be called an idealistic background, such as only a civilized nation can conceive. Italians might improve the land, but they could never improve the Arab; they are themselves not sufficiently wise, or even well-intentioned.

The Anti-Semitic agitation has died a natural death: you may curse the Jews, but you cannot crush them. They make good citizens, and are for ever trying to gain more political influence, which is surely to their credit, though it annoys a certain class in Tunis. As intermediaries between the Arab and the white man they are invaluable, their plasticity allowing them to ascend or descend in either direction, while their broad and active tolerance, fruit of bitter experience in the past, has honeycombed the land with freemasonry and scientific charity and liberalism. So far as I can see, their dirt does not detract from their astuteness—perhaps it aids it, by removing one source of mental preoccupation, cleanliness. The old distinction between Livornese and Tunisian Jews is slowly becoming effaced.

If there is one class of these immigrants whom the ordinary French employé hates more than another it is his own countrymen, the Corsicans. They have the gift of climbing into small but lucrative posts of administration, and there, once established, they sit fast like limpets, to the dismay of competing French office-seekers. Eject them? You might as well propose to uproot Atlas or Ararat. Not only can they never be displaced, but from year to year, by every art, good or evil, they consolidate their position. That done, they begin to send for their relations. One by one new Corsicans arrive from over the sea, each forming a centre in his turn, where he sits tight, with a pertinacious solidarity that borders on the super-human.

Cave-haunting savages at heart, and enemy to every man save their own blood relations, the Corsicans are the nightmare of the Arabs on account of their irreclaimable avarice and brutality. They would flay the native alive, if they dared, and sell his skin for boot-leather. They can play at being *plus arabes que les arabes*, and then, if the game goes against them, they invoke their rights of French citizenship in the grand manner. The Frenchman knows it all; he regrets that such creatures should be his own compatriots—regrets, maybe, that he is not possessed of the same primordial pushfulness and insensibility; and shrugs his shoulders in civilized despair.

As for the Maltese, they would be all very well if—if they were not British subjects. But such being the case, you never know! It is disheartening to find such babble in the mouth of respectable officials and writers.

I am well aware that there is a Sicilian *in fabula* who is not *mafioso*; that the crude banditism which sits in every Corsican's bones has raised him to the elysium of martyrs and heroes and not, where he ought to have gone, to the gallows; that the Maltese are not merely cantankerous and bigoted (Catholic) Arabs, but also sober, industrious, and economical. I have lived with all these races in their own countries and—apart from a fatal monkey-like apprehensibility which passes for intelligence but, as a matter of fact, precludes it—have found chiefly this to admire in them, that they are prolific and kind to their offspring.

Small praise? Not altogether. The same may apply to cats and dogs, but it does not always apply to civilized races of men. The Scotsman, for instance, can produce children, but is often unkind to them (*Read the papers!*); the Frenchman is kind to children, but often cannot produce them. It would seem that chiefly in half-cultured people are these two qualities, twin roots of racial and domestic virtues, to be met with side by side.

Whatever may be the cause of it—better food, a different legislation or climate, or contact with other nations—the suggestive fact remains, that the more objectionable idiosyncrasies of the Maltese, Corsicans and Sicilians become diluted on African soil. Can it be the mere change from an island to a continent? There may be some truth in Bourget's "*oppression des îles*". *Insulani semper mali*, says an old Latin proverb. . . .

"Do you know," the gaitered young ex-farmer was saying—"do you know how many French *colons* there are in the whole Regency? Eight or nine hundred, drowned in an ocean of Arabs, who own the land. And that's what we call settling a country. The Americans knew better when they cleared out the redskins! And how do the English manage in India? Why, they shoot them—*piff-paff*: it's done! That's the way to colonize (looking approvingly at me)—*supprimez l'indigène!* A nation cannot condescend to the idealistic ravings of an individual."

I observed that I had never heard of that method being actually adopted in India.

"You say that, Monsieur, because you fear it sounds a little drastic. But we are not in Paris or London just now; we can say what we think. Or better still" (glowing with enthusiasm), "they tie them to the mouth of a big gun, and then—*Boum . . . houplà! ! Biftek à la tartare.*"

"You are misinformed, my friend," said the voice from the other table. "That Indian cannon business was merely an administrative experiment."

I looked at the speaker, who was smiling mirthfully to himself. He was a fair-complexioned man of about forty-five, rather carefully dressed, blue-eyed, with a short, well-groomed beard—evidently an old acquaintance of the company.

"It's all right for you," the other retorted, "with your comfortable offices and your fat, ever-increasing salaries. You are not a harassed agriculturist, skulking in fear of his life, or a public servant, starving on four francs a day. Behold!" he went on, extracting a newspaper out of his pocket, "behold the latest portrait of yourself and your colleagues—you have an air of revolting prosperity. And your whole biography, too, in black and white; your wife, your children, your past career . . . what it is to be a capitalist!"

"*Tiens!* I never saw this. And printed in Paris a fortnight ago! But it may be lying somewhere about the house. I only returned at midday, you know. Not exactly a flattering likeness. . . ."

The document was handed round. It was a French journal devoted to mining interests, and contained a long article dealing with the phosphate industry of Metlaoui, near Gafsa, with views of the works and portraits of its principal representatives. Beneath that of the speaker were printed the words—

"*Paul Dufresnoy,*
Ingénieur civil des mines,"

and some other titles.

An odd coincidence, this meeting, on the eve of my departure.

I passed over to his table and mentioned that I possessed an introductory letter to him.

"How! And you are leaving to-morrow for the Djerid? You are not coming to see me?"

I replied that I would gladly give myself that pleasure. His family, he explained, was away just now, but if I could arrange to delay my departure for a little while he would accompany me as far as Metlaoui, which lies on the Tozeur route, and show me over the mines. He was to return to his work there in a week or so. The proposal was too tempting to be refused.

We spoke of the spirit of irritation and discontent that seemed rife among the Europeans in Gafsa.

"Yes, the wind," he said; "or perhaps Africa generally. I've often noticed that men, and women too, put on new faces and characters hereabouts. This contact with an inferior race upsets their nervous equilibrium. The lack of comfort and the need of abrupt action make them discard gentleness and other external husks of civilization. The mildest of us are liable to become brusque; and harsh ones, brutal. Only the native remains resigned."

Thereupon I propounded my hypothesis of the *Mektoub* or resignation doctrine: the intellectual burnous of the Arabs.

The theory, he thought, was so good that there must be someting wrong with it. His work brought him into daily contact with the natives, and, so far as he could judge, *Mektoub* was only one aspect of their general way of looking at things. It was bound up, for instance, with that idea of impenitence. Unlike ourselves, who approve of self-abasement, the Arab regards repentance as only fit for slaves. He does not hunt for his own sins; he hunts for yours, and hits you on the head when he finds them. There was something in the notion, he thought, for surely remorse was rather a provincial sensation; it implied that a man has really done something wrong, or that he thinks he has; in either case, what was there to boast of? He had little time for studies, nowadays, but it seemed to him that the trend of feeling was in the direction of Old Testamentary ideals. Men were growing tired of offering their other cheek to be smitten; they found it degrading, as do the Arabs. Why not import some of these sterner conceptions into our morality, as we import their peppery curries and kouskous and pilaffs into our cuisine?

He was inclined to say amiable things about the English race. The Anglo-Saxon, he thought, with his "constitutional non-morality", had come nearest to discovering a sensible working system of conduct—as a nation. It is his highest racial virtue to lead the Cosmic Life—to take all he can get, and ask for more. That is why every one, in his heart of hearts, envies and admires him. His chief defect, he thought, was a disdain of a knowledge of general principles, justifiable enough in the times of unsound teleological theorizings, but not nowadays, when we have at last set foot upon earth.

"And what do you say", I asked, "to our so-called national hypocrisy?"

"Well, we others are apt to stand aside and marvel whether you have succeeded by reason of it, or in spite of it. Of course it annoys us beyond words! But there is a form of it which is highly laudable: the Anglo-Saxon, it seems to me, often acts in apparently hypocritical fashion out of consideration for what he conceives to be the opinions of the majority. Profoundly self-respecting, he is equally careful not to impinge upon the feelings of others, however wrongheaded he may think them. In such cases, his hypocrisy is only a proof of civilization and genuine politeness. Hence also that shyness and reserve which I have often noticed in your countrymen— they are not signs of awkwardness or indecision, but of strength systematically controlled."

"That is very gratifying. And what of our snobbishness?"

"The English snobbishness", he replied, "may not be beautiful, but its origins are sufficiently venerable to inspire respect. It testifies to long political stability; it is rooted in Magna Carta. We foreigners, who upset our Governments and annihilate our aristocracies every ten years, will never attain that mellow stage. One may dislike it; one dislikes the by-products of many excellent institutions. Your Government, for example, does extraordinarily little to foster art or literature or research. Taken by itself, that is an evil. But as a by-product of the English cult of the individual— of that avoidance of pestilential State interference in everything which is the curse of continental Europe—it may be gladly endured, if not admired."

He added:

"When one lives out of Europe, Monsieur, one learns to know England better. To see things at their true perspective one must take up a stand at a proper distance from them. England only begins to show its true proportions at a point where other lands cease to be visible. Austria, for instance, can only be examined on the spot. Once you have crossed the insignificant Mediterranean, this immense and fertile country, with its long history of rulers and battles, has already faded into air. *Ça n'existe plus.* Your Gladstone explained the phenomenon correctly: Austria has never done good to the world."

I gathered that the Metlaoui phosphate company had modelled its principles on those of the "Anglo-Saxon". There is little "pestilential State interference" in its management; the board of directors takes all it can get, and asks for more. It is a paying concern, and consequently the shareholders admire it unreservedly —in the rest of mankind, this feeling is tinctured with a strong dose of envy.

VIII
POST-PRANDIAL MEDITATIONS

ONE dines early in Gafsa, and afterwards there is nothing, absolutely nothing, to do. Cafés become tedious with their card-games, cowboy politics and persistent allusions to *la femme*, that protean fetich which dominates and saturates the Gallic mind, oozing out, so to speak, at every pore of their social and national life. They never seem to grow out of the *Ewig-weibliche* stage. If only, like the Maltese, they would talk less and do more in certain respects, the *Comité du peuplement* might close its doors. But such recklessness would ill comport with the ant-like hiving quality which paid back, within I forget how few years, the German war indemnity.

After dinner, therefore, a short promenade about the streets and oasis, to court that illusive phantom, sleep, and to replenish the mind with new and peaceful images. I found a cloudless and relatively warm night. The wind had died down, and there was a brilliant comet (the Johannesburg comet) in the sky. Knots of natives were gazing at it with disfavour: I listened, and heard one of them attributing the Franco-Tripolitan frontier incident to its baleful fires. "And there is more to come," he added, "unless it goes away." Townspeople, of course; the cultivators are asleep long ago.

Why don't you settle down and make yourselves at home? With those words Dufresnoy had put his finger on the spot. The same idea must occur to every one who compares the French method of colonization with that pursued in English dependencies. Even our most ephemeral civil servants take pleasure in "settling down"; they acquire local interests in golf, or native folklore, or butterflies; they manage to surround themselves with an atmosphere of home. Among the *colons* of Tunisia you may find a home establishment of the most comfortable type, but Government employés regard the Regency in the light of an exile; they never try to make their life more endurable, as they easily could do, with a little co-operation.

In Gafsa, for example, where the summer temperature is 100, no ice can be procured unless you drive to fetch it from the station settlement, where the phosphate company has its servants; if you want good vegetables, you must telegraph *inland* for them to Metlaoui, whither they are brought from the sea-coast, via Gafsa, for the consumption of the "company"; fresh fish, which are caught in fabulous quantities at Sfax, and could be transported by every over-night train, are hardly ever visible in the Gafsa market. There is no chemist's shop in the place, not even the humblest drug-store, where you can procure a pennyworth of boric acid or court-plaster. So they live on, indulging all the time in a luxury of lamentation.

There would be better shops in places like Gafsa if foreign commercial settlers were not discouraged from establishing themselves. French ones, needless to say, refuse to "settle".

The hotels in the country places, too, would be better. At present they exist on a system of monopolism and favouritism; it is quite beyond the ambitions of their managers to collect a clientèle; most of these concerns are palpably run on the following principle: to keep the guest in such a state of chattering starvation that he is *ready to eat anything.* How often have I yearned, in these "Grand Hotels"—they are all *grand hotels*—for the material comforts and the decent fare of some little wayside hostelry in Finland, or a rest-house in the jungle of Ceylon!

Why do French travellers not complain oftener?

Well, the Frenchman is a patriotic creature and congenitally kind-hearted; the proprietors of these establishments are country people of his; they are poor devils who have got stranded, somehow or other, in Tunisia; one must have patience with them. Sometimes, however, your self-respecting Gaul is strained beyond the point of patriotic endurance by the concoctions of these Locustas and Borgias; then he unsheathes that dagger-like Neanderthal manner which he carries about with him for rare occasions of self-defence; and it warms the cockles of one's heart to hear how pertinently he discourses damnation to the cringing host. For we non-Frenchmen, be it understood, are all *des déséquilibrés* who demand toast, hot water and such-like exotics; our complaints need not be taken seriously; besides, foreigners are bound to pay in any case. But when a countryman begins to find fault there is not only a possibility that

something, after all, may not be quite right with the cuisine or
drainage, but even a chance that one or two items will be coldly
struck off the reckoning. And that hurts!

They will tell you that there is nothing to be procured in the
market; but if you proceed to the spot, you will at least see succulent
legs of mutton exposed for sale. The *chef* of the establishment, however, when making his morning purchases, passes by these with
scorn, and betakes himself to a little booth whose table is strewn
with dubious scraps of skin and bones, which have already been
fingered and contemptuously thrown aside by fifty dirty Arabs (I
speak as an eye-witness); he buys a few handfuls of these horrors for
three or four sous, and forthwith—hey, presto!—they are transformed into a "ragout à la bretonne" for the famished traveller.
Tunisia is a sheep-rearing country—there are sixty thousand sheep
in the *contrôle* of Gafsa alone—but you may live there a lifetime
before seeing a leg of mutton at a country table d'hôte. For all the
"gigots" that ever appear at my host's entertainment, one might
really think that the muttons of Africa were a peculiar species, a
species without legs: crawling, maybe, on their bellies, like Nebu-
chadnezzar.

"*Je m'en f—de vot' bon-homme*," said one of these gentlemen to me,
referring to Baedeker, with whose sacred pages I had threatened
him. "And as for the tourists, they'll come just the same."

And so they do! But they all end in discovering that even the
worm will turn, when suffering from the torments of *dyspepsia
tunesina veridica sine quâ non.* . . .

A good deal of amateurish talking is done, in Gafsa, in regard to
the profits that would be gained were the oasis to be given over to
Sicilian cultivators. Apart from the fact that the wealthy Kaid of
Gafsa, who is the chief owner of it, would have something to say on
the subject, these advantages would be limited to pruning the trees
and grafting some of them; introducing, possibly, a few more
vegetables, and having the ground more parsimoniously tended than
at present. The magnesia in the water is hostile to the majority of
delicate European growths. Something, no doubt, could be done in
the way of improvement, but as a set-off to a visionary project of
this kind, which is averse to the whole spirit of French rule in
Tunisia, there would be a great rise in prices: Italians would form
their inevitable ring. The extent of the gardens has almost doubled
since 1880, without their help.

As to the Arabs——

If the French looked to their prison system they would soon arrive at better results. For childish thefts and such-like trespasses, committed nearly always at the instigation of their parents, boys of ten and twelve are now locked up with hardened criminals, often for considerable periods: what is this but a State-aided manufacture of crime? Go to the prison of Sfax, and you will realize that there may be some reason for the absinthe-drinker's remark as to the "organized bands of assassins" at that place. I speak of what I have seen with my eyes. I found the prison of Souk-el-Arba, for instance, so tightly packed with men and young boys that there was not room for all of them to lie down at night, and such furious fights used to occur for the possession of places near the wall (the room was in pitch-darkness) that the warder was obliged to enter, every now and then, and restore order by beating those nearest the door about the head with a club.

The Arab boy, they will tell you, is full of guile, and must be repressed.

Granted, but——

A colony, furthermore, is *not an orchid*.

Granted.

Q.E.D.

IX

SOME OF OUR GUESTS

I SHALL be glad to leave for Metlaoui and the Djerid. Gafsa is losing its flavour; the novelty and pungency are gone. The same old faces, the same old *bouts de conversation;* quickly, indeed, does one live oneself into a place and learn, or think to learn, all its little secrets.

The hotel, too, has suddenly become an insufferable menagerie. Mysterious inspectors come and go, and commercial travellers of unappetizing looks and habits are far more frequent than formerly. But I shall regret the earth-convulsing laughter of the Greek doctor, who has latterly taken to putting in an appearance at meal-time. He is a gruff, jovial personage, and so huge in bulk that he can barely squeeze into the door of his little shop in the *souk* where he sits, surrounded by unguents and embrocations, to treat the natives for their multifarious distempers. He is quite straightforward about the business. "You come to this country to spend money," he tells me, "but I—to make it."

The profession is not all plain sailing, however, for the French authorities raise every kind of obstacle in his path; they tear his red advertisements down from the street walls and openly call him a quack. Were it not for the Greek Consul in Tunis, who happens to be an old friend of his, who knows how much longer they would allow him to practise in the land!

I sometimes go to watch his operations, which, so far as I can judge, are fairly remunerative, thanks to Achmet the interpreter, one of whose many duties it is to inform himself confidentially of the financial status of prospective patients. For the richest sheikh will don tattered clothes when he visits the surgery, and would doubtless be taken for some poor labourer were it not for Achmet, who sees through the disguise and gives a discreet sign to Æsculapius, whose services, of course, must be prepaid; it is *money down* before he will prescribe or give away a drop of medicine.

I was much interested in one of his methods as exemplified on the person of a native youth who was led in the other day. He was an Aissouiyah dancer, and had evidently overdone his part in the heat of enthusiasm; there were no less than forty-three sword-cuts across his middle. After receiving a handsome fee the doctor gave him some liniment which caused exquisite pain: the patient writhed in agony.

"That's good medicine," I heard Achmet telling him, reassuringly; "that's strong. See how it hurts!"

For a while he bore up bravely, but the pain growing worse instead of better, the doctor was at last persuaded, out of compassion and in return for a second fee, to give him something with a more soothing effect.

But eye diseases are his speciality. His *pièce de résistance* is a Jewish tradesman whom he has lately supplied with an admirable glass eye —a thing almost unheard of in these parts. This man and myself were sitting in the shop not long ago when a Moroccan happened to be passing who had known him in his one-eyed days; the stranger gave him a sharp look and then walked swiftly away, apparently suspecting himself to be the victim of some absurd hallucination as regards the new eye. But he returned anon, to make sure of his mistake, I suppose; while the Jew confronted him with a defiant glance of his two eyes. They stared at each other for some time in silence. At last the Moroccan enquired:

"Are you the man who sold me that piece of cloth three weeks ago?"

"I am he."

There was another long pause. Then:

"That new eye: how came you by it?"

The Jew, a dreadful scoffer, pointed heavenwards with one finger.

"A thing of God!" he said. "A miracle has been vouchsafed me."

The man of Mequinez answered nothing. He gazed at him once more, and then, slowly bending down his head, folded his hands across his breast in prayer, and walked away. . . .

Then there is the Polish Count, Count Ponomareff, who arrived four days ago. He is past middle age, with a drooping moustache and large red nose; a wistful and woebegone figure, but a brilliant conversationalist, when the mood is upon him. I have not taken very kindly to the man. Among other things, he disapproves of flint-collecting; he asks, rather scornfully, "whether one can sell such stones". And yet, for some obscure reason, he has singled me out among the men as the object of his favourable notice, affecting rather a distant manner towards the rest of us; the ladies, however, are charmed by his courtly graces. He wears profuse jewellery, to set off his title, no doubt. It is understood that he has held high Government posts, and is now only waiting for some letters before joining certain friends in a costly caravan expedition further south. Yet he seems poor—hopelessly poor. I surprised him, soon after his arrival, in a heated debate with the landlord on the subject of candles and *café-au-lait*. Then he enquired if the country was safe.

"Not if you go out with a *machine comme ça*," touching the Count's gorgeous watch-chain.

He knows, at least, how to handle his knife and fork, which is more than can be said of all the inmates of this hostelry. A town-dweller, evidently; he tells me he detests wild life of every kind and has come here only to oblige his friends; he calls the Arabs "ignoble savages".

Such, however, is not the opinion of another guest, my friend Monsieur M——. One must be careful how one criticizes the habits of the natives in his presence; not that he would be angry, for he is too gentle to feel wrath; or become argumentative—he is too sure of his ground for that; but he might be wounded on his most sensitive spot, and he would certainly think you—well, misinformed.

The motley crew of Gafsa have become his favourites ever since his arrival in the country two weeks ago, and he has a theory that it is a mistake to endeavour to learn their language—it only leads you astray, it spoils the "direct impression".

He is a well-known French painter, whom some eye trouble has forced—only temporarily, let us hope—to abandon the brush. Despite his patriarchal beard, he is an impenitent romanticist of contagious youthfulness; the entire universe lies so harmoniously disposed and in such roseate tints before his mental vision, that no one save Madame M——, a wise lady of the formal-yet-opulent type, whom Maupassant would have classed as "*encore désirable*", is able to drag him to earth again, with a few words of wholesome cynicism.

Just for the fun of the thing, and to while away his hours of enforced idleness, he is collecting facts for a book to be entitled *Customs of the Arabs*, as exemplified by the life of Gafsa. The idea came to him quite suddenly, after reading some descriptions which he considered sadly misleading. Customs of the Arabs! To tease him, I quote the authority of Bordereau, who says that there are practically no Arabs in Gafsa; that the customs of this town are one thing and those of the Arabs another, unless he applies the word Arab to all the Mohammedan races of these parts.

The objection is brushed aside; one word is as good as another, *n'est-ce pas?*

I point out a genuine Arab who happens to be passing; he has come down from the hills and is leading a camel loaded with halfa; he is gaunt and ill-clad, but walks with a fine swagger, and is evidently a valuable young person, to judge by his tattooings.

"That? That's only a young savage from the mountains. How are you to find out anything about him? And I make a point, you know, of only recording what I see with my eyes. No theories for me! I mean to see everything and to set it down; to describe the Arabs as they are—as they *really are*, in all the circumstances of their daily lives. One must see everything."

As a painter, I urge, he must have discovered how useful it is to restrict the field of vision now and then; to be deliberately half blind.

"Painting, Monsieur, is one thing, and writing another. It is one of the few advantages of growing old that things begin to fall, so to speak, into their proper places. When I go to my studio, I go for distraction; art, it seems to me, is there to create moods, pleasurable or otherwise; a painter must seize impressions. But I go to my library for information; the business of a writer is to collect and arrange facts; a book, as I apprehend it, should be—a book. That is my quarrel with this Tunisian literature; many of the things that have been written about the country are not books at all; while others are full of mistakes. Look at these two volumes, for instance! Impressionistic realism, I suppose they would call it, scrawled down by an excitable female journalist who, I am sorry to say, has created quite a rage for European and American lady tourists among these Arabs, to the great discredit of our civilization. Read them, Monsieur, as a warning example, and perhaps you will give me your Bordereau instead; there may be something in it, after all."

I gladly make the exchange, and regard the transaction in the light of an omen, an epoch. I have been craving for something different from the facts of Bordereau, who has been my companion all these days. A solid little piece of work, by the way, which often set me wondering whether our British public would care to pay four shillings for a technical account of the climate, history and natural products of some remote Egyptian oasis. But perhaps the cost of production has been defrayed by some Government department.

These two volumes by Isabelle Eberhardt—where have I heard that name before?—look tempting. I promise myself some hours of pleasant reading.

"And then, for downright misstatement," he continued, "look at this. Here is a Monsieur Kocher, who passes for an authority, and who, describing the Arab marriage customs, talks of the '*brutalité du viol dans le marriage—un drame lugubre*'. Now that comes of not examining things with one's own eyes. Since my arrival here I have already seen several Arab weddings and something of their married life, and I must say, candidly, that I find it full of romance. Say what you will, these Arabs are unconscious poets."

"And if you want still further information," I said, "ask the boy whom I saw blacking your boots this morning. He will describe to you the minutest details of his married life with surprising frankness. His father bought him a wife two weeks ago, under the condition, however, that his little brother is to be allowed to share in the joys of matrimony. That young savage from the mountains would blush, if Arabs ever could blush, to hear their revelations."

"Oh, oh, oh! You appal me! But I would like to make personal enquiries into the matter; that is, if I can make them understand me. It is my rule, you know."

"Do, Monsieur; question both the brothers, and write down their answers, the perusal of which will be a liberal education for our boys at home. Among other things, they say that whenever—— But here is Madame coming!"

"Never mind her! She takes an interest in Arab institutions, as I do. . . . Only imagine, Amélie, our shoeblack is said to be actually married; and so is his little brother, and they have one and the same bride! Two husbands to one wife, or half a wife apiece— what do you think of that?"

"I think it's quite enough to begin with. Remember, *mon cher*, they are only children."

9

X

THE OASIS OF LEILA

I RODE, for a farewell visit, to the small oasis of Leila, or Lalla, which lies a few miles beyond the railway station. It is one of several parasitic oases of Gafsa: a collection of mud-houses whose gardens are watered by a far-famed spring, the fountain of Leila.

The water gushes out, tepid and unpleasant to the taste—but health-giving, they say, like so many unpleasant things—from under steep banks of clay through which the railway to Sfax has been cut. It is a sleepy hollow of palms, a place to dream away one's cares. The picturesque but old-fashioned well at this spot has just been replaced by a modern trough of cement. I watched the work from beginning to end, ten or fifteen Arabs, supervised by a burly Sicilian mason, finishing the job in a few days.

"These Saracens!"—such was the overseer's constant lament—"these Saracens! You don't know, dear sir, what fools they are."

In never-ending procession of gaudy rags the village folk come to these waters, the boys mostly on horseback, the women afoot. Donkeys are loaded with the heavy black goat-skins of water; there is laundry work going on, and a good deal of straightforward love-making under the shade. These children of nature have a wild beauty of their own, and the young girls are frolicsome as gazelles and far less timid. They have none of the pseudo-bashfulness of the townsfolk. For the rest only the *dessus du panier* of womanhood goes veiled hereabouts—a few portly dames of Gafsa, that is, who are none the worse, I suspect, for keeping their features hidden. Perhaps the good looks of these Leila people are a heritage from olden days, for this oasis is known to be a race islet, inhabited almost exclusively by men of the Ellez stock—one of the three races that have chiefly contributed to the formation of the modern Gafsa type; a conquering brood of European origin, small but shapely.

But untold ages ere this the waters of Leila were already frequented by men of another kind, by the flint artists. Among the relics of their occupation I picked up, here, an unusually fine implement of the "amygdaloid" shape.

Not a soul in Gafsa, native or foreign, could tell me who was the lady Leila that gave her name to this fountain. On the spot, however, I heard this tale: She was a young girl, madly enamoured of an Arab youth, but strictly guarded. Her married sister alone knew of their infatuation, and used to help her by keeping a look-out for him at the water-side; and when he appeared, she would return home and sing to herself (as if it were a snatch of some old ditty)— Leila, Leila, your lover comes! But the maiden understood, and swiftly, under pretence of fetching water, she would run to meet him at the well, and take her joy. The story has an air of probability; such things are done every day, at every fountain throughout the land. This lingering at the well is one of the moments when their hard life is irradiated by a gleam of romance.

An old man also gave me the following account:

Ages ago, he said, when Gafsa belonged to the Sultan of Trablus (Tripoli) there was sad misgovernment in the land. The taxes became quite unendurable, and the city was half emptied of its inhabitants, who fled this way and that, rather than submit to the extortions of the Sultan's officers. And among those who escaped in this fashion was a god-fearing widow and her children. Her name was Leila. She took up her abode near this fountain, which was then little frequented. Here she dwelt, doing good works whenever occasion offered. And here, at length, she was received into the mercy of Allah and entombed. The country-folk gave her name to the water to perpetuate the memory of her pious life. . . .

The depression beyond this fountain is celebrated as the resort of game, and yesterday a French gentleman of my acquaintance went there, provided with all the accoutrements of sport, not omitting a copious luncheon-basket—there might be snipe or partridges, or perhaps a hare, a gazelle, a leopard—who knows? He returned in good time for dinner.

" Voilà ma chasse! " he said, opening his bag. It contained a bundle of wild asparagus, for salad, and fourteen frogs, which he had killed with a rifle.

"You can't get frogs as easily in my part of France," he told me. "If the sport were not forbidden for seven months out of the twelve, the species would long ago have become extinct."

I enquired whether the close-season for frogs was officially set down, like that of hares or wildfowl.

"Frogs", he explained, "are not considered game in the governmental sense of that word; they fall into the category of fisheries which, as you know, comes under the jurisdiction of the respective prefects. Hence the close-time, though officially fixed, varies according to the different provinces. In my department, for example, it begins on the 15th of January. At Gafsa, if I may judge by certain indications, it would probably be arranged to commence still earlier."

Far be it from me to decry the succulent hams of *Rana esculenta* (or rather *ridibunda*). I have been offered far more fearful wild-fowl nearer home—certain ornithological wrecks, I mean, that have been kept beyond the feather-adhering stage, and then reverently held before a fire, for two minutes, wrapped in a bag, lest the limbs should drop off.

There is considerable talk at Gafsa of the wild mountain sheep, the Barbary moufflon. They say that as late as the early nineties it was no uncommon thing to meet with flocks of over thirty grazing in the mountains. Although a special permit must now be obtained to be allowed to shoot them, their numbers have much diminished. But the accounts vary so wonderfully that one cannot form any idea of their frequency. Some talk of seventeen being shot in the course of two weeks' camping, others of three in a whole season. As a rule, they are not stalked, but driven, by an army of Arabs which the sheikh organizes for that purpose, towards certain openings in the hills where the sportsman takes up his stand. The desert lynx is sometimes met with, and hyenas, they say, occur as near to Gafsa as the Jebel Assalah. Arabs have told me that the fat of the hyena is used by native thieves and burglars to smear on their bodies when they go marauding. The dogs, they say, are so terrorized by the smell of it, so numbed with fear and loathing, that they have not the heart to bark. (Pliny records an ancient notion to the effect that dogs, on coming in contact with the hyena's shadow, lose their voice.)

Here, at the Jebel Assalah, I encountered a jackal—a common beast, but far oftener heard than seen. While resting in a sunny hollow of rock, I heard a wild cry which came from a shepherd who was driving the jackal away from his goats. The discomforted brute trotted in my direction, and only caught sight of me at a few yards'

distance. I never saw a jackal more surprised in my life. When a
camel expires in the plain near some nomads' tents, they sometimes
set a spring-trap for jackals near the carcase—they eat these beasts
and sell their skin for a few francs; the traps are craftily concealed
underground, with a little brushwood thrown over them to aid the
deception. It is impossible to be aware of their existence. But woe
betide the wanderer who steps on them! For the machine closes
with the shock of an earthquake, a perfect volcano of dust and iron
teeth leaping into the air. Its force is such that the jackal's leg is
often cut clean off, and he hops away on the remaining three. For
this and other reasons, therefore, it is advisable not to approach too
near a dead camel.

The desert hare is shot or coursed with muzzled greyhounds,
sloughis, who strike it down with their paws; unmuzzled, they rend
it to pieces. There are few of them in Gafsa just now, on account of
the cold to which they are sensitive; although muffled in woollen
garments they shiver pitifully. Of falconers, I have only met one
riding to the chase. It was the Kaid of Gafsa, a wealthy man of
incalculable political influence both here and in Tunis. It is even
whispered—— But no; one must not repeat all one hears. . . .

With the proprietor's permission I went over a young plantation
of trees and vegetables that has sprung up near the railway line,
about half-way between Gafsa and Leila. Excavating to a depth of
six metres at the foot of the bare Rogib hill, they encountered an
apparently unlimited supply of water, and here, where formerly
nothing but a few scorched grasses and thorns could be seen, is now
a luxuriant little oasis. More might be done with the place, but the
owner seems to have lost interest in it; the locusts, too, have been
rather destructive of late.

He had planted quantities of prickly pears, he said, but the
Bedouins' cattle had devoured them. These are useful growths in
Tunisia, requiring hardly any moisture and forming, when full-
grown, impenetrable walls of spiky green. They also bring in a
respectable revenue. In the district of Kairouan, for instance, many
families draw their entire income from them. A few have been
planted at Sidi Mansur and elsewhere near Gafsa, but they are
unprotected and liable to be trodden down in their early years, or
eaten. Barbed wire, herald of civilization, is almost unknown in
these parts.

Like most tradespeople, this proprietor was rather despondent about the future of Gafsa. There had certainly been some improvement within the last twenty years—slight, but steady; the building of the railway station so far outside the town he considered a disgraceful piece of jobbery, a crime which had permanently injured the prospects of the place. Merchants, he said, are entirely dependent on the state of the Metlaoui mines. If, like last year, these do well, then Gafsa also thrives. If there is a strike or over-production, as at this moment, Gafsa suffers.

Tourists come to this town, he said, but they leave next day. Nothing is done to make their stay agreeable.

The natives are not of a kind to take much interest in its welfare. Gafsa has gone through too many vicissitudes to be anything but a witches' cauldron of mixed races. Seldom one sees a handsome or characteristic face. They have not the wild solemnity of the desert folk, nor yet the etiolated, gentle graces of the Tunisian citizen class; much less the lily-like personal beauty of the blond Algerian Berbers. Apart from some men that possess, almost undiluted, the features of the savage Neanderthal brood that lived here in prehistoric times, the only pure race-type that survives is one of unquestionably Egyptian origin, one to which Monsieur Bordereau, in his book on Gafsa, has already referred. No wonder; since Egyptian invasions of this region went on for centuries, culminating in the extended sea-domination of Thotmes III at the end of the seventeenth century B.C.

A bastard Greco-Latin was the language of the place up to the thirteenth century A.D.

This confusion of blood has done one good thing for them—it has given them considerable tolerance in matters of religion. They are the least bigoted Orientals one could wish to meet. Only fifteen in a hundred, perhaps even less, perform the devotions prescribed by the Prophet. And it is part of their charming heterodoxy to be dog-eaters. They will catch and devour each other's dogs; they even breed them for the market, though they dare not expose the meat publicly, any more than that of swine, which they eat with relish. But up to a few days ago they had never ventured to touch the dog of a foreigner. On Wednesday evening, however, a fox-terrier belonging to a French official was found in the street, dead, with its throat cut. A stream of blood was traced from that spot to the door of a native eating-shop, and enquiries from the neighbours elicited the fact that the cook of the establishment had caught the beast and cut its throat; that the miserable creature, in its dying struggles, had escaped from his grasp and run in the direction of home, only to stagger by the roadside and expire from loss of blood.

There was a wild excitement over this little episode. The dog of a Frenchman killed, for culinary purposes, by an Arab; it was the *comble* of temerity! The owner of the animal, on hearing the news, buckled on his revolver and repaired to the shop with the avowed intention of shooting his man, whom the police, fortunately, had already conjured into some safe place of custody. If he is wise he will languish in prison for some days longer.

Gafsa lies high, and I ask myself whether its fierce shiftings of heat and cold, its nocturnal radiation that splits the very rocks and renders life impossible for many plants (outside the cultivated zone, which equalizes these extremes)—whether all this has not had a numbing and stupefying influence on the character of the inhabitants. Would not a man, under such perennial vexations, end in bowing his head and letting things take their course? I notice the climatic effect upon myself is a growing incapacity for mental effort. It is time to depart for the Djerid, where the sun, they say, still exhales a certain amount of warmth.

Add to this, Arab frugality and the cheapness of native living throughout the country, which removes all stimulus to work. A middle-class citizen tells me that he has just returned from Tunis, where a lawsuit has kept him for two years. He went there with an overland caravan which cost next to nothing; he slept in a *zaouiah*, where he also obtained a bath gratis; he spent on his food four sous a day, neither more or less, and by way of amusement took coffee with his friends or strolled down to the harbour to look at the ships. Six pounds in two years! And natives in authority, who are generally the richest, pay nothing whatever for their nourishment. Like the Kaid of Gafsa, they simply requisition it in the market; the sellers grumble, but conform to custom.

How quickly their looks can improve is shown by those who join the army. In a few months they grow fat, cheerful, and bright-complexioned, thanks to the hygienic life and better food. As it is, I have noticed single individuals among the poorest classes who look remarkably well as compared with their fellows. "They drink milk," was the explanation given me.

There is vitality enough among the young boys who play hockey —these ball games are non-Arabic, a relic of Berberism—and keep up the sport till late at night amid a good deal of ill-tempered fighting and pulling about. Their mothers' milk is still inside them; they have not yet succumbed to the ridiculous diet, clothing, and life-habits of their elders. But soon manhood descends upon them like a cataclysm; it tears them with a frenzy which is anything but divine and thereafter absorbs them, to the exclusion of every other interest. Hockey-sticks are thrown away. . . .

That witchery of Orientalism, with its immemorial customs, its wondrous hues of earth and sky—it exists, chiefly, for the delectation of hyperborean dreamers. The desert life and those many-tinted mouldering cities have their charms, but the misery at intermediate places like Gafsa (and there are hundreds of them) is too great, too irremediable to be otherwise than an eyesore. They have not solved the problem of the simple life, these shivering, blear-eyed folk. Their daily routine is the height of discomfort; they are always ailing in health, often from that disease of which they plaintively declare that "whoever has not had it, cannot enter the kingdom of Heaven", and which, unlike ourselves, they contract by their patriarchal habit of eating and drinking out of a common dish. They die like flies. Naturally enough; for it is not too much to say, of the poorer classes, that they eat dirt, and that only once a day. A fresh shirt in the year is their whole tailor's bill; two or three sous a day will feed them; sunshine, and the stone floor of a mosque or coffee-house by night, is all they ask for, and more than they sometimes get.

An old Arab song contains words to this effect: "Kafsa is miserable; its water is blood; its air is poison; you may live there a hundred years without making a friend." No doubt the plethoric Sicilian mason at the Leila fountain would thoroughly endorse this statement with his "Ah, signore—these Saracens!" . . . But one learns to like the people none the less. They are merely depressed; they are not deficient in mother-wit or kindliness; a little good food would work wonders.

The oasis people are milk-drinkers, and would be healthier than the townsmen but for the agues, fevers and troublesome "Gafsa boil" to which they are subject.

I go to these plantations at night-time, after dinner, when the moon plays wonderful tricks of light and shadow with the overarching foliage. The smooth sandy stretches at the outskirts of the gardens shine like water at rest, on which the leaves of an occasional

sparse tuft of palms are etched with crystalline hardness of deline-
ation.

This untilled region is most artistic, the isolated clumps shooting
up like bamboos out of the bare soil. The whole grove is still wrapped
in its wintry sleep, and one can look through the naked branches of
the fruit trees into its furthest reaches. Only the palm leaves overhead and the ground at one's feet are green; the middle spaces
bleak and brown. But, do what he will, a man who has lived in the
tropics becomes rather *blasé* in the matter of palms.

Besides, there are no flints to be found here. . . .

Yet such is the abundance of water that these Gafsa gardens have
a character different from most African plantations. They are more
artlessly furnished, with rough, park-like districts and a not un-
pleasing impression of riot and waste—waste in the midst of plenty.

Then there is a charming Theocritean bit of country—the
temperate region at the tail-end of the grove. Only olives grow here;
seventy-five thousand of them. Beside their silvery-grey trunks you
may see herds of the small but brightly tinted oxen reposing; the
ground is pied with daisies and buttercups, oleanders border the
streamlets, and the plaintive notes of the *djouak*, the pastoral reed
of the nomads, resound from some hidden copse.

There will be nothing of this kind, I fear, in the carefully tended
oases of the Djerid.

XI

A HAVEN OF REFUGE

THE cold being past all endurance and belief, I was tempted to fulfil my promise and call upon Monsieur Dufresnoy.

What kind of man was this that managed to survive it?

They led me to his house, which is one of the few two-storeyed buildings of the town and lies in a squalid street of mud-dwellings. Villainously dirty walls surround a massive entrance-gate studded with nails and bands of iron, intervolved in artful designs. No bell, no knocker, no door-handle; only an impressive lock. At the sight of this doorway I paused—it was grim, claustral, almost menacing; there was an air of enchantment about the mansion, as if once in a hundred years its forbidding portals might turn on their rusty hinges.

Finally, I fled away altogether, in a kind of godly panic.

M. Dufresnoy, on his way homewards, almost ran into me. I tried to explain the sensations his domicile had aroused in my mind; he laughed at first, and then admitted that he had often felt the same thing. The house was apt to look like that, he said, when his wife was away.

The inside appearance, once that portal has been passed, is quite different, and I was glad to have an opportunity of seeing the place, as it is one of the surprises of Gafsa, one of the few remaining town-houses that date from better days, being built originally for some Turkish grandee or governor—for him, I daresay, who drove the god-fearing widow to the sylvan seclusion of Leila. You step through the gate into an open square patio, surrounded, on the sides not abutting on the street, by an arched passage that reposes on old Roman columns. This covered loggia, running round three fronts of the court, is the feature of the house; wonderful how a few arcades and pillars will impart an air of distinction and even luxury! Almost nothing has been done to change the old appearance of this small but well-proportioned patio; the walls have been freshly whitewashed, the original mud-flooring replaced by tiles, a bright flower-bed set in the centre—nothing more.

The five or six lower rooms to which the loggia gives access must be delightfully cool in summer, but they are dark and chilly at this season. Luckily, the mansion possesses an upper storey where the family resides during the winter, in rooms that are actually floored with wood. From here, looking out of the windows, there is a wondrous view over a wilderness of decayed Arab dwellings upon the oasis beyond, and the distant purple mountains.

There is an irresistible air of geniality about this home: can it be the house itself? For a subtle influence, no doubt, penetrates to the heart of man from the mere form and disposition of inanimate things. I was prepared to be smothered in a profusion of local effects; of saddle-cloths, silk hangings, water-pipes, daggers and match-locks, dim nooks with divans, and those other decorations that suggest the glamour of the Orient to certain Western minds. Or again, I said to myself, this European wife will have imported certain tastes from over the sea; the house will be replete with trifles carefully disposed in negligent fashion, silver photograph frames and flower vases reposing on diminutive tables, and such-like indications of what our novelists call the "tender but indefinable touches of a woman's hand".

Nothing of the kind. The place is simply comfortable: it appeals to one's sense of propriety. There are carpets and genuine arm-chairs—unique phenomena in this part of the world; best of all, fire-places wherein ample logs of olive-wood glimmer and glister all day long.

And so the last few days have passed. Mentally, too, I am thawing once more; the hotel life and solitary walks of Gafsa had begun to affect me disagreeably. Such things are endurable and perhaps stimulating in youth and in the plenitude of health; but there comes a period when one lives less in future dreamings than in the experiences of the past—unpleasant company, for the most part; when one craves to see the faces and hear the opinions of rational fellow-creatures; when one requires, in short, to be distracted. This is the age, too, at which a man begins to realize the significance of those once-despised material comforts. Tunisian hotels can only be inhabited by young hopefuls.

The house contains a considerable library of local literature—mostly technical and dealing with Dufresnoy's Metlaoui district, but some of it intelligible to a simple traveller like myself. From certain books I have begun to make extracts concerning the places I am likely to visit: Metlaoui, the Djerid oases, and the Chott country.

Dufresnoy is essentially a mining engineer. He evidently knows his business thoroughly; he has been employed in various parts of the French dominions and likes the work; all of which has not prevented him from becoming a man of the world and keeping his other intellectual pores open. There is nothing of the professional in his conversation. He is rather undemonstrative, for a Frenchman.

He told me an odd thing about the native rising in Thala in 1896, when a marabout preached death to all foreigners, with the result that several white men were murdered (it was a hastily collected band of Italian tradesmen who put down the insurrection). They caught him, and in due time he died (?) in prison—they were probably afraid to execute him: perhaps he killed himself—and the odd thing is this: that although the necessary sum has been contributed for erecting a monument to these unhappy victims of native ferocity, yet the Franco-Tunisian authorities are averse to the plan, on the ground that such a public monument might offend Arab susceptibilities. This struck me as overdoing the "pacific penetration" policy; and he thought so too, more especially as there is a commemorative stone to some preposterous bigot at the very place. . . .

I shall be sorry to leave Dufresnoy at Metlaoui. In him I often admire that fine trait of his race: the clarifying instinct. He possesses —with no pretension at knowledge beyond his mining sphere— an innate rigour of judgment in every matter of the mind; he avoids crooked thinking by a process of ratiocination so swift and sure as to appear intuitive. Even as a true collector of antiques has quite a peculiar way of handling some rare snuffbox or Tanagra statuette and, though unacquainted with that particular branch of art, yet straightway classes it correctly as to its merits, so, to him, an idea of whatever kind is an *objet de vertu*, to be appraised with unfailing accuracy. He is a connoisseur of abstractions. What the Goth carves out grotesquely after a painful labour of mental elimination, the right deposited, as residue, after a thousand wrongs—what the Latin smothers under a deluge of mere words: this your Frenchman of such a type will nimbly disentangle from all its unessentials; he presents it to your inspection in reasonable and convincing shape—

purified, clipped, pruned. What is this gift, this distinguishing mark?

Discipline of the mind, culminating in intellectual chastity—in what may be called a horror of perverse or futile reasoning.

He mentioned, incidentally, the case of suicides among the natives to prove that the *Mektoub* doctrine is not wholly pernicious. Suicides were quite unusual, he said; the Arabs do not seem to be able to fall in with the idea, preferring to bear the greatest evils rather than take an active part in the undoing of themselves. That was *Mektoub*: to bow the head, dumbly resisting. And were they not right? Did not the great majority of European cases of suicide imply a neurotic condition—such as when men of business have suffered reverses on Exchange or lost some trivial appointment? How easily things could be bridged over, or repaired, or even endured! The most hopeless invalid could testify to the fact that some pleasure can still be extracted out of a maimed or crippled existence; a man, however impoverished, might still live in dignified and fairly cheerful fashion.

He thought that in the matter of suicides, as in that of remorse, we were too "spectacular and altruistic"; that we lived in a rather unwholesome atmosphere of self-created and foolish ideas concerning honour and duty; that the *Mektoub* practice of the Arabs pointed to an underlying primitive sanity which we would do well to foster within us.

XII

THE MYSTERIOUS COUNT

GAFSA, even Gafsa, has its enigmas.

I climbed this afternoon to the summit of the Rogib hill, which lies near the railway station, on the further side of the Oued Baiesh. This, presumably, is the site where Marius halted for the last time before attacking the town; and the spot was also interesting to me on account of its flint implements. . . .

A sad and barren range of hills. There was no sunshine, for a scirocco-storm raised clouds of dust and obscured the sky; the wind was bitterly cold. Finding it impossible to attune my phantasy to the picture of Marius and his soldiers, I descended once more.

On the station turnpike I overtook a solitary foot-passenger, who plodded slowly along. It was the Polish Count. He had been absent from the hotel for several days, and now appeared to be in the gloomiest of humours.

Where had he been?

For a promenade, he said. It was too dreary sitting indoors, all alone. He had left the hotel. The place was too noisy: the dogs barked incessantly. He had taken rooms with a Jew, and arranged to have his meals at a small Italian *trattoria*.

This was a half-truth, I felt sure. The dogs of Gafsa, no doubt, are past all endurance; they are worse than in any Turkish village where they howl at least in unison, and so continuously through the night that one ceases to take note of them; but the man's real reason for this change of domicile was probably another one.

"You must find that much quieter," I said, "and cheaper as well. These hotels are rather pretentious."

"Pretentious and dear. Here I am, stranded in an unknown place, without friends; remittances are due to me, and they never come" —he broke into the subject without reserve—"and it is hard, I assure you, to deprive oneself of things, of trifles, if you like to call them so, to which one is nevertheless accustomed and entitled, so to speak, by birthright. But I am talking to the winds, no doubt. You, Monsieur, are one of the fortunate ones; you don't know—you don't know——"

"Yes I do," I replied, trying to think of something to say in the way of consolation. "I know quite well——"

"How do you know?" he interrupted. And next, with needless vehemence: "*What* do you know?"

I was surprised at his sudden change of tone. It was awkward, all this. I gave utterance to such commonplaces on the instability of human affairs as occurred to me, and ended up by offering, I hope with sufficient delicacy, to assist him to the small extent that lay in my power.

"Ah!"

He seemed infinitely relieved by my words: he evidently expected some answer of quite another import. Turning his back to the wind, and pausing for a moment to adjust his clothing, he replied, with ambassadorial deliberation:

"You may be certain, Monsieur, that I would not easily forget a kindness of this nature; my lot in life has been far too unhappy to make me undervalue what you, a stranger, have just offered me. But I will decline: what are a few francs to me? Pray don't think me ungrateful, however. You have caught me in an almost delirious moment, and your friendly words just now, when I felt myself so abandoned and in so critical a state of mind, with this dreadful desert wind moaning and everything, as it seems, hostile to me: your kind words, I say, touched me more deeply than I can express." (Here he wiped away a genuine tear.) "But my luck may yet turn, and then, be sure, I will make you forget all my childish querulousness."

And he went on, almost gaily:

"I never could keep money! And the worst of it is, I hate work; I was not brought up to it, and you will admit that I am too old to begin life anew. Yet I object on principle to so-called charity, being intelligent enough to know that there is only one kind of charity, and Justice is its name. But what is justice? I suppose we all possess some kind of natural rights, according to our stations; justice, I take it, would consist in our being permitted to enjoy those rights. If this is correct, then—ah, Monsieur, the demoralizing effects of poverty, of non-justice, on a man like myself; how it lowers your self-respect and makes you capable of actions that you would reprobate, in your right mind——"

"In your right mind? Is a poor man, then, insane?"

"How can I make you understand? Tell me, is not poverty a kind of madness, an obsession that haunts you night and day? To puzzle, at every hour, how to meet this demand and how to shun that one; to deny yourself the necessities of life, and your friends those poor little pleasures that you are yearning to bestow upon them—is it not a mental malady, a fever; is it not damnation itself? The thousand meannesses: how they degrade you; how they suck away your strength, your ambition, your faith! To see no openings before you, save ever darker gulfs of despair! I cannot hope to make you conceive such a hell: one must have been there oneself. But note this, Monsieur: never judge an impoverished man by your own standards of right and wrong—never! For the old-established meanings of things shift for him—they shift: and his temptations become formidably subtle beyond belief. When rich, he says calmly *Non; ça ne va pas*. But to forgo an advantage, when poor, is the same as if—let me see . . . as if one asked you to leave lying some fascinating flint in the desert waste."

"That simile, surely, is all wrong, Count. Nobody can be injured by my flint-mania, whereas——"

"I know, I know; I am not trying to excuse things; I am only explaining how they happen. But how explain to others? We always talk of putting ourselves in our neighbours' place; idlest of phrases! since we cannot possibly avoid bringing our personal apparatus to bear on their problems. There is a gulf between man and man. You will hardly believe that I used to take an interest—quite superficial, you know, but none the less real—in all those questions of the day that absorb the ordinary man of ease, in politics and art and whatnot; but nowadays all my interests are centred on one single point. On what point, do you think? On keeping up the external appearance, and the manners, of well-being. I have no energy left for anything else; and even this effort quite exhausts me. Art and politics! What, in the name of heaven, do I care for art and politics, with the knife at my throat? I only utilize these things; yes, I utilize them for conversational purposes, in order to deceive others as to my true, incessant and miserable preoccupations. Laughable, is it not? Why don't you smile, Monsieur—you, who have never known the bitterness?"

We were crossing the broad Oued Baiesh, a stretch of yellow sand and stones. To obviate damage by sudden floods, the French

have covered this tract of the road with a coating of asphalt; but
the busy life here, the droves of camels and sheep, the Arab folk
laughing over their laundry-work in the shallow streamlet that
trickles through the waste—all these things were gone for the
moment. But for the torn line of Gafsa palms that confronted us
on the other side of the river-bed, we might have been in the veriest
wilderness. Although the wind was lulled, petulant little pillars of
sand still arose here and there among the boulders and sank down
again, as if exhausted; the descending sun had emerged, a lurid
disc, framed in a sulphureous halo that melted imperceptibly into
the gold of the west.

It was growing chillier than ever, and the Count, shivering with
cold, drew his burnous more closely about him; he had bought one
for fifteen francs, probably in imitation of myself, or because I once
jokingly called it "a garment for millionaires who need not use their
hands". He liked to be taken for a millionaire.

I looked at him awhile, wondering what thoughts were ruling the
expression of his perplexed and sorrowful features, and then tried
to turn the conversation into other channels.

"Are there interesting people at your Italian restaurant?"

"Well, there is Hirsch, the young German: you know him?"

"The police commissaire was talking to me about his case
yesterday."

"Ha, was he? Let me tell you that I have investigated it
thoroughly, and find it most instructive. This young fellow is not
yet twenty; he ran away from home for no discoverable reason,
then signed on a merchant vessel at Marseilles and, disliking the
work, slipped out as soon as she touched port at Sfax, and climbed
without a ticket into a night-train, thinking to reach Tunis. Instead
of that, he woke up in the morning and found himself at Gafsa!
Here, you see, are all the elements of wrong-doing, and the authorities have learnt his history from his papers which they seized. As a
German and a Jew, the French instinctively dislike him; as a Jew
and a foreigner—the Arabs; he is objectionable to look at, dull of
wit, and knows not a word of French or Arabic. But he is poor, and
therefore—every one loads him with kindness."

"And why not?" I asked.

"Why not, indeed? Your friend the magistrate has given him
some money out of his own pocket; the restaurant proprietress
refuses to be paid for his food, while another one, near the station,

sends word to say that he can have a plate of soup there whenever he likes; a young Arab boy—these Arabs are really incomprehensible—gives him as many cups of tea or coffee as he can drink; a Jewish lawyer has sent him some clothes; a gentleman in your hotel a quantity of linen; the Italian barber shaves him gratis; a certain shopkeeper sends him a bottle of liqueur—of liqueur!—every second day; the commissaire has given him, free of charge, a decent unoccupied bedroom in the prison, where he can go in and out as he pleases; best of all, the *Ponts et Chaussées* are now employing him at three francs a day—a princely income, they tell me—at some agricultural job; pure kindness, inasmuch as he has never handled a spade or pickaxe in his life. He can have a pleasant time in Gafsa; he can marry an heiress if so disposed; then, when the place begins to bore him, the German Consul in Tunis will repatriate him, at his Government's expense. 'He's a poor devil,' they say. Why do I tell you all this? Because—well—I am also poor—"

Always harping on the old theme!

"The cases are not quite parallel, are they?"

"No. He is young, and fit for work, whereas I am past the middle term of life. Old age—another horror! Besides, I am a gentleman——"

"Exactly. We should be ashamed to shave you gratis."

"I suppose you're right, Monsieur. I was only trying to explain—to explain myself—to myself, I mean. Pardon me if I speak too much of my wretched affairs. But I'll tell you what I think. To endure this revolting destitution a man must be an Arab. Now, I cannot pretend to be an Arab; I would not adopt their ideals if I could. And yet, alas! I am beginning to believe in predestination, as they do; to believe that our faults and our virtues are distilled beforehand in the silent laboratory of the past. A sad creed, to think of men born to misfortune; to be obliged to consider yourself—how do you say in English?—*a stepchild of nature*. . . ."

He was always a good talker, but it is impossible to describe the intensity of feeling in his speech to-day. He seemed to suffer from some imperious need of unburdening himself, even to a chance acquaintance like me; long days of loneliness, maybe, had worked on his nerves and produced a kind of congestion. But in his words and voice I detected lapses into other moods, into some other state of being; they gave me the impression as of two different individuals addressing me. The man did not ring true, altogether; he was mentally disorganized, disharmonious; those meretricious reasonings about justice, for example, struck me disagreeably.

And I could not help contrasting his rambling emotionalism with the logic—the relentless, diamond-like *justesse*—of the mining engineer. He is the very antithesis of that pellucid and homogeneous character. The sanguine temperament. . . .

What is a man of this type doing in Gafsa?

Mystery!

The rest of us, the cynical Greek doctor, the artist-sage and lover of Arab institutions, myself (flint-maniac)—to say nothing of men like Dufresnoy—we all contrive to fit, after a fashion, into the place; we have a *raison d'être*. But this composite, unadaptive city-dweller: how incongruous a figure against that background of palms and barren mountains!

An enigmatical creature, and yet not wholly unlovable; he may be unsound or even unprincipled, he may be deficient in qualities that go to make men respected and satisfied with the world in general, but he possesses, I think, certain citizen-virtues unintelligible to the self-centred, rustic type of mind. He could be stirred to acts of unworldly enthusiasm; he would share his last crust with some shipwrecked sailor, or shed his blood gaily for a generous idea. And he is plainly in hard case just now.

A stepchild of nature. . . .

"You have a very good English accent, Count."

"We were carefully brought up in languages. Not everyone understands Polish, you know."

"By the way, how does it come about that you, being a Pole, should have a Russian family name?"

The question seemed to astonish and perplex him. At last he said:

"Oh, it's about the same thing, isn't it? Nowadays, I mean," he added, with grandiloquent pathos, "ever since the misfortunes of my unhappy country."

At the entrance to the town we separated, and I watched for some time his bowed form as it crept along the wood-market in the direction of the Kairouan road.

This is one of the figures that will persist in my mind very clear and pathetic, and I shall long remember those plaintive remarks about poverty that welled up, surely, from the bottom of his heart. How far, I wonder, is such a man the author of his own calamities, and how far have they *made him?* Academic questionings, based on out-of-date philosophy! Our vices, he said, are distilled for us beforehand in the dim laboratory of the past. His vice, evidently, is to hate work of every kind; his faculties, therefore, never undergo the rhythmic joy of reaction, for he is too well nourished to live the *vita minor* of a starveling, to endure Arab acquiescence in non-production.

"I am only trying to explain myself—to myself." Half-truth, I imagine. He is probably conscience-stricken, or at least dissatisfied with his conduct for one reason or another, and endeavouring to justify some base plan of action by restating ethics in terms of hunger; a specious line of argument, since hunger is not the rule but the exception.

And then I shall think of his red nose and watery little eyes, his absurd jewellery—a fine presence, none the less, when he pulls himself together; there is about him an air of faded distinction that softly symbolizes the history of his adopted country.

The Count!

Why a count? Because all Poles are counts—those that are not princes. But why a Pole? Well, perhaps from the convenience of vagueness, inasmuch as there is something international about a Pole—international, and yet neither equivocal nor vulgar; every one sympathizes with them, for they all possessed, once upon a time, vast estates whose loss is borne in cheerful resignation, and never so much as alluded to; they know everybody, and everybody worth knowing is related to them, by marriage or otherwise, in this or some other century; as men of the world, they are ready to talk upon any subject with tolerance, geniality and a pleasingly personal note that withers up the commonplace, smoking, meanwhile, innumerable cigarettes out of mouthpieces which display a complex escutcheon contrived in gold and rubies upon the amber surface. Yes, his choice was good: Poles are gentlemen. But why caricature them? And why, above all things, select an inappropriate Muscovite name? That argues a lack of general intelligence and might easily spoil everything; so true it is, as a legal friend once observed to me, that "It takes a wise man to handle a lie. A fool had better remain honest."

What can be the meaning of this unlovely comedy? Some defalcation or forgery? Likely enough. But I think he lacks the cleverness requisite for a habitual criminal. Perhaps he is only a poor survivor, drifting about in lonely and distracted fashion while waiting for the inevitable end. Others may solve the enigma, but not I; for to-morrow we go to Metlaoui.

Yet I know that long after the palms and minarets of Gafsa have faded into the blurred image of countless other palms and other minarets, I shall be able to call up the figure of this forlorn and ambiguous fellow-creature, standing on the asphalt of the river-crossing with his cheap burnous wrapped around him, sighing, shivering, and setting forth certain views concerning human life for which there is, after all, a good deal to be said.

XIII
TO METLAOUI

I SHOULD be sorry to say how long the train takes to crawl through the thirty-odd kilometres that separate Gafsa from Metlaoui. My companion on the trip, M. Dufresnoy, tells me that the return journey is still slower, because the line runs mostly uphill and the trucks, thirty or forty of them, are loaded with minerals. Fortunately, the car in which we travelled—each train has only a single passenger carriage—was comfortable, being built after the fashion of the Swiss *Aussichtswagen*, with seats on the exterior platform whence one can admire the view.

It gave me some idea of the goods traffic (phosphates) along this line when he told me that during the past seven days 23,000 tons of mineral had been conveyed to the port of Sfax alone, to say nothing of those that had gone further on to Sousse and Tunis. And not long ago, he said, the company had an unpleasant surprise: sixteen new engines of a powerful type, which they had ordered from Winterthur, were suddenly discovered to be liable to a duty of 1000 francs apiece as "imported articles".

"We can afford it," he said. "Our five hundred-franc shares are standing at three thousand seven hundred francs."

But he thought that a grave error had been committed in selecting the narrow metre gauge; it was all very well for phosphate transport, but once the line over Feriana and the branch to Tozeur are completed, they would have to deal with other material, such as tourists, that require fast services.

They had an accident last year. The couplings of a train, climbing uphill from Gafsa past the Leila oasis, suddenly broke, with the result that the rear portion rushed backwards again, careered through the Gafsa station and up the artificial incline which leads towards the Oued Baiesh, crossed the bridge, and thundered at a vertiginous pace into the desert beyond. As luck would have it, another train was just then approaching Gafsa. They collided with terrific force and, telescoping being out of the question since both were loaded with minerals, escaladed each other in Eiffel-tower fashion. Arab eye-witnesses say that the stoker of the up-train was thrown out by the impact and flew across country "like a bird" for half a mile; he alighted on his feet, and was found, after a week or so, wandering about the plain in a dazed condition. The driver was killed outright, and his widow draws a respectable pension from the company.

Since then two engines are always employed to move the train up the few miles beyond Gafsa.

The cream-tinted level is speckled with white incrustations and sombre tufts of desert herbs; here and there, where the winter's rain lingers underground, are spots of brilliant green; short-lived crops of corn, sown by the nomads. The hills to the right of the line are bare and torn into wild ravines; lilac-hued patches, ever changing and fair to see, move among their warm complexities: cloud shadows. Here, if anywhere, one learns that shadows are not always grey or black; even those cast in moonlight have a certain ghostly coloration.

It was a marvellously clear day, and not many miles before reaching our destination we looked back upon the downhill route traversed which, so far as one could see, might have been a dead level. At a distance of nearly twenty miles Gafsa was plainly visible—white buildings piercing a dusky line of palms—an hour's walk, it seemed. I observed in the brushwood a couple of bustards, their heads peering above the herbage. These birds are rather rare hereabouts, and shy of approach. Arabs say that the bustard is like the camel: once it begins to run, you never know when it will stop. They surround them therefore cautiously, and gradually close the circle to within shooting distance.

Metlaoui is the name of two distinct villages which have been conjured out of the waste by the discovery of its phosphate deposits —the station village, and a mile or so further on, Metlaoui proper, with its big establishments for working the minerals.

Here already, at the station settlement, there is more life than in Gafsa, though the surroundings are decidedly unpropitious—a waterless plain, with low hills in the foreground, phosphate-bearing, and wondrously tinted in rose and heliotrope. There are respectable stores here, very different from the shops of Gafsa. I entered a large Italian warehouse which contained an assortment of goods—

clothing, jams, boots, writing-paper, sealing-wax, nails, agricultural implements, guns, bedding, mousetraps, wire, seeds, tinned foods— and vainly endeavoured to think of some article which a *colon* might require and not find here. The only drawback is that there are no "colons" in the district.

While waiting for a conveyance to take me to the industrial settlement, I strolled about and found my way across a sad stretch of ground littered with tin cans, bottles, and other refuse, to a slight eminence whereon lay a cemetery. In this forlorn square are about twenty tombs, already crumbling to dust, although not one of those I saw was five years old. Humble victims for the most part —Italians in the prime of life who had come to these regions to gain a little money; or little children, carried off by the harsh climate (yet the climate of this place is preferred to that of Gafsa). The enclosure is filling up with drift-sand; the inscriptions on the tombs, often a mere charcoal scrawl of some unlettered friend or parent, are soon effaced by winds and rain.

One is wholly unprepared for the appearance of Metlaoui proper. In ten years' time a village has sprung up here, partly of factories and smoky chimneys, but chiefly of trim bungalows, with white walls and red roofs, that are dotted over the uneven surface of the ground. The whole site is owned by the company, and inhabited by its officials and overseers. It has its own church, shops, schools, hospital, workmen's clubs, bakeries, and its air of neatness and well-being contrasts pleasingly with the forsaken landscape all around.

The higher posts are reserved for Frenchmen, but among the lower grades you may find a number of other nationalities; Spaniards and Sardinians—hardiest of white Mediterranean races —as well as some Italians, and not a few Greeks. The manual labour in the mines is performed by Africans.

Not long ago nearly every drop of water for this settlement had to be conveyed from Gafsa on the backs of camels. But the company has now captured a spring at the head of the Seldja Gorge, about eight miles distant, which brings a copious flow of water into the place. Thus they have been enabled to plant a great number of trees, but I wish they could be persuaded to adopt a little more variety in their choice of them. One grows tired of the eucalyptus, that doleful and dismal growth, and even of the eternal pepper trees, green as they are; and the results, in a few years' time, would be far more charming if they would take the trouble to copy some of the Algerian municipalities in this respect, or—better still—obtain professional advice from the Agricultural Institute at Tunis, which could furnish them with a large list of ornamental timber and shrubs that would thrive equally well, and convert Metlaoui into a veritable garden city. The plants suffer at first from the strong winds, but they acclimatize themselves by degrees.

Remembering what had been told me of the unsuccessful attempt of the French to appropriate the water springs of Sidi Mansur, near Gafsa, I asked Dufresnoy whether the Arabs had not contested the action of his company at Seldja.

"I should think so!" he said. "They raised the devil. But we are not civil servants here, who must humour the caprices of half a dozen savages: the health of the settlement was dependent on our getting this water, and we took it, *voilà!* The great ambition of the company is to fix its people on the spot; to make life here so pleasant for them that they don't want to leave."

"You must find it difficult. The Arabs, I suspect, run back to the desert as soon as they have earned a few francs; and as for the European tradesmen, no doubt they get rich quickly, and then return to their homes again as soon as possible."

"That is exactly what the company manages to avoid. Let them prosper, we say; but slowly. And we succeed."

"How so?"

"By manipulating the rates of merchandise transport. The railway to Sfax belongs to us, and we can regulate prices as it suits us; if we liked, we could choke off all trade. Ah, the company knows its business! Of course, that makes us many enemies; they call it high-handedness and brutality—a concern like ours is bound to expose itself to such remarks—*we* call it common sense. If the railway were not ours, if we were not practically dictators of the country, those Americans, with their immense phosphate importation into Europe, would eat us up; and then these local merchants would lose everything. That is the justification of our so-called tyranny. Are we to have nothing for our risks? Look at this installation of machinery—all built, too, with a view to future aggrandizement: does it strike you as a half-hearted speculation?"

Daring, on the contrary. Here are gargantuan sheds, capable of holding thirty thousand tons of mineral apiece; furnaces, miniature volcanoes, for drying them artificially in winter-time, when the sun's heat is insufficient; all around you a gehenna of mad industrial life, smoke and steam, a throbbing agglomeration of wheels and belts and pistons; there are chains of buckets, filled with phosphates, wandering overhead in endless progression or disappearing sullenly into the bowels of the earth; passionate electric motors; mountains of coal and iron contrivances; railway engines snorting and whistling, or bearing a load of minerals down from the hills to where an army of Arabs will tear them out of the cars to dry, amid clouds of tawny dust. One might grow crazy at the idea of the primary difficulties involved in grafting upon the desert soil this ordered mechanical efflorescence, this frenzied blossoming of human activity.

What is happening?

They are separating the crude phosphate from its natural impurities; drying, pounding, and loading it upon trains for removal to the sea-board.

XIV
PHOSPHATES

A LIGHT railway leads up to the hills where the phosphates lie. Here you may see the fiends at work. A legion of wild-eyed, swart and nearly nude creatures are disembowelling the hoary mountain: visions such as this must have floated before Milton's eye when he drew his picture of Mammon, who with his horde of demons, opened in the hill a spacious wound—

> Ransacked the centre, and with impious hands
> Rifled the bowels of our mother Earth
> For treasure better hid. . . .

The workers are chiefly of three races: Tripolitan, Khabyle (Algerian), and Moroccan; they live in separate clusters among the rocks, each with their peculiar national traits and mode of building; there is hardly a woman among them all.

Besides these tribes a certain proportion of Tunisian Arabs are employed, but they are too weak or timorous to relish underground work; a sprinkling of negroes, as well as some of the hill-folk from the district surrounding Metlaoui, who go by the quaint name of Boujaja.

"Good fellows," said Dufresnoy. "They will slit your throat for a sou."

The surface phosphates having already become exhausted, the mineral is now pursued into the dim recesses of the earth. Tunnels are excavated, whence smaller ones radiate in definite directions—all of them sustained by wooden beams; the amount of material to be extracted from a given spot is scientifically fixed; it is shattered by minute blasts of dynamite and, once the trolley cars have carried it away, the wooden supports are removed and these cavities filled up by the collapse of the roof. By this means accidents are forestalled such as that which took place some years ago when, owing to an oversight of some subordinate left in charge, an immense mass of mountain fell in, entombing about three hundred, miners, whose bodies are not yet recovered. The ill-fated engineer who was legally responsible for the mishap was in Paris at the time; he returned in all haste. After seeing the mischief, he tried to throw himself into an Arab well, and, baulked of this, lay down at night under a passing train and was decapitated.

They showed me a map of this subterranean world, variously tinted according to the regions already exploited and those yet virgin. It reminded me, with its regular street and blocks, of some model city in the Far West.

The underground workings here are about thirty kilometres in length. Beside these Metlaoui deposits, the company has begun to attack those of Redeyeff, and will shortly open an assault upon the others at Ain Moulares, which lie near Henchir Souatir, the present terminus of the Feriana line. It employs six thousand men; some of the mineral goes as far as Japan; the output of last year amounted to over a million tons.

One may well be interested in the discoverer of these phosphates, in the man who has revolutionized the trade of Tunisia. He is a veterinary surgeon in the French Army—Monsieur Philippe Thomas.

His record is of the best.

Born in 1843, he has taken part in twelve military campaigns, distinguishing himself particularly in the Franco-Prussian war.

But, above all, he is a savant.

He has written valuable treatises on the diseases of domestic beasts, describing, among other things, a hitherto unobserved infectious malady of goats. He is the author of a number of memoirs on the geology of Northern Africa, and has discovered no less than two hundred new species of fossil animals of that country; he has made numerous contributions to our knowledge of its ethnology, prehistoric tombs, and flint implements. Many of these writings date from the seventies and earlier; they have procured for him the membership of learned societies, as well as medals and decorations of all kinds.

A man of such distinction, one would think, coming to Tunisia in 1885 at the head of a scientific expedition sent by the Ministry of Public Instruction, would be received according to his merits. It was far otherwise. Whether from distrust of his capacities or some other cause, Monsieur Cambon, the Resident, assumed towards him a most chilling official manner, and the commanding military officer, General Boulanger, all but refused to grant the escort necessary for his expedition. In one of his papers he speaks of this reception as "several degrees below zero".

Then, in the same year, appeared his sensational report of the discovery of phosphate deposits which he had traced over a long line of country; realizing their commercial value, he insisted that they should be exploited "*pour le plus grand bien de l'agriculture française et algérienne*". Nevertheless, ten years passed ere a company could be formed, as financiers were diffident about the American competition and the risks of installation in a desert country.

A tardy recognition of his services to the company took the form of a pecuniary grant, in 1904, of fifteen thousand francs—little enough, in all conscience, considering the millions he has gained for them. They further honoured him by changing the name of the station settlement of Metlaoui into "Philippe-Thomas".

"It's very economical," Dufresnoy observed.

I am glad to think that another place of that name, the mining village, will continue to exist; it would seem a pity to erase from the map the tuneful word Metlaoui, which contains the five vowels in a remarkably small compass. . . .

Dufresnoy tells me that those barren slopes where the mines lie, and where the different races now work together in apparent amity, were once the scene of a sanguinary primitive battle. There is a steep gully at one point, a dry torrent; the Khabyles lived on one side of it, the Tripolitans on the other, and between these two races there occurred, on a starlit night in May, 1905, an affray of unearthly ferocity.

The Khabyles, prudent folk, many of whom had served in the French Army, had long been laying in a store of warlike provisions; their secret was well kept, although it was observed that piles of stones were being collected round their huts, and that a goodly quantity of dynamite and petroleum was missing from the stores; some of them possessed guns and revolvers, the rest were armed with knives, daggers and savage mining gear. They chose a Sunday for the attack, well knowing that the Tripolitans, who are good-natured simpletons, would be least prepared to resist them on that day, and half of them in a state of jollification; and they were so sagacious, that they actually induced a few drunken Tripolitans to insult them, before beginning the conflict. This, they knew, would be counted in their favour afterwards.

Hardly was the night come before they advanced in battle array
—the fighting contingent in front; behind them the boys and older
men, who kept them supplied with stones and weapons. A well-
nourished volley of missiles greeted the Tripolitans, some of whom
rushed to the fray, while others took refuge in their huts or with the
Moroccans who lived in their own village near at hand. It was now
quite dark, but at close quarters the stones began to take effect,
and hardly was a man down, before five or six Khabyles ran out of
the ranks to finish him off with their knives; others, meanwhile,
went to the locked huts and fired them, or burst them open with
dynamite.

The explosions and light began to attract attention in Metlaoui;
the whole sky was aflame; there were mysterious bursts of sound,
too, and a chorus of wild howls. Something was evidently wrong,
up there.

A party of Europeans, accompanied by a small force of local
police, went up to the mines to investigate. They found themselves
powerless; "keep yourselves out of danger," they were told, "and
let us settle our own affairs." The carnage was in full swing; it was
hell let loose. Not content with killing, they mutilated each other's
corpses, bit off noses, gouged out eyes, and thrust stones in the
mouths of the dead; burnt and hacked and slashed each other till
sunrise; no element of bestiality was lacking. The wounded crawled
away to die in caves, or were carried to nomad camps. The number
of the dead was never ascertained; Dufresnoy says "about a
hundred", which is probably below the mark, as an eye-witness saw
three railway trucks loaded with the slain. To this day they find
mouldering human remains, relics of that battle, hidden away in
crevices of the rocks.

Although, once roused, the Tripolitans fought like demons, they
were worsted—the others were too numerous. They had a brief
moment of revenge, however; for during their retreat, on Monday
morning, they encountered two young Khabyle boys who had been
on absence and were now returning to work at the mines, blissfully
ignorant of what was going on. These unfortunate lads were torn
to shreds.

I confess that, as a spectacle, I should have preferred that night's
engagement to anything in modern warfare. It must have been a
stupendous exhibition of the *bête humaine.*

The Khabyles meditated nothing short of a total extirpation of the Tripolitan stock; they sent to the mines of Redeyeff for auxiliaries of their nation, some of whom actually arrived in time for the slaughter; the rest were intercepted on the hill-paths by the police of Gafsa, who had been telegraphically summoned and despatched by special train. And soon afterwards, elated by success, the Khabyles fell foul of the Moroccans and sent word that they meant to fight them too for sheltering Tripolitan fugitives in their huts. The Moroccans were delighted at the prospect; but the management got wind of the project in good time, which was just as well, for the Moroccans are not only the most orderly of the native settlers at the mines, but also by far the strongest and fiercest, and it might have fared ill with the Khabyles. The Tripolitan village has now been moved to another site—a certain number of troops, too, are definitely stationed at Metlaoui.

"As usual," said Dufresnoy, "We came in for the blame. They say that we did not allow the real authors, the Khabyles, to be punished, because they are French citizens, and all the rest of it. Don't believe a word of that. If it had been the Tripolitans, we would have acted just the same; we cannot be bothered with decisions of civil courts, which would have satisfied nobody, besides depriving us, probably, of a number of good workmen. There was a little outcry about this too: that none of the wounded were treated in our hospital, but carried down to the native *funduk* near the station. 'The hospital', said our director, 'is for those who are injured in the performance of their duty, and not for blood-thirsty savages.' That's sound—that's military. One cannot afford to be sentimental in this country."

I asked what could possibly be the reason for such a ferocious outbreak of hostility.

"Long-standing animosities of race," he said, "and, as determining cause, *cherchez la femme*."

"But you said that there were no women on the place."

"*Eh bien, cherchez toujours. . . .*"

And then it also occurred to me that among the mass of local literature and newspaper files I had perused in his house there was not a single criticism of this affair. I thought it strange, I said.

He smiled.

"Local politics, my friend! We are obliged to keep the Press well under control, you know. Don't compare Tunisian life with life in England; there is no public opinion here, no idea of fair play.

These papers, if they were not subventioned, would print abominations such as no English journalist could conceive; they would alienate our best friends in the long run. The company must take account of things as they are, not as they should be—of Arab savagery, Franco-Tunisian malevolence; of journalistic venality and public credulity. Whoever is not for us is against us. That is why the only papers that dare to criticize our management are those which nobody reads; those, to put it bluntly, which are not worth bribing. For the rest, there is not a writer in the whole country capable of grasping either our aims or our methods; the poor fellows have not had the required education. They only want their mouths stopped."

"That must be more convenient than libel suits; and more economical as well."

"Just so. Above all things, we are bound to consider the interests of our shareholders."

XV

THE SELDJA GORGE

I T is good, after such visions of human infirmity and of death, to ride over the plain to the Seldja Gorge, an astonishing freak of nature. I was twice within its towering walls of rock; the first time on horseback, accompanied by a young Tripolitan miner, and in the evening; yesterday again, in the torrid noon, afoot, alone.

You will do well, in every case, to ride as far as the *bordj*, or rest-house, that stands near the entrance of the cleft, since there are about four wearisome miles of level country to be traversed after leaving Metlaoui. On the first occasion the Tripolitan ran for this whole long stretch beside my horse, which trotted briskly; he amused himself, none the less, in belabouring its hind-quarters with a club to make it go still faster, and I confess to being not scandalized, not inordinately scandalized, at this performance. We grow hard among the implacable desert stones. Besides, it was only a hired beast. Any true lover of animals will understand.

Skirting the foot of the hills that trend along, apparently closed, one suddenly encounters a broad stream-bed with a rivulet meandering down its centre; this is the Seldja-water (*arabice*, Thelja). It issues out of a gateway, hitherto unrevealed; and here you may turn aside from the plain and enter into the heart of the mountains, into a world of nightmare effects. This very portal is fantastic, theatrical; it leads into an arena of riven rocks that might serve as council-chamber for a cloud of Ifrits, and is closed at the further end. There is a second gateway to be passed before you can enter the gorge itself.

The track winds upwards—the whole length of the defile is about three miles—sometimes between walls of rock which are chiselled so smoothly by the gentle waters that one can hardly believe them to be of natural workmanship (and at these points, as a rule, your only path is the stream-bed itself); opening out again into wide amphitheatres, rose-tinted cirques of desolation, where masses of debris, slipped down from the heights, lie prone in Dantesque confusion. There are rock-doves and falcons fluttering about the sunny precipices; cliff-swallows build precarious habitations against the roof of yawning caverns; sandpipers and wagtails skim over the streamlet that glides in a smiling flood across reaches of yellow sand. The charm of water in the waste! This Seldja-brook is a true child of the sun; cold in the morning and evening hours, its restless little heart becomes tepid at midday with the glowing beams.

Spiky reeds and tamarisks trip alongside, and the wild fig thrusts demoniac roots into the crevices; here and there you may see a group of oleasters, descendants, maybe, of the now vanished Roman olive plantations in the plain, or a stunted palm that has shot up from the stone cast away by some passing caravan. For these Oueds are all highways dating from immemorial ages; there is a ceaseless passage of man and animals along them.

We passed numbers of camels, groaning and snorting among the slippery rocks, with the water splashing over their feet; higher up, a large descending flock of sheep, over six hundred of them, completely blocked up the valley. They were being led to the plain below, where, thanks to the recent rains, a succulent but ephemeral crop of green had sprung up. Their owner was a fine Boujaja, some six and a half feet in height, accompanied by a sturdy brood of children: milk-drinkers. The upland pastures could wait, he said. Strange to think that two more showers a year would make settlers of these vagrants.

It was among these rocks that Philippe Thomas first detected the traces of those phosphates that have made his name famous. Tissot, in 1878, already anticipated their discovery.

In point of sheer grandeur, of convulsed stratification and cloven ravine, of terrorizing features, I have seen gorges far finer than this of Seldja. Yet it contains one stretch of superlative beauty—a short defile or cañon, I mean, formed of two opposing precipices with a chasm of some thirty yards between them; they wind and curve, parallel to one another, with such accuracy that one would think they had been designed with mighty compasses from on high, and then carved out, sagaciously, by some titanic blade.

Here we halted; it was time to turn back. There was an indentation in the rocks near at hand, fretted away by hungry floods of the past and overhung, now, with creepers and drooping fernery, concerning which my Tripolitan companion told me a long and complicated legend. This shallowy hollow, he explained, was the bridal couch, in olden days, of an earthly maiden and her demon-lover. He was a simple fellow, unfortunately, who knew the story too well to be able to tell it coherently.

On my second visit, however, I pushed vigorously up the stream-bed in the heat of the morning, determined to reach the head of the waters. Gradually the aspect of the valley changes. It opens out; the rocks melt away into bare white dunes, the country assuming the character of a tableland; you begin to feel a sense of aloofness.

There was blazing sunshine in these upper regions, but a fresh breeze: this is the Ras-el-Aioun, where the French have bridled some of the wild waters, thrusting them into a tube that carries them in a mad whirl to their settlement at Metlaoui. Here, too, they have planted a promising youthful oasis, a kind of nursery garden of poplars and cypresses and tamarisks and mimosas, in whose shade grow geraniums, mesembryanthemum and other flowers and creepers, as well as a host of vegetables of every kind. I soon discovered a recess in this delectable pleasaunce, and began my solemn preparations for luncheon.

Out of the pool below there resounded a tuneful croaking of frogs; it spoke of many waters. . . .

Presently an Italian workman or gardener with curly grey hair and moustache—the ubiquitous Italian—came up and began to talk, *per fare un po' di compania*. He conversed delightfully, a smile playing about his kindly old face. He told me about the garden, about the French engineers, about himself, chiefly about himself, in limpid, child-like fashion. He had travelled far in the Old and New Worlds; in him I recognized, once again, that simple mind of the wanderer or sailor who learns, as he goes along, to talk and think decently; who, instead of gathering fresh encumbrances on life's journey, wisely discards even those he set out with.

Seldja, he told me, used to be a dangerous place for Europeans to traverse; many robberies and even murders had taken place there in times past; the new regime, of course, had put an end to all that. But there were still two perils: the frightful flies that bred diseases and made the gorge almost impassable in the hot months (every one suffered from fevers), and the serpents. Ah, those *maladette bestie di serpenti*—they swarmed among the rocks: they were of every kind and size; worst of all, the spleenful naja. He himself had killed one that measured two metres in length and was as thick as a man's arm. They don't wait till you can hit them, he said, but rush straight at you, swift as an arrow, upraised on their massive posterior coils, hissing like a steam-engine, and swelling out their throat with diabolical rage.

This is the beast that figured in the competition between Aaron and Pharaoh's conjurers, and it remains the favourite of modern African snake-charmers, who catch it after first irritating it by means of a woollen cloth wherein the fangs are embedded and broken. It is also, no doubt, the dreaded species which Sallust describes as infesting the region of Gafsa. But Lucan goes a little too far in his account of Cato's expedition into these parts; this veracious historian has inserted a few pages of sublime serpent nonsense, exquisite fooling. . . .

Of all the deadly worms that breed in these wildernesses the most formidable, because the most sluggish, is the two-horned nocturnal cerastes, the "pretty worm of Nilus". No sensible person, nowadays, goes into the bled* in summer-time unless armed with a phial of the antidote—Trousse Calmette or Trousse Legros—whose liquid is injected with a hypodermic syringe above and below the wound, and has saved many lives.

"And the scorpions, Signore! We have to tie cotton-wool round the legs of our beds so that these infernal creatures cannot climb up while we are asleep; they get entangled in it, ha, ha! And that is why we all keep cats and hens, who eat them, you know, just like the Arabs do. And sometimes it rains scorpions."

I had heard that story before, from natives; and it may well be founded on fact. The terrific gusts of desert wind overturn the stones under which the scorpions lie; the fragile beasts are exposed to the blast and, being relatively light, swept skyward across leagues of country with the flying sand. A similar explanation has been given for those old accounts of frog and fish rains.

"Yes; they drop from the clouds. During certain storms I have

---

* This is one of the many Arabic words which admit of no clear translation. As opposed to a town, it means a village or encampment; as opposed to that, the open land, a plain, or particular district. When colonists talk of "going into the bled", they mean their farms; in newspaper language it signifies the country generally, inhabited or not—what we should call "the provinces"; oftentimes, again, the barren desert or (more technically) the soil.

picked them off my clothes, three or four at a time. Rather a ticklish operation, sir."

So we discussed the world in that umbrageous shelter, to the music of the frogs. He condescended to partake of a microscopic share of my meal, and thereafter left me, with some old-world compliment, to irrigate his thirsty lettuces.

XVI

AT THE HEAD OF THE WATERS

I SAT alone, screened from the midday heat, drowsy and content. It was a pleasant resting-place, under that leafy arbour, through which only a few rays of light could filter, weaving arabesque designs that moved and melted on the floor as the wind stirred the foliage overhead. And a pleasant occupation, listening to those amiable amphibians in the mere below—they carried my thought back to other frog-concerts, dimly remembered, in some other lands —and gazing through the green network of branches upon that sun-scorched garden, where now a silvery thread of water began to attract my attention as it stole, coyly, among the flower-beds.

The day is yet young, methought; it is too hot to think of marching home at this hour. Now is the time, rather, for a pipe of *kif*— if only to demonstrate the difference that exists between man and the ape. For your monkey can be taught to eat and drink like a Christian; he can even learn to smoke tobacco. But he cannot smoke *kif:* the stuff would choke him.

Four pipes, reverentially inhaled . . . it was almost too much, for a mere dilettante.

But the mystery of the frogs, the when and where of it, was solved. Slowly and benignly the memories travelled back, building themselves into a vision so clear-cut and elaborate withal that I might have been holding it, as one holds some engraving or miniature, in my hand. It was in the Rhine-woods, of course; long years ago, in summer-time. But the frog-music here was not amiable at all; never have I heard such angry batrachian vociferations. They came in a discontented and menacing chorus from ten thousand leathery throats, and almost drowned our converse as we crept along through the twilight of trees that shot up from the swampy earth.

These Rhine-woods are like pathless tropical jungles: everything is so green and luxuriant; and morning grew to midday while we threaded our way through the tangle of interlacing boughs and undergrowth. Yet we knew, all the time, that something else was in store for us, some joy, some surprise. And lo! there was an opening in the forest, and we suddenly found ourselves standing upon the summit of a high bank at whose foot there rolled a sunlit and impetuous torrent. Too staid for the formation of ripples, too swift for calm content, the river seemed to boil up from below in a kind of frolicsome rage. A blissful sight.

"*Er spinnt*," my companion was saying.

In what obscure chamber of the brain had those words slumbered, closely folded, for thirty years? It was indeed an authentic weaving of arabesque designs upon the even texture of the living liquid mass; multitudinous rings and ovals and lozenges were cast up from the green depths as from a mighty over-bubbling cauldron; some fiercely engulfed again, others torn hither and thither into new and pleasing shapes, fresh ones for ever emerging; only a few contrived to linger unchanged, floating in sunny splendour down the face of the waters. A blissful sight! The dark and mazy woodlands, now, were left far behind—the croaking of the frogs sounded strangely distant. We gazed in ecstasy upon that shining flood. . . .

On my return journey down the Seldja Gorge, that afternoon, I had a narrow escape. It struck me that it would be more agreeable, instead of once more following the windings of the brook, to proceed along the railway—a single line—that climbs down from Ras-el-Aioun to within a few hundred yards of the *bordj*, where my horse was waiting. It was easier walking; it would also be shadier (in the tunnels) and, last and chiefest, I would enjoy a change of scene by looking down into the valley instead of up at the cliffs.

Plausible reasoning.

This line is a pretty little piece of engineering; there are bridges and steep embankments that afford fine views into the tortuous depths of the gorge; there are tunnels, blasted into the rock without lining of masonry, deliciously cool and all too short—all too short save one, that seemed never-ending. It writhed about, too, in that dark mountain; I saw no speck of light, either before or behind me; the iron roadway was raised about a foot, on rough stones, above the narrow path that followed the jagged, irregular wall of rock along which I was groping and stumbling. Rather an awkward place, I thought, to meet a train——

And as if in that reflection had lain the potency of a spell, there came upon me, at that moment, from behind, a distinct blast of wind and a low rumbling sound. I pricked up my ears. There was no doubt about it: a train, still invisible, was gliding in good-natured fashion, with steam shut off, down the gradient. A considerable number of ideas, incongruous and quite beside the mark, passed through my mind; but also this one—if I ran, I should inevitably stumble against a sleeper or some projecting stone; if I stumbled, I should lose my presence of mind, and then, perhaps——! Meanwhile, the noise grew louder, deafening; already, in imagination, I felt the monster's hot breath upon me.

Walking steadily, therefore, for a few more yards, I felt a little cavity in the rough-hewn wall of rock that appeared deeper than the others; there I compressed myself, feeling flatter than a turbot, and absurdly resigned. It was the nick of time. The earth was trembling under the mechanical horror; it passed me, with a roar and rush of wind, by I know not how many inches; there were flashes of light, a screeching of machinery, an acrid smell of mineral oils and heated metal. Then all was over again, save for a choking fit produced by a deluge of bituminous coal.

Just a little flutter.

Outside that tunnel, in the sunshine, I sat down and indulged in certain musings. *Suicide of an Englishman in Tunisia:* that was it; inasmuch as even they who know me well could hardly be brought to believe that such an act of abysmal foolishness, as this of not investigating on which side the safety-niches were, could be the result of accident An ignoble, ridiculous death.

It must have been a fit of temporary obliviousness, brought about by the unaccustomed heat of the sun.

Or possibly the *kif.* . . .

It affects people differently.

I must limit myself to three pipes in future.

XVII

ROMAN OLIVE-CULTURE

Now, on the former occasion, instead of descending into the *bordj* from the railway line, I rode with the Tripolitan once more out of the rock-portal into the plain, that glowed with the fugitive fires of sunset. It is a treeless waste, bereft of every sign of cultivation.

And yet, if you look on your left hand as you issue from the gorge, you will perceive, at the very narrowest point, some fragments of ancient masonry adhering to the cliff; they are all that remains of a Roman dam which blocked up the valley, regulated the supply of water flowing from above, and purified it from stones and sand. The inference is clear: the plain must have been cultivated in those days. Likely enough, it was covered, like many other parts of "Africa", with olives, that drew their life from this judiciously managed water-supply.

The Oued Seldja to-day fulfils no such useful function. Once the rock-portal is passed, it unlearns all its sprightly grace and trickles disconsolately through the sands, expiring, at last, in the dreary Chott el Rharsa.

Monsieur Bordereau thinks that the ancient "forest of Africa" was composed chiefly of olive plantations, and proofs of the former abundance of these trees can be found in certain local names, such as Jebel Zitouna—the Mount of Olives—clinging to localities where not a tree is now visible; there are also sporadic oleasters growing near many Roman ruins. Strong evidence; and still stronger is this: that Roman oil-presses have actually been found, buried in the desert sand. Up to a short time ago the Arabs deliberately destroyed the olives, to avoid paying the tax on them; the French have changed all this, and though I am not aware that they go so far as did the Romans, who encouraged tree-planting by exemption from imposts, yet they have inaugurated a severe regime; one reads with satisfaction of exemplary penalties inflicted for illicit timber-cutting.

10*

It is good to remember, also, that whereas the Romans had five centuries of peace to bring Tunisia to its high pitch of prosperity, the French only began yesterday. And they have a harder task before them, for in the interval the Arabs have arrived in the country. It is they, with their roving and pastoral habits, who have done the mischief, changing arable land into pasture, which grows ever poorer, and finally desert. The fertility of these regions may be said to have been annihilated by the goats of a nomad race, whose faith has made it improvident and mentally sterile.*

Yet it may be disputed whether the land was as thickly wooded under the Romans as some would have us believe. If so, how was it that after three centuries of their rule there should come a drought lasting for five years? Wood brings water, and if things were so satisfactory, why did they penuriously hive and distribute the element? They described Africa as a "waterless land"; Marius, when he made his forced march across country to surprise Gafsa, took in at one place a sufficient provision of water to last for three days. This, however, may be due to the fact that he purposely kept to the desert lest, by following the main route, his designs should be made public.

One thing strikes me as conclusive evidence that the "Africa" of olden days was a different country: they had no camels. These beasts were unknown there at the time of Julius Cæsar, and only came into common usage towards the end of the fourth century. The Africa of to-day, without camels, would be almost uninhabitable.

Some years ago, whilst staying among the magnificent forests of Khroumiria, forests such as certainly never clothed these southern hills, I grew interested in this question of the old African water-supply. Comparing the accounts of classic authors with what has been written by modern students like Bourde, Carton and others, whose very names have faded from my memory, I remember coming to the conclusion—a very obvious one, no doubt—that supposing all the ruined Roman hydraulic contrivances were now

---

* I have just re-perused Lapie's *Civilisations Tunisiennes*. He says that "*la chèvre est le génie malfaisant de la Régence . . . Plus que le despotisme, plus que le fatalisme, elle a ruiné le pays: c'est la chèvre, en effet, qui déboise et surtout qui s'oppose au reboisement, et l'on sait quelle influence a eue sur le régime des eaux et sur la fertilité du sol le déboisement de la province d'Afrique.*" Apropos of this pasturing by nomad cattle, it is a singular fact that whereas a large proportion of desert plants of northern Tunisia are poisonous to camels and goats, here, in the south, nearly all of them are edible.

in working order, supposing them even to be furnished with such improvements as modern science could suggest, still the French would be unable to obtain, at the present moment, the agricultural results of the Romans. The positive diminution in the supply of liquid has been too great. Archæologists, for instance, have discovered in the district of Gafsa alone over a hundred Roman wells and reservoirs, of every shape and size; but it would be sheer waste of money to re-activate many of these ancient works—there are wells which would remain dry fron one year's end to another; the watercourses, too, have shrunk or altogether expired.

Quite apart from what the French have taken from it, this Seldja brook must have carried down a larger volume of water in those days, helped, as is very probable, by small tributary streamlets which have now ceased to flow.

Old Arab authors say that one used to be able to walk from one end of North Africa to the other in the shade. Allowing for some exaggeration, this means that either the legendary African forest of the Romans continued to subsist, or that certain bare tracts covered themselves with timber in post-Roman periods of abandonment, before the Arabs and their goats had time—for it must have required time—to change the climate and aspect of the province.

These woodlands, at all events, cannot have been all of olives. There is Sbeitla, for instance, the Roman city whose remains I was unable to visit owing to the Arctic blasts of wind; viewed from the railway, its surroundings look so bleak and bare that nobody would believe they could ever have been timbered. Yet, concerning Sbeitla, we happen to possess the testimony of three independent older eye-witnesses, who visited the spot at different periods: first Shaw (about 1725), then Bruce, then the botanist Desfontaines. All three of them describe the region as wooded. And, as if to clinch the matter, Leo Africanus, writing in 1550, says that the inhabitants of Gafsa and its district made their boots out of the skins of stags. (These are no doubt the fortassa deer, a few of which still linger in the country north of Feriana.) Stags can only live in timbered regions. If these forests were still in existence there would be a greater abundance of water; the cold in winter would be less intense, and so would the summer heat, since forests are harmonizers of all climatic discords.

Now these woodlands were not composed of olives, but for the most part of junipers and of Aleppo pines, a precious growth to which the French began to pay attention some five years ago. These bright and graceful trees flourish on the poorest soil and multiply rapidly; they are valuable not only for their timber, but for their turpentine. You can buy, in the Gafsa market, a crude black tar made from this tree; the Arabs use it for impregnating the linings of their water-skins, like the Greeks for their receptacles of rezzinato wine.

The only drawback to these pines is that their inflammable branches are always suggesting a display of extempore fireworks to the Arabs, who are the veriest pyromaniacs.

XVIII

THE WORK OF PHILIPPE THOMAS

THE old olive plantations are creeping back again into regions that have been deserted for centuries. They follow the railway lines; and nothing is a fitter commentary on the mediævalism which deplores *the building of railways into the desert* than facts like that of the plain of Maknassy—a sterile tract up to a few years ago—which is now covered, for a distance of sixty kilometres, by olive groves. Why? Because the line from Sfax to Gafsa happens to pass through it.

The same will take place in due course along the Feriana and other southern lines, and thus one of the gravest problems that confront the Tunisian administration will be solved: the unstable nomads will fix themselves—they are already fixing themselves—round these new agricultural centres. In 1890 there were still eight tents to every five houses in Tunisia, but this proportion is rapidly changing. And besides this, the railway, with its facility for the rapid conveyance of troops, has given security to regions formerly so dangerous that no settler, however favourable the soil, would have dared to establish his home there; it has awakened the date industry and created halfa deposits all along the line.

There is one of them at Gafsa station, for instance—relatively small; and yet, in the season, two hundred camel-loads of this costly hay arrive there every day, to be dried, pressed and stored ready for transportation to the coast, whence it is shipped to Europe. In 1905 sixteen thousand six hundred tons of halfa were forwarded from the interior by the Sfax-Gafsa line alone!

And were it not for this railway the branch line to Tozeur would never have been contemplated; the oases of Souf and Djerid and Nefzaoua, with their teeming populations, would have slumbered the sleep of ages in their burning desert sands. And to realize what a change it has wrought in the appearance of the ports of Sfax, Sousse and even Tunis, one must have known these places in the olden days. The company pays yearly half a million francs to the Government; it contributes another yearly sum of 600,000 francs towards the harbour enlargement scheme of Sfax; indeed, it may be said to have created the modern town of Sfax, its hotels, banks, restaurants, theatres.

And what brought the railway?

The phosphates. But for their discovery no Utopian would have thought of constructing these lines just yet. An unlovely deposit of brown dust has worked a revolution upon the minds of men, upon the face of the country. It has even enriched the French vocabulary.

"Your friend, is he an *alfatier?*"

"No, sir; he is a *phosphatier*."

As I issued out of the rock-portal of the Seldja Gorge and beheld that strip of masonry which told so plain a story, with the now barren plain at its foot, it struck me that this spot was pregnant with a romance beyond that of mere scenery. It was well, here, to pause awhile and contrast old and new notions of African prosperity. The Romans had the same difficulties to contend with as have the French: a harsh climate, and fickle and faithless natives who "cannot be bridled by threats or kindness". They had the same ambitions; so Strabo tells us that they used every endeavour to make settlers of them and fix them to the soil, and "paid particular attention to Masanasses, King of Numidia, because it was he who formed the nomads to civic life and directed their attention to husbandry".

Both administrations are necessarily based on military rule. And if the now uncultivated plain affronts our eye, there is already a set-off to this apparent superiority of the ancient regime in the new line of railway which, at great expense, has been made to climb up the sinuosities of the Seldja Gorge itself.

Whither wending?

To fetch more phosphates!

Here they lie, the quintessential relics of those little Eocene fishes and other sea beasts, if such they were, that swam and crawled about the waters many years ago—piled up on terraces so high that the mind grows dizzy at contemplating their multitudes, or the ages required to squeeze them into this priceless powder; piled up for 500 miles along their old sea-beach—an arid inland chain of hills, nowadays, where hardly a blade of grass will grow;

sterile themselves, the cause of surpassing fertility elsewhere. These phosphates are something of a symbol: there are men and women fashioned after this model.

I question whether the men of the *Pax Romana* could ever have reached the phosphate-extracting stage. They were not trending in that direction. Eyes were turning inwards, and the age of sober thinking was past and over for the time being, since the Orient began to infect the world with the mephitic vapours of self-consciousness. Truth was a drug in the market; for twenty long centuries the Banu-Israel, with their ferocious contempt of craftsmanship and honest intellectual labour, were enabled to foul the stream of human endeavour. It is gratifying to think how thoroughly the modern Jews have shaken off their ancient bigotry—a good refutation, by the way, of those scholars who still argue about the "immutability of race-characters".

But those earlier and artless Galileans, methinks, must have been on the mental level of the Tripolitan savage running beside my horse: it needs no very cunning marabout to convince him that his little troubles will be set aright in a world hereafter, where he shall sit comfortably enthroned and listen to his enemies gnashing their teeth. For the poor in mind are like children in this, that they create realities to coincide with emotional states; and for such as these, they say, is the kingdom of Heaven reserved.

Nevertheless, though men sought the "inner light" and not phosphate deposits in those days, yet certain men of God, roaming about these same stony wildernesses, made discoveries in natural history no less surprising than that of Monsieur Philippe Thomas. Saint Anthony encountered a faun—half-man, half-goat; he spoke to the creature and was charmed by its edifying discourse. You will object that Saint Anthony is known to have been a hallucinated neuropath; that the story, therefore, may not be true. So be it.

But such a description can hardly be applied with decency to certain holier and wiser men, who saw with their own eyes things yet stranger. The great Augustine tells his congregation—it is in one of his sermons, I believe—that in these deserts there are men without heads, men who have one single eye placed in the centre of their breasts. You may suggest that the saint was quoting from the heathen pages of Herodotus, the *Father of Lies*. Nothing of the kind. He is too conscientious to speak from hearsay of such marvellous matters; he says that he personally went among these headless monocular folk; he says that he spoke to them and lived with them; that he made a study of their morals and social institutions, which, in this particular sermon, he holds up as an example to his two-eyed Christian hearers.

And Saint Augustine has the reputation of being a fairly truth-loving saint and *doctor ecclesiæ*.

No; phosphate-hunting was assuredly out of the question under such conditions; scientific curiosity and commercialism, parents of fair talk and fair dealing among men, retire discomfited when there are immortal souls to be saved. And soon enough they came, those Ages of Faith, of moral dyspepsia and perverse aspirations, when truth-seeking, useless under the *Pax Romana*, became much worse than useless—perilous, that is, to life and limb. So quickly do we forget past torments, that some of us continue to yearn for those picturesque days of burnings and thumbscrewings.

Meanwhile, if truth is found useful for the moment, it is due to the humanizing work of those quiet investigators like Philippe Thomas—to the men who have armed their country for the heroic task of cleansing the Augean stables.

Monsieur Dufresnoy had never met the phosphate discoverer, but another gentleman described him as follows:

"He is a simple fellow, and the devil for work. Married, and a good husband; clear eyes; spectacles, a short beard, rather stout, and not dark; never so happy as when he is examining old bones and trash of that kind. A *bon garçon*, mind you. And yet—Lord! what a simpleton. He could have become a millionaire if he had managed the thing properly. Too modest, perhaps—too unworldly; too foolish, or too proud: who can tell? You never know what is going on in the minds of these *savants*. He told them he was a veterinary surgeon, and not a man of business. Can you understand such an attitude?"

"I must think about it, Monsieur."

And so I did, riding home that evening from the Seldja Gorge—and next day too; but, somehow or other, have not yet attained a mature opinion on the subject. It may be, however, that there is nothing to prevent a man from being simultaneously modest and proud—nothing, save the fact that we have not yet coined a word for an alloy of these particular ingredients. We have words, always either too few or too many; words which are for ever emancipating themselves from our control and becoming masters instead of slaves, so

that our ideas, which ought to be formed by independent cere-
bration, are half derived from mere verbal symbols, which become a
kind of intellectual pepsine that weakens the strongest systems. So
when we speak of a man being "proud", that miserable expression
is apt to engross and dominate us, conjuring up an image which
excludes certain others: that of modesty, for instance.

It comes to this, that if we wish to describe a man who does not
seem to fit into any of the categories permitted by ordinary words,
we are driven to refer him to some exemplar recognized in legend
or history—we talk of his being Epicurean, Voltairean, and so
forth.

Let us say, therefore, that Monsieur Thomas, like Pasteur, is of
the Promethean type—a seeker after verity, a light-bringer.

POSTSCRIPT.—This is surely a land of coincidences. In a Tunisian
paper of this very morning I read of the death, on the 13th of
February, of Monsieur Thomas. It describes him as "one of the
most perfect citizens of our poor humanity". He only lived a year
to enjoy the annuity of six thousand francs which the Government
of the Regency, with belated thoughtfulness, had granted him.

XIX

OVER GUIFLA TO TOZEUR

A MULE, a sturdy beast, was waiting to convey me from Metlaoui to Tozeur. Leaving my heavier baggage to follow with some camels, I rode into the dawn.

Considerably less than half-way stands the rest-house of Guifla, kept by an Algerian with a pretty wife. Here I saw a few carved Roman stones which had been found, the man told me, in the neighbouring Oued Baghara. At Guifla, according to Valery Mayet, they killed an ostrich twenty years ago—a *rara avis* in these parts.

There were numbers of engineers and workmen at this place, engaged in laying down the line of railway which will unite Tozeur to Metlaoui. It cannot help being a paying concern, I should think, to judge by the traffic that passed me in the course of this day, for I was hardly ever out of sight of a caravan.

It was an ideal day for desert travelling—a grey, sunless sky, a gentle breeze. Another weary stretch brings one to El-Hamma, a small oasis fed by hot springs which the Romans long ago utilized, and where I had hoped to refresh myself with a Turkish bath. Alas! the hammam is only a shallow tank covered with palm-thatching; there were some twenty Arabs splashing about this establishment and soaping themselves and their boy-children—bathing was out of the question. Near at hand lies the women's bath, which is built on the same primitive lines. A pious legend runs to the effect that this water of El-Hamma used to be cold, but an Arab marabout was persuaded to spit into it and, lo! it suddenly became hot and mineral. . . .

As you approach Tozeur the landscape becomes more desert-like; mountains are left behind; stones are rarer; you wade in sand. One realizes how useless it would be to construct a good road in these parts, since every storm would drown it. And such storms are some-times of great force; there was a celebrated one in 1857 which lasted for seventy-two hours. It threw some of the riders of a French detachment off their horses, and finally obliged the whole company to stamp up and down for twenty-four hours in the twilight of raging sand for fear of being buried alive. It submerged several hundred palm trees of the Tozeur oasis *up to their crowns* (they are 60 to 100 feet high).

Notwithstanding these difficulties, an enterprising Maltese runs a motor-car from Metlaoui to Tozeur and Nefta for all such persons as are prepared to pay his price, and I hear that the speculation has paid well. There are moments during my ride when I regretted not having come to some understanding with him; when I grew tired of the jolting mule, the rough track and an Arab saddle which keeps one's legs at an angle of 179 degrees. True, my conveyance had only cost four francs. . . .

Straining my eyes at the water-shed beyond El-Hamma, whence one has the first view of Tozeur and its palm forest, I thought to detect, at an immeasurable distance, two minute dusky streaks, swimming in air—other oases, no doubt. They seemed to dangle, by some gossamer thread from the grey vault of Heaven.

This first view of the oasis of Tozeur, and the Chott Djerid beyond it, has often been praised. To me, arriving at the water-shed on a cloudy afternoon, that line of inky-black palm trees with its background of blanched sterility melting into a lowering, leaden-hued sky, conveyed a most uncanny impression: the prospect was absolutely familiar! Yes, there was no doubt about it: I had seen the place before; not in Africa, of course, but—somewhere else. Where—where? Suddenly I remembered: it was a northern land-scape, a well-known forest of sombre firs, rising out of the wintry plain. The white, salty expanse, filling up the interstices between the palms, helped to complete the illusion; it was powdered snow among the tree-tops. For a brief moment I was *transported*. . . .

It was not long before I found a companion at Tozeur. He was an Arab from the Souf, region of sand; dark-skinned, oval-faced, with straight eyelashes, straight nose, and an infectious, lingering smile; quite a worthless fellow; he had picked up a few words of French slang, and never tired of exhibiting them. We rode out to the Chott to see the extraction of the salt, which is a Government monopoly; the track leads past a famous lotus, a Methuselah among trees, whose shadow covers 120 square metres of ground and whose branches are so long, so weary with age, that they bend downward and touch the earth with their elbows—to rest, as it were—and then rise up again, refreshed. These salines are about three miles from Tozeur and an uncommonly simple establishment; they dig a ditch in the morass which promptly fills with water; the liquid evaporates, leaving the salt, which impregnates it, to be piled up in heaps on dry land. Next, they stow the mineral in sacks and transport it to Tozeur on donkeys. It undergoes no preparation whatever, but is sold as it comes out of the Chott, agreeable to the palate though rather yellowish in colour. Needless to say the Government runs no risk of the supply failing; there is salt, a swooning stretch of salt, as far as eye can reach.

Once you have issued from the oasis in this direction it is all a level of dried-up mud, speckled with low shrubs and dangerous watery spots, where a man may slowly sink down and disappear for ever. A strange desert lily, purple and golden, starts leafless, like a tall orchid, out of the bitter waste; camels eat its fat, bulbous, snowy-white root; the Arabs call it *tethuth*.

I saw some darker markings on the surface of the expanse which the workman at the salines declared to be the ruins of old buildings and quite inaccessible nowadays, but they may well have been small ridges of sand, magnified by mirage: those oasis-Arabs have rather indifferent eyesight. Plainly visible, however, was a line of palms about eight miles distant to the east; it was one of a group of oases of Oudiane. I looked at it, wondering whether I should pass that way on my homeward journey.

But my companion, with a languishing gesture, pointed in the other direction, towards his home.

Tozeur, he thought, was all very well, and so were Oudiane and all the rest of them, but Eloued was fairer by far. And only three days' journey! Why not leave this country and go to the Souf, to Eloued, instead? *Sacré nom!* I could return by way of Biskra if I liked. And if I paid him five francs for a camel he would accompany me the whole way, like a brother. The five francs, he explained, were only for the camel-hire; he did not want me to pay for his food; he liked me for my company—it seems I reminded him, in a way, of the folks at Eloued. They must be charming people, and I was almost tempted to follow his advice and make their acquaintance.

Later on we went to what they call the Roman *barrage* of the main oasis river; the large blocks of which it is composed are unquestionably antique, but they have been carried to this spot not by the ancients, but by Berber cultivators of long ago. Gazing upon these venerable stones we were led to talk of past times, of buried treasures and their wondrous lore. One of his uncles, he tells me, is versed in the black arts and an adept at raising hoards; he learnt it from a Moroccan. But bad luck had dogged his footsteps lately. He discovered a treasure whose guardian *jin* offered to surrender it if he brought three things: a white goat, certain materials for fumigation, and "the book". It seemed a very simple request, but each time, unfortunately, that he arrived at the enchanted spot, he found that, for some extraordinary reason, he had left at home one or other of these three articles; and when at last he managed to bring all three of them together, he accidentally—*sale bête!*—said a pious "bismillah" at the critical moment, which of course spoilt everything.

And here a wild craving came upon me: I wished to follow the winding of this brook and trace it to its source, which I judged to be not far distant. The companion smiled, as usual; he was ready for anything; but the undertaking proved to be rather arduous. We walked and climbed for long among the gardens, crawling under vines and thorny shrubs, wading tributary brooks and clambering up and down their steep earthen banks with a hundred dogs in full pursuit; there was no possibility of orientation; we doubled our tracks over and over again—it was like being imprisoned in the works of a clock.

At last, and doubtless by the merest of accidents, we emerged from the true oasis of orderly fruit trees and vegetables; the soil became sandy and uneven, with palms sprouting up in isolated clusters amid tamarisks and bristly reeds. The stream, meanwhile, continued to divide and subdivide into smaller rivulets. After a good deal of walking on this kind of ground, we finally reached the head of the waters—the eye, as the Arabs poetically call a fountain, alluding to its liquid purity, its genial play of light and movement.

It trickles out under a tall incline of sand, and the crowns of the palms at this spot are not quite on a level with the desert overhead. Looking down from these sandy heights, I found that we had followed a tortuous river of green palms, that flowed through yellow sands into a distant lake of the same green—the oasis.

But the companion had become quite silent. He was bewitched, apparently, by the rural charms of this place. At last he said:

"If only I had brought some *kif* to smoke!"

Your Oriental, as a rule, becomes hungry at the sight of a fair landscape; he manifests a sudden yearning for food. Not so these Souafa; they must have their native *kif* on such occasions. They are all, I am sorry to say, partakers of the pernicious drug.

"You have forgotten your *kif?*" I asked. "Well, that *was* an oversight!"

And, to his astonishment, I fumbled in my pocket, produced the stuff and lit a pipe. I smoked on placidly, looking at him and wondering what his thoughts might be.

"An Inglis"—perhaps he was saying to himself—"one of those who joke and talk in such friendly fashion, and then, when it comes to a sou's worth of *kif*—a single puff of his pipe. . . . ! *Sacré cochon!* That is how they grow rich."

Possibly he reasoned thus, but I fancy he reasoned not at all. There he sat, and kept his eyes fixed on the ground; a European might have feigned interest in something else, or cheerful indifference, but this desert-child did none of these things. He simply sat and suffered dumbly: it was a blow of fate, to be borne like all the rest of them. A fine exemplar (*édition mignonne*) of the mektoub profession.

Presently I made him a gift of the whole apparatus. He was quite speechless, at first, with surprise.

The spot was well chosen for indulgence in the divine herb, bland quencher of doubts, begetter of blissful images; impossible to conceive anything but a good genius residing amid these bubbling waters and gently stirring foliage. Everything was kindly and gracious, and yet——

"Yonder," he said, pointing dreamily with his pipe-stem to a place not far distant, "yonder they killed a man and a woman. They hacked them to little pieces."

And he unfolded a tale of love and revenge.

It was the usual intrigue; with this peculiarity, that the woman was quite a poor creature, of blameless past, married and mother of children; the man—though what we should call a "gentleman by birth"—had long ago become a vagabond, a child of iniquity, an outcast from the coast-towns, whom some wave of misfortune had left stranded on this green island in the desert. Listening to the hazy and rather disconnected recital, I tried to piece the story together as it really happened; to discover its logic, its necessity; the arts by which this decayed citizen, proficient only in the lore of vice and scorned by the whole populace, had gained his end; above all, how it came about that these two never wearied of their infatuation. Had he struck some latent and hideously defective chord in her motherly breast, that began to throb in response to his amorous complexities—was *that* their common bond?

Likely enough.

But I would prefer to think otherwise. I would prefer to think that this woman's very simplicity, and this green dell, had worked a miracle; purging and simplifying him, carrying him away from depraved memories of middle life towards certain half-forgotten and holier ideals of youth that revived, at last, and took shape in the prime features of this—as he may have called it—pastoral diversion; making him cling to them stubbornly, even as we might promise ourselves to cling to some friend of past days, were he ever to return. . . .

The idyll lasted for long, ere the awful retribution came—the element of insecurity acting, I suppose, as a cement. There is in most of us, Arabs or otherwise, a deep-seated sporting instinct (is that the right word?) which the system of legalized unions was contrived to curb, but cannot; if connubial life were a hazardous liaison there would be fewer divorces.

A perverse and sordid romance, you will say.

And yet it endured, like many of its kind.

XX

A WATERY LABYRINTH

TOZEUR is more than twice as large as Gafsa, and the inhabitants are a healthier race, good-natured and docile, with much of the undiluted Berber blood still in their veins. The houses are also of better construction, and not a few of them can boast of cool, vaulted chambers and an upper storey. Unfortunately for the artistic effect, new French buildings are rising up here and there; it is inevitable—the place cannot be expected to stand still; artists and dreamers must go now further afield.

And the oasis is a forest of sumptuous splendour, wherein grow bananas (absent in Gafsa), together with every other kind of fruit and vegetable, but chiefly date-palms, that give the highest and most constant return. They cultivate seventy different varieties. There are half a million trees paying taxes—the common variety sixty centimes, the delicate amber-tinted and translucent *deglat* twice as much; some trees produce more than fifty francs a year. But they require incessant care; "palms must eat and drink," say the Arabs; they drink, in the summer months, a hundred cubic metres of water apiece!

The export of these dates has been going on for centuries; in 1068 the geographer Bekri wrote that almost every day a thousand camels, or even more, leave Tozeur loaded with dates, and the trade will become still livelier when they have finished building the railway which is to connect this place with the present terminus Metlaoui. Maybe the Egyptians introduced the tree into these regions; they cultivated dates as early as 3000 B.C. It is perhaps the earliest fruit of which we have clear record, save that old apple of 4004 B.C. which gave some trouble to Adam and Eve.

In olden days they sold negro slaves here for two or three quintals of dates apiece.

The irrigation of these palms is a hair-splitting business. Water-conduits, varying in size from a brook to the merest runlet, cross and recross each other on palm-stem aqueducts at different levels; the properties are served with the precious element according to time. And inasmuch as the labourers have no clocks or watches, they have devised a complicated and apparently frivolous system of marking the hours; the water is cut off from a certain property, for instance, when a certain shadow shall have attained the length of three footsteps of a man, and so forth; the shadow varies according to the seasons, but, in the long run, everybody is satisfied. There is peace now under the palms; the days are over when the lean and hungry desert folk, who cannot climb trees, used to ride hither and, pointing their guns at the terrified cultivators, make them clamber aloft and throw down a month's provision of dates.

Arabs will tell you that there are 194 water springs at Tozeur; they are ready to give you the names of every one of them, and several more; these unite to form what might almost be called a river, which is then artificially divided into three rivulets—divided so neatly, says an old writer, that even some fragment of wood or other object drifting down the current is split up, perforce, into three equal parts, one for each of them; these three, later on, are once more subdivided into seven smaller ones apiece—twenty-one in all; and these, again, into a certain fixed number of almost miscroscopic brooklets. Allah is all-knowing! To me, wandering for the first time in this region, the irrigation canals seemed to flow from every point of the compass. I teased my spirit with the imaginary task of unperplexing the liquid maze, of drawing a map of this dædal network of intersecting waters.

You can stroll in every direction along shady paths in the oasis and never weary of its beauty. The tiller-folk are a happy people— one can see from their faces that they have few cares; those that are not at work under the trees may be seen splashing about the brooks or wending to market with donkeys that almost disappear under immense loads of green stuff; they will greet you with a smile and a "Bon soir, Moussié!" (It is always 'bon soir'.)

Seven little villages nestle under the palms; here and there, too, you enter unexpectedly upon gem-like patches of waterless, shimmering sand—mock-Saharas, golden and topaz-tinted, set in a ring of laughing greenery; there are kingfishers in arrowy flight or poised, like a flame of blue, over the still pools; overhead, among the branches, a ceaseless cooing of turtle-doves. At this season, a Japanese profusion of white blossoms flutters in the breeze and strews the ground; these peaches, apricots, plums and almonds are giants of their kind, and yet insignificant beside the towering trunks of the palms whose leaves shade them from the sunny rays; the fruit trees, in their turn, protect the humble corn and vegetables growing at their feet.

During the Turkish period these oases were in danger of their lives; the sand invaded them, choking up the waters and gradually entombing the plants. The nomads and their flocks and camels, pasturing at liberty round the cultivated tracts, had destroyed the scrub vegetation which hindered the flying desert sands from penetrating into the groves; they had trampled to powder the soil at these spots, so that every breath of wind raised it heavenwards in a cloud. But the peril is averted now by the system of *tabias* or sand-dykes introduced some twenty years ago—introduced, I believe, in accordance with the suggestion of Monsieur Baraban, whose book on Tunisia drew attention, among other things, to this deplorable condition of the oases and the threatened loss to the exchequer.

Now, if you look closely at this sand, you will see that it is full of minute crystalline particles, and that, in places where it lies undisturbed, these hard and jagged grains wedge themselves into the softer ones and form a coherent crust. It was observed that the wind cannot raise this crust, and the problem how to manufacture it in the neighbourhood of the oases was solved by enclosing the near-lying tracts of half-desert within low mounds crowned by upright branches, and forbidding all access to man and beast. The flying plague heaps itself against the palisade and submerges it; a new set of branches is then inserted, and so the structure grows higher and more efficacious every year. The soil within the enclosures, meanwhile, grows hard; wild shrubs sprout up to help in the work, and though the crust yields, like thin ice, at the slightest pressure of the fingers, the end is accomplished.

The protected districts are already assuming a different aspect from the true desert outside, which shifts with the breeze; apart from their tufts of vegetation, the soil has become quite dark in colour. Only the most reckless of nocturnal nomads will dare to violate these hallowed precincts in search of firewood; the citizens have already learned to regard them with reverential fear. At a long distance from the town I asked a small boy to climb over the palisade.

"Not if you give me a packet of cigarettes!" he said. "The *brigadier*"—in an awed whisper—"he sees everything."

Hearing that protective works of a new kind are being carried on at this moment, I walked yesterday to the bare slopes that lead down to the water-springs. A hundred or more Arabs were engaged, under the supervision of a keen-eyed young Frenchman, in digging a multitude of curved concentric ditches across the hollow of the catchment area, intersected by diagonal ones here and there; the general appearance of the work—the bright yellow of the newly excavated part set against the dark ground of the old—was as if some gigantic fishing-net had been carelessly thrown across the country. These little dykes were about two feet deep, and there must have been already some twenty miles of them. The overseer explained:

"You see what happens. Our putting this tract under the tabia-system had prepared us an unpleasant surprise. The rain formerly used to sink into the soft sand, but since the crust has formed, thanks to our efforts, it no longer sinks, but runs over the hard surface, pours in a flood down that steep incline at whose foot the fountains issue, and threatens to suffocate them with soil torn from its banks. The very life of the oasis was imperilled by our well-meant artifices. But now, with these little ditches, we hope to catch and tame the showers, and force them to wander about in these channels till they either sink into the earth or evaporate. Not a drop of liquid is to leave the catchment basin; it is exactly the reverse of what we desire in Europe."

It struck me as a simple and efficient device.

Midday came and the workers were paid off, each of them receiving a slip of printed paper for the half-day's work; the possession of four of these slips entitles them to exemption from the yearly tax of two francs forty centimes which they would otherwise pay: a good example of the *politique d'association*. They trooped away gleefully, and I could not help remarking on their cheerful humour.

"They are gentle as young girls," he said, "and far more tractable; thievish, of course, and untruthful—but so are all children! They attach themselves to me in a pathetic, dog-like fashion, without hope of preferment or any ulterior object. . . . Yes, they have established themselves in my heart, somehow or other; perhaps because I am an orphan and rather lonely and susceptible. . . . I really love these poor Arabs, as a father might love them——"

"That stick of yours: it looks business-like. May I ask whether you ever chastise them?"

"Why not? Would I not thrash my own children if they deserved it? This work in Africa," he went on, "attracts and interests me. At home I lose my personality and become a sheep in a herd, but here, in the desert, I can create and leave a mark, which has always been my ambition. I think I could live in this country for ever. Can you understand such a feeling? None of my colleagues can; their minds are in France, and they complain of a colonial exile, as if Tunisia were the Devil's Island; they call me an enthusiast, because I think well of this warm, palpitating soil in which I seem, I don't know how, to have struck deep roots."

And he gazed lovingly over the sea of glossy palm-tops, down yonder, on our right. This, I thought, was a most unusual type of Frenchman; and yet there was something in his language, or perhaps in his ideas, which was already familiar to me.

"To be Sultan of Tozeur, for example—ha! I would bend them to my will; I would lead them to battle and give them laws; I would have them about me as slaves and companions—they should sing to me and tell me stories while I go to sleep. This fair land seems like the realization of some old, dimly remembered dream of mine. How does it all come about, I wonder?"

Sultan of Tozeur—that gave me the cue, and I hazarded the guess that he had inherited his tastes from certain old rovers and conquerors of the northern seaboard.

"True," he said, "our family comes from Normandy, though we have lived in Paris for two generations. Now how on earth did you find that out?"

These are the men whom the Franco-Tunisian administration will do well to encourage as officials and settlers in the wilder parts.

XXI

OLD TISOUROS

THERE is a daily recurring spectacle at Tozeur which enchanted me: the camping ground at dawn. Here the caravans repose after their desert journeys; hence they start, at every hour, in picturesque groups and movement. But whoever wishes for a rare impression of Oriental life must go there before sunrise, and wait for the slow-coming dawn. It is all dark at first, but presently a sunny beam flashes through the distant palms, followed by another, and yet another—long shafts of yellow light travelling through the murk; then you begin to perceive that the air is heavy with the smoke of extinguished camp-fires and suspended particles of dust; the ground, heaving, gives birth to dusky shapes; there are weird groans and gurglings of silhouetted apparitions; and still you cannot clearly distinguish earth from air—it is as if one watched the creation of a new world out of Chaos.

Even before the sun has topped the crowns of the palms, the element of mystery is eliminated; the vision resolves itself into a common plain of sand, authentic camels and everyday Arabs moving about their business—another caravan, in short. . . .

And at midday?

Go, at that hour, to the thickest part of the grove; then is the time; it must be the prick of noon, for the slanting lights of morning and eve are quite another concern; only at noon can one appreciate the incomparable effects of palm-leaf shadows. The whole garden is permeated with light that streams down from some undiscoverable source, and its rigid trunks, painted in a warm, lustreless grey, are splashed with an infinity of keen lines of darker tint, since the sunshine, percolating through myriads of sharp leaves, etches a filigree pattern upon all that lies below. You look into endless depths of forest, but there is no change in decorative design; the identical sword-pattern is for ever repeated on the identical background, fading away, at last, in a silvery haze.

Here are no quaint details to attract the eye; no gorgeous colour-patterns of pleasing irregularities of form; the frosted beauty of the scene appeals rather to the intelligence. Contrasted with the wanton blaze of green, the contorted trunks and labyrinthine shadow-meanderings of our woodlands, these palm groves, despite their frenzied exuberance, figure forth the idea of reserve and chastity; an impression which is heightened by the ethereal striving of those branchless columns, by their joyous and effective rupture of the horizontal, so different from the careworn tread of our oaks and beeches.

Later on, when the intervening vines and fruit trees are decked in leaves, the purity of this geometrical design will be impaired. . . .

The origin of Tozeur is lost in the grey mists of antiquity, since a site like this must have been cultivated from time immemorial; the first classical writer to mention the town is Ptolemy, who calls it Tisouros; on Peutinger's Tables it is marked "Thusuro". The modern settlement has wandered away from this ancient one which now slumbers—together, maybe, with its hoary Egyptian proto-type—under high-piled mounds whereon have arisen, since those days, a few mediæval monuments and crumbling maraboutic shrines and houses of more modern date, patched together with antique building blocks and fragments of marble cornices: an island of sand and oblivion, lapped by soft-surging palms.

They call it Bled-el-Adher nowadays, and this is the place to spend the evening. I was there yesterday, perhaps for the last time.

It exhales a soporific, world-forgotten fragrance. There is no market here, no commercial or social life, save a few greybeards discussing memories on some doorstep; the only mirthful note is a swarm of young boys playing hockey on the sand-heaps, amid furious yells and scrimmages.

True hockey being out of the question on account of the deep sand, they have invented a variant, a simple affair: they arrange themselves roughly into two parties, and the ball is struck into the air with a palm branch from the one to the other; there, where it alights, a general rush ensues to get hold of it, clouds of sand arising out of a maze of intertwining arms and legs. The lucky possessor is entitled to have the next stroke, and the precision and force of their hitting are remarkable; they evidently do little else all day long.

I noticed an element of good humour and fair play not prevalent among the Gafsa boys; there was no peevish squabbling, and I only

saw one fight which was a perfectly correct transaction—nobody
interfering with the two combatants who hammered lustily at each
other's faces, and at last separated, satisfied and streaming with
blood. For some days past they had seen my interest in the game,
and yesterday I observed that it was suddenly suspended; a con-
sultation was taking place and presently one of the boys approached
me and politely asked whether I would not care to join; if so, I
might have his club; and he placed the weapon and ball in my hand.
The proposition tempted me; it is not every day that one is invited
in such gentlemanly fashion to wallow on all fours with young
Arabs. I made one or two strokes, not amiss, that called forth huge
applause; and then returned, rather regretfully, to my sand-heap,
to meditate on my own misspent youth, a subject that very rarely
troubles me.

There is a tall round building that stands within a hundred
yards of where I sat; they call it the "Roman" tower, and the
foundation-stones, though not *in situ*, are probably of that period;
it was a Byzantine bell-tower, then a minaret, now a ruin. And
here, confronting me, lie a few stones, that are all that remain of a
pagan temple which became a Christian basilica and afterwards a
mosque. In the fifth century Tisouros—this slumberous Bled-el-
Adher—was a dependency of the Greek "Duke of Gafsa" (how
strange it sounds!); Florentinus, its bishop, was executed by the
king of the Vandals; Christian churches survived, side by side with
mosques, as late as the fourteenth century. There seems to have
been no great religious intolerance in those days.

They showed me a gold coin of the Emperor Gordian—the same
who built the amphitheatre of El-Djem—which was found here, as
well as some lamps and sculptured fragments of stone. Bruce speaks
of cipollino columns; they are still to be seen, if you care to look for
them, split up, since his time, to mend walls and doorsteps. Tozeur
must have looked well enough under the later Empire.

And now, sand-heaps and a brood of young savages, shouting at
their game. It is long since these people knew the meaning of refined
things, although some of the houses, their fronts decorated with
gracious designs in brickwork, testify to a not extinct artistic
feeling—the citizens once enjoyed a reputation for delicacy and love
of letters. There is nothing like systematic misgovernment for
degrading mankind, and I think it likely that the gradual fusion of
the Arab and Berber races, so antagonistic in all their aspirations,

may have helped to abrade the finer edges of both parent-stocks. But the native civilization was not remarkable at any time.

The climate, and then their religion, has made them hard and incurious; it is a land of uncompromising masculinity. The softer element—thanks to the Koran—has become non-existent, and you will look in vain for the creative-feminine, for those intermediate types of ambiguous, submerged sexuality, the constructive poets and dreamers, the men of imagination and women of will, that give to good society in the north its sweetness and *chatoyance;* for those "sports" and eccentrics who, among our lower classes, are centrifugal—perpetually tending to diverge in this or that direction. The native is pre-eminently centripetal. His life is reduced to its simplest physiological expression; that capacity of reflection, of forming suggestive and fruitful concepts, which lies at the bottom of every kind of progress or culture, has been sucked out of him by the sun and by Mahomet's teaching.

A land of violence, remorseless and relentless; the very beetles, so placid elsewhere, seem to have acquired a nervously virile temperament; they scurry about the sand at my feet with an air of rage and determination.

So I mused, while the game went on boisterously in the mellow light of sunset till, from some decaying minaret near by, there poured down a familiar long-drawn wail—the call to prayer. It was a golden hour among those mounds of sand, and I grew rather sad to think that I should never see the place again. How one longs to engrave certain memories upon the brain, to keep them untarnished and carry them about on one's journeyings, in all their freshness! The happiest life, seen in perspective, can hardly be better than a stringing together of such odd little moments.

XXII

THE DISMAL CHOTT

HEARING that there are few or no tourists in Nefta just now, I left Tozeur three days ago, an hour or so before sunrise. This region, the Djerid, is all sand; an isthmus of sand thrust in between two Chotts of Djerid and Rharsa; the oases are scattered about the country, says some old writer, like the spots on a leopard's skin. . . .

The air was keen, and I shivered on my mule, looking back often at the dark forest of Tozeur, where I had spent some happy days.

After about five miles of comfortable wading through soft sand, I became aware of a ghostly radiance that hovered over the pallid expanse of the Chott. Abruptly, with the splendour of a meteor, the morning star shot up. Then the sun's disk rose, more sedately, at the exact spot where Lucifer had shown the way; and climbing upwards, produced a spectacle for which I was not prepared. For as it left the horizon, a counterfeit sun began to unroll itself from the true, as one might detach a petal from a rose; at first they clung together, but soon, with a wrench, parted company, and while the one soared aloft, the image remained below, weltering on the treacherous mere. For a short while the flaming phantasma lingered firm and orb-like, while the space between itself and reality grew to a hand's breadth; then slowly deliquesced. It gave a prolonged shiver and sank, convulsed, into the earth.

Light was diffused; the colour of daytime invaded the ground at our feet, flitting like some arterial rill through the dun spaces. Wonderful, this magic touch of awakening! It is the same swiftness of change as at sunset, when the desert folds itself to sleep, like some gorgeously palpitating flower, in the chill of nightfall; or rather, to use a metaphor which has often occurred to me, it hardens its features, crystallizing them into a stony mask, even as some face, once friendly, grows strangely indifferent in death.

11

My companion of this morning, who happened to be of a religious turn of mind, took the opportunity to glide off his beast and, standing a little apart, with his arms thrown through the reins to prevent the mule from straying, recited the dawn-prayer. The noble gesticulations looked well on that bare sandy dune, in the face of the Chott.

As for myself, I thought of the old god Triton, who dwelt in yonder foul lake and showed some kindness to Jason, long ago, when his ships were entangled in the ooze; I thought of Tritogeneia, the savage, mud-born creature who, cast into the purifying crucible of Hellenic mythopoesis, emerged as bright-eyed Athene, mother of wisdom and domestic arts. The Amazon maidens of the country used to have combats in her honour with sticks and stones, and the fairest of them, decked in a panoply of Grecian armour, was conducted in a chariot about the lake. A fabled land! Here, they say, Poseidon was born, and Gorgo and Perseus, Medusa and Pegasus and other comely and wondrous shapes that have become familiar to us through Greek lore.

These folks of Atlantis "saw no dreams", but they studied astronomy and navigation; their priests may well have been those Druids whose temple-structures, the senams and cromlechs, have wandered from the Tripolitan frontier as far as the chilly coasts of Brittany, and Salisbury Plain, and Ultima Thule. And every day, as the sun passed over their heads, they saluted him not as the Giver of Life or Lord of Earth, but cursed him with imprecations long and loathsome, for his scorching fires.

Shaw, I believe, was the first to identify the Chotts with Lake Triton.

There were islands in this sea; the sacred isle of Phla, for instance, which the Spartans were commanded by an oracle to colonize, and whereon stood a temple to Aphrodite. There are islands to this day, great and small; one of them is called Faraoun—evidently an Egyptian name, for Egyptian influence was felt early in these regions; at Faraoun grows a peculiar kind of date which, we are told, an Egyptian army had left there. The waters of the pool touched Nefta, whose Kadi gave Tissot a description of a buried vessel which, from its shape, could be nothing but a *galère antique*— it was dismembered for fuel, and metal nails were found in its framework.

Movers is probably correct in seeking at Nefta the Biblical Naphtuhim of the generation of Noah: an Egyptian document speaks of it as the "land of Napit". Arabs have another theory of its origin. According to a chronicle preserved in the Nefta mosque, the founder of the town was Kostel, son of Sem, son of Noah; he called it Nefta because it was here that water boiled, for the first time, after the Deluge. The Romans called it Nepte, but, in confirmation of this old story, I observe that the Arabs of to-day invariably pronounce Nefta as *Nafta*. It is quite likely, too, that the name Hecatompylos, the city of a hundred gates, which has been applied to Gafsa, is a misreading for Hecatompolis, the land of those hundred cities which, they say, studded the shores of this great lake.

For it was a lake, or series of lakes, and nothing else; geological evidence is opposed to the supposition that the Chott country was ever a gulf of the Mediterranean within historical times—it was merely a chain of inland waters. And another surprising discovery has been made of late, namely, that these depressions lie at different levels and have, each of them, its own system of alimentation. This fact came to light between 1872 and 1883, when a number of studies were undertaken with a view to the restoration of this ancient Libyan Sea. Men of middle years will still remember the excitement produced by this scheme which originated with Tissot, though another name will for ever be associated with it, that of Roudaire, a man of science dominated by an obsession, who clung to this project with the blind faith of a martyr, his enthusiasm growing keener in proportion as the plan was proved to be futile, fantastic, fatuous. True, the great Lesseps had taken his part.

Desolation reigns on this morass of salt, where the life of man and beast, and even of plants and stones, faints away in mortal agony. Unnumbered multitudes of living creatures have sunk into its perfidious abysses. "A caravan of ours", says an Arab author, "had to cross the Chott one day; it was composed of a thousand baggage camels. Unfortunately one of the beasts strayed from the path, and all the others followed it. Nothing in the world could be swifter than the manner in which the crust yielded and engulfed them; then it became like what it was before, as if the thousand baggage camels had "never existed." Yet it is traversed in several directions, and if you strain your eyes from these heights you can detect certain dusky lines that crawl in serpentine movement across the melancholy waste—caravan tracks to the south.

Unlike the living ocean, this withered one never smiles: it wears a hostile face. There is a charm, none the less—a charm that appeals to complex modern minds—in that picture of eternal, irremediable sterility. Its hue is ever-changing, as the light falls upon it; the plain, too, shifts up and down with mirage play, climbing sometimes into the horizon, or again sharply defined against it; often it resembles a milky river flowing between banks of mud. The surface is rarely lustrous, but of a velvety texture, like a banded agate, mouse-colour or liver-tinted, with paler streaks in between of the dead whiteness of a sheet of paper; now and again there flash up livid coruscations that glister awhile like enamel or burnished steel, and then fade away. These are the fields of virgin salt which, when you cross them, are bright as purest Alpine snow, and may blind you temporarily with their dazzling glare. Viewed from these uplands, however, the ordered procession of horizontal bars stretching into infinity, their subdued coloration, fill the mind with a wave of deep peace.

Walking from Nefta to the Chott, you will reach, on the burning plain, a maraboutic shrine that might serve as an asylum for some conscience-stricken, malaria-proof penitent. They go well together, maraboutism and the Chott—two factors that make for barrenness in man and nature.

And Nefta is full of such shrines. Another one, for example, has been built into the very heart of the rustling palm forest; the water glides under its walls wherein sits the aged impostor who, unlike his amiable colleague at Tozeur, is too holy even to speak to unbelievers (you are permitted to gaze upon him through a grated window). Yet another one is the humble Sidi Murzouk, the negroes' sanctuary, among the sand-hills on the middle heights. These are three representative types of a hundred at least.

It is hard to say why the French foster these Arab maraboutic tendencies as opposed to the saner ideals of the Berber stock; perhaps they think it politic to *arabize* the older race in this and a few other particulars, though it signifies, almost invariably, a retrograde movement of civilization.

Of these pious folk the paradox is true that the best are the worst; those, that is, who do not expose themselves to ridicule or adverse criticism, whose good intentions are self-evident, who carry out to the letter the apostolic injunction of clothing the naked, feeding the hungry, and succouring the distressed. It is they who pander to all the worst qualities of the Arabs, improvident and incorrigible loafers, besides affording an asylum to every criminal; their *zaouiahs*, like our own mediæval convents, are often enough mere menageries of deformed minds and bodies. As for the much-vaunted calm to be found within their walls, it is there, to be sure, together with certain other things—there and nowhere else, since the frantic religious passions, of which such monastic institutions are offshoots, have made peaceable living outside their walls an impossibility.

In a land where no one reads or writes or thinks or reasons, where dirt and insanity are regarded as marks of divine favour, how easy it is to acquire a reputation for holiness—(oral tradition alone can make a saint)—to turn the god-habit of your fellow-creatures into a profitable source of revenue: as easy as it was in Europe, in the days when we cherished such knaves and neurotic dreamers. Some of them are simple epileptics, verminous and importunate; others, shrewd worldly rogues who, having run away from home after a fit of discontent or homicide, cruise vaguely about Islamism for half a lifetime, and at last return, bearded venerables, to be stared at by their kinsfolk as portents, heaven-sent, because they have freighted themselves with a cargo of fond maxims such as "The World is Illusion: all Flesh is Vanity", and similar gnomic balder-dash, the wisdom of the unlettered.

No wonder they despise what they call the world. For the real world, the cosmos of rational thought and action, has never existed for them. At Tangier, Mecca, Jerusalem or Timbuctu, they have sat eternally in the same coffee-houses or mosques, and listened eternally to the same theological chatterings; which accounts for a certain "family likeness" between all those mentally starved creatures, who are nevertheless favoured of Allah so far as bodily comforts are concerned, inasmuch as (if they play their cards correctly) money, wives, and lands pour down upon them till, in old age, they become so fuddled with homage and holy mumblings that they themselves cannot exactly remember whether they are humbugs or not; this, I take it, must be the culminating point, the *dernier mot*, of maraboutic enlightenment.

And beside these ten thousand impromptu saints that spring up daily out of the fertile soil of Arab imagination and poverty, every one of the descendants of Mahomet's daughter is a marabout, and all their children, male and female, in *sæcula sæculorum*.

God alone, who numbers the stars, can keep count of their legions.

XXIII

THE GARDENS OF NEFTA

A PERSON unacquainted with tropical vegetation would be amazed at the prodigality of the oasis of Nefta; in point of exuberance it is as superior to Tozeur as that to Gafsa. But the cathedral-like gravity of Tozeur is lacking; there is too much riot and opulence, too many voluptuous festoons and spears and spirals, a certain craving, so to speak, after the purely ornate: if Tozeur represents the decorative style of Louis Quatorze, this is assuredly Louis Seize. One great drawback is that the thick undergrowth often obstructs the view; and another, that you cannot walk about in all directions, as at Tozeur, because there is too much running water—perhaps one should say too few paths and bridges.

For the last two days a sand-storm of unusual violence has been raging. On the ridges above the town one can hardly stand on one's feet; the grains fly upwards, over the crest of the hill, in blinding showers, mighty squadrons of them careering across the plain below. The landscape is involved in a dim, roseate twilight. But occasionally there comes a sickly radiance from behind the curtain of cloud that glimmers lustreless, like an incandescent lamp seen through a fog: it is the sun shining brightly in the pure regions of the upper air.

Here, under the trees, the wind is scarce felt, though you can perceive it by the fretful clashing of the palm branches overhead. And despite the storm there is a strange hush in the air, the hush of things to come, a sense of uneasiness; spring is upon us, buds are unfolding and waters drawn up forcefully from a soil which seems to heave under one's very feet. It is a moment of throbbing intensity.

And the scirocco moans to these pangs of elemental gestation which man, the creature of earth, still darkly feels within him.

The ground is cultivated with mathematical parsimoniousness

and divided into squares which made me think of the Roman *agrimensores*. But concerning this point, a civilized old native told me the following legend. Long ago, he said, these oases were wild jungles, and the few human creatures who lived near them little better than beasts. Then came a wise man who cut up and ploughed the watery district of Gafsa, Tozeur and Nefta; he planted trees and all the other growths useful to mankind; he divided the land into patches, led the water through them, and apportioned them among certain families—in short, he gave these oases their present shape, and did his work so well that up to this day no one has been able to suggest any improvements or to quarrel with his arrangement. The story interested me; it may be a variant of the old Hercules myth—it shows how much the Arabs, with their veneration for past heroes and prophets, and their sterile distrust in the possibility of any kind of progress, will believe.*

Yet the *deglat* palms which grow here in great abundance—the finest in the world—with their lower leaves pendent, sere and yellow; the figs, lemons, apricots and pomegranates clustering in savage meshes of unpruned boughs, among which the vine, likewise unkempt, writhes and clambers liana-fashion, in crazy convolutions—all these things conspire to give to certain parts of the oasis, notwithstanding its high cultivation, a bearded, primeval look. The palms, particularly the young ones, are assiduously tended and groomed by half-naked gardeners who labour in the moist earth by relays, day and night.

What nights of brooding stillness in summer, under the palms, when these leaves hang motionless in the streaming vapour as though carved out of bronze, while the surrounding desert exhales the fiery emanations of noontide, often 135 degrees in the shade. For the heat of Nefta is hellish. One might think that the inhabitants, whom Bertholon holds to be descendants, somewhat remote, of the old marrow-sucking, grandmother-devouring Neanderthal folk,

---

* It shows, also, that one cannot be too careful what one writes. I will take this little credit to myself, that, unconvinced of my own explanation, I made further enquiries and learned that—allowing for the inevitable exaggeration—the man actually existed! His name was Ibn Shabbath; he was a kind of engineer-topographer who lived about the thirteenth century; he wrote a commentary, in three volumes, on some well-known Arabic geographical poem—a commentary which exists only in a few manuscript copies, one of which is preserved at the Grand Mosque in Tunis, and another, I am told, in the library of Monsieur de Fleury.

would have become placid by this time; that all harshness must have been boiled out of them. Far from it! The faces that one sees are less friendly than those at Tozeur, and they were noted, in former days, for their vehemence in religious matters. I am sorry to hear it, but not surprised. The arts and other fair flowerings of the human mind may succumb to fierce climates, but theological zeal is one of those things which no extremes of temperature can subdue; it thrives equally well at the Poles or Equator, like that "Brown or Hanoverian rat" which Charles Waterton—a glorious old zealot himself—so cordially detested.

There are eight Europeans here, and thirteen thousand natives: I should not care to be in Nefta on the day when the Senoussi are to realize their long-deferred hopes. All the same, it is a relief not to hear the eternal gossip of employés or to see the soldiers loitering at street corners, like dressed-up chimpanzees. The better class of natives are sometimes of an astonishing immaculate cleanliness from head to foot; they are often remarkably handsome. The traveller Temple was struck, at Nefta, with the beauty of its "desart nymphs, whose eyes are all fire and brilliancy", and he might have said the same of the boys.

But I observe a defect in the eyes of all Arabs, namely, that they seem to be unable to utilize them as a means of conveying thoughts; they have no eye language, even among each other, and must express by words or by some gesture what other people can make clear with a glance. The best-looking youth or maiden has eyes which, beautiful as they are, might be those of a stuffed cow for all the expression they emit. They cannot even wink.

From the rising ground at the back of Nefta you look down into a circular vale of immoderate plant-luxuriance, a never-ending delight of the eye; the French call it by the appropriate name of *la corbeille*. Here the springs issue—152 of them—from under steep walls of sand; they form glad pools of blue and green that mirror the foliage with impeccable truthfulness and then, after coursing in distracted filaments about the "corbeille", join their waters and speed downhill towards the oasis, a narrow belt of trees running along either side. This marvellous palm-embroidered rift sunders Nefta, seated on the arid sand-hills overhead, into two distinct towns or settlements. The eye follows the stream as far as the low-lying plantations and into the Chott beyond, resting at last upon the violet haze of its mysterious southern shores.

Visible from here are also certain mounds at the eastern extremity of the oasis, near the Chott; they are marked on the map as "ruins of Zafrana". What this Zafrana was, or how it comes to have a name resembling that of a small Sicilian village, I cannot tell; thither, at all events, I bent my steps, having heard that ancient coins, as well as lamps, had been found there. So far as I can make out there is only pottery on this site, and none of it pre-Mohammedan; if a city ever stood here it has been completely entombed, or torn into shreds by the wind, the flying sands, and the heat. Nefta itself, built of soft loam, would crumble away in briefest time if left unrepaired. The acute Guérin was not more successful than myself at Zafrana, nor was Maltzan.

This being the most exposed corner of the oasis, the *tabias* have grown to a fine size; I climbed over the inner one, which must be ten yards high and at least twenty in breadth. From its summit one perceives distant forms of ruinous buildings rising up in the Tozeur direction, on the slope which inclines to the Chott. Was this, perhaps, Zafrana?

No. Riding up to them, I found they were merely turret-like eminences of hard bluish clay, the carapace of the desert, which the wind has carved into quaint semblances of human dwellings. In the evening light they catch the last rays of the sun and shine like diaphanous spectres upon the darkened ground, but at sunrise, when the yellow sands sparkle with light, they tower up grim and menacing: a mournful, ghoul-haunted region, like those veritable townships of the past, Dougga, Timgad and the rest of them, standing all forlorn in their African desolation.

Whoever has visited such sites will understand the impression they conveyed to men of simpler ages. He will realize how they must have inflamed the phantasy of those wandering mediæval Arabs who could make no distinction, in this respect, between the works of man and those of nature, nor bring themselves to believe that such titanic structures were reared by human hands or for any human purpose—were otherwise than an illusion, or a natural incongruity. That amphitheatre of El-Djem, for example, visible for leagues in the solitude around—what more apt to become a true mountain of wondrous shape, the haunt of some Ifrit imprisoned in its cup or soaring thence, a pillar of cloud, into the zenith?

These are the ruins whose report was carried to Baghdad by those early caravan traders, and there woven into the flowery tapestries of the *Arabian Nights*—nightmare cities, rising like an enchantment out of the desert sand; bereft of the voices and footsteps of men, but teeming with hoarded treasure and graven images of gods. They gaze down, inscrutable and sternly resplendent, upon the wanderer who, stumbling fearfully through a labyrinth of silent halls, suddenly encounters, in demon-guarded chamber, some ensorcelled maiden, frozen to stone.

XXIV

NEFTA AND ITS FUTURE

THERE are cities in the East where, from ramparts that support fairy-like palaces—complicated assemblages of courts and plashing fountains and cool chambers through which the breeze wanders in an artificial twilight of marble screens pierced so craftily, one might think them a flowing drapery of lace-work—where, from such wizard creations of Oriental pomp, you glance down and behold, stretched at your feet, a burning waste of sand. A fine incentive to the luxurious imagination of a tyrant, this contrast, that has all the glamour of a dream. . . .

Such abrupt transitions are not the rule. Midway between the pulsating town-life and the desert there lies, mostly, a sinister extra-mural region, a region of gaping walls and potsherds, where the asphodel shoot up to monstrous tufts and the fallacious colocynth, the wild melon, scatters its globes of bitter gold. For it is in the nature of Orientals that their habitations should surround themselves with a girdle of corrupting things, gruesome and yet fascinating: a Browning might have grown enamoured of its macabre spell.

No European cares to linger about these precincts after dusk; here lie the dead, in thick-strewn graves; here the jackal roams at night—it thrusts its pointed snout through the ephemeral masonry of townsmen's tombs or scratches downward within the ring of stones that mark some poor bedouin's corpse, to take toll of the carrion horrors beneath; so you may find many graves rifled. And if you come by day you will probably see, crouching among the ruins, certain old men, pariahs, animated lumps of dirt and rags. They are so uncouth and unclean, so utterly non-human, that one wonders whether they are really of the sons of Adam, and not rather goblins, or possibly some freak, some ill-natured jest on the part of the vegetable or mineral kingdoms. Day after day they come and burrow for orts among the dust-heaps, or brood motionless in the

sunshine, or trace cabalistic signs with their fingers in the sand—
the future, they tell you, can be unriddled out of its cascade-like
movements.

It is one of the complaints of sentimentalists that the French are
abolishing these picturesque Arab cemeteries in Tunisia; combining
firmness with a great deal of tact, they insidiously appropriate these
sanctified premises and deck them with timber as a solace for
coming generations. Let them go! The undiluted Orient is still
wide enough; and no one will appreciate the metamorphosis more
than the native citizens themselves, who love, above all things, to
play about and idle in the shade of trees; perhaps, in the course of
time, they will realize that not only Allah, but also man, is able to
plant and take care of them. Your Arab often has a love of nature
which is none the worse for being wholly unconscious.

At Nefta there is no impure region, properly so called. The
searching sunbeams and the winds are inimical to all the lush
concomitants of decay; the sand also plays its part; so every dead
dog, and every dead camel, arrests the flying grains and is straightway interred—transformed into a hillock, trivial but sanitary.

There are tombs, of course, tombs galore; but what strikes one
most are the numerous shrines erected to saints alive or dead, of
which I have already spoken.

You will do well to visit the Christian cemetery. It lies on an
eminence above the town and is almost buried under deep waves
of sand, which have risen to the summit of the surrounding walls
and drowned the three graves, all but their tall stones that emerge
above the flood. One of them is that of a *controleur* of the district
who died at his post while combating a cholera epidemic—there
may be more of them, for aught I know, submerged beneath the
drift.

It is surely in the interests of French prestige to pay a few francs
for the cleansing of such a place in a land where, as conquerors,
they live on a pedestal and are to assert their superiority in every
way. It will be long ere Arabs can appreciate French art and science,
but they understand visible trifles of this kind, and, conversing
with them, I have found that, like many simple-minded people,
they are disposed to contrast unfavourably their own burial-grounds
with our trim method of sepulture, which assures to the defunct
a few more years of apparent respect, while flattering the vanity of
the living. To a sensitive Christian this cemetery of Nefta must be

a sad and a scandalous sight; no humble nomad's tomb on the bleak hillside is more neglected than these memorials to his fellow-believers who have died, far from their homes, under the flaming sun of Africa.

From this point you can see the tail-end of the oasis. It lies in the Zafrana region, and is the worst nourished. This, I suppose, is inevitable; the gardens must be continually moving—moving away from the Chott towards their vital sources, which now lie under a respectable precipice of sand. It is hard to believe that the present site of the fountains is what one might call the natural, aboriginal one. I imagine that the cultivators, in the course of ages, must have tracked the element and followed it up, as a terrier will pursue a rabbit in its burrow, planting trees in proportion as they laid bare its once subterranean bed. Thus, the supply of liquid being constant, the oasis is impelled to wander in the direction of its springs; the more you add to the head, the shorter grows the tail. In prehistoric days, maybe, the water gushed out somewhere near the Chott; the charming depression of the *corbeille* is perhaps the work of human hands.

The same has struck me at Tozeur, which also marches horizontally away from its termination. An exquisite *corbeille* could be manufactured here; all the elements are present; it only requires a few thousand years of labour. And what are they, in a land like this?

And the oases are undergoing another and more curious progression—downwards. Strange to think that, while towns and villages rise higher every year, these gardens are slowly descending into the depths; they are already far below the circumambient desert, though not so deeply sunk as the verdant, crater-like depressions of some parts of Africa. For it stands to reason that as the stream-beds become excavated more and more—and this is what has brought them to their present position—the groves must irrevocably follow suit, since water escapes at the lowest level, while trees cannot be suspended in air. Supposing the system of dams, which now force the liquid to keep to a certain plane, fell into disuse, how would it end?

The imagination of an Edgar Poe might picture these Nefta gardens as the reverse of those of Semiramis—sunk, that is, further into the profundities of the earth than the already existing Sahara plantations—with this difference, that here, to obviate infiltration from the ooze of the Chott, sturdy walls must enclose them. Ages pass, and still the groves descend, while the defences grow so stout and high that, viewed from above, the palms down there, in that deep funnel, look like puny vegetables, and men like ants. And still they descend. . . . One day the pale population engaged in tilling this shadowy paradise will be horrified to perceive, in their encircling bulwarks, rents and crevices that ooze forth ominous jets of mud. The damage is hastily repaired, but the cracks appear once more, and, widening imperceptibly at first, soon burst asunder and admit, from every side, a wrinkled flood of slime which closes with sullen murmur over the site of the drowned oasis.

Or if the wells dried up? One of those geological displacements that have taken place in past times would suffice to wipe out the memory of this town—the palms would wither, the clay-built houses melt into the earth whence they arose.

Meanwhile, perched on the last wave of an ocean of shining sand, Nefta sits in immemorial contemplation of the desert and vividly green oasis which flows, like a grand and luminous river, into the very heart of its flat dwellings. There is a note of passionate solemnity about the place. All too soon, I fear, the railway to Tozeur will have done its work; dusty boulevards, white bungalows, eucalyptus trees and *bureaux de monopoles* will profane its strangely wonderful beauty, its virginal monotone of golden grey. Nefta will become a neurasthenic demi-mondane, like Biskra.

Such, at least, is the prognosis.

But one is apt to forget on how precarious a tenure these gardens are held, with the hungry desert gnawing ceaselessly at their outskirts; for the desert is hungry and yet patient; it has devoured sundry oases by simply waiting till man is preoccupied with other matters. And how rare they are, these specks of green, these fountains in the sand—rare as the smiles in a lifetime of woe! Beyond and all around lies a grave and ungracious land, the land of the lawless, fanatical wanderers.

These Romans and heathen Berbers, tillers of the soil, had remained in contact with phenomena; unconcerned, relatively speaking, with the affairs of the next world, they attained a passable degree of civilization in this one. But your pastoral Arab scorns a knowledge of general mundane principles. His life is a series of disconnected happenings which must be enjoyed or endured; he is incapable of reading aright the past or present, because he asks himself *why?* instead of *how?* Whoever despises the investigations of secondary causes is a menace to his fellow-creatures.

Face to face with infinities, man disencumbers himself. Those abysmal desert-silences, those spaces of scintillating rock and sand-dune over which the eye roams and vainly seeks a point of repose, quicken his animal perception; he stands alone and must think for himself—and so far good. But while discarding much that seems inconsiderable before such wide and splendid horizons, this nomad loads himself with the incubus of dream-states; while standing alone, he grows into a ferocious brigand. Poets call him romantic, but politicians are puzzled what to do with a being who to a senile mysticism joins the peevish destructiveness of a child.

It is an almost universal fallacy to blame the desert for this state of affairs; to insinuate, for example, that even as it disintegrates the mountains into sand, so it decomposes the intellectual fabric of mankind, his synthesizing faculty, into its primordial elements of ecstasy and emotionalism. This is merely reaction: the desert's revenge. For we now know a little something of the condition of old Arabia and Africa in the days ere these ardent shepherds appeared on the scene, with their crude and chaotic monotheism. The desert has not made the Arab, any more than it made the Berber. It would be considerably nearer the truth to reverse the proposition; to say that the evils which now afflict Northern Africa, its physical abandonment, its social and economical decay, are the work of that ideal Arab, the man of Mecca. Mahomet is the desert-maker.

INDEXES

INDEX TO SIREN LAND

INDEX TO FOUNTAINS IN THE SAND